Addicted to Oil

To Diana

ADDICTED TO OIL

America's Relentless Drive
for Energy Security

Ian Rutledge

I.B. TAURIS
LONDON · NEW YORK

New Paperback Edition Published in 2006 by I.B. Tauris & Co Ltd
6 Salem Road, London W2 4BU
175 Fifth Avenue, New York NY 10010
www.ibtauris.com

In the United States and Canada distributed by Palgrave Macmillan,
a division of St. Martin's Press, 175 Fifth Avenue, New York NY 10010

First published in hardback in 2005 by I.B. Tauris & Co Ltd
Copyright © Ian Rutledge, 2006

ISBN 10: 1 84511 319 5
ISBN 13: 978 1 84511 319 3

A full CIP record for this book is available from the British Library
A full CIP record for this book is available from the Library of Congress
Library of Congress catalog card: available

Typeset in Minion by Dexter Haven Associates Ltd, London
Printed and bound in India by Replika Press Pvt. Ltd

Contents

Acknowledgements

I should like to thank those colleagues who have read and commented on all, or particular, chapters of the book: John Hart, Walter Little, Bernard Mommer and Philip Wright. Special thanks go to my first 'editor', John Ellis, who hacked his way through the dense undergrowth of the book's initial version. Hanako Birks and an anonymous referee did some further hacking until eventually the book emerged in its present form. Finally I must thank my literary agent, John Parker of MBA Ltd and my publisher, I. B. Tauris, for keeping faith with a project which at times must have seemed rather inauspicious.

Note on Names and Terminology

OIL COMPANY NAMES

Most of the oil companies mentioned in the text changed their names during the period of time covered by this book: e.g. Standard Oil of California changed its name to Chevron Corporation. Since the new names will naturally be more familiar to readers than the old ones, in those chapters which contain a historical narrative, I have adopted the procedure of mentioning both in the first instance e.g. 'Standard Oil of California (later to become Chevron Corporation)' and thereafter using only the new name, irrespective of the historical period in which it is being used. In these later references I have also abbreviated the full company name: e.g. 'Chevron Corporation' to the simpler 'Chevron', as is common practice. A further complication is that over the historical period covered by the study some oil companies have merged; for example in 2001 Chevron merged with Texaco to become 'ChevronTexaco' (sic). In these cases I have used the appropriate name for the relevant historical period, i.e. before 2001 we refer only to 'Chevron,' thereafter 'ChevronTexaco'.

CRUDE OIL AND ITS REFINED PRODUCTS

The term 'oil' is used throughout to refer both to crude oil and to crude oil-plus-natural gas liquids. This is common practice in the oil industry (see e.g. BP Statistical Review of World Energy). Natural gas liquids (NGLs) are hydrocarbon liquids extracted from natural gas streams which are later processed into liquefied petroleum gases (LPGs) such as propane and butane. Today they constitute about 25 per cent of US 'oil' production.

The term 'petroleum' is used to refer to the products refined from oil (e.g. aviation fuel, heavy fuel oil, motor gasoline etc.), however in some contexts, for example when referring to import or export quantities, it is used to mean both refined products and crude oil. The term 'gasoline' is used to refer specifically to the fraction of refined crude used for motor vehicle fuel. I have used this term throughout in preference to the UK English word 'petrol'.

ARABIC NAMES

A few Arabic names and words appear in the text. I have followed the commonly used transliteration of Arabic whereby letters having absolutely no English equivalent (e.g. ayn and hamza) are simply omitted; those for which there are reasonable English equivalents, qaaf and ghain, are rendered as q and gh respectively; and the so-called 'hard' consonants (i.e. Saad, Daad, Taa and Dhaa) are transliterated as their 'soft' English equivalents. Finally, to avoid pedantry, some commonly used Arabic names (e.g. Osama; al Queda) have been retained.

THE 'PERSIAN' GULF

The US Department of Energy, from which we have drawn much of our data, still uses the term 'Persian Gulf' which modern atlases now simply refer to as 'The Gulf'. Ideally one would have omitted the 'Persian'. Unfortunately, in the world of oil there are two 'Gulfs' – the 'Persian' and the Gulf of Mexico, so although I have generally used the simple 'Gulf', on occasion, and for clarity, I have been obliged to use 'Persian Gulf'.

Preface to the
Paperback Edition

With the conflict in Iraq looking ever more intractable, debates continue to rage about how and why the US became embroiled in this situation. In *Addicted to Oil*, I tried to show that while the 2003 invasion of Iraq is explicable in terms of a number of oil-related factors, it was not a one-off bid to plunder Iraq's natural resources. Rather, it should be seen as the result of mainstreaming the goal of a stable energy supply into all aspects of US foreign policy decision-making. As the need for such a supply has grown more rather than less acute since the publication of the first edition of *Addicted to Oil* in 2003, it seems unlikely that the invasion of Iraq will be the last reckless act of US foreign policy.

Since publication of the first edition of this book in 2005, the patterns of energy consumption it outlined have continued to grow with worrying intensity, to the point where even the oilman-turned-president George W. Bush claims to find it a cause for concern.

Focusing firstly, on the most basic figures, according to the US Energy Information Agency (EIA) the consumption of oil (crude and petroleum products supplied) in the USA increased from 19.7 million barrels per day in 2001 to 20.6 Mb/d in 2005.[1] Over the same period net oil imports increased from 10.9 Mb/d to 12.3 Mb/d.[2] Therefore as a percentage of total oil supplies the US dependence on imports has increased from 55.3 percent to 59.7 percent. These figures reflect both the increase in consumption and the decline in US domestic oil production that occurred over the same period, falling from 7.7 Mb/d (crude and natural gas liquids) in 2001 to 6.7 Mb/d in 2005.[3]

As in 2001, the most recently published figures (for 2004) show that transportation (motor vehicles, aircraft, railways) remains by far the largest source of US oil demand, holding steady at around 68 percent of total petroleum consumption over this period. With respect to motor vehicle transportation, consumption of gasoline rose from 8.4 Mb/d to 8.9 Mb/d between 2001 and 2004[4] and consumption of total motor fuels increased from 10.7 Mb/d to 11.3 Mb/d.[5] These facts reflect the continuing motorisation of US society. The total number of registered motor vehicles in the USA increased from 235,331,000 in 2001 to 243,023,000 in 2004 and over the same period the average fuel economy of all US motor vehicles has remained static at 17.1 miles per US gallon.[6] Focusing only on light vehicles the average fuel economy of automobiles did improve slightly between 2001 and 2004, from 22.1 miles per US gallon to 22.4 M/gallon; but the average fuel economy of 'light trucks' (SUVs, pick-ups and minivans) fell from 17.6 M/gallon to 16.2 M/gallon.[7] And while US citizens continue their love affair with the car, the percentage of US employees using public transport to travel to work has fallen to an all time low of 4.4 percent.[8]

At the same time, the USA remains the largest world producer of motor vehicles, building 11,960,000 vehicles in 2004 – slightly up on 2001 – compared to its nearest rival, Japan (10,512,000).[9] Sales of motor vehicles in the USA, which were 17,368,400 in 2001 and that had fallen slightly in 2003, recovered strongly in 2005 to 17,444,600.[10] However, the percentage of lower fuel economy 'light trucks' (SUVs etc.) in the total figure for light vehicle sales, increased from 51.1 percent in 2001 to 54.8 percent in 2005, countering some anecdotal evidence that US consumers were switching to more efficient vehicles as a result of higher gasoline prices.[11]

The failure of US consumers to respond in any significant way to higher oil and gasoline prices by shifting to more fuel-efficient vehicles has been analysed in depth by Walter S. McManus, Director of the Office for the Study of Automotive Transportation at the University of Michigan. He first notes that the real (inflation adjusted) price of gasoline increased from $1.66/gallon in 2001 to $1.96 in 2004 and it would be reasonable to assume that an 18 percent real increase would have had some observable impact on motorists' choice of new vehicle. Nevertheless, during the period covered by McManus' study SUVs lost only 0.5 percent of market share while pick-ups actually held their share. Large pick-ups and large and luxury SUVs, which have the lowest miles/gallon, actually gained market share. Thus the increase in the price of gasoline between 2001 and 2004 'does not appear to have been associated with a shift towards segments with higher fuel economy'.[12] According to McManus the reason why no discernible shift to more fuel-efficient vehicles took place is because higher profit margins on SUVs etc. allowed retailers to offer greater discounts on such vehicles offsetting the impact of higher gasoline prices. This underlines the point made in Chapter 9 of *Addicted to Oil* that in analysing the phenomenon of US mass motorisation it is essential to consider not only the role of the consumer but also to appreciate the continuing significance of the US motor manufacturing and retailing industry (whether US or foreign-owned).

Most recently, and especially reflecting the surge in gasoline prices after Hurricane Katrina, there was a fall-off in sales of certain types of SUV in 2005. But writing in December 2005, the motor correspondent of the *Washington Post*, Warren Brown, wrote that, 'the sky isn't falling on the SUV market'. Instead, consumers were simply switching to different types of SUV and 'cross-over' vehicles combining SUV-like characteristics with more comfortable passenger car features. According to Brown, talk of the 'end of the SUV' is 'baloney'. Even the troubled General Motors Company is seeing a recovery in specific types of SUV.

> While news organisations were busy trumpeting declining SUV sales, GM was hauling in cash on sales of its Hummers, led by the new Hummer H3. According to the Automotive News Data Center, Hummer sales were up 122.5 percent in November. Sales of Land Rovers, led by the new Land Rover Sport rose 18 percent in November ... In fact all over the automotive landscape, there is ample evidence that the people at General Motors are not crazy for planning the 2006 rollout of a bevy of new, full-size SUVs such as the completely re-worked Chevrolet Tahoe.[13]

Turning to the future, the EIA's 'reference case' for its *Annual Energy Outlook 2006*, envisages US oil consumption increasing to 22.17 Mb/y in 2010 and to 24.81 Mb/y in 2020.[14] Over the same period net imports are forecast to increase to 12.33 Mb/y in 2010 and 14.42 Mb/y in 2020 , however these figures already appear to be a serious underestimate since provisional data for 2005 show net imports to have already reached 12.3 Mb/y.

In his 2006 State of the Union address, President Bush made the surprising statement that America is now 'addicted to oil'. It is difficult to know how seriously to take this apparent admission, but clearly the failure of his war for oil in Iraq will have brought home to his Administration the increasingly critical state of the nation's energy security, especially since – as we have seen – almost all the key indicators of America's 'addiction to oil' have deteriorated further since the Iraq invasion. Unfortunately the President's two proposed remedies for this unsatisfactory state of affairs not only displayed a remarkable ignorance of US government research but were, in one case, exactly the opposite of what the USA requires.

Bush's first 'solution' to America's oil addiction was the assertion that the problem could be dealt with solely via a technological fix. He characteristically avoided any suggestion that US citizens should change their lifestyle or that the state should promote radical new transportation and housing policies. 'By applying the talent and technology of America' Bush stated, 'this country can ... move beyond a petroleum-based economy.'[15] Nobody would deny the immense technological creativity of the American people, but the idea that technology alone can reduce America's oil dependence in a timely fashion by the introduction of new types of automobile engine (fuel cells etc.) is simply not realistic.

Indeed, the notion had already been demolished by the US Department of Energy's own study of future US highway energy use, published in May 2001, five months into Bush's own presidency.[16] That study underlined the central problem that, even if such new technologies were developed on an economically viable scale and the related infrastructure constructed, because of relatively slow car-replacement rates, the diffusion of such new technologies throughout the national vehicle stock might take as long as 38 years before on-road fuel efficiency doubled (see *Addicted to Oil*, Chapter 9).

Bush's second policy recommendation for curing his country's 'addiction' – or perhaps one should say, the economic dangers of that addiction – was a pledge to reduce dependence on oil imports from the 'unstable' Middle East by 75 percent by 2025. Seemingly Bush was again completely unaware of the views of the USA's own General Accounting Office, which had published a report in 1996 that demonstrated that because oil is a 'fungible' commodity, an oil supply/price crisis originating in the Middle East would impact US oil markets in exactly the same way as all other oil markets, even if the USA imported absolutely no oil at all from the Middle East. For example, if a Middle East supply crisis were to drive up prices in European markets, tankers carrying oil from, say, Angola to the USA, would divert to Europe (to take advantage of the higher prices) and sooner or later US prices would be dragged up to those European levels[17] (see *Addicted to Oil*, Chapter 10).

However, the belief that the USA can and should reduce its 'dependence' on Middle East oil is fallacious for a more fundamental reason: in future years America's energy security problem may not be that the Middle East plays too great a role in oil production, but rather that it plays too small a role. Here again we may refer to the US government's own Department of Energy. According to the latest edition of the EIA's *International Energy Outlook*, by 2025 the Middle East will need to more than double its current exports of oil to the USA if US oil prices are not to increase above the modest levels specified in the report's 'reference case' (real US import prices, $47.29/b in 2010 and $54.08/b in 2025).[18]

The inevitable growing dependence of the USA (and Europe) on petroleum exports from the Middle East has also been emphasised by observations that the Middle East (primarily Saudi Arabia) is one of the few places where substantial new refining capacity is being constructed. So, in future, America may not only need growing supplies of Saudi crude but also Saudi motor gasoline and other refined products.[19] The question (which we address below) is, however, will the USA be able to obtain these products and at what price?

The forecast of only moderate oil price increases in the EIA's *International Energy Outlook* is also based on the assumption that exports from areas outside the Middle East will increase from 38.8 Mb/d in 2002 to 50.6 Mb/d in 2025.[20] This seems highly unlikely. All the evidence points to the fact that the major multinational oil companies have already decided that there are few really profitable oil exploration and production opportunities in areas outside the Middle East and are consequently returning cash to shareholders rather than investing in new oil reserves. The last time that oil prices spiked at very high levels (1980–82) the oil majors spent more than 80 percent of their free cash flow on finding and producing new oil. Today they are only re-investing 40 percent. According to one oil analyst this is because, 'There is just not enough good stuff to invest in until foreign investment is allowed in areas of the Middle East currently closed…'[21]

In *Addicted to Oil* it was shown that in the first few months of Bush's presidency expert bodies of opinion, such as the James Baker III Institute for Public Policy and the President's own National Energy Policy Development Group chaired by Richard Cheney, recognised the extent to which the opening-up of the Persian Gulf countries to foreign (ideally US) oil investment was essential. Without this opening the additional oil supplies at moderate prices, essential to US energy security in future years, would not be forthcoming no matter how much the USA diversified its oil imports or increased domestic production. For this reason, Cheney's 2001 report stated that 'The [Persian] Gulf will be a primary focus of US international energy policy'[22] and two years later the USA embarked on its ill-conceived mission to 'force' the required opening under the guise of destroying Iraq's 'Weapons of Mass Destruction'.

Had the US invasion of Iraq been followed by a peaceful occupation; had US (and perhaps British) oil multinationals been able to sign production-sharing agreements, which would have boosted Iraqi oil output to around 3–4 Mb/y by today (as the US anticipated), with prospects of further major production increases in years to come as the relatively unexplored Iraqi territory yielded up its riches – then America's energy security problem would have been largely solved and its citizens' hyper-motorised way of life guaranteed for the foreseeable future. This would have been achieved not only through the direct impact on Iraq but also via the 'demonstration effect' upon Saudi Arabia and the other Middle East oil suppliers who, most probably, would have been taught the error of their ways in trying to resist the overwhelming might of the US Imperium and its attendant oil companies.

Instead, the continuing violence of the unanticipated insurgency – degenerating recently into low-level civil war – has not only obstructed the hoped-for inflow of foreign oil investment but has actually reduced Iraq's oil exports to a level lower than before the invasion.[23] Even worse, the hatred that has undoubtedly been engendered within Saudi Arabia and other Middle Eastern countries by the Abu Ghraib tortures, the destruction of Fallujah and the massive civilian casualties of indiscriminate US bombing and shelling, have made it even more unlikely that there will be any significant opening-up of the region to foreign oil capital.

So Saudi Arabia remains firmly closed to foreign oil companies (except for a handful of small gas exploration projects); Kuwait's parliamentarians are still equally opposed,[24] and most recently the conflict between the USA and its European allies with Iran over the latter's nuclear energy policy would certainly appear to stymie the very small, faltering steps that country has so far taken towards admitting foreign oil capital.

The final section of *Addicted to Oil* reflected upon the likely consequences of America losing its war for oil. One possible outcome considered was that Saudi Arabia – freed from any real or imagined threat from Saddam Hussein as a result of the US destruction of his regime – would now have little need for the kind of security guarantees implicit in its half-century-long pact with the USA. On the other hand, by failing to win its war for oil, the USA still remains dependent on Saudi oil supplies. We therefore speculated that Saudi Arabia might soon begin to demonstrate a significant shift in its strategic orientation away from the traditional US embrace. In particular we noted that Saudi Arabia might soon begin to look to the Chinese for security guarantees and military assistance in return for pledges of long-term oil supplies.

Sure enough, in January 2006, King Abdullah made the first official Saudi visit to Beijing where the King and Chinese President Hu Jintao signed a protocol on cooperation in petroleum, natural gas and minerals. Significantly, it was also the first official foreign visit of Abdullah bin Abdul-Aziz since he became King. Accompanying King Abdullah were a large contingent of Saudi businessmen who signed a 'host of agreements'. We do not know the details of the oil agreements signed but it is highly likely that they were similar to those announced in a further example of Saudi Arabia's 'turn to the East'. On 27 January 2006, the Saudi and Indian governments signed another strategic energy agreement which envisions increased volumes of crude oil supplies from Saudi Arabia to India via 'long-term contracts which would be renewed automatically'.[25]

According to Abdulaziz Sager, Saudi Chairman of the Gulf Research Center in Dubai, 'While some assert that the [Saudi-China] energy deals are simply the result of mutual economic interests others argue that they stem from new strategies in both Riyadh and Beijing.'[26] Reflecting this possibility, it was also reported that in the Saudi-China meetings the two sides also discussed 'possible military co-operation'.[27]

The second anticipated consequence of America losing its war for oil in Iraq was a steadily rising oil price, possibly leading to a major price acceleration towards the end of the decade, an event that would damage all highly motorised countries but for reasons explained in *Addicted to Oil* would be especially painful for US citizens. At the time of the US invasion, in March 2003, the price of US oil imports, (refiner acquisition cost) stood at $29.23/b; by November 2005 it had reached $51.60/b. This 77 percent increase in price is greater than we would have anticipated for this point in time and it would be incorrect to explain it entirely by reference to the problems in Iraq; clearly other events such as Hurricane Katrina, inadequate levels of refining capacity and the stand-off over Iran's nuclear facilities have played a part. Nevertheless, it is also true that had America won its war for oil on the sort of terms outlined above, the oil markets would have been much less tight and the impact of factors such as those mentioned above would have been much less pronounced or sustained.

Some economists remain relaxed about the extent of the damage to US consumers and the US economy generally by rising oil prices. The USA certainly seems to have taken a 77 percent oil price increase remarkably well (although high oil prices may be one of the factors currently depressing President Bush's popularity ratings). However, as the US economist Martin Feldstein has pointed out, the recent increase in oil prices has occurred at a particularly favourable conjuncture – one in which US consumers have been able to protect their standard of living and maintain consumer expenditures by massive releases of equity through re-mortgaging housing property. This however, can only be a one-off event; once 'released' the equity cannot be spent again. Feldstein concludes that,

> The powerful effect of mortgage re-financing on consumer expenditure was a happy coincidence for the American economy at a time when oil prices were depressing consumers' real incomes. If oil prices were to rise again in 2006 or 2007, the adverse effect on consumers' real incomes would not be offset by increased mortgage refinancing … The US was lucky after 2003 to escape the contractionary effect of an oil price rise even without an explicit change in monetary or fiscal policy. It would not be so lucky if a big oil price increase happened again now.[28]

Reference to US consumption patterns brings us to our final observation with respect to US foreign policy, the Middle East and the future of the world oil market. Only very recently has the fundamental link between globalisation and global energy requirements come into focus.[29] Globalisation is not merely the massive expansion of international trade but the extension of capitalist social and economic relations to all parts of the world including, first and foremost, the rapid spread of 'western' consumption patterns. Indeed the rapidly increasing consumption of an almost infinitely differentiated cornucopia of commodities is now, more than ever before, the motor force driving World GDP growth. Motorisation, while the preponderant element in that process is but one aspect of a globalised economy in which the most bizarre and wasteful 'needs' are cultivated by the great multinational companies to ensure that the motor does not stall. To give but one small example, millions of human beings with safe and secure water supplies have now been successfully convinced that they will be healthier by consuming 'mineral water' enclosed in plastic bottles. So in the USA, for example, over 40,000 barrels of oil per day are required to produce the petrochemicals needed to meet this particular 'consumer demand'.[30]

Driven by globalisation world oil demand is now increasing seemingly without limit. However, the major oil producing countries in the Middle East are unable or unwilling to invest sufficiently themselves or to admit foreign oil companies to do it for them. Consequently, the world oil market may be about to undergo a truly seismic shift. In Chapter 10 of *Addicted to Oil*, we noted signs that the end of the era of free oil markets may be approaching: that a race among oil consuming states to 'lock-in' long-term oil supplies at guaranteed prices by offering in return security guarantees, foreign aid and soft loans, or by acquiring equity stakes in foreign oil companies or oilfields, has already begun. Since 2003, China has continued to pursue a policy of securing equity oil by acquiring foreign oil companies or oil fields (not always successfully as the recent US rebuff to CNOOC's bid for Unocal demonstrated); and Chinese and Indian state oil companies reflecting the needs of the world's fastest growing oil consumers, have forged an alliance to cooperate in securing crude oil resources overseas.[31] Meanwhile, energy-hungry Japan also remains a contender in the race for oil resources. 'We all will struggle for Middle Eastern oil among the three of us – China, India and Japan', says Yoichi Funabashi, a leading commentator for Japan's *Asahi Simbun* newspaper.[32]

Yet while the race for oil resources appears to have already started, America, whose Government – and many of whose politicians – continues to manifest barely concealed visceral antipathy towards the human beings who inhabit the countries holding 65 per cent of the World's proven oil reserves is, after Iraq, now even further from the starting line.

Ian Rutledge
Chesterfield
14/2/2006

Preface

At the very end of *Plan of Attack*, Bob Woodward's account of the events leading up to the invasion of Iraq, the author asks President Bush, 'How would history judge his Iraq war?' In one respect the question was misguided. History does not judge; it analyses, and above all it looks for causes. In doing so it applies the general principles of all scientific investigation: it frames hypotheses based on the observation of previously observed patterns of behaviour. In the case of the USA, the most frequently observed pattern which emerges from a study of its foreign policy over the past eighty years is a fundamental and abiding concern for, and involvement in, the geopolitics of oil.[1]

Nevertheless, on 15 January 2003 the British Prime Minister Tony Blair derided as 'conspiracy theory' accusations that the coming war on Iraq would be in pursuit of oil. Similarly, two months later, a leading article in the US foreign affairs weekly, *In the National Interest*, declared that 'Nothing demonstrates the political and moral bankruptcy of the American liberal left more clearly than the current attempt to portray military action against Iraq as "for the oil".'[2] Yet millions of people throughout the world continue to believe that oil was indeed the most important factor in accounting for the USA's invasion and occupation of Iraq.

Addicted to Oil is a preliminary attempt to show why those millions of people are correct. I shall argue that the invasion of Iraq was indeed 'for the oil', although not for the reasons usually attributed to this 'oil theory' by its opponents. There was never any intention to 'steal Iraq's oil'; but control and domination can be achieved without the direct appropriation of Iraqi oil reserves by US citizens.

The historical evidence of that 'fundamental and abiding concern for, and involvement in, the geopolitics of oil' to which we referred above, in itself provides a sufficient reason for believing that oil was the key to the invasion of Iraq. But, as we shall argue, there is additional evidence that at the turn of the twenty-first century, many of those long-standing oil-related factors were combining to reach a critical mass. The remarkable extent to which America's economy and society had become dominated by the automobile, the country's ever-increasing dependence on foreign oil supplies, the record level of US oil imports from the Persian Gulf, the warnings of an impending major oil price crisis if the leading Gulf oil producers continued to refuse entry to foreign oil investment, and the intense desire of America's oil companies to gain access to the exceptionally profitable reserves therein – all these factors coalesced in a pressure force of unprecedented magnitude. Taken together they were the most important factors leading to the invasion, war and occupation of Iraq.

Of course, oil was not the only factor. States do not go to war for one reason alone. The desire to coerce the Palestinians into the kind of 'peace' favoured by the Bush Administration's Likud party allies, by a massive demonstration of US military might must surely be included in the list of factors behind the invasion. Similarly, a growing frustration with the increasingly counter-productive sanctions regime cannot be discounted among the causative factors. But this is not to say that some kind of rank-ordering of causative factors is impossible, nor that we are unable to distinguish the fundamental predisposing factors from those which are only the catalyst.

Certainly, the catalyst for the 2003 invasion of Iraq, and indeed for the whole 'war on terror' that began with the invasion of Afghanistan, was the 'Twin Towers' atrocity of 11 September 2001. But in both cases, this catalyst was acting upon a complex of underlying oil-related forces which had already inclined American decision-makers towards forceful intervention in both these regions. Most wars reveal similar short-term and long-term causes. In the First World War, for example, we are able to distinguish between Gavrilo Princip's assassination of the Austrian Archduke Franz Ferdinand on 28 June 1914, which acted as the catalyst, from the long years of imperialist and nationalist rivalry and the massive arms race which historians recognise as the fundamental predisposing factors leading to that war.

We must also distinguish the crucial predisposing factors leading to war from those 'causes' to which the leading actors themselves refer, in explaining their own behaviour. Where material interests – interests of business as well as interests of state – give rise to a particular definition of reality we may refer to this as ideology.[3] In Woodward's Bush at War and Plan of Attack, and other journalistic accounts, the President and those around him view their own behaviour and that of the wider world, through the prism of their conservative ideology.

Not only would invading Iraq remove weapons of mass destruction ('as grave a threat as can be imagined', according to Vice President Cheney) but it would also be 'a forward strategy of freedom in the Middle East', part of a US-led 'global democratic revolution'.[4] Indeed, according to Woodward, Bush saw himself as undertaking an 'ambitious reordering of the world through pre-emptive and, if necessary, unilateral action to reduce suffering and bring peace'.[5] Doubtless these beliefs were sincerely held. However, historical analysis would not get very far if it merely confined itself to an inquiry into why individuals, in their own estimation, acted as they did. We should remember the words of the great English Historian E.H. Carr: 'human beings do not always, or even habitually, act from motives of which they are fully conscious or which they are willing to avow.'[6]

In fact we do not need to probe too deeply beneath the layers of neo-conservative ideology to find indications that solid matters of state and business were at issue in the Gulf which had nothing to do with 'weapons of mass destruction', 'freedom' or 'democracy'. Long before the embarrassing failure of the so-called WMD to materialise, there were signs that the alleged threat posed by the crumbling wreck of Saddam Hussein's fascist regime was merely a convenient excuse for America's leaders to play the end-game in a decades-long struggle to satisfy the inexorable demands of its massively motorised society. For example, in September 2000, when the neo-conservatives Paul Wolfowitz, William Kristol, Dov Zakheim, I. Lewis Libby and other contributors to the report *Rebuilding America's Defenses*, discussed the role of US forces in the Gulf, they frankly acknowledged that: 'While the unresolved conflict with Iraq provides the immediate justification, the need for a substantial American force presence in the Gulf transcends the issue of the regime of Saddam Hussein.'[7]

This admission, that Saddam Hussein was only the 'justification' – the pretext – for establishing a new American Imperium in what the report's authors had aptly described as 'a region of vital importance', clearly indicates that there was another, more fundamental reason for military intervention in the Gulf: that reason was oil.

Addicted to Oil begins by explaining the crucial role of oil in the world economy and emphasising the extent to which oil, in spite of its environmental drawbacks, is still the world's most useful energy source. The extent to which America has become increasingly dependent on foreign oil supplies is explained and it is demonstrated that the fundamental reason for this lies in the USA's transportation sector.

In Chapter Two, the origins of America's addiction to oil are traced back to critical decisions taken by politicians and business leaders during the first half of the twentieth century, when America chose to motorise its cities. This choice was by no means inevitable and it is shown that it was hugely influenced by the large automobile and oil companies. Consequently, by the mid-1960s, the core of the US economy was vehicle manufacturing and oil refining, with a growing dependence on oil imports from the Middle East.

America's troubled relationships with the Middle East, and with Saudi Arabia in particular, are examined in the third and fourth chapters, showing how a region originally considered to be the solution to America's growing energy security problem eventually came to be seen as a potential threat to it. And in 1990–91 this threat became an all-out war for oil after Saddam Hussein invaded Kuwait and threatened American oil supplies from Saudi Arabia.

In Chapter Five, the focus switches to the three individuals who, ten years later, would set in motion the events leading to a second American war with Iraq – George W. Bush, Richard Cheney and Condoleezza Rice. It is also shown how these three were the 'Axis of Oil' in the Administration, the three individuals most intimately connected with US oil and energy interests and the commercial objectives of its large companies, objectives which would now take pride of place in the new Administration's geopolitical agenda.

In chapters Six, Seven and Eight, our attention shifts to looking at the USA's by now 'traditional' policy of trying to diversify its sources of oil supply away from the Persian Gulf. The objective was to replace Gulf supplies with oil from domestic sources, neighbouring 'hemispheric' suppliers – Canada, Venezuela and Mexico – and from the Caspian region of the former Soviet Union. But it is shown how these policies had only limited success and how America was soon thrown back, once again, upon a growing dependence on the Gulf.

Chapter Nine revisits the subject of motorisation and assesses the extent to which it now permeates almost every aspect of contemporary US society. But in spite of the fact that America, at the beginning of the twenty-first century, was already by far the most highly motorised society in the world, a continuous growth in US demand for transportation fuel throughout the next four decades was forecast by the US government's own energy experts.

Against this background, Chapter Ten describes how the appearance on the scene of a new and potentially huge oil importer – China – combined with the reluctance of the major Gulf oil producers to open their doors to foreign oil capital, led expert bodies of opinion in the USA to anticipate an approaching world oil supply and price crisis of unprecedented severity.

Serious concerns about such an oil crisis were exacerbated by the USA's growing struggle with militant Islamism. As Chapter Eleven explains, the events of 11 September 2001 convinced many conservative Americans that 'something had to be done about the Middle East', its recalcitrant oil producers and the fanatical terrorists it was believed to have nurtured. The answer, the subject of our final chapter, was the full-scale invasion and occupation of Iraq with the intention of establishing, through a kind of 'democratic imperialism', a friendly and compliant oil protectorate in that troubled region. Based on the evidence at the time of writing, this chapter judges that America has fought a war for oil in Iraq – and lost it. What that means for the USA, Saudi Arabia and the future world oil price is then the subject of a brief and necessarily speculative conclusion.

1 Oil and America

Powerful forces have worked mightily to shame people into believing that
consuming energy is bad, and that Americans should therefore feel guilty
about consuming so much.

Competitive Enterprise Institute, 2001

Oil is the world's most valuable energy resource. Perhaps sometime in the future
we shall be able to find something more environmentally friendly to fuel our
machines and to convert into all those useful products which are now part of
our everyday life, but for the time being the world wants oil. So desirable is it,
that it has come to be thought of as a 'strategic' commodity; one without which
no highly industrialised society can survive and whose availability must be
guaranteed, if necessary, by military force. Indeed, according to one expert on
military and security matters, 'Of all the resources ... none is more likely to provoke
conflict between states in the twenty-first century than oil.'[1]

Yet we rarely trouble to ask ourselves why oil is so crucial to our societies. So
let us spend a few moments investigating why oil is so useful and valuable. In
doing so we will also help to establish precisely why America, in particular, has
become so dependent on this substance. Oil is so prized because it has the best
physical characteristics of any energy resource. Energy is 'the capacity to do
work'. One cannot actually observe or measure it directly – it is a theoretical
entity – but you can study the effect which it has upon matter, for example the
process of heating. This 'energy effect' is measured in units called 'joules',[2] though
for convenience we normally count in 'megajoules' (millions of joules) or
'gigajoules' (billions of joules). Using this measure of energy we can relate a
particular fuel's energy value to three of its other physical characteristics: its
weight, its volume, and its natural state (liquid, solid, gas or 'field'). This gives

1

us three 'energy grades' for each fuel. For example, a kilogram of coal of average quality contains 24 megajoules (MJ) of energy (the 'weight grade'); a cubic metre of coal contains 27,500 MJ (the 'volume grade'); finally, we simply note that in its natural form coal is a solid (the 'state grade').[3]

If we apply this system of grading to all the currently available energy sources, oil is consistently superior to all the others. For example, the weight grade of oil is 43 MJ compared to 25.5 MJ for ethanol (made from grain), 24 MJ for 'average' coal, 18 MJ for wood, 4.4 MJ for oil shale etc.[4] Now consider the volume grade: a cubic metre of oil contains 35,000 MJ, a cubic metre of average coal around 27,500 MJ, ethanol about 20,000 MJ, and a cubic metre of natural gas only 35 MJ. Even where gas is compressed to 20 MPa,[5] a cubic metre of gas still has only 6,000 MJ. With respect to the state grade, we distinguish four states: liquid, gas, solid and 'field'. Oil is in the most convenient and adaptable state: it is liquid. By contrast, renewable energy resources like solar power and wind power, as well as nuclear power from processed uranium ore, are all in the 'field' category: they are all some type of pressure, energy or radioactive field. However, the field state is the lowest state grade because it is difficult to store energy in this form and it cannot be used inside an engine such as an internal combustion engine. All energy sources with field states must be first converted into electricity, at considerable expense, whereas energy sources in the liquid state are easy to handle and use. Although crude oil must first of all be refined into gasoline and other petroleum products, this is a relatively simple industrial process and much cheaper, for example, than converting uranium ore into electricity.

The superiority of oil in the weight, volume and state grades has one particularly important implication. As human beings have advanced from the more primitive to the more advanced stages of technological development, one of the most important indicators of technical progress has been the invention, and the continuous improvement, of Large Independent Mobile Machines (LIMMs).[6] From triremes and chariots, steam-powered ships, early automobiles and biplanes to the supersonic jets, off-highway trucks, sports utility vehicles and high-performance cars of the present day, LIMMs have shaped our lives and moulded our social organisation and culture. Indeed, according to the energy economist, Douglas Reynolds, 'It has often been characteristic of any leading society that they have the biggest and most advanced LIMM.'[7]

This is why oil is such a useful energy source. In a LIMM, the machinery has to carry its own fuel; so the higher this fuel's weight grade the better any LIMM will perform. One up for oil. But, the volume grade of oil is also important because the higher the volume grade the smaller will be the LIMM's fuel tank and the smaller the tank, the more space will be available for other functions, such as passenger and luggage space or, in the case of military LIMMs, weaponry and ammunition. Consequently, for a society in which LIMMs play a central role no other energy resource is as efficient as oil. It is compact and easy to use, in its natural state it is located in highly concentrated reservoirs, and it can be transformed into a usable energy product rapidly, cheaply and safely.

Many people sincerely wish that we were much less dependent upon oil. They point not only to the link between oil-related carbon dioxide emissions and global warming, but also to the many insanities of the petro-society: traffic congestion, the tens of thousands of fatalities from automobile accidents, non-bio-degradable plastic refuse. Nevertheless, there are few indications, as yet, that the citizens of modern capitalist society – of which America is the archetype – are willing or able to forego their addiction to the 'conveniences' which make oil such an essential and strategic commodity.

OIL CAPITALISM: THE COMPETITIVE STRUGGLE FOR RESERVES

Because oil is so useful a substance, those who can achieve control over it will be very rich. We first learnt this lesson from Rockefeller in the 1870s, and then from the 'Seven Sisters', the great multinational oil companies which carved up the world oil market between them and maintained their control from the 1920s to the 1960s.[8] Although the historical development of capitalism was based primarily on the growth of manufacturing, we often think of the oil industry, especially 'Big Oil' – the major multinational oil companies – as the archetypal form of capitalist enterprise. However, 'oil capitalism' (and to a lesser extent, mining capitalism) has two particular characteristics which distinguish it from manufacturing capitalism.

Firstly, the capitalist oil company is confronted by landed property to which it requires access in order to drill for oil. This in turn, means that oil companies must accommodate themselves to a set of customary rules and arrangements concerning the governance of access to this property and the subsoil resources underlying it. Throughout history, in almost every sovereign nation, land and subsoil resources have remained subject to the 'eminent domain' rights of the state. These rights are essentially threefold: firstly, the right to tax (or demand some other contribution in kind); secondly, the right to revoke a right to landed property already granted or conceded; and thirdly, the right to 'police' i.e. to control or regulate.[9] Of course where the oil- or mineral-endowed country is under colonial or semi-colonial domination by another state or group of states these rights of eminent domain can be overridden; but, even then, the capitalist oil company

3

from the colonial power will usually have to set aside some part of its gross profit to pay a tax or royalty payment to the colonial authority or collaborating native rulers. In this respect, therefore, oil capitalism is much more akin to agrarian capitalism than to manufacturing.

Secondly, in one important respect, oil companies differ from *both* agrarian and manufacturing capitalist enterprises. This is because the continuous depletion of their natural resource, as they extract and sell the oil, means that they are remorselessly driven by what one might call a 'territorial imperative'. The oil company must be continuously on the move, shifting its operations from region to region, country to country, constantly seeking new reserves of oil to replace those which it is depleting. If it fails to replace these depleted reserves, it won't be long before its share price will decline and its directors and managers will suffer accordingly. This is because it is primarily the company's proven oil reserves which provide the basis for its future cash flow and profits. Capitalist investors base their stock market valuation of the company on the size of these remaining reserves, together with various more or less plausible assumptions about future prices, costs, production plans and a 'discount' rate used to put a 'present value' on the future stream of net cash flow.[10]

Before the 1970s, when the major oil companies still had access to the almost limitless reserves of Middle East oil, adding new proven reserves was just a question of drilling some extra adjacent acreage. After the 1970s, when these huge reserves of oil were removed from their control and nationalised by the 'OPEC revolution', the major oil companies concentrated their search for new oilfields, to replace those they had lost, in what were deemed to be politically 'safe' areas, free from the threat of expropriation and nationalisation. Initially they had some successes: in Alaska and the North Sea, in Western Canada, Indonesia (under the control of a pro-American dictator) and the onshore areas of the USA. But, by the early 1990s, such 'safe' petroleum provinces offered very little prospect of finding the 'giant' oilfields they were seeking; fields with more than 500 million barrels of reserves whose huge economies of scale offer exceptional profitability.

Despairing of finding any new 'giants' in North America, the major US oil companies began to move more of their upstream operations abroad. A study carried out by the US Department of Energy's Energy Information Administration (EIA) in 1995, noted that, 'Since the oil price collapse of late 1985 and early 1986, the US oil and gas industry has changed dramatically. The major oil companies have shifted much of their exploration and development efforts to targets outside the United States.'[11] This process continued throughout the 1990s. In 1991, the group of 20 largest US oil-producing companies designated as 'majors' by the US Department of Energy accounted for 55.7 per cent of total US domestic oil

4

production. But, by 2000, this figure had fallen to 45.2 per cent.[12] This movement away from the USA was reflected in the geographical distribution of the US majors' oil reserves. In 1985, for example, 55 per cent of Chevron's proven world oil reserves were located in the USA. However, by 1999, this figure had fallen to only 22 per cent.

But as the major US oil companies (accompanied by the European majors) moved abroad searching for new giant oilfields, they were soon joined by a new group of reserve-hungry privatised or semi-privatised former state oil companies, which were proliferating during the 1990s. According to the chief executive of one such former state-owned company, Italy's ENI, the early 1990s witnessed 'an explosion of the number of competitors' struggling to get their hands on non-OPEC reserves. In his opinion, 'Everyone wants to be an international major.'[13]

This ambition even took hold of some of the smaller US oil companies, the so-called 'independents'.[14] As we shall observe in later chapters, historically, the interests of US oil capitalism have not been homogeneous. Indeed for many years the objectives of the integrated, multinational major oil companies owning refineries in the USA was in exploiting low-cost oil reserves abroad and importing these into the USA at commensurately low prices. This objective clashed with the interests of the independents whose higher-cost domestic upstream operations were often unable to withstand the competition from the flow of cheap foreign oil into the country. But by the beginning of the twenty-first century this sharp division between the majors and the independents was beginning to break down. Some of the larger independents – companies like Apache Corporation, Burlington Resources, Pioneer Natural Resources, Ocean Energy and Vintage Petroleum – now also went multinational, joining the worldwide competitive struggle to control what remains of the really promising oil reserves outside the Middle East. Indeed, of the 187 publicly listed small and medium-sized US oil companies surveyed in 2001 by the *Oil and Gas Journal* 31 already held proven oil reserves outside the USA.[15]

With the competitive struggle to acquire new oil reserves hotting up, and the extraordinarily profitable opportunities in the Persian Gulf still out of bounds, the jostling crowd of multinational companies were forced to seek out opportunities in the so-called 'new frontiers' of oil exploration: the deep waters of West Africa's Atlantic Coast and the Atlantic West of Shetland, Vietnam, Egypt, Malaysia, and the Caspian and Central Asian states of the former Soviet Union. But although one or two new very large fields were discovered, they were often high-cost operations and sometimes far from the oil-consuming nations, so costly transportation infrastructure was required to bring the oil to market. At the same time some of the rulers of these new oil states had no intention whatsoever of allowing foreign oil companies to walk away with huge profits at their expense. Instead they hired consultants who devised tough petroleum fiscal regimes to ensure that the lion's share of any oil wealth discovered went to them. For example, by the mid-1990s, an oilfield which might typically reward a company with a pre-tax rate of profit of 43 per cent would yield only 9.4 per cent *after tax* in Egypt's Gulf of Suez; one in Malaysia with the same pre-tax profitability would yield only 10.8 per cent post-tax; and one in Kazakhstan only 12.8 per cent post-tax.[16]

So in general, throughout the 1990s investment opportunities for the major oil companies were insufficiently profitable to adequately remunerate their investors. Correctly measured, their rate of return on capital was weak.[17] The strategic response of the companies was to unleash a wave of cost-cutting, share buy-backs and mega-mergers: Exxon merged with Mobil, BP with Amoco, Chevron with Texaco and Conoco with Phillips Petroleum. Nevertheless, according to a report published in 2003 by the UK oil consultancy Wood Mackenzie, the 25 largest multinational oil companies 'have destroyed value in 50 of the 80 countries in which they have invested over the past six years'.[18] Two of the worst performers were the US companies ChevronTexaco and Conoco.

What the oil companies really needed was to return to the source of those former riches which they had enjoyed before the OPEC Revolution – the fabulously oil-rich lands of the Middle East. In the countries bordering the Gulf, in Kuwait, Saudi Arabia, the Emirates, Iran and Iraq, both capital and operating costs are but a tiny fraction of those in the 'frontier' and 'safe' oil regions to which the oil companies were then restricted.[19] Moreover in those Gulf states so bountifully endowed with petroleum wealth, the companies could easily hand over to their rulers as much as 90 per cent of the net profit and still enjoy a return on capital of over 40 per cent. Unfortunately, although the major US oil companies had so far used all the political and diplomatic influence at their disposal to try to prise open the upstream oil business of Saudi Arabia and Kuwait, these efforts had been to no avail and as for Iran and Iraq, existing legislation and the prevailing political conjuncture meant that for the time being these countries were strictly out of bounds to US businesses.

Historically, oil companies have rarely shrunk from utilising political power to achieve their economic ends and this was particularly true in relation to the Middle East.[20] However, circumstances do not always favour such manoeuvres and the political conjuncture is not always accommodating. For example, during the 'oil crisis' of the 1970s, the American public became intensely suspicious of the behaviour of the major oil companies and since then US administrations have generally become less willing to do the bidding of 'Big Oil'.

6

Nevertheless, at the turn of the twenty-first century, what was probably the most oil-dominated US administration in the history of the USA was elected, in spite of acute public awareness of the extent to which it was beholden to corporate interests in general and to the oil and energy business interest in particular. With the election of President George W. Bush, oil capitalism was now at the very heart of US power and its requirements were soon high on the agenda of the new regime.[21] Moreover, at this particular conjuncture, a significant change was taking place in the world oil market. After many years of low prices, world demand for oil was beginning to accelerate (for reasons which we shall explore in Chapters Nine and Ten). In these circumstances the historic division between the interests of the US major oil companies and the independents began to further erode, as the prospect of generally higher oil prices made the latter less fearful of 'cheap' foreign oil imports. Instead it was now the US oil consumer that became fearful – fearful of the country's rapidly growing dependence on foreign oil, and in particular dependence upon those major sources of oil which remained outside the control of US oil companies, large or small.

Increasing dependence on imports from the Persian Gulf, where America maintained a staunchly pro-Israeli foreign policy, carried with it the risk of major supply disruption such as the one which occurred as a result of the 1973 Arab oil embargo. Moreover concern was already mounting about the political stability of America's major source of Gulf imports, Saudi Arabia.

Thus, the accession to power of the Bush Administration occurred at a time when the interests of US oil companies and oil consumers were rapidly moving closer together. In these circumstances a relentless drive for 'Energy Security' dictated a new strategic focus on the Middle East, one which might accommodate the interests of both groups: unfettered access to new, highly profitable reserves for the companies; guaranteed security of supply at moderate prices for the consumers. The objectives of oil capitalism we have already discussed. We now turn to the factors underlying the American consumer's voracious demand for oil.

LIFE, LIBERTY AND THE PURSUIT OF OIL

For years external observers had expressed their exasperation at American energy profligacy and the geopolitical risks which it entailed. For example, a few days after Iraq's 1990 invasion of Kuwait, Anthony Harris, the *Financial Times'* correspondent in Washington, wrote an unusually angry article in which he drew attention not only to the remarkable extent of America's oil dependence but also to its reluctance to do anything about it. In particular he was referring to the almost unanimous rejection by Congress of a recent proposal by the Administration to introduce a small energy consumption tax. According to Harris, 'The American domestic response to the Gulf crisis has so far shown a combination of childishness and evasion of reality so complete that serious political leadership no longer seems possible in this poll-dominated democracy...' American motorists, he pointed out, already enjoyed by far the cheapest fuel in the developed world 'yet to listen to the phone-ins, an increase of about 10 cents on this bargain price is an intolerable threat to life, liberty and the pursuit of happiness'. As a result of its petroleum profligacy, the USA had become 'highly vulnerable, a permanent hostage to events in the Gulf' and yet, to the amazement of this distinguished *Financial Times* journalist, the US public was apparently quite happy to expose thousands of its young soldiers to a desert war, and at a huge cost to the nation, 'but will not face the bill for self-reliance'.[22]

One might have assumed that the USA would have learned the lesson of the 1991 Gulf War and taken steps to reduce its degree of oil dependence in the decade that followed. But far from curtailing its already gargantuan appetite for the world's oil, in the ten years following the Gulf War, US oil consumption increased by 18 per cent and in 2000 reached an all-time record of 897.6 million tonnes per year (19.7 million barrels per day).[23] With the Asia-Pacific region increasing its oil consumption by 45 percent between 1991 and 2000, and with China, in particular, more than doubling its consumption from 2.4 million to 5 million barrels per day, one might also have reasonably assumed that while Asian economic development required a certain 'catching-up' in oil consumption, a mature capitalist economy like the USA would perhaps be relinquishing part of its share: in fact, at 25 per cent, America's share of rapidly increasing world oil consumption, had remained more or less constant since 1991.

The problem was that in spite of the fact that throughout the 1990s the USA was still the second largest world oil producer – a fact we are often inclined to forget – since the early 1970s America had lost the ability to supply all its oil requirements from domestic sources. By 1950, America was already consuming more oil than it produced itself and during the next two decades the gap between consumption and production widened. However this picture is somewhat misleading because, as Chapter Four explains, for decades America was producing its own domestic oil at below capacity, partly to sustain domestic oil prices and partly in the belief that America should conserve its own oil reserves.

Gradually, however, the USA moved towards full capacity production. In 1970 domestic oil production peaked at 11.3 million b/d, and by 1972 every oil well in the country was producing at its full capacity rate. Then in 1973–1974 the world experienced the great 'energy crisis' induced by the actions of the Arab

OPEC countries, to be followed by the turmoil of a second oil price shock after the Iranian Revolution of 1979.[24]

Initially, the economies of all the industrialised oil-consuming nations were damaged by these 'oil shocks' but after a while their oil balances improved. High oil prices discouraged consumption and encouraged production in those countries which had domestic oil to produce. In America during the early 1980s, petroleum consumption actually fell, as oil used for generating electricity and for space heating was replaced by alternative fuels; and because the country's economic growth slowed down, it used less energy overall. Moreover, domestic oil production stopped falling and seemed to be stabilising.

However, by the second half of the 1980s, America's 'oil balance' had begun to deteriorate again. This time, not only was consumption growing strongly, but oil production was now on a steady downward path. Something had gone seriously wrong with America's energy policy and to a degree which had certainly not been anticipated. For example, Melvin Conant, one of the USA's leading experts on energy security matters, writing in 1981, believed that through increased development of domestic energy resources, improved energy technologies and conservation, US oil imports could be greatly reduced over the 1980s. Conant thought that a goal of cutting oil imports generally by 50 per cent by the decade's end was entirely possible for the USA, 'and it could eliminate dependence on the Gulf well before then'.[25]

But after falling in the early 1980s, net petroleum imports began to increase once again. By 1998, for the first time in its history, more than 50 per cent of the USA's oil requirements were provided by other oil-producing countries and by 2001 this figure had already increased to 54.3 per cent – a new all-time record of 10.6 million b/d.[26] Even more disturbing, the proportion of total US oil supplies (both domestic and foreign) which was coming from the Persian Gulf – 14.1 per cent – was now the highest in the nation's history.[27]

This remarkable increase in petroleum imports was all the more disturbing because, as we have mentioned above, the USA had been particularly successful in substituting coal, natural gas and nuclear energy for heavy fuel oil in the generation of electricity. In addition, a major programme of investment in nuclear energy was undertaken and, in spite of the setback from the near-disaster at Three Mile Island in 1979, electricity generation from nuclear energy also grew rapidly throughout the last two decades of the twentieth century. More recently there had also been a large amount of gas-fired generating capacity coming on-stream as a result of the technological breakthrough in combined-cycle gas turbines. Consequently, between 1977 and 2000 petroleum consumption by the US electricity-generating sector fell by 69 per cent, while coal burning increased by 99.8 per cent, natural gas by 97.2 per cent and nuclear energy by 196 per cent (albeit from a much lower base than coal).

OIL AND MOTORISATION

If electricity generation had been the only market for oil, Melvin Conant's 1981 forecast for oil imports might have been easily achieved. In reality, of course, oil is consumed in many other ways: by households and commercial enterprises (for central heating), by industry (in steam-raising boilers, furnaces and various non-energy uses like plastics) and in transportation. But while demand for oil from the residential, commercial and industrial (including electricity) sectors has remained more or less unchanged since the 1980s, demand from the transportation sector was soaring.

In 1950 the share of total US oil consumption attributable to the transportation sector was 54 per cent. By 1970 it had risen to 56 per cent, by 1980 it had jumped to 60 per cent and by 1990 it had reached 67 per cent. But it did not stop there. By 2001, 69 per cent of US oil consumption was accounted for by the transportation sector as a whole (including motor vehicles, aircraft, shipping and railways) and 53 per cent of total US oil consumption was accounted for by motor vehicles alone. Indeed, the rate of increase in America's consumption of motor vehicle fuels (gasoline plus diesel) was prodigious: in 1960 it was 3.76 million b/d, in 1980, 7.1 million b/d and by 2001, was running at 10.1 million b/d.

The reasons for this are clear. Oil, as we have already observed, is by far the most convenient energy source for LIMMs. In the twentieth century, American capitalism emerged and rose to phenomenal prosperity primarily through the manufacture and sale of the motor car – the archetypal LIMM. Other industries played their part – steel, plastics, and of course, the petroleum industry itself; but, as often as not, these were ancillary to the motor industry. Their products constituted the derived demand which emanated from the great car and truck factories. More than any other brand names, Ford and General Motors encapsulate the achievements of US manufacturing industry in the twentieth century.

Of course most other industrialised countries are motorised in varying degrees – but to nothing like the extent which characterises American society. This is a theme we shall examine in greater detail in Chapters Two and Nine, but for the time being it will suffice to underline one simple statistic which indicates the huge gap between the USA and the other industrialised countries. Motor gasoline and diesel consumption in the USA is 2,043 litres per inhabitant. That is three times greater than Japan and two and half times greater than Germany, France and the UK.[28] Moreover this is only partially the result of geography – distances travelled – because energy consumption per 1,000 vehicle/kilometres, 183 kg of oil equivalent, is twice that of France and the UK and 1.8 times greater than Germany and Japan.[29]

For the past forty years the automobile has imprinted itself upon the psychology and personality of the American citizen to a degree which no other society has experienced. By the beginning of the twenty-first century, America had become the motorised society par excellence and its working, shopping, recreational and family life reflected the personal mobility Americans enjoy. Not only did Americans drive to and from school, work, worship, shopping malls and friends and relatives' homes; they also stayed in motels and refuelled not only their cars at drive-in service stations, but also their bodies at drive-through restaurants. They even had access to drive-through dry-cleaning, pharmacies and funeral-home visitations. At an ideological level, words describing America's relationship with cars typified the American spirit in the eyes of many: 'freedom, power, autonomy, mobility, importance, liberty and adventure'.[30]

In 1992, President George Bush Sr, a reluctant participant at the Rio 'Earth Summit', declared that 'the American Way of Life is not negotiable.'[31] Ten years' after Bush Sr's, remarks, his sentiments were being endorsed even more strongly among conservative Americans. For example, in 2001 the Competitive Enterprise Institute, a right-wing 'think tank', inveighed against the 'anti-energy zealots' and complained that, 'powerful forces have worked mightily to shame people into believing that consuming energy is bad, and that Americans should therefore feel guilty about consuming so much.'[32]

Unfortunately, this completely motorised 'American Way' made the USA uniquely vulnerable to the forces of radical Islamism which, nurtured by the very regimes upon which America had come to depend for its energy security, now threatened the lifeblood of modern US capitalism.[33] American consumers needed Gulf oil and American oil companies intensely desired it; but political circumstances in the region threatened the interests of the former and obstructed the objectives of the latter.

But for the leaders of the world's only twenty-first-century superpower, increasingly conscious of their country's overwhelming military might, a solution seemed to be available. What was required was the establishment of a new American Imperium in the Middle East: one in which American-selected local rulers would invite American oil companies to make super-profits for American investors under the protective shield of the American military, while at the same time satisfying the voracious demands of the motorised American oil consumer.

And, by now, there were voices on the ideological fringe of the new US Administration, already whispering in their ear, reminding them that only fifty years ago it was Americans who controlled the oil flowing from the Middle East.

The automobile, this supposedly wonderful, freedom-giving, autonomy-providing symbol of US prosperity had turned into an economic and political juggernaut whose owners would increasingly have to subordinate and control the rest of the oil-producing world in order to ensure the continuing enjoyment of their 'non-negotiable' way of life. The 'juggernaut' of American motorisation had been trundling forward for decades but by 2001 it was gathering pace, sucking in vast quantities of imported oil as it advanced. The implications of this for the Middle East form the central theme of our book.[34] However, in the next chapter we explore precisely how the 'juggernaut' came into existence in the first place; how, during the years 1910–1960, it came to dominate so completely the lives of the vast majority of Americans; and the extent to which the large automobile manufacturers and the oil companies, sometimes acting in concert, were the juggernaut's real drivers.

2   The Die is Cast

Cities must be remade. The greatest automobile market today, the greatest untapped field of potential customers, is the large number of city people who refuse to own cars.

Paul Hoffman, President, Studebaker Corporation, 1939

America is the most highly motorised country in the world. It has 834 registered vehicles per 1,000 population, more than 50 per cent higher than Western Europe.[1] By the early years of the twentieth century, the USA was already leading the world in both the ownership and production of gasoline-powered motor vehicles. As early as 1907, there were 143,200 registered automobiles in the USA and a motorisation rate of 1.65 per 1,000, greater than the UK (1.56), France (1.02) and Germany (0.26). By 1913, there were 1,258,060 registered automobiles and a motorisation rate of 12.9, double that of Canada, its nearest rival. In the same year, 15 separate US car manufacturers produced 388,096 automobiles, about 13 times the number produced by European manufacturers.[2] By 1929, the US motorisation rate had increased to 219 per 1,000; 55 per cent of American families owned a car, and 10 per cent owned two or more.[3] A mere 25 years after commercial production of gasoline-powered vehicles had begun (the 1901 Oldsmobile), automobile production had become the USA's largest industry absorbing 80 per cent of national rubber production, 75 per cent of glass and 20 per cent of steel. Fully 25 per cent of the nation's machine tools were used in the manufacture of automobiles.[4] And by 1929, US automobile factories produced 85 per cent of the world's cars.[5]

In the economic slump of the early 1930s, the motorisation rate declined, but after 1936 it resumed its upward trend. The economic crisis had hastened industry consolidation and now three large companies, Ford, General Motors and Chrysler controlled 90 per cent of US automobile production. Already they had ruthlessly stamped their mark upon America's economy and society. Their innovations in both production and marketing were truly revolutionary – the production line, standardisation of parts, strict control over the labour process, advertising (by 1923 the car industry had become the largest advertiser in the USA), instalment credit, controlled sales outlets – all these new developments reflected the dynamism of this new mode of production.

During the Second World War, car ownership fell again as private consumption took second place to the demands of military production, but when manufacturing industry switched back to consumer goods, between 1945 and 1955, motor vehicle ownership increased yet again to 377 per 1,000 population. But there was an additional factor underlying this rapid post-war rise in motorisation. Behind the dramatic increase in car ownership lay the almost complete motorisation of US cities, with the decimation of their once flourishing public transit (transport) systems[6] – a phenomenon which, generally speaking, did not occur in Europe, certainly not to the same extent.[7]

THE MOTORISATION OF AMERICA

The motorisation of American cities, which was carried out in a number of discrete stages between 1925 and 1960, is conventionally explained by US economists and historians as the consequence of sovereign consumers exercising their freedom of choice. As one former presidential science adviser put it, 'Society decided it wanted the automobile, and it bought the automobile.'[8] As Americans got richer, so the argument goes, their personal preference for the private motor car over the public transport systems – streetcars, light railways and motor buses – expressed itself in a growing demand for the former and a falling demand for the latter. Private travel by automobile was simply more desirable than public transport.

It would be foolish to deny the utility, personal comfort and freedom of movement that cars provide. This, however, is not the issue. 'The relevant question', as the American historian David St Clair, puts it, is not 'whether people did or did not prefer the automobile, but rather to what extent, and for what purposes, and at what cost they preferred the automobile.'[9] Just because Americans liked cars does not mean that, from the outset, they wished to use them to the exclusion of all other forms of transport or for all transportation purposes. The complete motorisation of US cities was not inevitable. The problem with the conventional 'consumer sovereignty' argument is that it omits any mention of the other main actors. Much as orthodox economists would like to believe that the consumer is king, the history of the automobile in the USA shows that it was the giant capitalist enterprises – the car-manufacturing companies and, to a lesser extent, the large oil companies, which were really in the driving seat.

The interests of the oil industry were, of course, closely tied to the expansion of the automobile industry. At the beginning of the twentieth century, 57 per cent of all refined US petroleum was kerosene for oil lamps and only 12 per cent was gasoline. But by 1930, 44.8 per cent was motor gasoline and only 5 per cent was kerosene.[10] In 1907, the first drive-in gasoline station had opened, but for a time most gasoline continued to be sold by grocers and general merchants. However, between 1919 and 1929, the number of drive-in gasoline stations increased from about 12,000 to 143,000. The consumption of gasoline increased from 101 million barrels in 1920 to 394.8 million in 1930. In turn, this rapidly rising demand for gasoline led to a doubling of domestic crude oil production over the same period.[11]

It was a recognition of the common interest between the automobile and oil industries which led General Motors Corporation and Standard Oil Company of California (later to become Chevron) to develop a strategy which would first acquire and then dismantle a large proportion of the existing public transport systems in American cities, in particular, on the west coast of America. As we shall see, public transport in America did not die because of competition from the automobile – it was killed to make way for it.

The problem facing the automobile and oil companies, as the US economy began to recover from the slump of the mid-1930s, was that hitherto the principal source of demand for automobiles had come from customers living in rural areas. It was the farmers, rural doctors and lawyers who were initially most attracted to the motor car and the small truck. In a sparsely populated US hinterland the arrival of the automobile was a truly liberating factor for thousands of early-twentieth-century rural Americans.

However, America was urbanising fast. In 1910, 45.7 per cent of the US population lived in urban areas but by 1930 this had increased to 56.2 per cent. The automobile industry began to see this as an obstacle to further market penetration unless something could be done to raise the car ownership rates in the cities to those in the rural areas and small towns. As the President of Studebaker Corporation[12] revealingly admitted in 1934, 'Sales resistance to further absorption comes from inability to use automobiles effectively rather than from inability to own them.' He acknowledged that many well-to-do people did not own automobiles, not because they could not afford to own them, but because, 'as they will tell you, the ownership lacks advantage. They can use mass transportation more conveniently for many of their movements.'[13]

GETTING RID OF THE STREETCARS AND REMAKING THE CITIES

The first stage in dealing with this 'problem' of public transport was elimination of the electric streetcar systems (or light railways) which, by the early 1920s, were common to most American cities, and their replacement by gasoline, and later diesel-fuelled, motor buses. In 1922, there were only 1,370 miles of urban motor bus routes in service compared to 28,906 miles of street railway track; but, by 1940, there were 78,900 miles of motor bus routes, while operational streetcar track had fallen to 15,163 miles. Passengers carried by streetcar fell from 13,569,000 in 1923 to 7,290,000 in 1942, whereas passengers carried by urban motor bus increased from 661,000 to 7,245,000 over the same period. By 1955, there were only 5,478 miles of streetcar track in operation in the USA.

However, all this had little to do with consumer preferences. Existing streetcar systems were predominantly privately owned, but publicly regulated monopolies. Like other US public utilities they were subject to control of their rate of return on capital and were therefore safe but not particularly lucrative investments. This made them vulnerable to hostile takeover. General Motors developed gasoline-fuelled motor buses in the 1920s and in the early 1930s began to buy-up electric streetcar companies via a number of small, affiliated 'front' companies. Conversion from streetcar to motor bus swiftly followed, as General Motors cancelled orders for new streetcars and scrapped existing ones, replacing them with its own gasoline, and later diesel buses.[14]

At first this strategy was aimed only at smaller towns but once it was decided that larger targets should be attacked, a more highly capitalised form of company was required for the purpose. In 1936, National City Lines was established through the amalgamation of a number of smaller motor bus companies in which General Motors had equity, or whose managements were controlled by General Motors through interlocking directorships. Then National City Lines' stock was sold to General Motors itself, to Chevron and to Phillips Petroleum.[15] Two years later, Pacific City Lines, another transit-acquiring company, was set up by General Motors and Chevron.

Although the purpose of National City Lines and Pacific City Lines was ostensibly to replace streetcar public transport with motor buses, it has been convincingly argued by a number of US transportation historians that the real intention was to clear the way for the mass introduction of the automobile to urban areas.[16] It has been shown, for example, that motor bus operation was actually considerably less profitable than the other alternative form of electric public transport which was becoming available in the 1930s – the trolley bus – and less profitable even than the existing streetcars.[17] This was because motor

16

buses required far more frequent repairs than either trolley buses or streetcars, and had a much shorter working life. So General Motors' strategy of forward integration into motor bus operations must have been driven by some motive other than a desire to become a public transport operator. Certainly, the front companies set up to run the new motor bus systems would provide a captive market for General Motors' bus division and to a lesser extent for gasoline and diesel fuel supplied by Chevron, but these markets were economically insignificant compared to the far greater volumes of automobiles and gasoline which would be sold once the steel rails were ripped up, the electric cables and pantographs were removed and the streets of US cities fully opened up to the motor car.

The destruction of efficient and profitable public transport systems based on streetcars and electric trains by General Motors/Chevron front companies was carried out most thoroughly and ruthlessly in California between 1946 and 1958. The electric streetcar and light railway systems of East Bay, San Jose, Fresno, Sacramento, San Diego and Los Angeles were all bought up by Pacific City Lines or National City Lines and then closed down. The policy was far from popular and there is evidence of widespread public opposition to the destruction of the streetcar systems. City Councils tried to block the motorisation plans of Pacific City Lines, local newspapers described the new motor buses as 'stink wagons' and, according to St Clair, in Los Angeles, 'the public clamoured to bring back the old streetcars.'[18]

Of course, General Motors and Chevron would have been well aware of the unsatisfactory nature of the motor bus public transport systems, but that was not their primary concern. In many cases conversion of streetcar systems to motor bus was followed by cutbacks in the new bus services or fare increases so severe that passenger numbers started to fall. Soon a vicious spiral of decline set in, with reduced services leading to higher fares leading in turn to further service cutbacks. These, in turn, pressured people to buy a car. For example, cutting evening bus services meant that people of that neighbourhood could no longer go out at night, unless they purchased a car and 'once they had a car, there was little incentive to take the bus even when it was running.'[19]

At the same time as older parts of the cities were losing their existing public transport systems, the new suburbs being constructed for the rapidly growing urban population were rarely provided with new ones. By 1940, 13 million US citizens, about one tenth of the population of the USA at the time, now lived in sub-urban communities without access to any kind of public transportation system.[20]

As the motorisation campaign advanced, it became clear that the major increase in urban automobile use which the car manufacturers were seeking would still be constrained unless large new roadways were constructed linking together the rapidly growing urban centres and penetrating their conurbations with fast radial freeways. To achieve this objective the automobile companies astutely linked their own interests to those of the military who were seeking a vast new federal interstate highway system for reasons of national defence. But their interests did not entirely coincide. For those sections of the planned system which entered urban areas the military wanted circumferential highways which would by-pass the city centres, while the car-makers wanted radial highways which would penetrate through to the central zones. These new roads must 'gash...ruthlessly through built-up sections of overcrowded cities', in the words of Studebaker's president Paul Hoffman who argued that, 'Cities must be remade. The greatest automobile market today, the greatest untapped field of potential customers, is the large number of city people who refuse to own cars, or use the cars they have very little, because it's a nuisance to take them out.'[21]

In 1951, with the US automobile industry now producing over two thirds of the world's cars, a massive publicity campaign for the industry's version of the interstate highway system was initiated by the innocently named National Highway Users Conference (the motor industry's lobbying organisation). It employed the dubious argument that, in the event of an atomic bomb attack, radial urban freeways attached to the interstate would enable the population to quickly evacuate the cities. When congressional hearings on interstate legislation began in 1955, the automobile industry, represented by James Nance, president of Studebaker and William Hufstader, vice-president of General Motors, made formidable presentations, arguing the need for an urban-oriented interstate highway system to meet the increased traffic flows into and out of the cities. However, while arguing that the urban interstate was needed to cope with increased traffic flows, it was clear from the auto manufacturers' comments that the huge number of automobiles which so urgently required the major new road network would, in fact, only materialise once the new road system was built – a circular argument not infrequently used by supporters of motorisation to this day. However, James Nance had another argument, which he expressed in a forthright manner, and which may have carried more weight than the one based on traffic-flow 'predictions'. Pointing out that the health of the US economy was tied to the expansion of the automobile industry he argued that, 'We have to have the roads if we are going to make wage-earners and car buyers out of these people.'[22]

Adding macroeconomic arguments to civil defence considerations swayed the legislators. The Federal Highway Act of 1956 provided for the building of what was to be the world's most expensive piece of civil engineering, constructing 42,500 miles of roadway at a total cost of $41 billion, about 90 per cent of which flowed directly from the Federal Government.

WHAT'S GOOD FOR GENERAL MOTORS

By 1960, the critical economic importance of the automobile industry could not be denied. It had become 'the keystone of the American economy'.[23] This is why Nance's argument on this point was highly persuasive; and that well-known assertion by General Motors' president, Charles E. Wilson, that what was good for General Motors was also beneficial to the country, contained a solid core of economic truth. The dynamism of America's capitalist economy now depended to a very large extent on the success of its key manufacturing sector, at the heart of which was the automobile industry, now producing a record 6.7 million cars each year, together with 1.2 million light and heavy trucks. In *Fortune Magazine*'s rankings for the year 1960, General Motors, now the largest US car-maker, was also the largest US corporation with annual sales worth $12.7 billion and net profits of $959 million.[24] The second largest corporation was Standard Oil of New Jersey (later to become Exxon), the largest oil refiner in the USA. The third largest corporation was the Ford Motor Company; the sixth largest was Mobil; the seventh the Chrysler Corporation; the eighth Texaco; and the ninth Gulf Oil. This was indeed, an economy based on cars and oil.

Around the big three automobile manufacturers – General Motors, Ford and Chrysler – and the few remaining smaller manufacturers, such as American Motors Corporation and Studebaker-Packard, there were about 3,000 companies supplying them with vehicle parts. The motor industry was also the principal market for US steel producers. At the other end of the commercial spectrum there were thousands of small businesses involved in automobile retailing, gasoline service stations, repair shops and breakdown recovery. We must also acknowledge the large service sector which developed out of the motorisation boom – out-of-town shopping malls, drive-in cinemas, motels and tourist attractions. Indeed, the last-named 'industry' was one which was to be of enormous cultural significance to Americans. With an automobile they could 'see America'.

Between 1950 and 1960, the total number of registered motor vehicles increased from 49.1 million to 73.9 million, an astonishing 50 per cent increase in only 10 years. By 1960, 78 per cent of American families owned at least one car and 21.5 per cent owned two or more.[25] There were now 401 motor vehicles per 1,000 US citizens: American society was firmly set in a mould created by the automobile industry. Writing of the 'average American' living in the USA of the early 1960s, John Rae noted that first, he lived in a metropolitan area, and most likely in a suburb; second, he owned an automobile; and third, 'he and his family were almost completely dependent on their car for transportation beyond walking distance, or frequently within walking distance.'[26]

Business ownership of heavy trucks also increased. Between 1950 and 1960, the volume of intercity freight carried by truck rose from 173 billion to almost 300 billion ton-miles – an increase from 16 to 22.5 per cent of the national total, while volumes carried by railroad fell from 56 to 43.5 per cent over the same period. Massive new diesel-fuelled trucks, carrying loads of twenty tons or more, now made their appearance, some of them combination vehicles, towing huge trailers. By 1960, over a million such 'combination' vehicles were in service.

To supply the huge quantities of gasoline now required by American motor vehicles, US refining capacity had to rise from 6.7 million barrels per day in 1950 to 9.8 million b/d in 1960.[27] In these same years, total petroleum supplies to US industries and consumers increased by 51 per cent, domestic oil output rose from 5.9 million b/d to 8 million b/d, while net oil imports rose from 0.5 million b/d to 1.6 million b/d, another all-time record. Although Venezuela was still the largest supplier of foreign oil at this time, providing 474,000 b/d in 1960, the Middle East was beginning to be a significant exporter to the USA. Between 1950 and 1960, imported oil supplies sourced from American and British oil companies in Kuwait, Saudi Arabia, Qatar and Iran rose from 114,000 barrels per day to 310,000 b/d.

So, by the early 1960s, the die was cast. The whole socio-economic structure of American society – and the geo-strategic consequences of that structure – had been constructed in a manner which would make it virtually impossible to modify in future years without a major effort of political will. However, as yet there seemed few reasons to veer away from what seemed a glorious exhibition of American industrial prowess and the American dream of unfettered individual freedom. But this freedom – to drive anywhere, to any extent, whenever and wherever, would eventually come at a heavy price and one which would leave America increasingly dependent upon a far-off region of which its ordinary citizens knew little and cared even less, so long as they could fill up their gasoline tanks for a few cents. Indeed, according to Daniel Yergin, shortly before the eruption of the oil price crisis of 1973, few Americans had any idea that their country imported any oil at all!

But there were other Americans, the directors and managers of the country's major multinational oil companies and the political power elite with whom they were intertwined, who knew a great deal about that far-off land; who, between them, had spent the past thirty years ensuring that most of the stupendous oil wealth lying hidden below the deserts and shallow waters of the Persian Gulf would fall into American hands. How that occurred is therefore the subject of our next chapter.

3   How America
Got Control
of the Gulf

The national policy of the United States should aim at securing for American
nationals access to the world's oil resources.

Petroleum Industry War Council, 1943

Hundreds of millions of years ago, gigantic seas pounded the mountainous
landmass of what is now the western part of Saudi Arabia and which geologists call
the Arabian Shield. Extending far beyond the present-day Gulf, these primordial
waters flooded north, intermittently covering the regions now known as Iraq,
Jordan, Lebanon and Syria. Through age after age, the seas alternately flooded and
retreated over this vast area, exposing the bare sediments to the erosion of wind, rain
and sun and then covering them once again. These sediments left behind once the
ancient seas had retreated, constitute the second and younger geological province
in the Gulf, the Arabian Shelf.[1]

The sediments of the Arabian Shelf outcrop on the eastern flank of the Arabian
mountains; then, along with progressively younger overlying beds, they dip gently
and thicken as they head towards the great deserts of the Rub Al Khali. As they
slope below the shoreline of the present-day Gulf they reach a thickness of around
6,500 metres. Stacked within this immense slab of sedimentary rock are a few
narrow slices – each of them less than 30 metres thick – which are the 'source rocks',
the origin of all the gigantic petroleum resources of the Gulf. They were formed in
the Jurassic age, about 150 million years ago, as a progressive change occurred in
the sedimentary environment. The seas began to withdraw, first from the area
which is now central Iraq, and then from the remainder of the region. As dinosaurs
waded in the shallow coastal waters of the late Jurassic, fine-grained muds rich in
the detritus of tiny marine animals and plants were deposited offshore in the

oxygen-starved waters. There they decomposed and became part of the seabed, beginning a sedimentary cycle in which organic-rich limestone rocks were laid down in alternate floodings and desiccations of a gradually receding sea. Finally the shallow salty seas evaporated to form impermeable anhydrite rock, sealing off the organic-rich limestones which lay below.

As the rocks containing organic matter were buried under further successive layers of newly deposited sediment, their temperature increased. By the time these source rocks were more than 2,000 metres below the surface, at temperatures exceeding 50 degrees centigrade, the micro-organisms began to cook into the substance we now call oil. Millions of years later, in the Cretaceous and Eocene periods, massive tectonic forces buckled and bent the strata of the Arabian Shelf as it collided with the Asian plate and partially slid beneath its western rim. Then the oil migrated into 'traps', where gently folding anticlynes of impermeable rock obstructed the natural upward movement of the oil. And here it remained for the next forty million years.

GIANTS, SUPER-GIANTS AND MEGA-GIANTS: THE OILFIELDS OF THE GULF

In a flicker of time, great civilisations rose and fell in the lands bordering the Gulf and some of the oil leaked to the surface where it turned into bitumen. Occasionally, the strange black substance oozing from the Mesopotamian lands ignited, providing inspiration for Zoroastrian fire-worshippers. The Summerians of Ur set decorative stone squares in it. The Babylonians used it to strengthen their walls and Alexander the Great, in a spirit of inquiry, burned a slave with it to further explore its practical uses. Yet none could have any idea of the liquid treasure that lay in the vast underground reservoirs from which the bitumen seeped.

And vast they still remain. The Ghawar oilfield in Eastern Saudi Arabia, for example, is the largest oilfield in the world and is one of only two classed as 'mega-giants'. It is 280 kilometres long and 16 kilometres wide at its greatest extent. In places the column of oil within it is over 300 metres tall. Discovered in 1948, it began production in 1951 and by 1990 had 219 flowing oil wells. In spite of continuous production ever since, the field still contains around 70 billion barrels of oil, more than twice the total oil reserves of the USA. The other mega-giant, Greater Burgan field in Kuwait, began production in 1938 but is still rated at just under 70 billion barrels of reserves. Of the 40 'super-giant' fields (50 billion down to 5 billion barrels), Kirkuk, in northern Iraq, still contains 10 billion barrels despite being in production since 1927. As for the 328 mere 'giants' (5 billion down to 500 million barrels), over one hundred of them are found in the Middle East.

There are only 417 giant, super-giant and mega-giant oilfields in the world out of over 42,000 discovered fields, but together these 417 fields account for three quarters of all the world's recoverable oil. Both the mega-giants, two thirds of the super-giants and one third of the giants are located in countries bordering the Gulf.[2] Together they contain 65 per cent of the total proven world oil reserves of 1,050 billion barrels. When all the other oilfields in the world have passed their peak and their long slow decline has begun, the owners of the Gulf oilfields will be waiting to reap the full advantage of their still vast reserves.

Yet none of this subterranean wealth was remotely conceivable when the first oilfield of the Middle East, Masjid e Suleiman, was struck in the early hours of 26 May 1908, on a remote plateau in the foothills of Iran's Zagros Mountains. Within a year, the British investors who had backed the venture made a public offering of its stock and the Anglo-Persian Oil Company (later to become British Petroleum) was born. During the first year of operation, in 1913, Masjid e Suleiman produced a modest 5,000 barrels per day, increasing slowly to 108,734 b/d by 1927 as new wells were sunk. At that time Iran was still the only source of Middle East oil. However, just before the First World War, German engineers working on the Ottoman railway system reported to the Deutsche Bank that surface features of the area around Mosul, in what is today north-east Iraq, appeared highly propitious for successful oil exploration. To further this objective, the Turkish Petroleum Company was established with German and British capital. But Turkey's entry into the First World War as an ally of Germany and Austria threw the company into disarray.

In 1916, under the terms of the Sykes-Picot Agreement, whereby the British and French divided the post-war Middle East between them, the Mosul oilfields were given to France. However, on 15 November 1918, a fortnight after hostilities had ceased, a British force under General Marshall advanced and occupied Mosul. The French reluctantly acceded to this *coup de main* but, in 1920, when the Allied Supreme Council met at San Remo to settle their many outstanding differences, the French were given a 25 per cent share in the reconstituted Turkish Petroleum Company, now stripped of its German owners and henceforth known as the Iraq Petroleum Company.

OIL AND AMERICA: THE DRIVE FOR ENERGY SECURITY BEGINS

The Americans did not attend the San Remo conference. They were already becoming disillusioned with the selfish behaviour of the other victorious powers and increasingly suspicious of British and French dominance in the new oilfields of the Middle East. The war had demonstrated, beyond any shadow of doubt, just how crucial petroleum was to the modern armed forces and, during the war, American refineries had supplied 80 per cent of the Allied requirements for petroleum products. In government offices, military HQs and elected assemblies all over the world, the linkages between oil, foreign policy and national security were now being discussed and for the first time the Americans began to worry about the resilience of their own oil reserves in the face of rapidly increasing consumption.[3] Of particular concern were the demands which would be made upon the nation's oil reserves by the large number of oil-fired capital ships which the US Navy was planning to build.

But the issue was more than just military requirements. A whole new era was dawning, what Daniel Yergin has aptly described as the 'Age of Hydrocarbon Man'.[4] As we have seen, the automobile industry was already a major force shaping the destiny of American society. Between 1910 and 1920, the annual factory sales of motor cars rose from 181,000 to 1,905,000 and over the same period the registered ownership of motor cars in the USA increased from 458,300 to a staggering 8,131,500. Between 1918 and 1925, annual consumption of gasoline increased from 74.5 million barrels to 223.9 million barrels of which 90 per cent was used as motor vehicle fuel.[5] Demand was soon expected to outpace supply.

The threat which this seemed to pose to the nation's oil reserves was heightened by the rather primitive state of geological knowledge at that time. Today, the remaining proven oil reserves of the USA are estimated to be around 30 billion barrels. But in 1919 the chief geologist of the United States Geological Survey believed that the nation's total proved reserves were only 6.7 billion barrels. It was reckoned that in about 23 years, at the current rate of consumption, the available supply of petroleum in the USA would be exhausted.[6]

Alerted to this seemingly critical situation, the US Secretary of State, Alvey Adee, issued new consular instructions in August 1919 which dealt specifically with oil supplies. His statement emphasised, 'The vital importance of securing adequate supplies of mineral oil both for present and future needs of the United States' and noting that the development of proven fields and exploration of new areas was being aggressively conducted in many parts of the world by nationals of other countries and that concessions for mineral oil rights were being actively sought, Alvey Adee instructed his officials to provide his department with 'the most complete information regarding such activities either by United States citizens or by others'.[7]

In response to the anticipated energy crisis, men like V.H. Manning, Director of the US Bureau of Mines, concluded that the government should set up its own international oil corporation, following the British Government's initiative in acquiring majority control over the Anglo-Persian oil company in 1914. Others, however, feared the precedent which this might set, at a time when socialist ideas were fuelling opposition to capitalist business throughout the world and not least in America itself. Instead, Franklin K. Lane, Secretary of the Interior from 1913 to 1920, advocated a more laissez-faire approach. In his annual report of 1919 he acknowledged the rapidly expanding demand for oil in the USA which would have to be met by gaining access to foreign oilfields. However, he argued that the government should refrain from any direct intervention in the oil business, either at home or abroad and should let the oil companies themselves do the job of locating and exploiting foreign oil reserves. The government did, however, have an important role to play, acting as protector for the oil companies and when necessary compelling foreign governments to give US companies equal access to their oil resources. Lane's robust pro-business position made him a favourite of the US oil industry and the cosy relationship between the industry and the government soon became apparent when Lane left office to become the vice-president of the Mexican Petroleum and Pan-American Transport Company, one of the principal oil exploration companies of the time.

PRISING OPEN THE DOOR TO THE GULF

It was pretty clear who Lane had in mind when he advocated equal access to foreign oil. British politicians and government officials had begun to boast about their growing control over the new oilfields of the Middle East, control assured through majority ownership of both the Anglo-Persian Oil Company and the Iraq Petroleum Company. Indeed, the First Lord of the Admiralty, Walter Hume Long, had rather unwisely told a meeting of the Institute of Petroleum Technologists in October 1921 that, 'if we secure the supplies of oil now available in the world we can do what we like,' a remark which was reported to the US Secretary of State by his Consul General in London.[8] Moreover, US oil company executives were deeply embarrassed by the fact that British businessmen appeared to have got their hands on what looked like being an oil province of the premier class, whereas US oil company interests abroad were at that time restricted to less desirable oil properties in Mexico and Rumania.

The US companies' initial response was to organise themselves into the American Petroleum Institute (API) in March 1919, with a 'Foreign Relations Committee' being set up the following July. The first Chairman of this committee was the energetic Walter C. Teagle, President of the Standard Oil Company of New Jersey (later to become Exxon). At this particular time, Teagle's company was primarily a refining operation with only 16 per cent of the crude it processed coming from the company's own wells. Standard Oil was therefore particularly keen to acquire upstream crude-producing assets, and the Middle East now appeared to be the most promising location.

The API was not the only body urging action from the government to support US entry into the Middle East oilfields. An older organisation, the American Institute of Mining and Metallurgical Engineers which had its own petroleum section, also urged action from the government. In March 1920 it presented a petition to the President and Congress entitled, 'Imperative Need of Aggressive Foreign Policy as Regards the Oil Industry', in which it was argued that the government should make representations to foreign governments about equal access to new oilfields and if they refused then 'the free entrance of foreign capital in the American development of natural resources will be reciprocally restrained.'[9] Indeed, this 'reciprocal' action was duly taken, at least in part. After intensive lobbying by Teagle and others, Congress passed the Mineral Leasing Law of 1920 which denied access to US Federal oil lands to citizens of any country which excluded US oil companies from oil-bearing lands which that country controlled. The law did not apply, however, to privately owned mineral lands.

In 1921, a new Republican Administration came to power and for a time professed itself equally concerned about the nation's oil requirements. In case any of the US oil companies still had not got the message about the nation's strategic need for oil, the Secretary of Commerce, Herbert Hoover, invited their representatives to Washington where they were told in no uncertain terms, 'to go out and get it'.[10] But exhortation apart, there was little more that the US government could do about Middle East oil and, as the 1920s wore on, the widespread clamour for an energetic foreign oil policy began to abate, largely because by this time it was becoming increasingly clear that there were, after all, still many new, very large oilfields to be discovered in the USA itself.

In the end, the initiative to broaden the national ownership of the Iraqi oilfields appears to have come from the British themselves, in the belief that the probability of a challenge to their rather shaky legal rights to Iraqi oil would be reduced if the USA was involved as a co-owner of the concession.[11] In 1922 the principle of US admission to the Iraq Petroleum Company was accepted, although diplomatic notes regarding the details of American participation continued to be passed back and forth across the Atlantic during the next few years. However, in 1927, the Iraq Petroleum Company struck its first oil, six miles north-west of Kirkuk, and the urgency of a settlement became apparent to all. Consequently in 1928, five US companies, Exxon, Socony Oil Company (later to become Mobil), Gulf Petroleum Corp, Atlantic Refining and Mexican Petroleum, were allowed to acquire 23.75 per cent of the Iraq Petroleum Company. Moreover, from then on it was American geologists who took charge of the company's exploration efforts and who were responsible for discovering several new fields in Iraq which pushed the company's production rate from 926 b/d in 1927 to 84,359 b/d in 1939.

So by the late 1920s American companies had established their first foothold in the Middle East. To their Iraqi interests they subsequently added Bahrain, in 1930, where Chevron acquired exclusive rights to a 100,000 acre concession and two years later struck oil at the Awali field. In 1934, Gulf Oil Company acquired a 50 per cent share in Kuwait's first oil concession, in partnership with British Petroleum. In both these acquisitions the American oil companies worked hand in hand with the State Department to prise open the British colonial control of the Gulf sheikhdoms.[12] In doing so, the oil companies firmly linked their own commercial interests to those of the nation as whole portraying their fiercely capitalistic motives as a patriotic endeavour.

Like the twenty-first-century neo-conservatives, American oilmen in the 1920s and 1930s saw their presence in the Middle East through an ideological prism – as part of a philanthropic and civilising mission. Men like Charles W. Hamilton of the Gulf Oil Company, who took part in many of the negotiations which gained the USA access to the oil of the region, saw themselves as continuing the work of a long line of American missionaries, doctors and educationalists who had dedicated themselves to the Middle East since the middle of the nineteenth century – men like the Reverend Daniel Bliss, the first President of the Syrian Protestant College, which opened its doors in Beirut in 1866; Samuel Zwemer of the Arabian Mission, who travelled up and down the Gulf, exploring and preparing the ground for the establishment of American mission hospitals; and the Rev. John Van Ess, Head of the American Mission in Basra who published an outstanding grammar and dictionary of colloquial Iraqi Arabic in 1917.

While denying, rather unconvincingly, that he judged his own compatriots to be more worthy or dedicated than their counterparts from Europe, in Hamilton's opinion, 'Americans sought to help, not to dominate – to lead and not to drive.' They inspired the indigenous Arab peoples to 'believe in the dignity of man', and 'they demonstrated that good will towards all men is a mightier force than armed conflict.'[13] Naive and sanctimonious though they might have been, these views were sincerely held – although Hamilton's 'dignity of man' was little in evidence when European and American oil companies confined their local workers to dismal 'native quarters' and subjected them to what was effectively a police regime. Indeed, even those educated 'natives' who were favoured with scholarships and bursaries to study abroad as petroleum engineers, geologists, etc. were swiftly re-inserted into an apartheid-like regime when they returned to work in the company concessions.

Such, for example was the experience of Saudi Arabia's future oil minister, Abdallah Tariki. He had even married an American girl but, on return from studying at the University of Texas to take up a position in the Arabian American Oil Company (ARAMCO), was excluded from the American managers' compound and cold-bloodedly relegated to the inferior 'native quarter' and a stark cubicle with hard beds and no refrigerator.[14] Denied the company of fellow Americans, his wife eventually left him, taking their small son, an experience which left Tariki understandably bitter and emotionally scarred.

In Chapter One we briefly referred to the customary right of sovereign nations to exercise 'eminent domain' over their landed territory and its subsoil resources. But this did not apply to the Gulf states, whose oil wealth was now being extracted by foreign oil companies. For they were either under direct colonial rule or semi-colonial control – Iraq under the British Mandate, Bahrain and Kuwait also under effective British rule, and Iran divided into spheres of British and Russian influence. Within a few years Saudi Arabia – nominally an independent kingdom – was also to fall under a form of semi-colonial rule by the USA, albeit with the connivance of its ruler. Not surprisingly therefore the oil concession agreements won by the British, French and American investors in these countries flagrantly ignored the basic precepts of 'eminent domain'.

Each oil concession covered vast areas of these countries, sometimes the whole country itself. Concessions were granted for remarkably long periods of time – 75 years in the case of Iraq and Kuwait. Provisions for the relinquishment of these concessions were virtually non-existent. Moreover royalty payments to the host governments (four gold shillings per ton – originally about one eighth of the per barrel price) were fixed by contract and for the duration of the concession. As such, any increase in royalties or taxation would have to be submitted to international arbitration. The contract was based on the 'international law of civilised nations' and no relevant national law was acknowledged.[15]

Not surprisingly, as these colonial or semi-colonial oil-producing countries gained independence these 'rights' became the focus of bitter disagreement. As we shall show in the next chapter, within twenty-five years it had become the principal objective of the newly independent oil producers – in the Gulf as elsewhere – to reverse this situation and establish 'permanent sovereignty over natural resources'.

The penetration of Iraq, Bahrain and Kuwait by American oil capital was a major achievement, but it paled into insignificance compared with the strategic relationship which was to be established between the major US oil companies, the US Government and the Kingdom of Ibn Saud – present-day Saudi Arabia. Since the troubled history of this relationship is a major theme of our book, it will be necessary to digress slightly at this point to say a little about its origins.

AMERICA AND THE HOUSE OF SAUD

In the early 1920s, a tribal ruler of the province of Nejd in the north-east of the Arabian Peninsular, Abd al-Aziz Ibn Saud, began a series of small local wars intended to take control of the Arabian Peninsular and in particular the two holy places, Mecca and Medina. It was also his firm intention to reinstate Wahhabism, the puritanical and ascetic brand of Islam for which his forefathers had fought and died.[16] By 1930 he had defeated Britain's former allies, the Hashemites of the Hejaz, made himself Protector of the Two Holy Places, and crushed a major uprising of his erstwhile followers, the fanatical *Ikhwan* (Brotherhood). To celebrate the consolidation of his rule over the entire Arabian peninsula, this Bedouin tribal chieftain announced, in 1932, the establishment of the *Mamlaka al-Saudiyya al-Arabiyya*, the Kingdom of Saudi Arabia.

In order to maintain the loyalty of his followers and the welfare of his numerous family, Ibn Saud required cash, preferably gold. So, in 1933, he signed a concession agreement with Chevron which, in return for exploration rights to 360,000 square miles of territory with a duration of sixty years, provided the King with a loan of £155,000 in gold to be paid in instalments and repaid out of the royalties which the King would receive once production of oil had commenced. In 1936, Chevron sold a 50 per cent share in the Saudi concession to Texaco.

Although oil was discovered at the Dammam field in 1938 and the first small shipment made out of the Ras Tanura terminal in May 1939, the outbreak of the Second World War led to a partial shutdown of facilities and the end of any further exploratory drilling for the time being. However, during the war, the US Government despatched the eminent petroleum geologist E.L. Golyer to further appraise Saudi oil potential. Using his expert knowledge of surface structures and the newly developed techniques of seismography, he concluded that Saudi reserves were around 5 billion barrels. But this was a very conservative figure and he recognised that the country was potentially far richer in petroleum resources, his overall judgement being that 'The centre of gravity of world oil production is shifting...to the Middle East – to the Persian Gulf area, and is likely to shift until it is firmly established in that area.'[17]

This appreciation of the petroleum potential of Saudi Arabia, and indeed of all the territories which bordered the Gulf, coincided with a recurrence of that fear about the adequacy of its own oil reserves which had so troubled the USA at the end of the First World War. As the extraordinary demands on domestic US oil production became apparent in the middle of the Second World War, the belief that the USA might 'run out of oil' once more came to dominate official thinking. As a result the so-called 'conservation theory' became current, according to which the USA would need to acquire and develop sources of oil outside the country in order to 'conserve' the nation's domestic reserves for the future, possibly for a future war. It was now absolutely clear where those extra-territorial oil reserves were to be found – in the Middle East.

In December 1943, the Petroleum Industry War Council, a broad-based advisory group which linked the US government's wartime Petroleum Administration to the oil industry, recommended that 'the national policy of the United States should aim at securing for American nationals access to the world's oil resources.' But in an almost exact reprise of Interior Secretary Franklin Lane's 1919 pronouncement, the Council added that 'any direct participation by the Government will discourage private enterprise and retard the orderly development of the world's oil resources.'[18] However, in another echo of Lane's earlier position, it was accepted that there remained an important role for government in supporting the efforts of US oil companies operating abroad. In similar vein, in December 1944, the Navy Secretary James Forrestal pronounced that it was the job of the State Department to work out a programme for substituting Middle Eastern oil for American oil and to promote the expansion of US oil company holdings in the Gulf.

Yet Chevron and Texaco remained nervous about the durability of their oil assets in the Gulf and in Saudi Arabia in particular. Something more than just State Department reassurance was required to support their confidence in what still appeared to many to be a rickety feudal state which could easily be overthrown by some rival Bedouin war lord or, worse still, by a nationalist or communist movement of the type that was beginning to emerge in other parts of the old colonial world. So, in what one US academic has referred to as 'one of the most extraordinary occurrences in modern American history',[19] in February 1945, shortly after the Yalta Conference, President Roosevelt met with King Abd al-Aziz Ibn Saud on a US warship in the Suez Canal. Although full details of their discussion were never disclosed, it is generally believed that Roosevelt offered

Ibn Saud military support to put down any external attack or internal challenge to his rule in return for privileged access to the Kingdom's vast oil resources – in other words American, not British or French oil companies would get the oil. To further cement the alliance between the USA and the House of Saud, in 1946 a $10 million loan to the Kingdom was arranged.

Meanwhile the State Department's own response was to quietly encourage and oversee a broadening of US ownership of the Saudi oilfields. The existing owners – Chevron and Texaco – lacked sufficient refining capacity in the USA to process the future oil production from the Saudi fields. On the other hand, Exxon and Mobil had the US refining capacity but insufficient reserves of crude. The obvious solution was to bring the four US multinationals together in a new Saudi-based, but American-owned company. So in 1947, the Arabian American Oil Company (ARAMCO) was established with the two owners of the original concession reducing their joint share to 60 per cent, while Exxon got 30 per cent and Mobil 10 per cent. For its part, the State Department viewed this merger as a private means for assuring US control over the Saudi Arabian concession.[20] Indeed, there was now 'a growing realisation that the US goals of security and access could be realised through the private operations of the major oil companies', and that instead of direct involvement in oil matters, 'the United States should focus on maintaining an international environment in which US oil companies could operate with security and profit.'[21]

Meanwhile two additional giant fields, Abqaiq and Qatif, were brought into production and the company began the construction of the Trans-Arabian Pipeline, across Saudi Arabia, through Jordan and Syria and onwards to the Lebanese coast. The pipeline was completed in September 1950 and, a few months later, the first oil tanker was loaded at the new terminal a few kilometres south of the ancient city of Sidon.

Years later, the immense value of the ARAMCO concession to the USA was acknowledged by the chief executive of one of its owners. Giving evidence to the US Senate Foreign Relations Subcommittee on Multinational Corporations, Chevron's Otto Miller declared that ARAMCO was, by far, the most important and valuable foreign economic interest ever developed by US citizens. When company officials first recognised the significance of the ARAMCO finds, 'it was immediately appreciated that its significance went beyond mere commercial implications. The finds were recognised as being of tremendous importance to our country.'[22]

THE PALESTINIANS – A COMPLICATING FACTOR

There remained only one source of friction between Ibn Saud and the Americans. On 2 November 1917, the British Foreign Secretary, Arthur Balfour, had declared that 'his Majesty's government views with favour the establishment in Palestine of a national home for the Jewish people.' The declaration also contained the proviso that 'nothing should be done which may prejudice the civil and religious rights of the non-Jewish communities in Palestine.' Nevertheless, it seems as though Balfour had little idea how numerous and well-settled these non-Jewish communities were.

A mere 59,000 people of the Jewish religion resided in the British Mandate of Palestine at the beginning of the First World War compared to 657,000 Muslim Arabs and 81,000 Christian Arabs.[23] But, by end of the 1930s, driven by the steely determination of Zionist political organisers, abetted by the foul anti-Semitism of Central and Eastern Europe, and facilitated to a considerable degree by the British Mandate itself, Jewish inhabitants of Palestine had increased tenfold, to half a million persons. In February 1947, after various proposed partition plans had failed in the face of Arab insistence on a unitary state, Britain referred the matter to the United Nations General Assembly which voted by 33 to 13 in favour of a new partition plan. The USA voted for the partition (as did the USSR).

King Ibn Saud, like all Arabs – Muslim and Christian alike – totally rejected the establishment of a Jewish state in Palestine. As he said to Roosevelt, when they met in 1945, surely the appropriate future homeland for the Jews, after their persecution by the Nazis, would be Germany not Palestine?[24] So in 1948, while the troops of the Jewish National Council were battling with those of the Arab League in the streets of Jerusalem, Ibn Saud made it known to the State Department, via ARAMCO's management, that public opinion in his country might soon compel him to apply sanctions against American oil concessions in retaliation for American recognition of the state of Israel.

In the event, the King did nothing. Much as he opposed the Zionists he had other enemies of whom he was considerably more fearful: the atheistic communists, whose shadowy presence he believed he already detected in the embryo forces of radical Arab nationalism; and his old dynastic foes – the Hashemites, who he had driven out of Arabia but who now ruled as British-supported kings in Jordan and Iraq. It was therefore tacitly understood that no action would be taken against ARAMCO so long as the USA ensured the survival of the House of Saud. In September 1950, to address the King's anxieties, the US President Harry Truman wrote guaranteeing the security and independence of his Kingdom. In doing so, Truman formalised the secret understanding which his predecessor had made with Ibn Saud five years earlier. In return, the consortium of four US companies which made up ARAMCO would have the huge Saudi oil reserves to themselves in perpetuity, or so it was believed at the time.

And for a time, that 'complicating factor', the tragic fate of the 750,000 Palestinian refugees from the 1948–1949 conflict, appeared to recede, as they settled, despondent and demoralised, in their camps, brooding on the *Nakba* – the catastrophe – which had befallen them. They were by no means entirely forgotten however. The remainder of the deeply humiliated Arab world felt a rising anger – towards the Jewish state itself, and towards the incompetent behaviour of their own leaders, who had succumbed to this audacious Zionist enterprise; but also towards the western powers, led by the USA who, so it was believed, had deliberately created the state of Israel as a 'watch-dog for Western interests in the Middle East',[25] among which interests Middle East oil was paramount. Indeed, although American politicians and some American oilmen of the 1950s had serious concerns about the USA's increasingly open-ended commitment to defending the state of Israel, especially when the latter opportunistically seized Egypt's Sinai region during the short-lived Anglo-French invasion of 1956, 'the buttressing of Israel as the Prussia of the Arab East' was soon to become a crucial element in America's plans for an oil Imperium in the region.[26]

AMERICA GETS CONTROL OF THE GULF

On 4 July 1954, the US Embassy in Tehran held its traditional Independence Day party. Charles Hamilton, a senior executive of Gulf Oil, recollected the scene in which the American Ambassador 'and his gracious lady' were 'charming hosts to a gathering of some 2,000 persons of all nationalities and walks of life – statesmen, diplomats, princes, government officials, officers of the various armed services...and the consortium group'. According to Hamilton, it was a gala occasion in a very friendly atmosphere. While this 'delightful lawn party' was held to commemorate America's Declaration of Independence in 1776, as subsequent events demonstrated, '4 July 1954 marked the beginning of a new era in Iran – when, for the first time, Americans would be admitted on equal footing with the British.'[27]

A year before the delightful lawn party, Iran's attempt to take control of its natural resources had been crushed in a coup organised by the CIA, ostensibly to stop Iran 'going communist'. The country's prime minister, Mohammad

Mossadegh, who had nationalised BP's Iranian oil business in 1951, was overthrown by a mob of paid hoodlums led by officers of the royal guard and consigned to one of the Shah's dungeons.[28]

The man widely credited with organising the successful coup which returned the Shah to power and restored the British to their oil was Kermit Roosevelt, chief CIA operative in Iran and the grandson of President Theodore Roosevelt. However, the efforts of the major US oil companies were also crucial in mounting a successful blockade of the nationalised Iranian oil industry which caused great economic hardship to Iran and undermined popular support for Mossadegh. That delightful garden party held in Tehran was, at least in part, to celebrate the British pay-off to their erstwhile competitors. In return for the assistance of the US oil companies and the CIA, BP had to give up 60 per cent of its former Persian oil business, of which 40 per cent was handed over to the US major oil companies – Gulf, Exxon, Mobil, Texaco, and Chevron. Shortly after the coup, Kermit Roosevelt joined Gulf Oil as a 'government relations' director and in 1960 Gulf Oil named him vice-president.[29]

Of course the oil companies, like any capitalists, were primarily driven by the search for profits, which were particularly easy to extract from the exceptionally productive Middle Eastern oil wells. But in the oil business matters of private profit and matters of state had a tendency to become interlinked, a factor which became considerably more pronounced in the 1950s, as the cold war intensified. Indeed, the Truman and Eisenhower Administrations deliberately used American-controlled multinational oil companies as instruments of US foreign policy. The companies had three main tasks. Firstly, they were to provide a reliable source of oil at reasonable prices to the USA and its allies; secondly, they were to provide a conduit for providing financial support to favoured Middle East regimes; and thirdly, they were to generally enhance the USA's economic and political presence in the region and to prevent the southward spread of Soviet influence. In return for performing these functions, not only were the major US oil companies allowed to make huge monopoly profits, but also these profits were effectively shielded from US domestic anti-trust actions.[30]

Since the entry of American companies into the Iraqi oil business in 1928, their situation had been radically transformed. By 1960, five of the seven giant multinational oil corporations which dominated the Gulf were US companies – Exxon, Chevron, Mobil, Gulf and Texaco. Between them, these companies controlled 60 per cent of the 164 billion barrels of proven Middle East oil reserves, with shares ranging from 23.75 per cent in Iraq and Qatar, to 100 per cent in Saudi Arabia.[31] Just how important these Middle East reserves were, compared to America's own domestic reserves was now clear to all. In 1944, informed geological opinion had stated that Middle East proven oil reserves were about three quarters of those in the USA. However, by 1950 Middle East reserves were reckoned to be 30 per cent greater than those in the USA and by 1960 over four times greater.[32]

CHROME, TAILFINS AND V-8 ENGINES

This was all to the good because, as we saw in the previous chapter, in the 1950s and 1960s the motorisation of American society, with its consequent pressure on domestic oil supplies, was now experiencing unparalleled growth. This was the era of the eight-cylinder V-8 automobile engine with a capacity rarely less than 3 litres and occasionally as much as 8.5; it was the apotheosis of the twin-tailed chrome-coated monster sedan; it was the time when America fell in love with big flashy cars like the 1959 Dodge Lancer whose elaborate steel architecture consciously echoed the lines of a jet plane.

There was also a new market emerging for the US automobile industry, encouraged and celebrated by popular TV dramas like *Route 66*, first shown in October 1960 and which featured two young men looking for fun and adventure, driving a Chevrolet Corvette across America. By this time the Baby-Boom generation was coming of age and young men and women of white America were enjoying unprecedented personal wealth and freedom. Looking for a way to capture the hearts and minds of this new youth market, Ford launched its celebrated and racy Ford Mustang in 1966. In the first 18 months, the company sold more than 1 million Mustangs, the fastest car launch in history. Adding further horse-power (and fuel consumption) as the 1960s progressed, the Mustang became the embodiment of the aptly named 'muscle car'.

And as the pace of motorisation increased so did the consumption of motor fuel: between 1960 and 1970, US consumption of motor gasoline and diesel increased from 3.76 to 5.76 million b/d while per capita consumption of gasoline increased from 1,082.5 to 1,432 litres per head.

In the 1930s and 1940s the motorisation die had been cast; but by the 1950s and 1960s it was rolling out not just millions of cars but also millions of infatuated car-lovers many of whom would indeed, 'get their kicks on Route 66' as it 'winds from Chicago to LA. More than 2,000 miles all the way.' This enormous cultural revolution would later have significant political implications as many of those adventurous post-war baby-boomers would mature into 50-year-old 'automobile addicts' for whom, in the hierarchy of modern American needs, 'the car falls somewhere behind food, clothing and shelter, but not by much.'[33]

Meanwhile, however, America's political and business leaders of the early 1960s were supremely confident that control of Middle East oil would underpin the future petroleum requirements of this new and remarkably vibrant economic, social and cultural way of life. It would guarantee the nation's energy security and with it the newly affluent lifestyle of America's consumers, epitomised by its steel and chrome gas-guzzlers. But those US leaders could not imagine that in little more than ten years this energy security solution would unravel in a great world oil crisis; that within thirty years the USA would have to fight a major war in the Gulf to protect its 'energy security'; and that within forty years, New York and Washington would be under attack by fanatical young men from Saudi Arabia invoking the old creed of Muhammad Ibn Abd al-Wahhab.

4 Energy Security and the Gulf: From Solution to Problem

The most fundamental ... is to reduce dependence on the Gulf

Melvin Conant, US Council on Foreign Relations, 1982

In the years immediately after the First World War, Americans feared they were going to run out of oil, but by the end of the 1920s they had suddenly found that they were faced with exactly the opposite situation – a major over-production crisis which brought with it catastrophically low prices and widespread social unrest in the oil-producing states. Between 1926 and 1929, a string of major oil discoveries in Oklahoma and California brought unanticipated new oil supplies onto the market and the US well-head price began to tumble, falling from $1.88 in 1926 to $1.17/b in 1928. But it was the smaller oil producers, those with proportionately greater numbers of low-productivity stripper wells, who suffered the most. When the larger oil companies, organised in the American Petroleum Institute (API), began to talk about concerted production cuts to support the price, the small oilmen took fright. Fearing that such a cure might be worse for them than the original disease, they broke ranks and set up their own rival organisation, the Independent Petroleum Association of America (IPAA), thereby setting the scene for decades of strife between 'Big Oil' and the 'Independents'. Instead of production cuts, the IPAA demanded a tariff on imported oil, most of which at this time was coming from Venezuela and Mexico. Their initial efforts in this respect were unsuccessful. Later, however, the pressure for a tariff on imported oil became irresistible as the crisis worsened.

On 3 October 1930, a wildcat oil well drilled in what came to be known as the East Texas field broke through into a vast reservoir of oil, the largest field ever to be discovered in the Lower 48 states (the USA excluding Alaska). By April

1931, the field was producing at a rate of 340,000 barrels per day. Coinciding as it did with a major depression in the economy as a whole, this sudden and massive increase in the supply of oil drove the price into a vicious downward spiral. From $1.19 per barrel in 1930, the average US oil-well-head price collapsed to 65 cents per barrel in 1931. Although this crisis of falling prices was severe in every US oil-producing state, it was particularly acute in Texas and seemingly intractable because there were by now thousands of small, under-capitalised oil-well operators at work who had little option but to continue producing oil, whatever the price. In May 1931, the well-head oil price in Texas was down to less than 15 cents per barrel and, at a time when East Texas was producing over a million barrels per day, equivalent to almost half of the total American demand. The outcome of this truly calamitous situation – which led to the declaration of martial law in East Texas and its occupation by the National Guard – was the setting in place of a comprehensive system of production regulation and control, commonly known as 'pro-rationing', which lasted until 1972.

The first move was for Texas and Oklahoma to introduce their own 'pro-rationing' rules whereby each state's oil producers were allocated production cuts, 'pro rata' with their existing production capacity. Each oil well was allowed a number of days per month on which it could pump oil, but for the remainder of the month the oil had to be shut in. However, small stripper wells, whose natural pressure drive had ceased and which now relied on pumping to extract the oil, were guaranteed a market for their production. Another advantage of the pro-rationing system, from the point of view of the small independent oil producer, was that the major integrated oil companies whose refineries provided the market demand for oil, were prevented from taking oil only from their own affiliated upstream producers. Instead, pro-rationing meant that the pain of production restraint was shared more or less equally by all oil producers. Next, pressure from the small oil producers across the nation to exclude oil imports became irresistible. In 1932 a tariff of 21 cents per barrel was imposed on all imported oil.[1]

Then, in July 1933, building on these earlier production-control initiatives introduced by the oil-producing states themselves, Roosevelt's Administration used its constitutional powers to regulate interstate commerce to establish a radical regime of state control over the national oil industry. Now the government itself set monthly production quotas for each state and these, in turn, were shared out among the pro-rationed producers. In 1935, Congress went one step further and passed the so-called Connally Hot Oil Act which put an end to illicit sales of 'hot oil' (oil produced in excess of that which had been pro-rationed) across state boundaries. It followed this by approving the formation of an Interstate Oil Compact Commission (IOCC)[2] with the necessary staff and authority to coordinate national pro-rationing and to function, in effect, as a national board of control over the domestic oil industry. From then until the beginning of the 1970s, the US oil industry operated with a substantial margin of spare capacity, as much as 4 million barrels per day in some years. It was left to a future Secretary General of OPEC, Ali Rodriguez, to point out that the IOCC was in fact 'the immediate and logical precedent for OPEC', since its clear objective was the raising of the oil price above the level dictated by purely market forces by means of production restraint.[3]

RIVAL VERSIONS OF 'ENERGY SECURITY':
BIG OIL VERSUS THE INDEPENDENTS

By the late 1940s, the Middle East oilfields acquired by the Americans over the preceding two decades had at last begun to export significant amounts of oil, a growing portion of which started to enter the US market. Although Venezuela still remained the largest source of US oil imports, supplying 265,975 barrels per day in 1949, the second largest supplier was now Kuwait with 52,269 b/d, and with the Middle East oilfields as a whole supplying America with 99,642 b/d. As these Middle East supplies began to arrive at US refineries in growing quantities – but at half the cost of domestic oil – those government officials, oil industry leaders and military men who were attempting to formulate a national energy security policy at a time of growing cold-war confrontation faced a perplexing dilemma.

Since foreign oil was so much cheaper than domestic, US consumers would obviously prefer to buy the latter. But since foreign oil would then inevitably displace domestic oil, the eventual result would be external energy dependence. Of course, the fact that US oil reserves would still be there underground, would mean that 'long-run' energy security was assured since these oil reserves would be available for future exploitation; this was the essence of the so-called 'conservation theory'. In the short run, however, the country might become extremely vulnerable to a sudden geopolitical or military crisis with America being cut off from its foreign oil suppliers without having the domestic production capacity to immediately make up the shortfall. For some oil industry observers, with memories of the vulnerability of tankers to submarines during the Second World War, this meant that truly secure oil supplies could only be obtained from a domestic industry incentivised by a high price and protected from foreign competition.[4]

However this dilemma over 'cheap' versus 'secure' supplies was exacerbated by the fact that the US multinational oil companies which had obtained concessions in the Middle East, were at this time under severe pressure from their host countries to rapidly increase oil production and with it the royalty and tax payments upon which their rulers depended. But at this time there was really only one market large and dynamic enough to absorb all this additional oil production – the USA.

Faced with these conflicting positions, the US Government tried to find a compromise between the fiercely anti-import stance of the independent oil companies and the desire of the integrated oil majors to use as much cheap foreign oil as possible in their US refineries. The first attempt at reconciling what eventually proved to be the irreconcilable, was made by the Petroleum Industry War Council. In 1945, anticipating the growing problem of oil imports, it published a 'Petroleum Policy for the United States', in which an effort was made to satisfy all sides of the industry and which declared that 'it should be the policy of this nation to so restrict amounts of imported oil that such quantities will not depress the producing end of the domestic petroleum industry.' In other words, oil imports would not be prevented but would be limited to an amount 'absolutely necessary to augment our domestic production when it is produced under conditions consonant with good conservation practices'.[5]

Four years later, the National Petroleum Council, the peace-time successor to the Petroleum Industry War Council, came up with an equally opaque statement about the proper role of oil imports. 'The nation's economic welfare and security,' it declared, 'require a policy on petroleum imports which will encourage exploration and development efforts in the domestic industry.' 'The extent to which imports are desirable' was to be determined, at least in part, by 'the availability of petroleum from domestic fields, produced under sound conservation practices'.[6]

However, whatever practical consequences were meant to flow from these vague policy statements, the reality was that in 1949, for the first time, US oil imports exceeded exports. Between 1948 and the second half of 1950, imports of crude oil and petroleum products increased from 514,000 barrels per day to 831,572 b/d, of which 781,424 b/d were accounted for by 11 major US oil companies. Texaco, for example, increased its imports from 16,977 b/d to 66,000 b/d, an increase of 289 per cent. Since the total demand for oil, as determined by the US Government's Bureau of Mines, remained unchanged, the compensating industry-wide production cuts required by pro-rationing bit deeper into the livelihoods of the domestic oil producers.

Faced with this challenge the Independent Petroleum Association of America made known their own particular interpretation of 'energy security', arguing that 'Middle East oil could not be defended in time of war and that these fields were only six hours bombing time from Russia.'[7] In response, the major oil companies hit back with their own 'energy security' rhetoric, using the now familiar 'conservationist' argument. The exploitation of domestic oil reserves, they argued, was now so intense that, given the current rate of depletion, they would be rapidly exhausted, in which case, argued Texaco's chairman, 'our national security would certainly be put in jeopardy.' For this reason it was essential for America to have access to foreign sources of oil which couldn't function economically if they were to be 'turned on and off like a faucet'.[8]

Although the onset of the Korean War in 1950 stimulated both domestic and military demand for petroleum fuels and, for a time, reduced the pressure of oil imports upon the domestic producers, from 1953 onwards the problem returned with a vengeance. In 1954, imports of crude oil and refined products were running at 1,050 thousand barrels per day (13.6 per cent of total supply). By 1955, imports were 1,250 thousand b/d (14.8 per cent of supply) and in the following year 1,430 (16.3 per cent). Under severe pressure from the political representatives of the oil-producing states, Congress added a 'National Security Amendment' to the 1955 Trade Act which gave the President the power to control the level of oil imports where these were deemed to be threatening the nation's security or its economic well-being. Subsequently, in April 1957, the Director of Defense Mobilization reviewed the amounts which the importing companies planned to import during the remainder of that year and reported to the President that these volumes did indeed pose a threat to national security. President Eisenhower then appointed six members of his cabinet to serve as a Special Committee to Investigate Oil Imports. The recommendation of the committee was that crude oil imports should be restricted to 12.2 per cent of domestic production, but that this restriction should be achieved by voluntary means.

However, by 1958 it was becoming clear that there was little chance of any voluntary oil import control being achieved. Indeed, imports was still increasing and, exacerbated by a recession in the US economy, demand for domestic crude was running nearly one million barrels per day below that of the previous year. In Texas, allowable production was reduced to just eight days per month. Eventually something had to give. In February 1959, the Director of Defense Mobilization again advised the President that crude oil and petroleum products were now being imported in amounts sufficient 'to impair the national security'. Ten days later, Eisenhower imposed a system of mandatory oil import quotas, which was to remain in force for the next 14 years. The battle had been won by the independents.

However, because America's overall demand for oil was now rising steadily, the quotas imposed on the importers did not prove particularly troublesome.

Between 1960 and 1965, total petroleum demand in the USA rose from 9.8 million barrels per day to 11.5 million b/d. Domestic production rose from 7.96 million b/d to 9.01 million b/d, but oil imports also increased – from 1.81 million to 2.47 million b/d. In the same period, exports to the USA from Saudi Arabia increased by 88 per cent, from 84,000 to 158,000 b/d.

MIDDLE EAST OIL – NOT SO SECURE AFTER ALL

Although Americans generally felt secure in their control of Middle East oil during the 1950s and early 1960s, a few US defence experts began to question the political stability of the area. In 1963, the Rand Corporation published the first detailed study on the security of Middle East oil supplies, as part of a programme of research being carried out for the US Air Force.[9] The study noted that 'twice in the past decade there has been a major disruption of the flow of Middle East oil to the non-Soviet world; and given the rising intensity of nationalist sentiment in the Middle East, further interruptions are to be expected.'[10] The two episodes in question were the nationalisation of the Iranian oil industry by the Mossadegh Government in 1951, after which the flow of oil was reduced by around 700,000 barrels of oil per day for 44 months, and the Suez crisis of 1956, when the flow was reduced by around 2 million barrels per day for 4 months.[11]

The general tone of the Rand Corporation study was remarkably hostile towards the Arab and Iranian peoples of the region (described as 'excitable', 'xenophobic', prone to 'economic irrationality', etc.) and reflected a prejudice in favour of the state of Israel that was soon to become the cornerstone of US foreign policy in the region.[12] In addition to the tensions arising from the creation of the Israeli state, the study drew attention to two further problem areas which could become the focus of future confrontations between the West on the one hand and Arab and Iranian popular aspirations on the other: conflict over the distribution of oil revenues between the US and British oil companies and their Middle East host countries; and the West's support for autocratic rulers like the Shah of Iran and the House of Saud.

However, in one respect the circumstances prevailing at the time of the Rand report were markedly different from the present day. The only serious threat to *American* interests which was foreseen was the possible nationalisation of ARAMCO in the event of a major upsurge of Arab nationalism in the Gulf, because compared to Europe, America's dependence on Middle East oil was still quite small at this time. Nationalisation of ARAMCO would certainly have been a serious blow to US business interests, but as far as the continuation of oil supplies was concerned, the kind of Middle Eastern crisis which the study envisaged would, it claimed, have no significant impact upon the USA. It was viewed as being primarily a problem for America's European allies, because the USA's own large domestic oil industry would insulate it from Middle Eastern oil disruption. Benefiting from that substantial margin of shut-in spare capacity in the domestic US oil industry whose origins we have described above, Americans were convinced that they could survive a disruption of oil exports from the Middle East, or anywhere else for that matter, at this particular time.

Nevertheless, this state of affairs was coming to a close. Between 1957 and 1963, the amount of shut-in oil-producing capacity averaged around 4 million barrels per day. But by 1970 it had fallen to only 1 million b/d and by 1971 it had virtually disappeared altogether. In early 1972, the Texas Railroad Commission, which administered pro-rationing, felt compelled to make a fateful decision – although it went largely unnoticed at the time. Because US oil demand had risen to such an extent that it threatened a price explosion, the Commission authorised full-capacity production. And that seemingly technical adjustment, Henry Kissinger acknowledged many years later, 'signalled the end of America's ability to set the world oil price'.[13]

'PERMANENT SOVEREIGNTY OVER NATURAL RESOURCES'

Meanwhile, as the Rand report had indicated, the countries of the Middle East were becoming increasingly dissatisfied with their share of the rapidly growing oil revenues. To give just one example: in the case of Iraq, between 1925 and 1950 the traditional royalty payment of four gold shillings per ton had only provided the country with 35 per cent of the net profits from oil.[14] So, to placate the rulers of the Gulf while doing nothing to prejudice the dividends of the US major oil companies, the US Government approved a clever arrangement whereby the companies would pay 50 per cent of their profits in tax to the host countries, but the whole of these tax payments would be classified as a tax credit against the companies' US tax liabilities. In this manner the rulers of the Gulf got their 50 per cent, but this was, in effect, paid not by the oil companies, but by the generality of US taxpayers.[15]

However, in conditions of exceptional productivity such as the Gulf, a seemingly equitable share in the net profits may still confer a gigantic *rate* of profit to the company (a point we shall return to in our final chapter) and by the late 1960s it was becoming evident that company rates of profit (return on capital) after deducting tax and royalties, were between 60 and 100 per cent.[16]

Moreover, by 1968 US oil firms in the Gulf and North Africa combined were earning around $1.3 billion per year of which only $263 million was reinvested with the remainder being repatriated to the shareholders in the USA.[17] However, the companies' lucrative Middle East assets were soon to be threatened by the dramatic events taking place in the developing countries of the Third World, and in the Arab oil-producing countries in particular.

The world was changing. Throughout Africa and South East Asia, national liberation movements were gaining ground and newly independent nations were emerging from colonial and imperialist rule. In the Middle East the first blow in the struggle against the prevailing post-war neo-colonialism had already been struck in 1951, when the Iranian Government nationalised the Anglo Iranian Oil Company. As we saw in the previous chapter, this first attempt at oil nationalism failed, but it set in motion a worldwide campaign to reassert national control over domestic mineral resources and their related infrastructure. For example, in 1952, a revolution in Bolivia nationalised the country's tin mining industry, and in 1956 Nassir's Arab nationalist regime in Egypt nationalised the Suez Canal. Two years later, there was a bloody revolution in Iraq which overthrew the pro-western Hashemite royalty and briefly installed Brigadier Abdul-Karim Qasim, a left-leaning military officer, supported by the Iraqi Communist Party. In 1961, his government issued Public Law 80 requiring the Iraq Petroleum Company to relinquish 99.5 per cent of its original concession area, an increase in the share of profits going to Iraq and an equity participation in oil production.[18]

Fearing the rapid spread of radical Arab nationalism to the pro-western rulers in Jordan and Lebanon, on 15 July 1958 American troops from the Sixth Fleet landed in Beirut, and a British parachute regiment arrived in Amman two days later. Although they later withdrew, President Kennedy's Administration now decided to begin quietly encouraging an anti-Qasim coup by rebel Army officers supported by the Baath Party and on 8 February 1963, just a few days before the Public Law 80 was to be put into effect, Qasim was overthrown and shot, and with the assistance of the CIA, the Baath Party began a bloody pogrom of all Iraqi communists and leftists.[19]

But these early defeats for natural-resource nationalism were coming to an end. In 1962, a key event took place in the General Assembly of the United Nations. The Assembly passed Resolution 1803, which for the first time enshrined the right of independent states to 'Permanent Sovereignty over Natural Resources'. Inseparable from this was the principle that such critical matters as taxation, equity participation and national control were the rightful objects of *national* law – not international arbitration of the kind which had underpinned the traditional oil-concession system.

The ground had now been prepared for the OPEC Revolution. In 1969, a group of radical young officers led by Muammar Qaddafi overthrew the Libyan monarchy. The following year, Qaddafi compelled the foreign oil companies operating in his country to raise the posted price of oil by 30 cents per barrel and Libya's share of oil profits from 50 to 55 per cent.[20] But the real significance of this event was much broader, in that it 'decisively changed the balance of power between the governments of the oil producing countries and the oil companies'.[21]

The dominoes began to fall. In December 1970, OPEC ministers met in Caracas and agreed that henceforth their minimum tax-take from oil company profits should be 55 per cent. In February 1971, led by the charming but formidable Saudi oil minister Sheikh Zaki Yamani, the OPEC countries met with representatives of twenty leading oil multinationals in Tehran. The companies conceded not only the 55 per cent tax-take but also an increase in the posted price of oil from $1.80 per barrel to $2.62/b over the next five years. The combination of these measures would raise the average government tax-take per barrel from $0.91 to $1.53. Ten days after the conclusion of these negotiations, Algeria nationalised 51 per cent of French oil concessions. On 2 April, Libya, negotiating on behalf of itself, Saudi Arabia, Algeria and Iraq obtained further price increases for oil delivered to Mediterranean ports. On 5 December 1971, Libya nationalised BP's concession. On 20 January 1972, Abu Dhabi, Iran, Iraq, Kuwait, Qatar and Saudi Arabia compelled the oil companies to make an 8.5 per cent increase in posted prices to offset a decline in the value of the US dollar. On 1 June, Iraq's Baathist regime – now proclaiming 'socialist' values – nationalised the Iraq Petroleum Company whose fields accounted for the bulk of the country's production. On 30 September 1972, Libya acquired a 50 per cent holding in two concessions belonging to Italy's state-owned oil company, ENI. Finally, and perhaps most significantly of all, on 5 October 1972, the oil companies reluctantly signed up to a 'General Agreement on Participation', whereby Kuwait, Qatar, Abu Dhabi and Saudi Arabia would nationalise 25 per cent of all western oil interests in their countries on January 1973, followed by further acquisitions taking the government stakes to 51 per cent over the next ten years. The complex provisions of this agreement also added a further 9 cents to the average price of Saudi crude.

Against this background of OPEC muscle-flexing, and without the safety margin previously provided by shut-in capacity, concern began to grow in America about the possibility of much higher oil prices and even a future oil shortage. As we noted in Chapter One, one result of this was the growing belief that the USA and its allies must begin to look for new, 'safe' sources of oil, outside the Middle East. The US State Department appears to have begun the search for these 'safe' sources of oil at the instigation of Secretary of State Henry Kissinger in 1972, as awareness grew of the new, radical turn in Arab politics. In a secret report prepared by James Akins, Director of the Office of Fuels and Energy at the State Department, it had been concluded that the balance of power in the world petroleum industry was now passing from the consumers to the suppliers. On 9 March 1972, the State Department reported its anxieties to the White House. Akins had recommended a strongly interventionist policy which included conservation, measures to increase domestic oil production and a deliberate policy of increasing oil imports from 'secure sources'.[22] It would appear that this was the first occasion on which such a policy objective was stated.

In April, Akins, whose opinions had been treated with considerable scepticism by some members of the Nixon Administration, went public with a major article in the prestigious journal *Foreign Affairs*, entitled 'The Oil Crisis: This Time the Wolf is Here'. He presented a dramatic statistic – that world consumption of oil for the next twelve years was expected to be greater than the total world consumption of oil throughout all history up till 1973. He also argued that the price of oil, then around $2 per barrel, was likely to rise to $5 per barrel before 1980 and that the Arab countries were now in a favourable position to use oil as a political weapon.[23]

So the search began for new sources of oil. Richard Funkhouser, one of the State Department officials who had helped to draw up the Akins Report to the White House, was sent to London to check out the prospects for the North Sea, where oil had been discovered in 1969. Funkhouser had few doubts about his role – to help to get the oil out as fast as possible from a 'safe' province, and in May he cabled the State Department declaring that 'North Sea oil is a vital factor in western economic survival.'[24] Even though it would be many years before the UK would become a net oil exporter, its ability from 1975 onwards to begin serving its own domestic oil needs would partially remove the necessity of diverting US supplies in that direction in the event of a crisis like that envisaged in the Rand Corporation study of 1963.

By April 1973, tightness in US domestic oil supplies had become so acute that the Nixon Administration was able to overcome the opposition of the domestic oil producers' lobby and abolish the import quota system. Oil imports, which had been 2.2 million b/d (19 per cent of total oil consumption) in 1967, surged to 6 million b/d by 1973 (34.8 per cent of consumption) and by 1976 had reached 7.1 million b/d (40.6 per cent of consumption). This threefold increase in the volume of oil imports within a mere ten years was not the only shock to America's image of itself as an oil-rich nation. 'The razor's edge,' as Daniel

Yergin puts it, 'was the ever-increasing reliance on oil of the Middle East'. In 1972, imports from the Gulf area contributed about 5 per cent of total US consumption, but by 1976, they had reached 1.8 million b/d and the following year accelerated to 2.5 million b/d – 13.3 per cent of total US consumption and 29 per cent of net oil imports.

Even a seemingly small 5 per cent dependency could have drastic ramifications, as became evident during the energy crisis of 1973–1974. In the twelve-month period beginning in April 1973, the western world witnessed a continuation of the creeping nationalisation of foreign oil interests throughout the Gulf and North Africa, a major war between Israel and Egypt/Syria, an embargo on oil supplies to the USA, unprecedented queuing for gasoline in the USA and a 350 per cent increase in world oil prices.[25] In the words of one of the main protagonists in this drama, Secretary of State Henry Kissinger, 'Never before had nations so weak militarily – and in some cases politically – been able to impose such strains on the international system'.[26] Later, Kissinger also observed that a century earlier the consuming nations would have responded by seizing the oilfields. According to Kissinger, 'From time to time...the United States threatened to do just that but never received any support from the other industrial democracies.'[27]

Indeed, recently declassified UK documents covering this period reveal that the British Government believed that America was seriously considering an invasion of the Gulf states in order to seize the key oilfields. The US Secretary of Defense at the time, James Schlesinger, was reported as saying that 'it was no longer obvious to him that the US could not use force.'[28] In the event, wiser heads, including Kissinger himself, drew back from this drastic response, fearing that it might provoke the intervention of the Soviet Union.

In 1979, while America agonised about how to deal with the continuing oil crisis, four critical events occurred which forced America and the House of Saud to reaffirm their historical strategic pact which, for a time, had seemed to be on the point of disintegrating. After months of unrest which had begun the previous year, the Shah of Iran was overthrown by a revolution led by Shia Islamic clerics and on 16 January 1979 fled the country. Next, in November, three hundred *Wahhabi* extremists seized the Great Mosque in Mecca in an attempt to spark a revolt against the Saudi Monarchy, a rebellion which was only suppressed with considerable difficulty and much bloodshed. The following month the House of Saud was confronted by a second revolt, this time among the downtrodden Shia inhabitants of the eastern oil-producing al-Hasa region; this too was crushed but the hidden hand of the Iranian revolutionaries was perceived as the underlying cause. Then, finally at the end of December, the Soviet Union mounted a full-scale invasion of Afghanistan to ward off the impending collapse of the country's communist government.

President Carter's response was to issue a formal declaration which extended even further America's strategic commitment to the House of Saud, asserting that, 'the region which is now threatened by Soviet troops in Afghanistan is of great strategic importance: it contains more than two-thirds of the world's exportable oil.' According to this so-called Carter Doctrine, any move by a hostile power to acquire control over the Gulf region would be regarded 'as an assault on the vital interests of the United States of America' which would be opposed 'by any means including military force'. The declaration was backed up by the creation of a 'Rapid Reaction Force' based in the USA but on high alert for any necessary military intervention in the Gulf.

At the same time Carter authorised covert support for the Afghan *mujahidin*, a programme which was to further unite America and the House of Saud in opposing the communist common enemy. The Saudi contribution was to be, as usual, in hard cash; but a few young men, educated in the religious schools which had been generously funded by Ibn Saud's successors, set off to join their Islamist brothers in the mountains of Afghanistan. After many years they, and their companions, would return to Saudi Arabia and the other Arab states, with deadly consequences.

REDUCING DEPENDENCE ON THE GULF

The Iranian Revolution of 1978 reduced the flow of Middle Eastern oil by around 3.5 million b/d for six months, and was followed by a second world oil price surge the following year. Coming on top of the 1973 Arab oil embargo, this seemed to further underline America's now problematic dependence on Middle Eastern oil. Although the Carter Doctrine offered a robust challenge to any force which contemplated a threat to America's position in the Gulf, to many it now appeared that what had originally been a means of ensuring energy security – importing Middle East oil – was now a poisoned chalice which could ultimately prove highly toxic to America's interests, especially its long-standing interest in supporting the state of Israel. In short, America might now have to trade its support for Israel against its need for oil.

Concern over the vulnerability of Gulf supplies was heightened even more by the outbreak of the Iran–Iraq War in October 1980, when oil supplies were again interrupted, this time by 3.3 million b/d for three months. Against this background, Melvin Conant, former Senior Government Relations Counsellor for Exxon and the Federal Energy Administration's Assistant Administrator for International Affairs during the 1973–1974 oil crisis, published the first comprehensive analysis of the USA's energy security problems in a monograph sponsored by the Council on Foreign Relations.[29] Among the policy measures Conant identified as being of critical importance 'the most fundamental ... is to reduce dependence on the Gulf.'[30]

Conant also argued that a major contribution to this objective would be a 'hemispheric energy effort' linking oil producers in Canada, Mexico and Venezuela to the US market. 'The American interest,' Conant argued, 'is clearly in maximising supply from these countries to reduce dependence on the Gulf.'[31] In this context, Conant applauded President Reagan's proposal for a 'North American Accord' (eventually realised in 1993 as the North American Free Trade Agreement – NAFTA), which was intended to integrate the energy economies of the USA, Canada and Mexico. Conant believed that there should also be 'an invitation to Venezuela to think through the implications to itself of participating in an accord.'

We shall look in greater detail at Venezuela and the idea of the hemispheric 'accord' in Chapter Seven. For the time being, let us examine the extent to which the USA did succeed in diversifying its oil imports away from the Gulf at this time. Total US oil imports fell between 1980 and 1985, from 6.4 million b/d to 4.3 million b/d, partly as a result of the general downturn in the US economy following the steep oil price increase in 1979–1980. Imports from the Gulf also fell substantially, from 1.5 million to 0.3 million b/d. At the same time, imports from what might be considered the 'safe areas', the UK, Canada, Venezuela and Mexico, which in 1980 had been approximately the same as those from the Gulf, increased and began to replace Gulf sources during 1981–1985. By 1985, as little as 2 per cent of total US petroleum supplies came from the Gulf.

THE SAUDIS TURN ON THE TAP AND
IRAQ TURNS ON ITS NEIGHBOUR

And now, at the very moment when the threat of a Middle-East oil stranglehold appeared to have significantly diminished, Saudi Arabia itself chose a strategy which seemed to herald a new era in which damagingly high oil prices would no longer threaten the USA and other oil-dependent western economies. Hitherto, in order to support the world oil price, Saudi Arabia had been compelled to progressively reduce its own output, which fell from 6.7 million barrels per day in 1982 to 3.6 million b/d in 1985. But, by January 1986, Saudi Arabia had tired of shouldering the burden of production restraint and raised its production to 5 million b/d. Immediately, prices plummeted by over 50 per cent, the spot price of Arabian Light crude tumbling from $27.53 per barrel in 1985 to $12.97 in 1986. The Saudis apparently hoped that this would discipline some errant OPEC over-producers as well as undermining large parts of higher-cost non-OPEC oil production, in particular the UK North Sea. However, although the move at first caused consternation in some of the non-OPEC oil-producing regions (ironically, as we shall see in the next chapter, including oil-producing regions of the USA), it failed to deal a death blow to the North Sea, where the new lower prices still exceeded the producers' marginal operating costs.

Although prices recovered slightly in 1987, when a demoralised and con-fused OPEC for the first time introduced a quota system, the following years saw little improvement, with persistent price weakness exacerbated by serious quota cheating by some OPEC producers. Kuwait in particular adopted a peculiarly arrogant policy of production expansion. Then, in a development totally unforeseen by America, Saddam Hussein, long considered a brutal but useful ally of the USA, shattered its complacent assumptions about a new world order in which the strategic advantages of a disintegrating Soviet Union would be combined with those of a demoralised and passive Middle East, by turning viciously upon Kuwait.

Kuwait was denounced as a treacherous ingrate. After Iraq had shed its blood in a war with Iran for eight dreadful years, ostensibly to defend the Arab world against 'the Persians' led by the fanatical Khomeini, Kuwait now had the effrontery to demand repayment of its war-time loans while at the same time continuing to undermine the oil price upon which Iraq's recovery crucially depended. In a further intensification of the crisis, Saddam Hussein dusted off old territorial claims against Kuwait and charged it with 'stealing' oil from a major Iraqi field lying on the Iraq-Kuwait border. Then, on 2 August 1990, after Kuwait had rejected all Saddam Hussein's demands, 100,000 Iraqi troops poured over the border. Five months later, on 16 January 1991, the US-led Coalition began the counter-attack with devastating air strikes on Iraq itself. In Daniel Yergin's words, 'the first post Cold-War crisis turned out to be a geopolitical oil crisis.'[32]

5   The Axis of Oil

Dick gives us a level of access that I doubt anyone else in the oil sector can duplicate.

David J. Lesar, President, Halliburton, 1998

When the US National Security Council convened on the day of the Iraqi invasion, 2 August 1990, oil was on the agenda from the very beginning. This first meeting of George Bush Sr with his strategic advisers, confirmed that at issue were crucial US interests as well as international law. Calculations revealed that with its control over Kuwait, Iraq now had access to 20 per cent of the world's proven oil reserves and if it overran Saudi Arabia's small and ill-prepared armed forces this figure would double.[1] The time had come to put into practice the USA's long-standing pledge to defend the House of Saud and its oilfields – 'laying down a line in the sand concerning Saudi Arabia', as Colin Powell, Chairman of the Joint Chiefs of Staff put it.[2]

The following day, the National Security Council met for a second time, to discuss America's response. Present at the meeting, in addition to President George Bush, were Defense Secretary Richard Cheney, Richard Haass, Special Assistant to the President for Near East and South Asian Affairs, Deputy Secretary of State Lawrence Eagleburger and Brent Scowcroft, National Security Advisor. Cheney, Eagleburger and Scowcroft, having first agreed the line they should take in advising the President, argued that Saddam's invasion was 'a far more important issue than Kuwait...it was about oil, in that with access to Kuwaiti reserves, Saddam would be able to wield unprecedented influence over the world oil market.'[3] The oil argument – that with 20, and perhaps even 40 per cent of world oil reserves under his control, Saddam Hussein could hike the price of oil to an unprecedented level, convinced Bush that war was inevitable;

and this oil argument was particularly efficacious in persuading the President because Bush knew all about oil.

Although coming from an eastern state, ivy-league background (his father was Senator for Connecticut), Bush had made his fortune in the Texas oilfields. Having established himself in the booming oil town of Midland in the late 1940s, he set up a successful medium-sized oil and gas exploration and production company called Zapata Oil. By the mid-1960s, Bush had made enough money from oil to follow his own father into politics, rapidly rising to become US ambassador to the UN, Chief of the US Liaison Office in China, and Head of the CIA. In 1980, he became Vice President to Ronald Reagan, and in 1988 President; but he never abandoned his interest in oil matters.

Bush also understood that the oil argument would have a powerful appeal in winning ordinary American citizens to support the war. On 15 August 1990, he delivered a dramatic rallying cry to America in a speech to Pentagon employees reported in the *New York Times*: 'Our jobs, our way of life, our own freedom and the freedom of friendly countries around the world would all suffer if control of the world's great oil reserves fell into the hands of Saddam Hussein.'[4] Moreover, there was an additional and deeply troubling significance to Saddam's oil grab. In the words of Daniel Yergin, 'A greater Iraq which had succeeded in absorbing Kuwait, would be well on its way to turning itself into a formidable nuclear state.' In other words, and to use the terminology of a later confrontation with Saddam Hussein, commanding the oil revenues from both Iraq and Kuwait would provide him with the economic wherewithal to build, and possibly use, 'Weapons of Mass Destruction'. 'This was the real significance of the "oil factor",' argued Yergin, 'the way that oil would be translated into money and power: political, economic – and military.'[5] Oil was fundamental to the crisis, 'not "cheap oil" but rather oil as a critical element in the global balance of power'.[6]

In the event, however, Saddam Hussein was driven out of Kuwait, by a US-led Coalition, his army largely destroyed, his country devastated. On 17 January 1991, the Coalition launched Operation Desert Storm. US Tomahawk missiles rained down upon selected military targets around Baghdad. For more than a month, F-117 Stealth jet fighters, B-52 bombers and a variety of aircraft from America's Coalition allies destroyed much of Iraq's infrastructure along with thousands of Iraqi civilians. On 24 February, General Norman Schwarzkopf followed this up with a blitzkrieg land attack, surrounding the Iraqi army and blocking its line of retreat. Kuwait City was recaptured and Iraqi forces retreating north towards the Euphrates river were incinerated on what became known as the 'highway of death'. By the end of the war, American forces had lost a mere 148 troops killed in action and another 467 wounded. So, having accomplished a mission with clear but limited objectives at so little cost in US lives, President Bush and his advisers decided to end the campaign rather than see US troops become bogged down in a bloody battle for Baghdad.

Saddam Hussein was left to his own devices, to mercilessly crush an uprising of Shia Arabs in the south and Kurdish rebels in the north. But these brutal demonstrations of his dictatorship only served to underline the basic weakness of Saddam's regime – how could a country so devastated, brutalised and divided ever again prove a threat to its neighbours, let alone to the world's only superpower? Furthermore, while it is undoubtedly true that the UN sanctions which followed Saddam's defeat soon came to be manipulated by Saddam and his entourage for their own purposes and the UN weapons inspectors never completed their job, by the beginning of the twenty-first century, Iraq's military capacity – despite Saddam's fascistic posturing – was dilapidated, broken, demoralised and utterly feeble, as indeed future events were to demonstrate.

However, ten years later, with Bush Jr now in the White House, the strategic logic behind the first Gulf War was suddenly and conveniently forgotten. In 1991, it had been believed that a Saddam Hussein emboldened by his conquest and enriched with the oil revenues of both Iraq and Kuwait (and perhaps Saudi Arabia) might use them to acquire weapons of mass destruction: in other words, greater oil power would bring even greater military power. But now, in 2001, the message emanating from the White House was quite different: Americans were to be told that they were indeed facing an imminent and devastating threat of nuclear, chemical and biological attack from Iraq – but this time from an Iraq which had not only been denuded of Kuwait's massive oil reserves long ago but whose domestic oil industry was struggling even to maintain a production level below that of 1990. In short, America and the world were being asked to believe that Saddam Hussein without oil power was equally as dangerous, if not more dangerous than a Saddam Hussein *with* oil power.

In fact, 'regime change' in Iraq was the number one item on the agenda of President Bush's first National Security Council meeting held on 30 January 2001.[7] In what Treasury Secretary Paul O'Neill was later to describe as an obviously 'scripted' discussion between Bush and his National Security Advisor Condoleezza Rice, the other members of Council were informed that, 'Iraq is destabilizing the region' and that 'Iraq might be key to reshaping the entire region.'[8] The Pentagon was soon put to work 'developing a military option for Iraq'.[9] Then, only nine months into George W. Bush's presidency, the opportunity to invade Iraq presented itself in a horrific manner. The terrorist attacks on the Twin Towers and the Pentagon, in Bob Woodward's words, 'gave the US a new window to go after Hussein'.[10]

Ten weeks later, on 21 November 2001, the three members of the Administration most determined to use that window of opportunity, President George W. Bush, Vice President Richard Cheney and National Security Advisor Condoleezza Rice, conversed and agreed that Secretary of Defense Donald Rumsfeld should get to work on the detailed battle plan for a second war against Saddam Hussein.[11] The three individuals responsible for that fateful decision were also the three members of the Administration whose occupational experience, political connections and personal wealth were most closely aligned with the interests of the US oil industry, Just how strong were those ties, we shall now relate.

THE AXIS OF OIL: GEORGE W. BUSH

George W. Bush wanted to become a rich and successful oilman like his father; but his performance in that business must have been something of a disappointment, both to himself and to his father. He had founded his own oil company, Arbusto Energy Inc. in 1977. However, in spite of the fact that Bush Sr, family friends and right-wing business magnates poured thousands of dollars into Arbusto, it didn't find much oil. Then the world oil price began to slide and Arbusto's condition deteriorated even further. However, in 1984, as Arbusto reached the nadir of its fortunes, the company was purchased by Spectrum Energy 7 Corp, a small oil exploration company owned by William DeWitt and Mercer Reynolds, two staunch and generous supporters of the Reagan and Bush Administrations. As part of the deal, and in spite of his hitherto unimpressive performance as an oil company executive, Bush Jr was made Chief Executive Officer of Spectrum at an annual salary of $75,000 and with 16.3 per cent of the company's stock. To many, the Spectrum-Arbusto transaction simply looked like a bail-out of Bush Jr by his father's friends.[12]

Unfortunately, the decline in oil prices which had caused problems for Arbusto, suddenly became a complete collapse following the Saudi move, in January 1986, to discipline the world oil market. Before long, Spectrum too was in serious trouble. In its last six months of trading it lost $402,000 and the company had more than $3 million in bank loans and other debts with no hope of paying them off in time.

It was at this point that the attention of Vice President George Bush returned, somewhat controversially, to the oil business. He had been planning a trip to the Gulf for some time, originally to show political support for 'moderate' Arab states like Saudi Arabia. But with the 1986 world oil price down to around $10 per barrel, his thoughts turned to the plight of his fellow Texan oilmen – not least his son. So in April 1986, to the surprise of many, he arrived in Riyadh, urging the Saudis to cut production and raise oil prices. It wasn't put quite so bluntly and there was much talk about 'letting the market do its work' but at a meeting with American businessmen in Dharan, a day after his visit to King Fahd, Bush made it clear that he considered very low oil prices were *also* a threat to America's national security.

Conditions in Texas and in the industry were now as bad as or worse than any he had seen during his own days as an oilman and the economic crisis in his own political base in the Southwest, particularly Texas, was suddenly very intense. Nor was Bush alone with his concerns in the Reagan Administration. With echoes of those 1950s arguments, Energy Secretary John Herrington was warning that 'the fall in oil prices has reached the point of threatening national security.'[13] From the perspective of America's own oil industry – an industry which in 1990 was still the largest oil producer in the world and whose daily output of oil exceeded that of Saudi Arabia by 2.2 million barrels per day – the pendulum could sometimes swing too far in the interests of the US motorised consumer.

If we take a brief look at the structure of the US domestic oil industry we can see why there was a problem. According to a study carried out by the Department of Energy a few years after the end of the Gulf war, the US domestic oil industry was unlike any other oil industry in the world. In addition to a handful of 'major' fully integrated oil companies (Exxon, Chevron, Texaco etc.) there were thousands of much smaller, so-called 'independents'. The census of 1992 had shown that the country had nearly 8,000 separate companies involved in oil and gas production; but of these only 427 were publicly traded companies listed on the US stock exchange.[14] The remainder were tiny businesses, many of them 'mom and pop' outfits, whose producing wells were mainly 'strippers' – wells producing fewer than 10 barrels per well per day. Cash operating costs for such wells were typically around 9–10 dollars per barrel so when well-head prices fell below this level, as they did in early 1986, thousands of small oil producers in Texas, and throughout the so-called Lower 48 states of the USA, looked ruin in the face.

In the event, the Saudis did nothing in response to the Vice President's pleas, understandably concluding that if the US oil industry was in pain, the pressure they were exerting on non-OPEC oil production was working. But in the meantime the plight of Bush Jr and Spectrum Energy was getting worse by the day.

This time a saviour appeared in the form of Harken Oil and Gas, a Dallas-based medium-sized 'independent'. Harken merged with Spectrum in a stock-only deal according to which Bush Jr and his business partners were given $2.2 million of Harken stock, Bush Jr became a Director of Harken at $2,000 per board meeting, with stock options worth $131,250 and a job as 'consultant' to the company with an annual salary of $80,000 a year, rising to $120,000 per year in 1989.[15]

Once George W. Bush came on board, Harken's business began to pick up. Harvard Management Company, the institutional investor representing Bush's Alma Mater, agreed to invest $20 million in Harken. Then, on 30 January 1990, Harken was offered a remarkable new business opportunity – an exclusive deal with the Government of Bahrain to explore for oil offshore and, if discoveries were made, to develop it through a production-sharing agreement with Bahrain.[16] As one US energy expert put it in an article in *Forbes Magazine*, 'This is an incredible deal for this small company,' particularly for a small, obscure, money-losing company which had never before drilled an offshore well. Although there have been allegations, then and since, that the deal was a sweetener to encourage the Bush Administration to establish a permanent military base in Bahrain – an agreement to that effect was signed in October 1991 – a rather simpler explanation suggests itself. According to a report in the *Washington Post*, Yousuf Shirawi, Bahrain's Minister for Development and Industry, who gave the production-sharing contract to Harken, 'had a link to the administration dating to the days when George Bush was Vice President'. In other words, Shirawi and Bush Sr were on friendly terms, and at a time when Bahrain was moving ever closer to the USA in matters of defence and security, doing a favour for the son of the US Vice President would probably have seemed quite natural.[17] In fact the Bush family, both father and son, were by now developing a strong relationship with a variety of Gulf oil business magnates – especially in Saudi Arabia, to such an extent that various members of the House of Saud and other members of the Saudi elite would soon become frequent guests and trusted confidants. Crown Prince Abdullah, later the de facto ruler of the Kingdom would eventually be writing personal letters to President George W. Bush, addressed to 'My Dear Friend' and the Saudi Ambassador, Prince Bandar bin Sultan would be shown top secret US plans for America's 2003 invasion of Iraq.[18]

Not surprisingly, the 1990 deal with Bahrain made Harken's stock look particularly attractive and although the company had, as yet, nothing to show for its new strategy, potential buyers factored-in expected future oil earnings from what was believed to be a tried and tested Middle East oil province. Then, on 22 June 1990, shortly after he had been shown a weekly 'flash' report on the company's current financial situation, Bush Jr sold 212,140 of his Harken Stock for $835,307, a profit of 200 per cent on their original value. Two months later and just a few days after Iraq invaded Kuwait, Harken Oil and Gas (now renamed Harken

Energy) announced a quarterly earnings loss of $23.2 million and the value of Harken stock dropped by 21 per cent. By the end of 1990 Harken stock had lost 66 per cent of its June value. Bush Jr had got out just in time and made a nice profit on the deal. As for Harken, it drilled two dry holes offshore Bahrain and left.

Unfortunately Bush Jr failed to inform the US Securities and Exchange Commission (SEC) promptly about his sale of Harken stock, waiting 34 weeks before doing so – a breach of US securities law. When questioned about the incident by the SEC, Bush said he had filed in time, but that somehow the paperwork had been lost, a reply which one observer likened to the school student who said that 'the dog had eaten his homework'. After a perfunctory SEC investigation carried out by an attorney who had previously been Bush Jr's own lawyer, and under the direction of an SEC Chairman who was a Bush Sr appointee, the investigation was abandoned in October 1993 with Bush Jr escaping any legal action. In any case, the shenanigans surrounding the Harken Energy affair seem to have had no impact on loyal Republican oilmen and voters in Texas and the scion of the Bush dynasty easily won the Governorship of the State in 1994 and re-election to that position in January 1999.

Bush Jr's re-election coincided with a replay of the low oil-price crisis which had nearly wrecked his own oil business career back in 1986. The problem had started with the Asian economic downturn of 1997. With some OPEC members, especially Venezuela, already substantially exceeding their quotas, the organisation decided it would do no harm to regularise matters by officially countenancing increased oil output levels. However, in the face of sluggish world demand for oil, the decision soon proved a disaster. Before long a free-for-all had developed with Saudi Arabia and Venezuela increasingly involved in a feverish price war. On 3 October 1997, the value of West Texas Intermediate (WTI), the US crude spot price, stood at $22.78 per barrel. By May 1998, it had fallen to $14.86, and Texan and other US domestic oil producers, with their ten-barrels-a-day wells and high production costs, began to see economic ruin staring them in the face once again. Although the oil price recovered slightly in October 1998, it then began to tumble once more, reaching a low of $10.73 on 10 December. Moreover, the actual well-head price, a more realistic indicator of what the oil producer received, was down to $9.20 in Texas at the 1998 year-end.

There was no doubt about the extent to which Texas was suffering. As the largest US oil-producing state, but with the largest number of low-productivity stripper wells in the country, the once great oil state appeared to be heading for terminal decline as a petroleum producer. True, the great Texan cities like Houston and Dallas were still benefiting from the computer and telecoms boom, but in the rural, oil-producing areas the local economy was in severe distress. During 1998, 2,127 oil wells were shut down, 11,500 oil industry jobs disappeared, drilling permits issued fell by a third, new oil well completions in February 1999 dropped by 70 per cent on the previous year and new gas wells down 35 per cent. Revenues from the oil severance tax, a local levy on oil production which supported the State's public expenditure, had fallen by $137 million.[19]

But the crisis ran even deeper. Unlike the rest of the world, the USA has a system of private royalty owners. This means that the royalty payment, typically between 12.5 and 20 per cent of the oil price and in theory a compensation for the depletion of the natural resource, is paid not to the government, but to the private individual who owns the land on which the oil well is drilled. Nationally there are around 4.5 million royalty owners, of which about 2.5 million are residents of Texas.[20] As one oil industry observer put it 'oil producers and royalty owners are Siamese twins – joined at the pocket book.'[21] So the impact of the 1998–1999 oil price collapse affected a much larger group of individuals than just those working directly in the oil industry.

Governor Bush had limited room for manoeuvre, but did what he could. On 2 February 1999, he designated a temporary $45 million tax break to low-productivity stripper wells, declaring an 'emergency' so that it could be taken up without delay by the State Legislature. The emergency legislation, which came into effect the following March, provided severance tax relief to low-productivity oil wells when the oil price fell below $15 per barrel.[22] Shortly afterwards, the world oil price began to recover and the crisis faded. But Bush had proved himself a reliable supporter of the domestic oil interest in his home state.

While measures like oil severance tax relief showed that Governor Bush knew how to retain support among the many small Texan oilmen and royalty owners, the support from the more rich and powerful Texan energy interests initially came without a price, in anticipation of what Bush might do for them if – as now seemed likely – he became the next President of the USA. Chief of these rich and powerful interests was Kenneth Lay, President and CEO of Enron Corporation and 'Kenny Boy' to his friend Bush. Enron Corporation had an oil and gas production subsidiary, Enron Oil & Gas Company, which had carried out joint drilling activities with Bush Jr's Spectrum Energy in 1986.[23] But Enron was also something new in the world of oil and gas companies. It had been created a year earlier out of a merger between two large interstate natural gas pipeline companies, Houston Natural Gas Company and InterNorth Inc., and when Enron went on to acquire a large electricity company, Portland General, in November 1996, it became clear that the US energy business was witnessing the emergence of a new phenomenon – the 'energy mega-marketer'.[24] The mega-marketer traded in *any* type of energy product – natural gas, liquefied petroleum gas, oil, electricity, even coal; and unlike the 'asset-heavy' large integrated oil companies like Exxon and Chevron, it purported to avoid the permanent ownership of fixed assets. Moreover, companies like Enron and its imitators claimed they were part of the 'New Economy' that was touted to be sweeping all before it during the last years of the twentieth century. In the energy sector the two key 'New Economy' elements were deregulation at home and privatisation abroad. Enron's projects in both spheres would benefit considerably when Bush Jr became President: the first directly, through the drafting of a new energy policy in which Lay intended to play a major role, and the second indirectly through the exercise of US state pressure upon developing countries which needed US financial assistance. To this end, Lay and Enron contributed \$550,025 to Bush's gubernatorial and presidential electoral campaigns over a number of years.[25]

In the event Lay only had a very short time in which to get a return on this investment. A few months after Bush Jr's election to the Presidency, the US stock market began to fall and Enron's crooked accounting practices began to come to light. Nevertheless, as Enron's crisis worsened through the first nine months of Bush's presidency, Lay got help from the President in a number of ways. The latter personally joined the fight against imposing price caps on the soaring price of electricity in California where Enron was manipulating both the electricity and gas markets; he granted Lay broad influence over the formulation of the Administration's energy policy, including the choice of regulators to oversee Enron's businesses; and he got his National Security Staff, headed by Condoleezza Rice, to put pressure on the Indian Government to accommodate Enron's operations in that country.[26]

Of course, many other super-rich executives of US energy companies supported Bush's political campaigns. In fact no other candidate for Federal office has ever received as much financial support from the oil and gas industry as Bush did during his 2000 campaign. Chairman of this campaign was Donald Evans, CEO of Tom Brown Inc., a medium-sized, Colorado-based oil and gas 'independent', who was to be rewarded with the post of Commerce Secretary once Bush was elected. From the energy and natural resources sector as whole, Bush received almost \$3 million of which \$1.9 million in contributions came from the oil and gas sector.[27] Executives from energy companies were the second largest industrial group of donors included in the list of Bush's so-called 'Pioneers' – individuals who had personally donated more than \$100,000 to his campaigns.[28]

In addition to chief executives of large Enron-like, Texas-based, energy trading companies, such as Reliant Energy and TXU Corp, it is noticeable that the 'Pioneers' list also includes a significant number of owners/CEOs of smaller domestic oil and gas exploration and production companies, contract drilling companies, and other companies dependent on a prosperous domestic US oil and gas industry.[29] Indeed the second largest individual donor to Bush's campaigns was Tony Sanchez Jr, CEO of Sanchez-O'Brien Oil and Gas Company, a relatively small independent oil and gas producer and contract drilling company. As we have already observed, the domestic 'independent' oil and gas sector typically has higher exploration and production costs than the major oil companies like ExxonMobil and ChevronTexaco and the 'independents' and the contract drilling companies who work for them are generally more vulnerable to persistently low oil prices than the major oil companies with international oil and gas assets.[30] Of course, Bush could not be seen to be pandering entirely to local oil and energy interests. While he was on the campaign trail in New England states, far from the oil-producing South West, and world oil prices were currently higher than they had been for many years, he criticised President Clinton for his failure to demand that OPEC 'open the spigots', increase production and reduce oil prices. However, once elected, his position soon changed. According to a report in the *Oil and Gas Journal* relating to OPEC's agreement to reduce quotas by 1 million barrels per day from 1 April 2001, Bush 'put into reasonable perspective the latest quota reduction by OPEC.' Bush, it was reported, 'apparently accepts the view that OPEC more likely acted to defend its members against another ruinous price crash than hike prices in defiance of economic forces and consumer interests'. And the President described as 'comforting' the Saudi oil minister's reassertion of a $28 per barrel ceiling on the price band against which OPEC was managing production.[31]

In a subsequent article in the *Financial Times*, an OPEC analyst with the Petroleum Finance Company in Washington is reported as saying that Bush's acceptance of an OPEC-determined price was 'the most significant statement by this administration on oil' and that 'it excited a lot of OPEC Ministers'.[32] No doubt it also excited the thousands of petroleum producers and royalty owners throughout Texas and the 23 other oil-producing states of the USA.

THE AXIS OF OIL: CONDOLEEZZA RICE

George W. Bush's choice for National Security Advisor had been a Director of Chevron Corporation since 1991. Condoleezza Rice even had one of Chevron's oil tankers named after her in 1993, a 129,915 ton vessel, now re-christened the *Altair Voyager*. Why Chevron should have chosen a black female academic, albeit one with pronounced right-wing views, to join its board becomes clearer when one examines Rice's particular sphere of academic expertise and the year in which she was appointed.

For her academic interest was cold-war politics. She had researched and published on various topics relating to the changing nature of the Soviet Union and the collapse of communism. During the key period between 1989 and 1991, the period of German unification and the final days of the Soviet Union, her Republican politics and academic achievements brought her into the Administration of Bush Sr, where she served as Senior Director of Soviet and East European Affairs in the National Security Council.

Her entrée to the board of Chevron was at the instigation of George P. Schultz, Reagan's Secretary of State, who was himself a director of Chevron in the late 1980s and whose abiding influence has been described as 'forming the bedrock of US foreign policy' in George W. Bush's Administration.[33] Schultz was familiar with Rice's academic interests and ideological stance and no doubt thought she would be the ideal person to advise Chevron in its planned forays into the former Soviet Union. Indeed, two years after her appointment, Chevron announced the formation of Tengizchevroil, a 50/50 joint venture with a subsidiary of the national oil and gas company of Kazakhstan, to develop the huge Tengiz oilfield, and in the years that followed Chevron made further investments in the Caspian region, a subject to which we will return in Chapter Eight.

Reporting directly to Rice, as chief NSC official for the Persian Gulf and Central Asia, was Zalmay Khalilzad, an Afghan-born US citizen who had served in the Reagan and Bush Sr Administrations, worked for the Rand Corporation and served as counsellor to Donald Rumsfeld. He had also been a consultant to Unocal Corporation, the large US multinational oil company, and played a part in that company's negotiations with the Taliban to build oil and gas pipelines across Afghanistan, from the Caspian to the coast of Pakistan, negotiations which only came to an end when the Clinton Administration launched missiles against Osama bin Laden's camps in August 1998.[34] Like Rice herself, Khalilzad had long been an advocate of military action against Saddam Hussein's Iraq.[35]

THE AXIS OF OIL: RICHARD CHENEY

Richard Cheney, who had strongly encouraged Bush Sr to go to war over oil in 1991, was not at that point in time directly involved in the oil business himself. But he was certainly looking forward to the opportunities in this field which the post-Gulf War settlement would bring. Hitherto, Cheney had spent almost all of his adult life in politics. He had entered public life as a relatively minor civil servant in the Nixon Administration, after which he rose through the ranks to serve briefly as President Gerald Ford's White House Chief of Staff from 1975 until the end of his presidency in 1977. He was then elected to the House of Representatives as Republican Congressman for his home state of Wyoming, a position to which he was re-elected five times. Wyoming is an oil- and coal-producing state and it seems likely that Cheney developed his interest in, and knowledge of, energy matters during this period. Continuing to rise through the ranks of Republican politics and demonstrating indefatigable support for conservative causes, in 1989 he became Secretary for Defense in the Admin-istration of George Bush Sr.

On leaving office in 1993, Cheney became a senior fellow at a Washington-based conservative 'think tank', the American Enterprise Institute, a role which would allow him to maintain his public profile while awaiting the offers of lucrative corporate posts which must sooner or later come his way in recognition of the portfolio of worldwide contacts which he had assembled during his years in government. Cheney was particularly energetic in pursuing the opportunities opening up in the territories of the former Soviet Union, since its collapse in 1991. He was soon reported to be 'courting politicians and business leaders through the booming Caspian Sea region in an all-out effort to secure key political ties with Azerbaijan and Kazakhstan'.[36] In 1994, these efforts yielded one particularly solid result: he was appointed by President Nursultan Nazarbayev of Kazakhstan to his twelve-member Oil Advisory Board, where he helped to broker the deal which set up the Caspian Pipeline Consortium to transport Chevron's oil from the Tengiz field.[37] Cheney also became one of the seven-strong Honorary Council of Advisors for the Azerbaijan-US Chamber of Commerce. This innocuous-sounding body was in reality almost entirely concerned with promoting the interest of US oil companies in the exploitation of that Caspian country's oil and gas reserves.

In October 1995, Cheney got his reward and the Dallas-based Halliburton Company appointed him as Chief Executive Officer. As Halliburton's President, David J.Lesar put it, 'Dick gives us a level of access that I doubt anyone else in the oil sector can duplicate.'[38] Halliburton is primarily an oil industry service company and is the largest such company in the world. In 2001, Halliburton had total revenues of $13,046 million and net income (profit after tax and interest payments) of $809 million. It employed 85,000 people and had around 7,000 customers in more than 100 countries.[39] Oil industry service companies do not directly own oil- and gas-producing properties; they are not oil companies in precisely the same way that, for example, ExxonMobil is. Instead they perform

THE AXIS OF OIL

the essential engineering and technical services which companies like ExxonMobil increasingly rely upon to carry out their day-to-day operations. They provide contract drilling services, construct oil and gas pipelines and operate oil production platforms; they provide geophysical and seismic exploration technologies and many other oil and gas industry-related functions. In a sense they are more at the 'sharp end' of the oil industry than the oil majors themselves with the latter increasingly becoming more like banks which set up deals with governments and then farm out the actual work to major subcontractors like Halliburton. One particular advantage of this is that the majors thereby free themselves from some of the tricky industrial-relations issues which are transferred to the contractors. These in turn, being less in the public eye, can often get away with anti-union and union-busting tactics which might be embarrassing for the more publicly exposed major oil companies. Halliburton, needless to say, is a non-union company, in fact the largest non-union employer in the USA.

Ex-Defense Secretary Cheney knew exactly how to convert his political assets into contracts and cash for Halliburton. As he himself said, during a 1998 speech in Corpus Christi, Texas, carrying out the top job at Halliburton had been greatly helped by his experience at the Pentagon, for after all, 'in the oil and gas business, I deal with many of the same people.'[40] Cheney moved fast, embarking on months of globe-trotting throughout the oil-producing world. According to the *Washington Post*, 'Soon he was on a first-name basis with oil ministers all over the world, building on the ties he had developed in the Middle East during his Pentagon days.'[41] It wasn't long before these top-level contacts paid off in the form of a string of major international contracts. Between 1994 and 2001, Halliburton's revenues increased by 127 per cent. But their composition also changed markedly. In 1994, before Cheney's appointment as CEO, only 43.8 per cent of revenues derived from the oil and gas services segment (the remainder being engineering, construction and insurance), and only 40.5 per cent of total revenues were earned overseas. But by 2001, oil and gas services provided 66.9 per cent of revenues and 62.4 per cent of total revenues were earned overseas.[42] A number of these new international oil service contracts, and some of the largest, were in the Caspian region – in Kazakhstan, Azerbaijan and Turkmenistan.

Halliburton also vigorously pursued its interests in the Russian Federation and Eastern Europe. It did so, moreover, with the aid of generous US government credit lines and contracts which Cheney appears to have been expert at manipulating. During his five-year stewardship of Halliburton, Cheney, the archetypal 'get-the-government-off-my-back' conservative, obtained for the company at least $3.8 billion in government contracts and guaranteed loans. The $2.3 billion of government contracts included in this figure was roughly double the value of contracts received by the company in the five years preceding Cheney's arrival.[43]

The received image of Cheney, as an uncompromising patriot obsessed with national security and the defeat of the 'Axis of Evil', is considerably at odds with his earlier behaviour as an oilman. During the 1990s, Cheney repeatedly pursued oil contracts in countries which were, officially or unofficially, 'out of bounds' to US companies. In a speech entitled 'Defending Liberty in a Global Economy' delivered on 23 June 1998, at a conference organised by the free-market Cato Institute, Cheney explained that, 'We oftentimes find ourselves operating in some very difficult places. The good Lord didn't see fit to put oil and gas only where there are democratically elected regimes friendly to the United States... we go where the business is.'[44]

Aside from the crafty linking of 'democratically elected' with 'friendly to the United States', this is a candid expression of what, for Cheney, had so far been a consistently held position. Indeed, as an oilman he had always professed an opposition to sanctions against countries and regimes of which the USA disapproved on the ground that they were ineffective. As CEO of Halliburton, Cheney was a strong supporter of USA*Engage, a corporate coalition of 50 affiliated companies and 600 individual members whose mission was to promote business 'engagement' with countries whose human rights record was under attack by Congress – countries like Myanmar, where Halliburton's subsidiary, European Marine Services, was helping to build the Yadana gas transmission pipeline. He also argued that unilateral sanctions imposed only by the USA, such as those against Iran and Libya, simply resulted in US companies losing ground to European and Asian competitors who, so it was claimed, had fewer scruples about doing business with 'rogue states'. Cheney lobbied strongly against the Iran-Libya Sanctions Act and also against Congressional sanctions aimed at Azerbaijan. At times, Cheney's position on sanctions against Iran and Libya even earned him rebuke from the US Israeli lobby, in spite of the fact that in all other respects he was strongly pro-Israel.[45]

On the other hand, Cheney maintained that Halliburton would accept multilateral sanctions such as those imposed on Iraq after the 1990–1991 war. However, in 1998, the UN passed a resolution allowing Iraq to buy spare parts for its dilapidated oil and gas industry. Cheney moved fast to take advantage of this relaxation, while concealing his company's move from the American politicians and public. During the 2000 presidential campaign Cheney denied any dealings with Iraq: 'I had a firm policy that we wouldn't do anything in Iraq, even arrangements that were supposedly legal,' he said in a July 2000 interview on ABC television's *This Week* programme, adding that, 'We've not done any business in Iraq since UN sanctions were imposed on Iraq in 1990, and I had a standing policy that I wouldn't do that.'[46] In fact, Halliburton had been trading with Iraq for some time, via two European-based subsidiary and associate companies. From September 1998 until it sold its stake in February 2000, Halliburton owned 51 per cent of Dresser-Rand. It also owned 49 per cent of Ingersoll-Dresser-Pump until its sale in December 1999. During the period when these companies were owned and controlled by Halliburton and during which Cheney was Halliburton's CEO, the two companies sold $23.8 million of oil production equipment and spare parts to Iraq.[47] With the help of Cheney's companies, Iraq was able to restore its oil production from 1.2 million b/d in 1997 to 2.6 million b/d in 2000, and responding to the rapidly accelerating demand of its motorised society, the USA was able to use the opaque and corrupt oil-for-food programme to substantially increase its oil imports from Iraq to 795,000 b/d, making the latter the USA's sixth largest source of foreign oil – greater than the UK's North Sea.

But what US sanctions did prevent Cheney from doing was to gain a foothold in the actual *production* of Iraqi oil at a time when Saddam Hussein was beginning to hand out potentially highly lucrative oil production contracts to companies from France, Russia and China. This must have been particularly irksome to someone who liked to claim that his company's main objective was to 'go where the oil is'. So when Bob Woodward described Cheney, in November 2001, as harbouring 'a deep sense of unfinished business about Iraq',[48] it was indeed, 'business' that Cheney was most concerned about. The image formed of Cheney from a study of his years with Halliburton is therefore of a single-minded representative of oil capitalism. Someone who, given the opportunity, would not hesitate to mould US foreign policy into a form conducive to the business opportunities and profit maximisation so earnestly sought after by the huge energy multinationals of which his own company was a leading representative.

CHENEY'S ENERGY POLICY

In August 2000, Cheney accepted George W. Bush's offer to be his vice-presidential running mate. Cheney had previously stated categorically that he would never return to politics. We do not know what changed his mind, but possibly it was the realisation that with Bush as President, *he* would be the real power behind the throne.

Returning to political office in January 2001, Vice President Cheney ensured that he would oversee what was intended to be one of the most important pieces of policy-making for several years – the formulation of a national energy policy. America hadn't had an energy policy since Jimmy Carter's presidency, back in the years of soaring oil prices. What appears to have triggered the return of this endangered species of policy-making was the largely fortuitous coming together of two quite separate developments: firstly the now unavoidable evidence of America's dependence on foreign petroleum; and secondly the emergence of a powerful cabal of economic interests determined to make the most of Bush's narrow and controversial victory. These were the large energy companies, both the new mega-energy-marketers like Enron, TXU and Dynegy, and the 'traditional' oil majors like ChevronTexaco, ExxonMobil, Conoco and Phillips Petroleum, together with the oil service companies like Halliburton and Schlumberger.

Significantly, it was at a Republican Party fund-raising dinner attended by numerous representatives of major oil and energy companies that Cheney first announced his plan to formulate a new energy policy. On 27 September 2000, at the 6th Annual Senate Majority Celebration dinner, he attacked the Clinton Administration for 'a lack of leadership' since they were 'without an energy policy' and promised that the Republican Party presidential nominee, George W. Bush, would rectify this situation; observing that, 'We have seen a lot of talk on reducing our dependence on foreign oil,' he pointed out that the reality of the situation was that 'we are producing less oil at home now than we have at any time since 1954. We are more vulnerable to having those supplies cut off.'[49]

Once elected, Cheney began a series of meetings with the chief executives of the major oil and energy companies which had supported the Republican ticket, in order to discover precisely what they wanted to be included in the report of his newly established National Energy Policy Development Group. At the time of writing, the Administration has still refused to disclose the identity of those present at these meetings, or any details of the discussions which took place, and has been supported in this refusal by the ruling of a federal judge. We know, however, that Enron's Kenneth Lay was present at four of these meetings and we can detect unmistakable signs of his influence in at least one of the Energy Policy Group's recommendations.[50]

While paying some lip service to the need for conservation and demand-side measures, Cheney's 2001 Energy Policy report concentrated on providing 'something for everyone' in the world of energy big business.[51] It was a mouth-watering cornucopia of potential deals, promotions and exemptions for US oil, gas, coal and electricity companies with whose projects the organs of state are repeatedly required to collaborate and provide support. For example, the Secretary of the Interior is required to 'consider economic incentives' for US offshore oil development and, working with Congress, to authorise oil development in the Arctic National Wildlife Refuge. The Secretaries of State, Commerce and Energy are required to 'continue working with the relevant companies' and to 'support the efforts of private investors' in the Caspian region. The Secretary of Energy is required to 'propose appropriate funding' for energy efficiency research and development, provided this is 'modelled as public-private partnerships'. Moreover, in what is perhaps the most bizarre piece of intervention on behalf of an individual company, the Report required the Secretaries of State and Energy to 'work with India's Ministry of Petroleum and Natural Gas to help India maximise its domestic oil and gas production', a sudden and unprecedented interest in the fuel supplies of a particular country, hitherto of minimal interest to US policy-makers, which only makes sense when it is recalled that at precisely this time, Enron was trying to establish itself as a key player in the Indian energy sector.[52]

So far, we have emphasised the extent to which the contents of Cheney's energy policy report were a reward for the corporate funding of the Bush/Cheney election campaign. Nevertheless, steering our way through the rich pickings of US corporate welfare, we can also discern three substantive policies, all of which address the key problem underlined by Cheney in his Senate majority celebration dinner speech quoted above: the problem of how to deal with America's dependence on imported oil, especially from the Gulf, and the perceived threat that this posed to America's energy security. Cheney knew full well that the USA would never again become self-sufficient in oil, nor was it ever likely to significantly reduce its current requirement for foreign oil; but America might slow or even halt the drift to even greater external energy dependence and it could use its enormous economic and geo-strategic influence to leverage political control over the world's major oil-producing regions outside the Gulf.

To achieve these objectives, firstly, the USA must increase it own domestic oil production. This objective is to be pursued, *inter alia*, by aggressively dismantling barriers to the leasing of Federal (i.e. Government-owned) lands and waters to oil- and gas-producing companies. This recommendation is hedged about with platitudinous statements about being 'consistent with good environmental practice', but the basic rationale is clear. Royalty reductions, tax breaks and other 'economic incentives' are also included in the list of recommendations.

Secondly, the USA should intensify its efforts to promote greater 'energy integration' with nations within the western hemisphere. Oil producers Mexico and Canada are referred to, but Venezuela is also mentioned as a target for agreeing a 'Bilateral Investment Treaty'. 'Energy Integration' means (in the case of Mexico and Venezuela) opening these countries to US oil companies with a view to increasing US imports from these relatively 'safe' sources.

Thirdly, the objective of switching US oil imports away from the Middle East is reflected in a series of recommendations aimed at promoting the Caspian region as a new American-friendly source of petroleum. Other areas are mentioned as contributing to the diversification of US oil imports, for example, West Africa, but it is absolutely clear in the Report that the Caspian holds pride of place in this respect. In the list of recommendations at the end of Chapter Five of the Report ('Strengthening Global Alliances: Enhancing National Energy Security and International Relationships'), five separate recommendations, the largest number relating to any one particular topic, relate to the Caspian oil and gas fields.

In fact, these three energy security strategies – increasing domestic oil production, solidifying hemispheric energy ties and a Caspian strategy to diversify the source of America's oil imports away from the Middle East, had already been initiated during the 1990s. As we have already observed, Cheney himself had already played a key part in one of them (the Caspian strategy). What Cheney was therefore advocating, in early 2001, was a deepening and strengthening of these strategies and this was because, to date, they had only been partially successful. Indeed, there were some ominous signs that the advances on these three fronts might even be running out of steam. Why this should have been so we examine in the next three chapters.

6 Energy Security Begins at Home

I'm adamantly opposed to energy conservation – we're not running out of oil. All we have to do is go out and find it and produce it.

Stephen Moore, Club for Growth, 2002

To secure the supply of oil for future national security needs, in 1923 President Warren Harding created a 23-million-acre Naval Petroleum Reserve on Alaska's North Slope. He took this action in response to the sudden upsurge in anxiety about future oil supplies after the First World War which had first propelled US oil companies towards the Middle East. Thereafter oil 'wildcatters' carried out a certain amount of desultory exploration in Arctic Alaska, followed in the 1940s and 1950s by a more extensive, government-sponsored exploration programme. In 1957, the Eisenhower Administration opened up a further 20 million acres of Alaska's North Slope to oil exploration and development. However, in 1960 Eisenhower's Secretary of the Interior, Fred Seaton, designated 8.9 million acres of coastal plain and mountains in north-east Alaska as the 'Arctic National Wildlife Range' with the intention of protecting its 'unique wildlife, wilderness and recreation values'.

Seven years later, on 26 December 1967, a massive new oilfield was discovered at Prudhoe Bay by the US oil company Atlantic Richfield (ARCO). A 10 billion barrel super-giant, it was to be the largest oilfield ever discovered in North America. Soon, plans were made to build the Trans-Alaska Pipeline System (TAPS) from the North Slope to Valdez, on Alaska's southern coastline, from where oil would be carried by tanker, to US markets on the West Coast. However, in 1969, there was a serious oil spill at Santa Barbara, California. This incident energised the newly emerging US environmental movement, which argued that the TAPS pipeline should be put on hold until America had exhausted the possibilities of greater energy conservation. Some environmentalists argued that the pipeline project and associated oilfield developments were so threatening to the Arctic ecosystem that they should be permanently banned. To the oil companies' dismay, in 1970 the environmentalists convinced a Federal court to issue an injunction blocking construction of the TAPS pipeline.

And there the matter would probably have remained had it not been for the great energy crisis of 1973–1974. Since 1960, the US motorisation rate had continued its remorseless increase, from 401 vehicles per 1,000 US inhabitants to 528 in 1970. America was now importing over 3 million barrels per day accounting for 21.5 per cent of total US consumption; and 42.5 per cent of these imports were coming from OPEC countries. By 1973, with the motorisation rate advancing by 12 per cent in just three years, America had doubled its net imports of foreign oil to 6 million b/d of which 14.1 per cent (848,000 b/d) now came from the Gulf.

The 1973 Middle East oil embargo gave BP, Exxon and ARCO the opportunity they had been waiting for to press their case for oil development in Alaska and at the same time provided the higher oil prices which would ensure its profitability. Permission for TAPS was granted and on 20 June 1977, oil began to flow along the Trans-Alaska Pipeline. By the following year, the North Slope was producing 1.2 million barrels per day and within ten years daily output had risen to nearly 2 million barrels.

The status of the Arctic National Wildlife Range now became a subject of disagreement and debate between the two houses of Congress because it was believed that the coastal part of the range also contained large oil deposits. In 1980, the Alaska National Interest Lands Conservation Act (ANILCA) was passed which doubled the size of the Range and renamed it the Arctic National Wildlife Refuge (ANWR). However, the coastal strip, now referred to as Area 1002 because of the reference to it in section 1002 of ANILCA, was not yet designated as 'Wilderness' pending detailed environmental impact reports.

These were carried out in the subsequent six years and in February 1987 the final environmental impact report was published. The following month, the Secretary of the Interior recommended that Congress authorise an oil- and gas-leasing programme in Area 1002, provided strict measures were taken to minimise any environmental impact. However, Congress remained undecided and failed to take any action. In 1989, the pendulum of influence swung back towards the environmentalists, following the catastrophic oil spillage from the tanker Exxon Valdez in Prince William Sound and, in 1991, the provision to open the ANWR to development was dropped from the National Energy Policy Act. By now it was also becoming clear that Alaskan oil production had passed its peak and that decline had set in. In 1995, Congress passed budget legislation which included a provision to allow drilling in the Refuge, but in December of that year President Clinton, after intense lobbying by the environmentalists, vetoed the Act.

In May 2001, Richard Cheney's Energy Policy Report asserted that: 'Measures to enhance energy security... must begin at home... The first step towards a sound international energy policy is to use our own capability to produce, process and transport energy resources we need.'[1] Five months later, the Interior Secretary Gale Norton, announcing the start-up of a controversial new oilfield in Alaska's Beaufort Sea – the Northstar field operated by BP – declared, 'In the aftermath of the 11 September terrorist attacks, Americans charged our Government to strengthen national security. This is a positive step in that direction.'[2] The Northstar project had been strongly opposed by US environmentalists and Norton's declaration demonstrated a new willingness to ride roughshod over them. Bush and his team had already kicked sand in the faces of the domestic supporters of the Kyoto agreement which aimed to limit greenhouse gases, and busting open the ANWR was next on the agenda. Indeed, opening the ANWR to oil development was one of the key elements contained in the fifth chapter of Cheney's energy policy report from which we have already quoted. In it, the President was advised to 'direct the Secretary of the Interior [to] work with Congress to authorise exploration and, if resources are discovered, development, of the 1002 Area of ANWR'.

THE ANWR: OIL VERSUS THE ENVIRONMENT

The 19-million-acre ANWR lies in the north-east corner of Alaska. The entire refuge lies north of the Arctic Circle and 1,300 miles south of the North Pole. Along the coastal area, the plain is an almost featureless expanse, barren and dotted with thousands of unconnected small lakes and ponds. To the south, the area changes to gently rolling, treeless hills which eventually merge into the foothills of the Brooks Range mountains. Apart from a small Inuit community at Kaktovik, adjacent to the coastal plain, the ANWR is completely uninhabited.

According to the US Government's Fish and Wildlife Service, as well as being the largest unit in America's National Wildlife Refuge System, it is the country's finest example of an intact, naturally functioning community of arctic and sub-arctic ecosystems. Such a broad spectrum of diverse habitats occurring within a single protected unit is, according to the Fish and Wildlife Service, 'unparalleled in North America, and perhaps in the entire circumpolar north'.[3] Indeed, the completeness and proximity of a number of arctic and sub-arctic ecological zones in the ANWR provides for greater plant and animal diversity than in any other similar-sized land area on Alaska's North Slope.

Area 1002 of the ANWR – the area explicitly cited for oil development in Cheney's report – is only 10 per cent of the total ANWR acreage but includes most of the Refuge's coastal plain and foothills. It is a 100-mile-long belt of tundra, compressed between the mountains of the Brooks Range and the Beaufort Sea and stretching between 20 and 40 miles inland. Nevertheless, Area 1002 is critically important to the ecological integrity of the ANWR as a whole. It provides essential habitats for numerous internationally important species such as the 129,000 strong porcupine caribou herd, musk oxen and polar bears. Some 135 species of different birds are known to use the 1002 Area including up to 300,000 snow geese, which feed on the Arctic tundra for three to four weeks each autumn, on their way from the nesting grounds on Banks Island in Canada to wintering grounds primarily in California's Central Valley.

Sixty miles to the west of Area 1002 lies Prudhoe Bay, on Alaska's North Slope. It is the site of America's largest oilfield, owned and operated by BP. Adjacent to it are a number of smaller fields owned by BP and a number of US oil companies such as PhillipsConoco and Anadarko Petroleum. This oil-producing industrial complex extends across a 1,000 square mile region, nearly 100 miles from east to west, and is continually expanding as new oilfields are developed. Linking the North Slope oilfields to the port of Valdez, on Alaska's southern coast is the 800-mile Trans-Alaska Pipeline System (TAPS). According to the National Resources Defense Council (NRDC), a major opponent of oil drilling in the ANWR, Prudhoe Bay offers a stark example of what such drilling would mean to Area 1002. The NRDC describes it as

> A gargantuan oil complex that has turned 1,000 square miles of fragile tundra into a sprawling industrial zone containing 1,500 miles of roads and pipelines, 1,400 producing wells and 3 jetports...a landscape defaced by mountains of sewage, sludge, scrap metal, garbage and more than 60 contaminated waste sites that contain – and often leak – acids, lead, pesticides, solvents and diesel fuel.[4]

According to an academic study of the impact of oil development on the area, during recent years there has been about one oil spill a day at Prudhoe Bay. The Prudhoe Bay oilfields and Trans-Alaska Pipeline have caused an average of 409 spills annually on the North Slope since 1996. Roughly forty different substances from acid to waste oil are spilled during routine operations: over 1.3 million gallons were spilled between 1996 and 1999, most commonly diesel and crude oil, the former being highly toxic to plant life. In addition, Prudhoe Bay is a major source of air pollution and greenhouse gas emissions. The oil industry on Alaska's North Slope annually emits approximately 56,427 tons of oxides of nitrogen, which contributes to smog and acid rain and North Slope oil facilities release roughly 24,000–114,000 tons of methane, a greenhouse gas.[5]

In fact, the environmentalists argue that the potential for ecological mayhem is even stronger in the ANWR. This is because studies carried out by the US Geological Survey have indicated that unlike Prudhoe Bay, where one massive super-giant field was discovered, it is more likely that oil in the ANWR is scattered across the coastal plain in more than thirty smaller deposits, in complex geological formations.[6] Consequently development in the 1002 Area would probably require a large number of small production sites spread all across the Refuge landscape, requiring a vast network of roads and pipelines that would fragment the animal and bird habitats and cause major disturbance to the wildlife.

The general categories of environmental damage which would be the likely consequences of oil exploration, development and production in the ANWR coastal plain have been listed in detail by the US Fish and Wildlife Service. They include:

> Blocking, deflecting or disturbing wildlife; loss of subsistence hunting opportunities; increased predation by arctic fox, gulls and ravens on nesting birds due to introduction of garbage; alteration of natural drainage patterns causing changes in vegetation; deposition of alkaline dust on tundra along roads, altering vegetation over a much larger area than the actual width of road; local pollutant haze and acid rain from nitrogen oxides, methane and particulate emissions; and contamination of soil and water from fuel and oil spills.[7]

The area's wildlife will suffer the most damaging effects. Arctic conditions dictate that oil exploration operations take place in the winter months when the ground is solid. But this is the time when polar bears retreat to their dens. It is estimated that 22 of the 53 Alaskan and Canadian polar bear dens on the mainland coast are located in Area 1002. Noise and vibration will seriously disturb the dens located in the zone, causing potentially fatal human-bear conflicts and exposing the cubs to increased mortality due to the harsh winter conditions for which they are not yet prepared. Also about 250 musk oxen live all the year round in Area 1002. During the winter months they huddle together to retain body heat. Here again, human activity and machine operations will most probably disturb the herd and put it to flight, leaving the calves to die.

Once full-scale oil production operations gets underway, human and machine activity will impact the wildlife on a year-round basis. In the spring the caribou would suffer as they migrated into the coastal plain to give birth to their young. The caribou's preferred food during the calving season is much more available within Area 1002 than other parts of the Refuge. To successfully reproduce they must move around freely without interruption or disturbance. Otherwise they cannot produce healthy calves. Oil development, and particularly the pattern of development considered most likely by the US Geological Survey, would reduce the amount of preferred forage available during and after calving, would restrict access to important coastal insect-relief habitats, would expose the herd to higher predation and would alter the ancient migratory pattern, the effects of which cannot be predicted.[8]

MR HUBBERT AND HIS PEAK

Given that these environmental consequences – detailed by the US Government's own Fish and Wildlife Service – are potentially so serious, we might well wonder precisely what has driven the Bush Administration to place oil development in the ANWR at the top of their domestic energy policy agenda. The answer begins with a Mr Hubbert and his 'Peak'.

In 1956, a certain M. King Hubbert, a Texan geophysicist working at the Shell research laboratory in Houston, published a scientific paper in which he forecast the year in which the production of crude oil from America's so-called Lower 48 states would peak and thereafter decline.[9] Hubbert employed a mathematical model of cumulative oil production whose shape is called 'logistic'. If the rate of increase of this logistic curve is calculated – what mathematicians call its 'derivative' – plotting this on a graph produces a bell-shaped curve for successive years of annual oil production. Annual production rises to a peak and then declines in a pattern which is symmetrical with that of the increase. The crucial conclusion of the theory is that the year of peak oil production – be it for a field, a country, or the whole world – occurs where approximately half of the original endowment of oil has been extracted. Using what he thought to be the best estimate of the USA's original oil endowment – 200 billion barrels – Hubbert predicted that the peak would occur in a mere 16 years – in 1972.[10]

Initially, Hubbert's ideas were derided. 'Utterly ridiculous' was a typical comment and this was not entirely surprising. From the very beginnings of US oil production, Cassandras had been forecasting the imminent exhaustion of the US oil reserves. Indeed, in Chapter Three we saw how such forecasts had impacted upon American energy policy in the early decades of the twentieth century, but we also saw how wide of the mark they had been.

However, to the surprise and shock of many, Hubbert's gloomy prediction for the year 1972 came true, or to be more precise, it occurred two years earlier, in 1970, when daily production of US crude oil reached a maximum of 9.6 million b/d and then began to fall. Of course, Hubbert's Peak was not actually 'visible' until some years later, but an important clue was provided in 1972 when pro-rationing was ended and every oil well in the Lower 48 states moved to full capacity production. Finally, as oil imports began to rapidly increase during the mid-1970s, the truth dawned: Hubbert had been right after all.[11]

Tracing the downward path of US domestic oil production thereafter is rather complicated because the total consists of three principal parts which have not always moved in the same direction: crude oil produced in the Lower 48 states, crude oil produced in Alaska, and natural gas liquids (NGLs) extracted from raw gas streams (which can be further processed into petroleum products).

Crude production in the Lower 48 states peaked in 1970 at 9.4 million b/d, as did total crude production and total petroleum production (at 11.3 million b/d). But as production from the Lower 48 states began a rapid decline, Alaskan production from Prudhoe Bay began to increase, slowing and then reversing the overall decline for a few years. However, in 1988, Alaskan production also peaked and thereafter the decline in total crude production was irreversible, only mitigated by the steady increase in natural gas liquids production which reached a record 1.9 million b/d in 2000, amounting to 25 per cent of total US petroleum production.

All in all, by the end of the twentieth century, US domestic production of petroleum, at 7.7 million b/d, had fallen by 32 per cent since its peak in 1970, and although there were some small signs of recovery in Lower 48 production as the oil industry moved into the deep waters of the Gulf of Mexico, no one had any illusions that these would, for long, stem the remorseless overall decline. Alaska, on the other hand, was another matter. Whereas the Lower 48 states had been drilled more intensively than anywhere on earth, there were vast areas of Alaska where, to date, no oilman had ever ventured.

'ARCTIC POWER' CAMPAIGNS BUT OIL COMPANY DOUBTS GROW

While Cheney's National Energy Policy Development Group was getting to work on its Report to the President, pressure to open up Area 1002 of the ANWR began to build once again. This time the campaign to open up the ANWR was led by Arctic Power, a lobbying organisation amply funded by the State Government of Alaska, certain oil companies and a number of private individuals. Alaska had done well out of oil development – at least in the material sense. For many years, a tough royalty and taxation regime had channelled considerable wealth to individual Alaskans. In February 2001, Republican Senator Frank

Murkowski, Senator for Alaska and Chairman of the Senate Energy and Natural Resources Committee, introduced his 'National Energy Security Act 2001', Title V of which outlined a programme for the development of oil and gas resources thought to be present under Area 1002 of the ANWR, calling it 'the starting point for what will be an important debate during this session of the 107th Congress'. Introducing his bill, Murkowski announced:

> Today is the first step in ending America's dependence on other nations to power our progress...Each day more than 8 million barrels of crude oil come from foreign shores. That is a dangerous strategy by anyone's measure. This bill spells out a national energy strategy with a critical goal – to finally reduce to 50 per cent the amount of oil we import.[12]

A variety of conservative organisations lined up behind Murkowski and Arctic Power. For example, Stephen Moore of the Club for Growth, told the *New York Times* that 'there is a belief on the environmentalist side that we are running out of oil, that we have to conserve energy. I'm adamantly opposed to energy conservation – we're not running out of oil. All we have to do is go out and find it and produce it.'[13]

Arctic Power claimed that the ANWR's coastal plain contained, 'from 9 billion to 16 billion barrels of recoverable oil'.[14] Cheney's energy report, referring to a recent study by the US Geological Survey, estimated that 'the total quantity of recoverable oil...is...between 5.7 billion and 16 billion barrels...with a mean value of 10.4 billion barrels.' Without doubt 16 billion barrels of oil would be a remarkable addition to America's reserves (proven reserves currently estimated at 30.7 billion barrels). However, the Cheney report and others which talked of 'up to 16 billion barrels', were playing fast and loose with the definition of 'recoverable reserves'. The figures quoted are referred to in the original 1998 US Geological Survey report as 'technically recoverable'. The fraction of technically recoverable reserves which are 'commercially recoverable' varies hugely depending on the current price of oil. Using an oil price at the high end of most companies' 1998 expectations – $24 per barrel – the amount of commercially recoverable oil in Area 1002 assessed at a 95 per cent probability, was only 2 billion barrels, increasing to 5.2 billion assessed at a 50 per cent probability, and with an outside chance (5 per cent probability) that there might be as much 9.4 billion barrels.[15] In other words, given that the USA consumes 19.6 million barrels of petroleum products per day (7.2 billion barrels per year), there was a 50 per cent chance that Area 1002 would provide between eight and nine months consumption, providing the price was no lower than $24 per barrel, and only after an exploration and development period of seven to ten years. However, if the oil price were to fall to something like the free-market level – ironically, something which Cheney's report presented as a 'good thing' – then there would be no commercially recoverable oil at all in the ANWR.[16]

Throughout 2001 and 2002, in addition to Murkowski's energy security bill, a number of additional bills and amendments were placed before both houses of Congress, some supporting drilling in the ANWR, others opposing it. The debate soon became entangled with broader issues involving the Middle East, terrorism, support for Israel and the impending military campaign against Iraq. A common theme among the pro-drilling legislators was that oil from the ANWR would allegedly replace oil imported from Iraq and other Middle East countries. In the House of Representatives, Congressman Billy Tauzin of Louisiana argued, 'You might not like oil companies at home, but it's a lot better if we have it instead of getting it from Saddam Hussein.'

Senator Murkowski sought to widen support for his proposals by announcing the formation of a group called 'Jews for Drilling' at a rally in support of Israel.[17] An aide to Senator Murkowski claimed that supporting drilling was 'a moral issue', because cash paid to Iraq for its oil 'is used by Saddam Hussein to pay $25,000 to the families of suicide bombers'. Shoshana Bryen, representing the Jewish Institute for National Security Affairs, urged Jewish groups 'to support any legislation that provides for the diversification of sources of energy. That includes the ANWR.' Murkowski's rather desperate attempt to swell the ranks of the pro-drillers was intended to persuade one or two Democrat Senators to back his attempt to win a procedural Senate vote on 17 April 2002. If he lost the vote his campaign to open up the ANWR would be stymied for the time being. On the usual assumption that certain Democratic congressmen were dependent on the Jewish vote, the idea was to get some of them to change sides. However the move misfired. Murkowski was accused by Mark Jacobs, director of the Coalition on the Environment and Jewish Life, of 'manipulation of Jewish concern for Israel'. According to Jacobs, 'The focus on the Refuge is a dangerous distraction from what we really need to be doing about energy security.'[18] In the event, Murkowski failed to get the required number of Senate votes on 17 April.

And by now some of the oil companies were becoming a little wary of the way the debate was going. Indeed, their commitment to an ANWR drilling programme was never as wholehearted as some of the its vociferous conservative supporters, for whom the issue was an ideological crusade against the 'tree-hugging' environmentalists. In November 2002, Arctic Power lost one its most important corporate members. BP announced it was leaving the organisation, its spokesman saying, 'we don't want to be involved in the debate any more. It's not BP's decision. It's up to the President and the American people.'[19]

There were a number of factors behind BP's decision; for example, it was currently receiving a lot of bad publicity about its safety record at Prudhoe Bay. In August 2002, an explosion at a BP well had caused serious injury to a worker and an oil spillage. Since then, 16 per cent of BP's Prudhoe Bay wells had been identified as potentially problematic and a representative of the company's oil workers accused it of running a 'shoddy operation'. Given the sensitivity of the whole pro-drilling campaign to accusations of environmental recklessness, this kind of publicity was embarrassing to say the least However, economics was probably the primary factor in BP's decision.

In February 2002, BP experienced a serious setback at a key Alaskan oil project. The Liberty field in the frozen Beaufort Sea was intended to add 65,000 barrels per day to the company's US production, but in February 2002 the company announced that it was shelving the project indefinitely because of serious cost overruns.[20] BP was apparently not alone in its doubts about the profitability of new Alaskan oilfields, especially when constrained by tightening environmental standards. In April 2002, the *New York Times* reported that the oil companies were 'not particularly enthusiastic' about supporting the campaign by Arctic Power to open up the ANWR, 'because of the high cost of producing oil and gas'.[21] Similarly an anonymous oil company spokesman acknowledged to the Associated Press Agency that compared to Alaska, 'there are many fields around the world where development would come more cheaply.'[22]

NATIONAL SECURITY = UNIMPEDED MOTORISATION

Earlier in the chapter, we referred to BP's inauguration of the Northstar oilfield at Prudhoe Bay and the Interior Secretary's declaration that the new field would make a significant contribution to 'national security' in the aftermath of the 9/11 terrorist attacks. By way of further explanation, the Interior Secretary had added that, 'oil coming from the field will be enough to fuel nearly one million US automobiles for six years.'[23] The statement provides us with a window into the mindset of America's new leaders as they embarked on their campaign for the 'New American Century': 'National security' meant energy security and the latter, in the mind of the Interior Secretary, meant unimpeded motorisation.

Between 1970, when US domestic oil production peaked, and Bush's electoral victory in 2000, the US motorisation rate increased from 528 vehicles per 1,000 inhabitants to 800, by far the highest rate of motorisation in the world. Moreover in the final decade of the century the profligacy of America's motor transport system was also increasing. Motor gasoline consumption per capita increased from 1,488 litres in 1990 to 1,570 litres in 1997; and energy consumption per 1,000 vehicle/kilometres, a key indicator of 'transportation efficiency' deteriorated, increasing from 155 kg of oil equivalent in 1990 to 183 kg in 2000, whereas in Germany, France and the UK this indicator declined from 98.5 kg to 88.7.[24]

The complete subordination of US society to the motor car, the increasingly sedentary, consumption-rich but time-poor lives of its citizens and their new fascination with the gas-guzzling sports utility vehicles which were by now pouring from the factories of Ford and General Motors were factors which had begun to threaten the integrity of America's long-cherished and protected wildlife and wilderness. But these factors were also driving the nation inexorably towards a foreign policy in which achieving control over the world's oil resources – always an important objective – had become an overwhelming imperative, as we shall see in the following chapters.

7 Canada, Venezuela and Mexico: A Hemispheric Solution?

The Administration may...want to consider leverage tools that could be brought to bear to assist political leaders in Mexico who advocate that Mexico open its energy sector to foreign investment

James Baker III Institute for Public Policy and the
Council on Foreign Relations, April 2001

In addition to its domestic oil agenda, Cheney's National Energy Policy Development Group also recommended the development of 'closer energy integration among Canada, Mexico and the United States', and a similar policy towards Venezuela.[1] That such 'integration' needed to be 'closer' reflected the rather chequered history of this particular strand in America's long-running quest for energy security. This is not really surprising when we examine precisely what was meant by 'energy integration' in relation to these three oil- and energy-rich countries. Firstly, it meant the overcoming of any nationalistic tendencies in these countries which might elevate questions of sovereign interest over and above the energy needs of the USA; secondly, the dismantling of any legal barriers to the acquisitions of these countries' energy resources by US companies; and thirdly, insofar as this was possible in the changing political climate within the three countries, the privatisation of their state oil companies – ideally in a manner which would facilitate the sale of their equity to US companies or citizens. Indeed, in 1996, the US Department of Energy's Energy Information Administration published a detailed guide to world privatisation trends, prepared specifically for the benefit of US energy companies, which underlined the 'impact that privatisation might have on maintaining a secure and affordable energy supply to US consumers'.[2] As we shall see, these objectives have been largely achieved in the case of Canada, but met with failure in the case of Mexico. Venezuela represents an intermediate situation where the process of integration, which appeared to be advancing at a rapid pace, was stopped and then reversed by surprising and largely unforeseen political developments within that country.

FROM CANADA FIRST TO CANADA SECOND

When the world oil crisis struck in 1973–1974, oil-producing countries outside the Middle East were not long in realising that oil was now such an important and strategic commodity that it was essential for them, too, to follow the example of the Middle East in making the exploitation of their reserves a matter of supreme national interest. The circumstances dictated some form of direct government intervention in, and control over, the oil sector. In practice this meant the establishment of a state oil company with a remit to participate directly in the development of the national oil industry, either by automatic right to an equity share in any new oilfield developments or through acquisitions of equity in other, private-sector oil companies.

In 1975–1976, the UK, Norway, Canada, and Venezuela created state oil corporations with varying degrees of monopoly power over oil production and refining.[3] (Mexico already had a state oil company, whose origins we shall briefly explain below.) Venezuela, Norway and Mexico still retain their 'national oil flagships'. However, the British foray into oil nationalism was soon abandoned by Labour politicians submissive to the American political will.[4] Similarly the Canadian experiment in oil nationalism, although initially appearing well established, eventually also proved to be a temporary phenomenon.

Canada only became a significant oil producer in 1947, when substantial quantities of light oil were discovered in the western province of Alberta. During the 1960s and early 1970s, it became a net oil exporter but by 1976 it had once again become a net importer, consuming 1.79 million barrels per day but producing only 1.6 million b/d. So in 1980, facing the record world oil price resulting from the Iranian Revolution, the Liberal Party government of Pierre Trudeau, backed overwhelmingly by public opinion, established a National Energy Policy (NEP) explicitly designed to ensure Canada's energy security. Its main objectives were to achieve self-sufficiency in oil production by 1990, to achieve 50 per cent Canadian ownership of all energy resources (at a time when US companies received 64 per cent of Canadian oil and gas revenues)[5] and to obtain a greater share of oil revenues for the national (federal) government. Meanwhile, the new state-owned oil company, Petro-Canada, set about energetically acquiring exploration rights and, more controversially, the take-over of a number of Canadian subsidiaries of foreign oil companies.

The general philosophy behind the NEP was that Canada was in danger of becoming a raw-materials-exporting satellite of America and was missing out on many of the value-adding 'linkages' which greater national control over the energy industries would provide.[6] A number of the NEP's provisions were explicitly discriminatory towards US and other foreign owned oil companies. This was because many Canadians felt that the USA was treating the Canadian oil industry as a 'cash cow' – spending little on exploration for new reserves while remitting substantial profits from their existing operations back to their head offices.[7]

Indeed, there was at this time a strong left-nationalist tendency in Canadian politics which was also reflected at the provincial level, notably in Saskatchewan where a government of the left-leaning New Democratic Party established its own publicly owned oil company, Saskoil. Like Chileans in the years prior to the nationalisation of their copper industry, many Canadians resented the fact that the power to decide matters of vital national interest appeared to lie outside of the country. To many it was as incredible to allow the energy sector to be alienated from the national domain as it would be to allow the armed forces or the federal or provincial courts to be controlled by foreigners. 'In a word such alienation is seen to be a violation of sovereignty, however vaguely understood that concept may be.'[8]

However, the influence of this left-nationalist political movement began to wane in the early 1980s as oil prices began to subside and, with them, the anxiety about energy security. Meanwhile, a new, self-confident, free-market ideology emanating from Thatcher's Britain and Reagan's USA began to impress itself upon Canadians and led to the election of Brian Mulroney's 'progressive conservative' government in 1984.

Once in power, Mulroney moved swiftly to mollify the Americans, travelling to New York to reassure Wall Street that Canada would now be 'open for business' and the NEP would be swept aside. In 1989, to the applause of the Reagan Administration, Mulroney signed a 'Free Trade Agreement' (FTA), the terms of which ensured that Canada would now become firmly integrated into a continental (later a hemispheric) energy market in which she surrendered any future possibility of putting her own energy security before that of the USA.[9] The same terms were included in the North American Free Trade Agreement (NAFTA), signed in December 1992.

Most remarkable in this respect was Article 904 of the FTA which obliged Canada to continually export to the USA a proportion of its oil and gas output equivalent to the average proportion exported over the preceding 36 months, with no provision at all for exceptional circumstances such as a major world energy crisis or national emergency.[10] Of course, theoretically, the clause also applied to the USA vis-à-vis Canada. But, since the USA's energy exports to Canada were minuscule compared with those flowing in the opposite direction, Article 904 clearly involved a massive loss of sovereignty by Canada in an economic sector which, by general agreement, was of great strategic concern. Edward Ney, the US Ambassador to Canada at the time, said later that Canada's oil and gas reserves were the prime motivation for the USA in negotiating the FTA or, as one high-ranking US Commerce Department official subsequently admitted, America could now count on Canada to support her wasteful gas-guzzling and delay the moment when fuel conservation would be required.[11]

In the event of a serious curtailment in world oil production and exports from the Middle East, Canada's obligation to continue supplying the USA under FTA/NAFTA rules could be seriously disadvantageous to it. This is because Canada's own oil balance is more precarious than would appear from simply noting its production (2.7 million b/d) and export (1.8 million b/d) volumes. Canada too is a highly motorised society and its own consumption of oil in 2001 ran at 1.9 million b/d, such that its total required supplies (consumption plus exports: 3.7 million b/d)[12] exceeded its production by around 1 million barrels per day. This shortfall had to be imported each year, some of which came from the Middle East. This unusual arrangement still pertains and is partly determined by Canada's geography, with the western provinces exporting oil to the USA and the eastern provinces importing oil from abroad, 582,000 b/d coming from the North Sea and 145,000 b/d from the Middle East. Thus, in spite of the fact that Canada is a net exporter (exports of 1.8 million b/d exceed imports of 1 million), the country still has a 'gross' dependence on foreign oil of about 27 per cent (imports of 1 million b/d as a percentage of the total required supplies of 3.7 million b/d) remembering of course, that under the FTA/NAFTA, Canada must continue to export oil to America whether it wishes to or not.

With the exceptionally low oil prices prevailing, after Saudi Arabia's 1986 refusal to continue shouldering the major burden of production restraint, the financial position of Petro-Canada, the state oil company, worsened, largely because it had been spending aggressively both on exploration drilling and asset acquisitions. The company was condemned as a failure by Canada's business-oriented press and, in 1991, Mulroney's government announced its forthcoming privatisation. However, fearing a renewal of nationalist sentiment if wholesale privatisation led to a takeover by a major US oil company, the conservative government initially restricted the privatisation sale to only 20 per cent of the company's equity. It also stipulated that total foreign ownership should not exceed 25 per cent, and ruled that no individual shareholder should acquire more than a 10 per cent stake.[13] Over the next decade, the state holding in Petro-Canada was whittled down to 18 per cent, and in 2000 the government changed the rules to remove the restriction on foreign ownership exceeding 25 per cent of the company's equity. At the time of writing, the restriction on the amount of equity which may be owned by one individual shareholder (10 per cent) is still in place, although how long this final obstacle to a US takeover will survive, remains to be seen.

US OIL COMPANIES INVADE CANADA

Between 1997 and 2001, there was a massive wave of US takeovers of Canadian oil and gas companies: the total buying spree was estimated to be worth C$40 billion.[14] Canadian companies acquired by US corporations included a string of smaller companies (Velvet Exploration, Courage Energy, Chieftain International, Archer Resources, Gulfstream Resources, Berkeley Petroleum and others) as well as relatively large oil companies like Norcen Energy. According to a report in the *Oil and Gas Investor*, the Canadian government was willing to encourage investment in Canada's hydrocarbon industry – even if the companies developing and owning those assets were non-Canadian. The *Oil and Gas Investor* observed 'Gone are the days of Canada's... National Energy Policy – outgrowths of the energy crisis of the 1970s,' adding that 'Those programmes were viewed by US exploration and production companies as nationalist, protectionist and interventionist.'[15]

Another oil industry report described the laissez-faire attitude of the Canadian Government towards US acquisitions in Canada more colourfully. 'It's rape and pillage to your heart's content.'[16] Biggest of all the acquisitions was the takeover in 2001 of Gulf Canada, one of only a handful of remaining large multinational Canadian oil and gas companies, by Houston-based Conoco Inc. But, according to one oil industry correspondent, Gulf Canada, 'certainly won't be the last of the majors in Alberta's oil and gas patch to fall into the hands of Dick Cheney's chums'.[17]

By 2001, the dismantling of Canadian energy nationalism and the integration of the country's oil and gas sector into a hemispheric energy system had been more or less entirely achieved. Its *raison d'être* was to guarantee the safety and security of an important part of America's oil supplies, while providing US companies with unfettered access to the profits which would flow from extracting Canada's oil and gas reserves. By 2001, Canada had overtaken Saudi Arabia, Venezuela and

Mexico to become the USA's largest foreign oil supplier, exporting 1.79 million barrels per day to the USA out of a total production of 2.76 million b/d.

OIL NATIONALISM IN VENEZUELA

With a production capacity of around 3.4 million b/d, Venezuela is the western hemisphere's third largest oil producer after the USA (7.7 Mb/d) and Mexico (3.6 Mb/d). It is also the western hemisphere's largest oil exporter. During the 1920s Shell and Exxon, faced with revolution, rising costs and salt water intrusion in their Mexican oilfields, moved into Venezuela beneath the protective shield of its cruel and cunning dictator, General Juan Vicente Gomez. By 1928, Venezuela had overtaken Mexico to become the second largest world oil producer, with an annual output of 137 million barrels as well as the largest world oil exporter.[18] In the same year, for the first time, US oil imports from Venezuela exceeded imports from Mexico and thereafter, through to the 1970s, Venezuela became America's principal foreign oil supplier.

After Gomez's death, a generation of young politicians who had suffered persecution as student opponents of the regime, planned to overturn the comfortable status quo which the foreign oil companies had enjoyed under the dictatorship. Some of them formed the Accion Democratica party which initially had strong liberal/socialist ideals.

Although the Venezuelan Congress passed a New Hydrocarbon Law in 1943, which achieved a modest redistribution of oil income in favour of Venezuela, in 1945, a coup by dissatisfied young military officers acting in collaboration with the young radicals of the Accion Democratica Party resulted in substantial revisions to the Hydrocarbon Law which ensured that from now on, the oil companies were obliged to pay 50 per cent of their profits to the government.

Although another brutal dictator, Colonel Marcos Perez Jimenez, seized power in 1948, with the backing of the oil companies and the Eisenhower Administration, ten years later, one of the leading intellectuals and oil industry experts of that earlier democratic interlude, Juan Pablo Perez Alfonzo, returned to power as Minister of Mines and Hydrocarbons when the dictatorship collapsed.

Perez Alfonzo, an austere and determined figure, set the country on a path which would lead towards a new nationalism in its oil affairs and a major role in shaping the future of the world oil industry. The 1945 Government had increased Venezuela's tax-take from oil to 50 per cent, but Perez Alfonzo raised it to 65 per cent. Next, in April 1959, Perez Alfonzo met with Abdallah Tariki, Saudi Arabia's radical new Director of Oil and Mining Affairs, and made a 'gentleman's agreement' with him which contained a raft of proposals to place before their respective governments. These proposals were to form the basis for the creation of OPEC the following year, when representatives of the major oil exporting countries, Saudi Arabia, Venezuela, Iraq, Iran and Kuwait, met in Baghdad and set in motion the train of events which was to culminate in the 'OPEC Revolution' of the early 1970s.

Also in 1960, Perez Alfonzo created Venezuela's first national oil company, the Corporacion Venezolana de Petroleo. Eleven years later, Venezuela introduced a law which required that on expiry all existing foreign oil concessions would revert to the state. Finally, in 1976, urged on by Perez Alfonzo now in retirement, Venezuela reached the apex of its nationalist oil policy with the full nationalisation of foreign oil interests and their incorporation into one new state-owned oil company, Petroleos de Venezuela S.A.(PDVSA).

The following year PDVSA began a massive programme of investment in oil exploration and development operations whose economic impact spread throughout the whole economy. At the same time, the fruits of the new petroleum wealth arising from the dramatic increase in world oil prices were distributed to a rapidly growing urban population, mainly via an oil-price sustained over-valuation of the national currency.

However, by the late 1980s, Venezuela's experience of oil wealth was turning sour. During the oil boom years, a large urban middle class had developed and grown comfortably rich. But their cultural and consumer tastes were increasingly dictated by their North American neighbour. Consequently, their rapidly growing consumer expenditures sucked in vast quantities of US-manufactured consumer goods, inhibiting the growth of domestic manufacturing industry and creating a growing burden on the current account balance of payments. Investment and economic development outside the oil sector languished.[19] Corruption, was by general acknowledgement, widespread. As time went on, the low world oil prices prevailing after 1986 led to increased public and private borrowing and successive currency devaluations. Consequently, in 1989 the Accion Democratica government agreed to submit to an IMF 'structural adjustment programme' which seriously worsened the living conditions of the poorer sections of the community provoking widespread rioting in which hundreds were killed and wounded by government security forces, an operation which was observed with disgust by a certain officer of paratroops named Hugo Chavez. In addition, the IMF informed the Venezuelan Government that PDVSA's borrowings would now be considered part of the public sector deficit which the country was committed to reduce.[20] The lesson was clear: Venezuela would have to open the doors to foreign oil companies if it wanted further investment in its national oil industry.

APERTURA – RE-OPENING VENEZUELA TO THE OIL COMPANIES

Between 1993 and 1998, a policy of *Apertura* (opening) set Venezuela on a course which was markedly different from that which it had followed in the preceding fifteen years. Not only was foreign investment permitted but it was 'incentivised' by exempting certain projects from the basic petroleum fiscal regime.[21] At the same time a new vision of Venezuela's petroleum future was emerging. Under the direction of Luis Giusti, appointed President of PDVSA in 1994 and 'widely considered the architect of the so-called opening policy',[22] it was increasingly the state oil company rather than the government which would determine national oil policy. This American-educated petroleum engineer began to convert the state company into his image of a modern multinational: efficient, profitable and ripe for eventual privatisation. Indeed, according to a biographical note on Giusti published by the Center for Strategic and International Studies, a Washington-based 'think tank', 'Mr Giusti has come to be seen as a champion of privatisation initiatives aimed at adjusting the positions of state oil firms to the demands of a new globally competitive age.'[23]

As for national oil policy, the strategy was clear. Backed by proven conventional oil reserves of 77.7 billion barrels and a further 100 billion of up-gradeable 'heavy' oil, the plan was to increase production as quickly as possible with the aid of foreign, especially US, investment. At the same time, PDVSA's own investments in refining capacity in the USA and its refining alliances with US oil majors would help to absorb the large increases in Venezuelan oil production which would follow the success of the *Apertura*.[24] While those on the Venezuelan Left saw the new policy as 'helping to dig OPEC's grave',[25] Giusti and those who supported his mission barely troubled to conceal their growing animosity towards OPEC and 'the Arabs'. Indeed many oil industry experts now believed that Venezuela was on course to massively ramp up its oil production and break with OPEC.[26]

Indeed, between 1991 and 1997, Venezuelan oil production increased by 33 per cent, from 2.5 to 3.3 million b/d. At the same time, Venezuelan oil exports to the USA rose from around 1 million b/d in 1991 to 1.8 million b/d in 1997, providing 17 per cent of total US oil imports. President Clinton's National Security Council celebrated this new breakthrough in energy security declaring that 'we are undertaking a fundamental shift away from reliance on the Middle East' and that Venezuela had now become 'our number one foreign supplier'.[27]

As if to give blessing to Venezuela's new credo of market share *à l'outrance*, OPEC itself announced a 10 per cent increase in production quotas at its meeting on 29 November 1997, ostensibly to help the world economy in the aftermath of the Asian economic crisis. Venezuela's new quota was 2.583 million b/d, but

PDVSA had no intention of limiting itself to this modest level. Then, in December 1997, just as Giusti's grand project appeared to be achieving its objectives, PDVSA fell victim to hubris.

In an interview with the US bulletin *Oil Daily* on 3 December 1997, unnamed PDVSA officials demonstrated that their ambitions stretched much further than simply becoming a leading oil supplier to the USA. They announced that Venezuela's intention was to expand production, push down oil prices and squeeze US marginal producers out of the market allowing PDVSA to gain a larger market share. The story was all the more credible since Giusti had earlier told the Reuters news agency that 'continued low crude oil prices would drive about 1 million b/d of US and Canadian oil production out of the market in the next few months.'[28] The story also fitted neatly with PDVSA's declared plans to increase production from 3.3 million b/d in 1997 to 6.2 million b/d by 2006.

'SAFE' OIL SUPPLIES – TOO MUCH OF A GOOD THING?

In the following months, Venezuela's behaviour in the US oil market seemed to confirm this strategy. Venezuelan oil continued to flow into the US market in near-record volumes putting further downward pressure on US oil prices. In order to protect their own shares of the US market, Saudi Arabia and Mexico also started to aggressively discount their oil sales.

As a consequence of these developments, between October 1997 and December 1998, the world oil price collapsed and the well-head price for US oil fell to a mere $8.03, the lowest real oil price for 53 years. Although, with hindsight, we can see that this was a short-lived conjuncture, at the time it did not look that way. By early 1999, the consensus among oil industry observers and oil company executives alike was that there would be a continuation of very low oil prices into the foreseeable future. The American Petroleum Institute, saw 'little firm basis for sustained recovery in market conditions for several years'.[29]

The immediate impact of the oil price collapse was felt by those smaller independent US producers whose lifting costs (cash operating costs) exceeded the well-head price net of royalty payments and state severance taxes. Well-head prices were below $8 per barrel in many states at the end of 1998, whereas about two thirds of the oil wells belonging to small and medium US oil companies were marginal wells with lifting costs of around $9 per barrel.[30] Between November 1997 and January 1999, 136,000 oil wells and 57,000 gas wells were shut down. Production fell substantially in every oil-producing US state and by December 1998 crude oil production was nearly 600,000 b/d (9.1%) below the same period in 1997.

The expectation of a long period of low oil prices was also reflected in a major cutback in capital spending and development plans, which only became evident in the following year. During 1999, in spite of the fact that prices had actually recovered by mid-year, exploration and development expenditures in the USA by the major oil companies fell by $9 billion and the number of onshore wells completed by the majors in 1999 was the lowest since 1974. Aggregate data are not available for the independent oil company sector but it seems probable that capital spending by this group fell even more sharply. Reflecting this fall in capital spending, between April 1997 and April 1999 the number of US drilling rigs in operation fell from 901 to 496, considerably lower than the lowest level in the previous 'crisis' year of 1986 (686 rigs). The lowest daily figure for operational rigs (488) since records began in 1940 was recorded on 23 April 1999, and the monthly average for US drilling rigs in operation during 1999 (622) was also the lowest monthly average on record.[31]

The oil crisis impacted upon wider sections of the community than just the producers themselves. The combination of lower production and lower prices resulted in substantial reductions in severance tax revenues in the states affected. In January 1999 it was estimated that the sustained low oil price had, in turn, resulted in the loss of more than $1.8 billion in lost severance taxes and royalties to America's 33 oil- and gas-producing states and to the Federal Government.[32]

The income accruing to the USA's 4.5 million private royalty owners was also falling along with the oil price. An example was given in February 1999, in testimony before the US House Subcommittee on Ways and Means, of a typical Oklahoma royalty owner whose royalty income fell from $8,600 in 1997 to $5,300 in 1998. It was, said the testimony, a 40 per cent drop in one year for someone already living near the so-called poverty level pointing out that there were approximately 200,000 other Oklahomans in the same boat who depended on investments or assets in oil and gas mineral royalties. Royalty income had sustained countless families, small farms, ranches and rural towns for decades. Royalty dollars circulate many times through the local economy by way of the grocer, the pharmacist, the feed store, small shops and those who provide services to the elderly. So 'when those dollars disappear whole communities can be financially devastated.'[33]

SAVE DOMESTIC OIL!

The Venezuelan oil officials, and the US oil and chemical multinationals which imported Venezuelan oil, should have checked their history books. They would have discovered that it was the threat of cheap Venezuelan oil which had first galvanised the small and medium US domestic oil producers to set up the Independent Petroleum Association of America in 1927. With echoes of this distant past, a small-time Oklahoman oilman named Harold Hamm launched an attack upon the Venezuelan oil industry and, by implication, upon the major US oil-importing companies and the US Government. In January 1999, making good use of the Internet to rally support, he set up 'Save Domestic Oil' (SDO), an organisation of small- and medium-sized oil companies which announced that it would take legal action against Venezuela on the grounds that the latter was deliberately pricing below cost and hence 'dumping' oil in US markets with predatory intentions. Saudi Arabia, Mexico and Canada were also included in the initial 'charge sheet', although Canada was later replaced by Iraq, no doubt to add a little political spice to the mixture.

Hamm's website railed against both the Venezuelans' 'Grand Plan' and the US Government. If the 'Grand Plan' worked, Hamm said, America's small oilmen would all be out of business. But surely the US Government would never allow this to happen? Wrong, said Hamm. 'Our Government loves cheap oil. The mission of our own Department of Energy is to create an abundance of foreign supply from a myriad of diverse sources... Their job is to keep us awash in crude oil.'[34]

Hamm now expanded his coalition with the support of 32 state oil- and gas-producer associations and associations of private royalty owners. His petition, filed in Washington with the US Department of Commerce and the International Trade Commission, requested the imposition of tariffs upon oil imported from Venezuela and the other named countries. But while SDO's action were supported by the Independent Petroleum Association of America, the American Petroleum Institute (API) firmly opposed it. For the large integrated US oil companies represented by the API had, by now, a much-reduced interest in US domestic oil production. As we saw in Chapter One, their share of total US oil and gas output had fallen considerably since the mid-1980s. Not only did they themselves import substantial quantities of oil from Venezuela and elsewhere for processing in their US refineries, they were also deeply concerned that SDO's action would, if successful, prejudice their plans to acquire exploration and production licences in the countries named in the petition. To date only Venezuela had actually 'opened up', but at the time it was hoped that Saudi Arabia (and other Gulf producers) might also eventually follow suit.

SDO's petition was not actually heard until 29 June 1999. But in the meantime, in February, its contents had been leaked to the press. A jubilant Hamm described how: 'within three days time, Venezuela issued a press release denying dumping. Within a week it cut its production by 500,000 b/d, stated that it would abide by its OPEC quota, and conceded defeat for its bid to increase its US market share.'[35]

Hamm and SDO claimed that Venezuela's dramatic policy shift was the result of their campaign and the threat of import duties. In fact, it was nothing of the sort. The reversal of Venezuela's previous oil policy was entirely due to a completely independent and equally unexpected turn of events: the election of Hugo Chavez as President of Venezuela in December 1998.

VENEZUELA RETURNS TO THE OPEC FOLD

Elected with 58 per cent of the popular vote, Chavez was a man from the *barrios,* whose indigenous racial origins provoked both anxiety and hatred among his overwhelmingly white-skinned political opponents – the Venezuelans of European origin who had dominated the country's political and economic life since the country's independence at the beginning of the nineteenth century. His campaign against the two incumbent and largely discredited 'official' parties, Accion Democratica and COPEI was backed by a coalition of smaller left-leaning and populist groupings in the National Congress. Among the individual politicians who supported Chavez's 'Bolivarian Revolution' was the former guerrilla-turned-lawyer, Ali Rodriguez Araque, President of the Permanent Commission on Energy and Mining in the Chamber of Deputies.

Chavez and Rodriguez were long-standing opponents of PDVSA President, Giusti. They criticised both the tax concessions of his *Apertura* policy and the gold card culture of PDVSA's bosses. PDVSA had become 'a state within a state', declared Chavez.[36] Ali Rodriguez also accused PDVSA of favouring foreign oil companies when joint oil ventures with the private sector were set up, claiming that the qualification criteria set by PDVSA were designed in such a way that Venezuelan companies were largely excluded from the business.[37] Chavez had promised to sack Giusti if he was elected President and he kept his word. Giusti was forced to resign in February 1999, after which he swiftly moved to a directorship with Shell and a senior position with Riverstone, the energy company belonging to the secretive US Carlyle Group.[38] Meanwhile Ali Rodriguez became Chavez's first Minister of Energy and Mines.

On 23 March 1999, OPEC met in Vienna to discuss the lamentable state of world oil prices. The presence of Ali Rodriguez, who firmly pledged Venezuela's determination to be a loyal OPEC member once more, radicalised the assembled oil ministers and gave confidence to the organisation that it could now deliver the necessary production cutbacks which would restore world oil prices. A further 1.7 million b/d of cuts were added to the 2.6 million b/d agreed in the previous year, with non-OPEC producers Mexico, Norway, Oman and Russia promising an additional 400,000 b/d in cutbacks.[39] By the end of the year, oil prices had more than doubled and the US crude spot price, which had begun the year at $12.47/b, ended it at $25.60/b.

As for the domestic US oil producers, the majority of them organised in the Independent Petroleum Association of America, knew exactly who to thank, regardless of the aggressive and jingoistic posturing of the SDO campaigners. In June 1999, the Association put on record its 'respect and gratitude to these countries Saudi Arabia, Venezuela and Mexico for production restraint'. Mentioning, in passing, that the Association had already had talks with Venezuelan energy officials earlier in the year 'to explore areas of mutual interest', it stated that 'IPAA believes it is critical to have this kind of exchange with all oil exporting countries if we are to avert another price collapse … Constructive dialogue with oil exporting countries will remain a top priority for IPAA.'[40] Little wonder that Robert Mabro, the Director of the Oxford Institute For Energy Studies, should dryly remark some months later, that it had now become evident 'that the USA is a non-subscriber member of OPEC'.[41]

While both the Clinton Administration and its Republican successor were quietly pleased by the recovery in world oil prices – as we have seen already, Bush subsequently said that he 'gave credit to OPEC' for supporting the world oil market – they were not at all happy with the new Venezuelan Government's oil taxation policy, especially Ali Rodriguez's statement that the tax concessions offered to foreign oil companies in the contractual clauses of *Apertura* agreements were 'forbidden by our constitution and our tax laws'.[42] While he promised to respect all existing commitments made by Venezuela he also served notice that in future contracts foreign oil companies would not be given the tax privileges enjoyed under the previous regime. Not surprisingly, the foreign oil companies were reported to be 'dismayed' by this news.[43]

Chavez was re-elected for a six-year term in July 2000. By now all the major US oil companies – Exxon, Mobil, Amoco, Chevron, Conoco, Texaco and Phillips Petroleum – had participated in the *Apertura* programme and were looking forward to further, more lucrative investments as the policy widened and deepened. They were now confronted with an oil minister who was determined, in the words of one of Ali Rodriguez's closest allies, 'to implement a policy aimed at recovering the state's control over natural resources'.[44] By the time Ali Rodriguez had moved to take over the post of OPEC Secretary General in January 2001, he had firmly established the basic principle upon which future oil and gas taxation would be based: a major switch of emphasis towards higher royalty payments, compensated by a lower tax on profits. Royalties, calculated as a simple percentage of the sales value per barrel, are easy to calculate and make it difficult to cheat. Profit taxes on the other hand, require complicated calculations of allowable costs and provide more scope for tax avoidance.

The new Hydrocarbon Law decreed in November 2001 established that henceforth all oil companies, including PDVSA itself, would pay the government a royalty of 30 per cent, except in the case of economically marginal projects where a reduced rate of 20 per cent was payable. In addition, the Hydrocarbon Law stated that the government must in future take a majority 51 per cent stake in any joint ventures with foreign oil companies. These fiscal policy reforms were long overdue and were principally targeted at the state oil company itself, whose management had, for many years, developed a number of devices – including transfer pricing to its overseas refinery companies – to deliberately divert profits away from the Ministry of Mines and Energy.[45] Giusti and those around him thought *they* should control the revenues of PDVSA, not the elected Congress or Government; as a result PDVSA's contribution to the country's fiscal revenues had fallen from 71 cents per dollar of gross income in 1981 to 39 cents by 2000.[46]

Nevertheless, the introduction of a new royalty-based petroleum fiscal regime was portrayed by the overwhelmingly hostile news media, in Venezuela as well as the USA, as an attack on foreign capital, even though the new tax regime was not to be applied retrospectively to existing foreign oil investments. They made it appear as though Chavez's government was deliberately thumbing its nose at the US oil companies at a time when the most oil-company dominated Administration in US history had just taken office. To make matters worse, Chavez made well-publicised visits to fellow OPEC members Iraq and Libya.

After the terrorist attacks of 11 September 2001, the Bush Administration needed no further reminder of the extent to which America's national security was inextricably linked to events originating in the Middle East. Yet when the government's national security experts made their regular, by now almost routine, perusal of the Energy Information Administration's data on the sources of America's oil imports they would have had a rather nasty shock. For whereas the figures had regularly shown a steady decline in Gulf oil dependence since 1990, the trend had now gone into reverse. Propelled by a frantic increase in motorisation, US demand for petroleum rose from 17.7 million b/d in 1995 to 19.7 million b/d in 2000. Even when total oil demand fell back slightly, to 19.6 million b/d in 2001, oil imports continued to rise: in that year they reached a record high of 10.9 million b/d of which 2.8 million barrels were from the Gulf. At 14.1 per cent the proportion of total US oil consumption supplied by the Gulf was now the highest in the nation's history, while as a share of total imports supplies from the Gulf were 25.3 per cent.

As America began the year 2002, the fevered imagination of Bush, Cheney and Condoleezza Rice, obsessed with the prosecution of the 'War on Terror', began to focus upon Chavez, this rabble-rouser who had the temerity to consort with America's enemies and criticise America's bombing of Afghanistan as 'meeting terror by terror'. And now that the USA was once again apparently in the thralls of oil dependence to the detested 'sheikhs', it seemed that any useful function Chavez had previously performed – by preventing the total collapse of oil prices – was now superseded by the need to discipline another rogue state, or rather as one US journalist explained in this particular case, a 'rogue democracy'.[47]

So when Pedro Carmona, a private-sector petrochemical boss, and Head of Fedecameras, the Venezuelan Businessmen's association, arrived in Washington in February 2002 with plans to overthrow the Chavez Government in a *coup d'état* which would be supported by the senior officer corps, Bush Administration officials and the Pentagon listened to their ideas with considerable interest. As one Administration official put it, 'we were not discouraging people.'[48]

Chavez's enemies, both inside and outside Venezuela, now initiated a campaign to get rid of him. The privately owned Venezuelan news media and TV channels, uniformly hostile to Chavez and his government, began to demand his resignation. On 10 December 2001, a coalition of business and trade union groups, drawing support mainly from the middle classes and higher-paid workers whose leaders remained loyal to the former ruling political parties, staged a one-day 'strike' demanding the reversal of planned legislation and repeal of the new Hydrocarbon Law.

During the first three months of 2002, the media cries against Chavez, both in Venezuela and in the USA, grew ever more strident. At the same time the opponents of Chavez's pro-OPEC oil strategy came out into the open. Men like Francisco Monaldi, a leading advocate of oil privatisation and advocate of Thatcher-style 'popular capitalism' and Andres Sosa Pietri, a former president of PDVSA, demanded a comprehensive energy alliance with the USA in which Venezuela would grab the share of the US market currently held by Saudi Arabia and the other Gulf states. On 3 March 2002, six weeks before the coup attempt against Chavez, Francisco Monaldi published a fierce attack on the government's 'left-wing thinking' in the pages of the daily *El Nacional*. A few days earlier, Chavez had replaced the current president of PDVSA Guaicaipuro Lameda and four board members who had objected to the implementation of OPEC quotas. This had proved a catalyst for a new national mobilisation by Chavez's predominantly white middle-class opponents. Celebrating the resistance of PDVSA managers who had rallied to their directors' defence, Monaldi attacked the 'anachronistic and restrictive thinking of those who govern us and are trying to use PDVSA as their instrument'. He condemned Venezuela's 42-year-old participation in OPEC as a disaster for the country, one in which Venezuela 'had sacrificed our share of world oil production in order to protect the oil price'. Instead, he proposed a new national oil policy which he described as a 'Continental Self-Sufficiency Accord'. It would take advantage of what he believed to be a deteriorating relationship between the USA and Saudi Arabia and 'in exchange for massive [US] investment' Venezuela would increase its oil production to 10 million b/d, most of which would flow to the USA.[49]

A few weeks later, once again in the pages of *El Nacional*, Monaldi elaborated further on his proposal, this time adding a crucial new element, that the 'Treaty of Continental Self-Sufficiency' would embody a tariff against 'foreign' oil, thereby 'guaranteeing the market and investment to produce, within one decade, eleven million barrels daily'.[50] Presumably Monaldi had now remembered the 'Save Domestic Oil' affair, and that the US domestic oil producers would hardly be delighted to hear that they were about to be deluged by a flood of imported Venezuelan oil. Consequently the self-sufficiency agreement had to be supplemented by a tariff which would mitigate the damage done to US producers by excluding oil from the Persian Gulf. No doubt Monaldi thought this plan would appeal to US politicians reeling from the attacks of 11 September 2001 and now deeply suspicious of anything 'Arab'. In a similar vein Andres Sosa Pietri, now a leading member of the self-styled 'Alliance for Liberty' bitterly attacked Venezuela's OPEC membership and announced that, 'It is necessary for us to distance ourselves from the organisation of Oil Exporting Countries and from the Arab countries and to move closer to the western world, to which we belong.'[51]

FIASCO – THE COUP FAILS

On 7 April 2002, management and union members at PDVSA began a strike against the removal of PDVSA's anti-OPEC Board of Directors. The role of the state oil company's employees – Venezuela's 'labour aristocracy' – is not difficult to understand. Led by officials loyal to the old political parties which had been kicked out by Chavez's election, they regarded the OPEC-supporting production and investment cuts which Chavez was implementing as detrimental to their own economic interests, regardless of any benefits accruing to the nation as a whole as a result of higher oil prices. Three days later, Fedecameras, the businessmen's organisation, declared a 48-hour 'strike' and during the street demonstrations by middle-class opponents of Chavez which followed, a number of people were killed in circumstances which have yet to be accurately determined, but which were instantly blamed on Chavez by the Venezuelan media. This was precisely the opportunity the plotters were anticipating.

On 12 April, President Chavez was seized by rebel military officers and taken to a secret location from where it was announced that he had resigned. Pedro Carmona was then appointed President by the plotters and immediately announced that the National Assembly would be closed down and that all Chavez's economic and social reforms – including the 30 per cent petroleum royalties – would be cancelled. Carmona himself would be Dictator until order was restored and in the opinion of the *Financial Times* the 'interim government' was 'likely to be well disposed towards relaxing oil production curbs within OPEC and easing fiscal constraints on foreign investors'.

Unfortunately for Venezuela's new dictator, his power lasted for one day only. Loyal paratroopers and thousands of Chavez supporters from the impoverished *barrios* of Caracas cornered Carmona in the Presidential Palace and demanded Chavez's release; but not before the US Government, displaying barely concealed glee at Chavez's downfall, had implicitly given recognition to what it described as 'a transitional civilian government'.

Following the failed coup attempt, Chavez asked Ali Rodriguez to return from OPEC HQ in Vienna to take the helm of the state oil company. It was a sound decision. Ali Rodriguez quickly won the support of many of the lower-paid grades in the oil company and some of the middle management. However, the opposition parties were still determined to oust Chavez. On 2 December 2002, Fedecameras began yet another 'strike' and a few days later, it was again joined by large sections of the PDVSA management and white-collar staff. As the PDVSA strike entered its third week, Venezuelan oil production fell to below 1 million b/d compared to the pre-strike level of 3 million b/d.

BUSH'S DILEMMA: GET CHAVEZ OR GET SADDAM

The Bush Administration was now in a quandary. Fanatical anti-leftists like Otto Reich, the Cuban émigré recently appointed Assistant Secretary of State for Western Hemisphere Affairs, wanted to give maximum support to the anti-Chavez movement. But Bush and his entourage were focused on the coming war against Iraq; it was not a good time to be encouraging a major oil-supply disruption just when the markets were already anticipating a severe war-induced increase in oil prices. Moreover, the situation was complicated by some local oil industry fundamentals.

As we have already made clear, for many years the conventional assumption about US energy security had been that the country's oil imports should be diversified away from the 'unstable' Middle East. Oil coming from western hemispheric sources like Venezuela is classed as 'short-haul' oil, being at sea for a few days only, whereas oil from the Middle East is 'long haul', taking several weeks to arrive at US markets. The problem is that short-haul oil is not, in the short term, substitutable by long-haul oil. As JP Morgan's oil expert, Paul Horsnell explained at the time of the PDVSA managers' strike, there was one drawback with the view that energy security would be enhanced by having less reliance on the Middle East. Energy security is also enhanced by having more reliance on long-haul imports, giving more time to make adjustments after a shock. More dependence on short-haul sources in Latin America and West Africa reduces the flexibility of the supply chain by cutting the amount of inventory at sea held in that chain. 'A disruption from Venezuela, five days sailing away, feeds straight through, while one from the Middle East, five weeks sailing away, is more manageable.'[52]

However, Horsnell also underlined a second local difficulty. Venezuela was not only the fourth largest supplier of US oil imports, but the type of oil it supplied – heavy crude – was virtually unobtainable from anywhere else (except Mexico which was already producing flat out). The problem was that the US refineries on the Gulf coast which used Venezuelan and Mexican oil were geared *only* for heavy crude and couldn't easily substitute lighter grades; and 42 per cent of their throughput came from Venezuela. The potential price impact of the Venezuelan stoppage was therefore severe indeed. Horsnell cautioned that markets should not underestimate the gravity of the Venezuelan oil stoppage for the USA and, choosing his words very carefully, he warned that, 'scenarios in which there is a change of government without prior recourse to the ballot box appear to hold some severe dangers, given that the fault lines are so based in terms of income levels.'[53]

In other words, open class warfare in Venezuela would not be exactly conducive to a smooth restoration of oil supplies to US energy markets nor, for that matter, to Bush's war preparations. Indeed Horsnell considered that, it was not possible to rule out a scenario where Venezuelan events become as important to oil markets in 2003 as the unfolding situation in Iraq. If the political situation in Venezuela continued to deteriorate then a steep increase in the oil price might become inevitable, 'and without a swift resolution, we will soon be in a situation where the use of US strategic reserves almost becomes forced.'[54]

With problems mounting by the day for Bush's Iraq strategy, a relatively low profile on the Venezuelan social conflict seemed advisable. Meanwhile, Chavez had isolated right-wing elements in the armed forces, and there were no signs of the second coup attempt which the opposition demanded. By mid-January, the businessmen's 'strike' was weakening and on 23 January 2003 in the centre of Caracas, hundreds of thousands of Chavez supporters celebrated its collapse.

In spite of the post-strike dismissal of most of PDVSA's rebel managers, by March, managers and workers loyal to PDVSA President Ali Rodriguez had succeeded in restoring national oil production to around 2.5 million b/d. This was reflected in oil prices. Although the average price of US oil imports briefly touched $31.35/b on 28 February 2003, by late March, as US and British troops began their major push into southern Iraq, the price had fallen to around $26/b. While this was partly due to the rapid success of the invading forces, the timely restoration of Venezuelan oil production also clearly played a part.

Ironically, then, because of the abject failure of the pro-American Venezuelan opposition, Bush was able to launch his invasion of Iraq relatively untroubled by the threat of a major world oil price increase and without having to release any oil from the US strategic reserve.

MEXICO NEUTERS NAFTA

The Mexican Revolution of 1917 promulgated the most socially and economically advanced constitution of its day, including the declaration that all subsoil mineral resources belonged to the people. But the practical implementation of this concept, which required the largely American- and British-owned Mexican oil industry to agree to a new system of mineral rights, royalties and taxation was strongly resisted by the companies.[55] Backed by the military power of the USA, the US and other foreign oil companies were, on the whole, left relatively unmolested by the turbulent events in much of the country throughout the 1920s.

Between 1919 and 1926, Mexico became the world's biggest oil exporter and the second biggest world oil producer after the USA, with a record production of 193 million barrels in 1921 accounting for about one quarter of world production. Fully 65 per cent of Mexico's production was exported and three quarters of its exports were delivered to the USA.[56] Mexico remained the largest world oil exporter until 1928. However, after this date, saltwater intrusion into many Mexican oil reservoirs and the attractions of 'political stability' under Gomez's brutal Venezuelan dictatorship led US and British companies to run down their Mexican exploration and development operations and move to the richer prospects of Lake Maracaibo.[57]

The oil companies' declining investment in the country, together with their refusal to negotiate with the government-backed unionised oil workers, were among the factors which led to Mexico becoming the first country in the world to nationalise its oil industry. In 1938, while the governing Partido Revolucionario Institucional (PRI) was briefly under the leadership of a left-nationalist president, Lazaro Cardenas, the country's predominantly US-owned oil companies were taken into public ownership. Thereafter the state oil company, Petroleos Mexicanos (PEMEX) became a symbol of the Mexican Revolution, hailed by both left and right in the country as the touchstone of national dignity and independence. It was therefore clear from the start that PEMEX, with its exclusive rights to explore and produce oil and gas in Mexico, was going to be a tough nut to crack for the USA's hemispheric energy integration project.

At 26.9 million barrels, Mexico's proven oil reserves are the third largest in the western hemisphere after Venezuela (77.7 billion) and the USA (30.4 billion).[58] If Mexico could be compelled to sign the same sort of 'Free Trade' agreement as Canada had, then this would certainly underwrite the USA's energy security for many years to come. However, once negotiations for NAFTA got under way, the Mexican Government made it absolutely clear that there was no question of it agreeing to the same kind of 'proportional supply guarantee' that Canada had accepted in the earlier FTA and which had now been incorporated into Canada's obligations under NAFTA. At the same time, any question of Mexico opening up the exploration and production sector of its oil industry to investment by US companies was also completely ruled out. Only in natural gas transportation and distribution was it agreed that foreign companies could bid for licences to build and operate such facilities. US companies stated they were not interested in this part of Mexico's hydrocarbon industry unless they were also given access to upstream gas reserves.

Mexico's attitude towards OPEC has remained ambiguous. It is not a member of OPEC, but Mexican oil officials have, on occasion, welcomed efforts by more radical OPEC members to reduce production and raise prices. For example, when Iraq confronted Kuwait and the United Arab Emirates in July 1990, accusing them of deliberately ignoring production quotas and demanding that OPEC raise its target oil price to $25 per barrel, officials at PEMEX were said to be, 'greatly encouraged' by Iraq's belligerent stand. Referring to Saddam Hussein, a senior PEMEX executive enthused, 'He has become something of a folk hero amongst us.'[59] Moreover, on two occasions in March 1988 and March 1999, Mexico agreed to concerted production cuts along with OPEC in order to strengthen prices.[60]

Although, as we have already noted, there are occasions on which the USA is not averse to Mexico intervening to help OPEC prevent a world oil-price collapse that would be disastrous to high-cost US domestic oil producers, in general 'the USA wants Mexico to increase oil production to decrease its Middle East exposure.' So said Jose Alberro, a Mexican political scientist at the University of California and referring to the US-Mexico NAFTA negotiations, Alberro also described how, 'The USA pressured Mexico, to the point of almost breaking the negotiations, that opening the energy sector to foreign investment was in Mexico's self-interest.'[61] Mexico, however, resisted.

In spite of the USA's failure to dragoon Mexico into an *apertura* policy, there is considerable evidence that it continued to contemplate similar schemes to achieve this objective. The report of an independent taskforce on the USA's Strategic Energy Policy sponsored by the James Baker III Institute and the US Council on Foreign Relations and published in April 2001, one month before Cheney's Energy Policy Report, made a number of recommendations about Mexican oil and gas. Having first noted how, 'Mexico's resources are closer and maybe more economical to develop than those in Alaska', and regretting that 'Mexico's constitution blocks ownership participation in oil and gas fields by foreign entities and Mexico's oil workers unions are heavily set against any foreign participation,' the taskforce openly canvassed suborning members of the Mexican elite to acquiesce in US objectives, suggesting euphemistically that the US Government might want to consider 'leverage tools' that could be brought to bear to 'assist political leaders in Mexico who advocate that Mexico open its energy sector to foreign investment'.[62] And with further disdain for Mexican public opinion, the taskforce advocated keeping discussion of opening Mexico's hydrocarbon sector 'within a hemispheric focus…in order to diffuse attention from the negative aspects of Mexican popular opinion regarding US-led investment in Mexican resources'.[63] Reading these policy recommendations, it should surprise no one that one of the key members of the James Baker III taskforce was the deposed ex-president of PDVSA, Luis Giusti, now openly committed to promoting the strategic energy interests of the USA.

By 2001, the concept of the hemispheric accord as a strategy for ensuring America's continuing energy security, was proving elusive, at least insofar as Mexico and Venezuela were concerned. However, America hadn't entirely given up on its hemispheric strategy. In June 2002, two months after the failed pro-American military coup in Venezuela, the Bush Administration won Congressional agreement to expand President Clinton's $2 billion programme of military assistance to the Colombian Government, known as 'Plan Colombia', by dispatching 70 green beret special forces troops to the province of Arauca to train Colombian troops and help fight left-wing guerrillas.

The reason? Around 50 per cent of Colombia's oil production (600,000 b/d in 2002) is exported to the USA. However, Colombian oil production and supplies to the USA have been falling steadily since 1999, largely as the result of guerrilla attacks on the pipeline from Occidental Petroleum's Cano Limon oilfield, the country's second largest. Because of civil strife in the Colombian countryside which has lasted almost continuously since the 1950s, much of the country remains unexplored and could well contain some major oilfields like that at Cusiana, Colombia's largest field operated by BP, which was only discovered in 1988.

Bush's supporters, like Congressman Mark Souder of Indiana (described by the *Congressional Quarterly* as one of the 'conservative true believers'), urged intervention in Colombia, backing their case in explicitly 'energy security' terms. 'Clearly we have an energy threat,' he declared in May 2002. 'Colombia is either our seventh or eighth largest supplier of oil. We already have instability in the Middle East. We have more compelling reasons to be involved in Colombia than almost anywhere else in the world.'[64]

So while the Bush Administration was planning its invasion of Iraq it had not forgotten Latin America; and while it continued to rail against the government of Venezuela, with over 400 troops and DynCorp mercenaries in Colombia, the Axis of Oil was also 'stepping into another foreign war'.[65]

8 The Caspian and Central Asia: A New Middle East?

The trouble with diversifying outside the Middle East...is that it is not where the oil is. One of the best things for our supply security would be to liberate Iraq.

Sarah Emerson, Energy Security Analysis Inc., 2002

The collapse of the Soviet Union in 1991 brought independence to its former southern republics lying between the Caucasus and the Chinese frontier. Conventionally referred to as 'Central Asia', Kazakhstan, Kyrgyzstan, Tajikistan, Turkmenistan and Uzbekistan form a landmass of over 1.6 million square miles, most of it unimaginably hostile terrain, with a total population of 56.4 million – slightly less than the UK. On the western flank of this Central Asian region lies the Caspian Sea, a vast sedimentary basin around whose shores lies the hydrocarbon wealth of the region. On the western shore of the Caspian, the Caucasian states of Azerbaijan, Armenia and Georgia form the bridge between Central Asia and the USA's NATO ally, Turkey. On Georgia's northern border lies Chechnya, a country struggling for independence but whose position, originally straddling Soviet-era oil pipelines from Baku and southern Astrakhan, made military intervention by Russia virtually inevitable.[1] On the southern shore of the Caspian, Iran, the region's only OPEC member, stretches hundreds of miles southwards to the Gulf and the Arabian Sea. Finally, on the eastern flank of the Central Asian region, lies strife-torn Afghanistan, whose function as an energy pipeline conduit from Central Asia to the Indian Ocean was mapped out some years ago by Unocal, a major US oil and gas multinational.[2]

This whole vast region bordering the Caspian Sea and beyond has rapidly become a human disaster area, with whatever health, education and infrastructural investments made under the Soviet regime collapsing into disarray. Most of the inhabitants live in poverty with per capita national income for the new states of the Caspian and Central Asia at around $700 per annum.[3] The result has been domination by local mafiosi, large-scale drug- and people-smuggling enterprises, gun-running, Islamic fundamentalism and reciprocating repression by the US-supported corrupt oligarchies who have firmly embedded themselves and their relatives in the commercial life of the region. In the words, of Fiona Hill, a Brookings Institution fellow in foreign policy studies, 'Independence has not been kind' to the new southern states of the former Soviet Union.[4]

THE CASPIAN BECOMES 'STRATEGICALLY SIGNIFICANT'

However, America had plans for these benighted populations. In the words of Richard Cheney, speaking to an audience of US businessmen in Washington in 1998, 'I can't think of a time when we've had a region emerge as suddenly to become as strategically significant as the Caspian.'[5] Cheney seemed to have good reason to be excited. American oil companies, with Chevron (and Condoleezza Rice) in the lead, had by now secured what appeared to be a treasure trove of hydrocarbon wealth. The US Government's Energy Information Administration (EIA) had just published their first estimate of the oil reserves believed to be located around the shores of the Caspian Sea. According to the EIA, 'the Caspian Basin is an area of vast resource potential.'[6] Total oil resources of the region were put at 218 billion barrels, of which 32.5 billion were already said to be proven.[7] However, attention inevitably focused on the uncertain 'total' reserves figure, and while the EIA cautioned that 'the concept of potential oil resources is much more speculative,' this didn't stop them from making favourable comparisons with Saudi Arabia.[8] Moreover, while they also pointed out that exploitation of these reserves was conditional on the timely construction of a network of pipelines required to transport this oil from the landlocked Caspian, they nevertheless took what they described as 'an optimistic view' of this requirement. After the building of some of the pipelines, which the EIA anticipated would take place by the end of the decade, and in particular after the building of a pipeline through Turkey to the Mediterranean which would come on stream 'after the turn of the century', Caspian oil production was forecast to reach around 3.3 million barrels per day by 2005, 4.5 million b/d by 2010, and 5.8 million b/d by 2015.[9] In other words, within seven years, the Caspian would be producing as much as Venezuela, within twelve years its production would rival that of Iran and Qatar combined, and in twenty two years its production would be nearly as much as Iran and Iraq combined. Moreover, the Caspian contained considerable reserves of natural gas. According to the EIA's 1998 *International Energy Outlook*, Turkmenistan had the largest proven reserves with 101 trillion cubic feet (Tcf) – in energy terms equivalent to around 17 billion barrels of oil. Uzbekistan had 66 Tcf and Kazakhstan 65 Tcf. Together, these three new states held more gas than the USA and Canada combined although, as in the case of oil, new pipelines would have to be built to transport the gas to markets outside the former Soviet Union. Overall, it seemed that at last the USA had found a major source of additional oil and gas supplies which would give it powerful motivation to take control of the region and possibly even a 'new Middle East'.

Initially, US policy towards the Caspian and Central Asian states evolved in a largely ad hoc fashion. At the time of the USSR's break-up, there was no coherent strategy towards the Caspian and Central Asia. Prior to 1991, the USA had no vital national interest in either the Caucasus or Central Asia. Indeed, as Fiona Hill pointed out, had it not been for the rediscovery of the energy resources of the Caspian Sea, and the collapse of the Soviet Union, 'the regions would have likely remained a marginal backwater for crafters of US foreign policy'.[10] She also pointed out that it was not until major oil contracts were signed between US oil companies and the governments of Kazakhstan and Azerbaijan in 1993–1994 that the region really began to register on the radar screens of the American public. It was the commercial interests of US oil companies in exploiting new energy reserves that gave US policy-makers a specific interest to protect in the Caucasus and Central Asia. 'The US has come to see Caspian resources as one of the few prospects for diversifying world energy supply away from the Middle East.'[11]

However, during the two Clinton Administrations between 1993 and 2000, these two primarily oil-related US objectives – protecting the interests of US oil companies in the Caspian and diversifying oil-supply sources – became entangled with a third, geo-strategic objective: that of detaching the newly formed Caspian and Central Asian states from both the Russian and Iranian spheres of influence. Growing US pessimism about the likelihood of Russia restructuring into a US-style 'model' economy and society appears to have prompted a new, more antagonistic attitude towards that country during the mid-1990s. Similarly, President Clinton's 1995 Executive Order prohibiting US companies from conducting business in Iran, followed by the passing of the Iran-Libya Sanctions Act in 1996, dictated an intensification of America's already hostile political posture towards the Islamic Republic.

A key figure highly influential in directing the Clinton Administration's attention towards the alleged geo-strategic importance of the Caspian and

Central Asia, was the former National Security Advisor to President Jimmy Carter, Zbigniew Brzezinski. In the early 1990s, Brzezinski made extensive visits to the region as a consultant to the US oil company Amoco. He had long been a mentor to Clinton's Secretary of State, Madeleine Albright, and he warned the White House that the USA would be making a serious mistake if it ignored what he claimed were its crucial strategic interests in the region. Consequently, covert CIA officers, some of them well-trained petroleum engineers, were despatched to travel through Southern Russia, Azerbaijan, Kazakhstan and Turkmenistan in order to gain further understanding of both their oil potential and their general political situation. In August 1997, Albright and her State Department colleagues received a full CIA briefing on the Caspian/Central Asian region, after which Albright concluded that working to mould the area's future was 'one of the most exciting things that we can do'.[12]

Possibly the most important outcome of these discussions in the State Department was the decision about the role which future oil- and gas-pipeline construction would play. The Department acknowledged that some new pipelines from the region would probably have to pass through Russia, but insisted that 'Russia should not be able to turn a valve and shut off all or most of the Caspian flow.' Above all, there was to be no weakening in the USA's determination to block any pipeline construction southwards, through Iran. 'The last thing we need,' one White House aide observed, 'is to rely on the Persian Gulf as the main access for more oil.'[13]

Little wonder then that Cheney viewed the Caspian region as 'strategically significant' and, by 1998, the strategy was becoming clear – to incorporate the inhabitants of the Caspian, Central Asia and the southern Caucasus (with the exception of Armenia)[14] into a vast US dependency, anchored upon the construction of a massive new oil and gas pipeline infrastructure stretching along an East-West energy corridor that linked Turkey, Georgia, Azerbaijan, Kazakhstan, Turkmenistan, Uzbekistan, Tajikistan and ultimately Afghanistan, Pakistan and India.

CASPIAN OIL BECKONS

Caspian oil beckoned; but not for the first time. What was occurring at the end of the twentieth century was in many ways a reprise of those events which had occurred at the end of the nineteenth. By the early 1880s, the Nobel Brothers' Petroleum Producing Company, to which the Tsarist authorities had granted an exclusive licence to explore and develop the oil seepages around Baku, was producing and refining around 30,000 barrels per day. By 1888, Russian oil produced at Baku, supplemented by new oilfields around Grozny in present-day Chechnya, equalled about four fifths of US production and in spite of the immense difficulties of transporting oil from the Caspian, oil exports from Russia provided 22 per cent of world supplies. By the early 1900s, Russia produced about half of the world's oil.

However, the onset of the First World War, followed by the Russian Revolution and the occupation of Baku by Turkish forces in 1918, spelt the beginning of a period of decline until 1925, when production began to recover. By 1938, the contribution of the Caspian fields to Soviet oil production was still around 75 per cent, but by 1950 it had fallen to 45.2 per cent.[15] And as the cold war began to intensify, Stalin's customary paranoia led him to believe that the geographical location of the Baku fields made them an insecure source of oil. As Stalin informed the US Ambassador to Moscow, 'Beria and others tell me that saboteurs – and be it only one man with a box of matches – could cause serious damage.'[16]

Successive Soviet Governments shared Stalin's anxiety about the vulnerability of the Baku oilfields and during the 1950s and 1960s the focus of Soviet oil production shifted to new oil-producing zones in the Volga-Urals region. By 1965, the Azerbaijan Soviet Socialist Republic (containing the Baku oilfields) contributed only 9 per cent of total Soviet oil output,[17] Later still, the focus of the Soviet Union's oil development policy shifted to the huge, newly discovered oilfields of Western Siberia. However, during the late 1970s, Soviet geologists identified some exceptionally large oil- and gas-bearing structures in the Caspian region, including the giant Karachaganak (gas-condensate) and Tengiz (oil) prospects, although by the time the Soviet Union collapsed these had not been developed for production.

One other legacy of the Soviet era which has survived to complicate the USA's Caspian-Central Asian energy strategy is the legal status of the Caspian Sea itself. A Treaty of Friendship between Iran and the Soviet Union in 1921 agreed that the Caspian was a shared lake, with the implication that all the natural resources of the Caspian were to be divided equally between the two countries. However, the emergence of three new littoral states in 1991 – Azerbaijan, Kazakhstan and Turkmenistan – with a combined length of Caspian coastline which exceeded that of Russia and Iran – led these new states to demand a redefinition of the Caspian's legal status as a sea rather than a lake. General principles of international law provide that seas can be partitioned, while lakes are treated as legal condominiums. If the Law of the Sea Convention applied, full maritime boundaries for the five littoral states would be established, based on a division of the sea and its sub-sea resources into equidistant national sectors. The Americans, with their plans for massive investment in offshore oil and gas, clearly favoured the 'sea' interpretation which would confer clear and unambiguous property rights for sub-sea resources.[18] However, although there have been various attempts to find a solution to this problem, so far there has been no agreement between the five littoral states. In April 2002, another conference of the littoral states failed to make any headway on the subject, although afterwards bilateral agreements to divide up the northern part of the Caspian were reached between Russia and Kazakhstan, and Russia and Azerbaijan, appearing to signal a willingness to press on with their respective oil and gas developments on the assumption that the Caspian will eventually become accepted as a sea.

By now, Caspian oil production, which had severely declined by the mid-1990s, was increasing once again reaching a total of 1.46 million barrels per day in 2001[19] and the oil exports from this region which had previously been either extremely small or negative (i.e. net imports) were also increasing, most notably in the case of Kazakhstan. However, the failure of the five littoral powers to agree upon the legal status of the Caspian seriously complicated the task of creating a unified oil and gas pipeline network in the region. Until such an agreement could be reached, it would not be possible to construct any new underwater pipelines crossing the Caspian Sea and linking Kazakhstan and Turkmenistan to Azerbaijan and the western markets.

ENTER THE OIL COMPANIES

The recovery in Caspian hydrocarbon production was entirely the result of the influx of major foreign oil companies, mainly American, into the region after 1993. Even before the final death throes of the mighty Soviet Union, western oil companies were circling the dying super-state waiting to close in for the feast; but as in nature, it was the cheetahs of the oil world that reached the prey first, leaving the major companies to take the lion's share at a later date: it was a small Aberdeen-based oil services company, Ramco, which arrived in Baku in 1989 and rediscovered a giant group of oilfields – Azeri-Chirag-Gunashli – in the southern Caspian.

Five years later, on 20 September 1994, after a coup launched by ex-KGB general, Heydar Aliyev, the new government of Azerbaijan signed what became known in oil circles as the 'Contract of the Century', a production-sharing agreement with the newly formed Azerbaijan International Operating Company (AIOC) to exploit the 4.3 billion barrels of estimated oil reserves in the Azeri-Chirag-Gunashli fields, at a cost of $13 billion. Presiding over the assembled dignitaries from Azerbaijan and the world of multinational oil at the contract-signing ceremony were Bill White, US Deputy Energy Secretary and Tim Eggar, UK Energy Minister. In addition to tiny Ramco and the State Oil Company of Azerbaijan, the AIOC's members included three US oil multinationals, Amoco, Pennzoil and Unocal, together with the US energy services company McDermott, and the US-Saudi partnership, Delta Hess; the consortium also included Britain's BP, Norway's Statoil, Russia's Lukoil and the Turkish State Oil Company.[20]

The central role of Azerbaijan and its oil in US geo-strategy in the region is clearly revealed by checking the membership of an innocuous-sounding body called the 'US-Azerbaijan Chamber of Commerce'. Originally established in 1996, by the end of the decade this body was controlled by key members of the US political establishment, along with senior managers from all the major US oil companies. Its 'Honorary Council of Advisors' consisted of Dick Cheney, Henry Kissinger and Zbigniew Brzezinski, along with former members of Bush Sr's Administration, Brent Scowcroft, James Baker and Lloyd Bentsen. Future Deputy Secretary of State in George W. Bush's Administration, Richard Armitage, was a member of its Board of Directors, while Richard Perle, soon to be Chairman of the Defense Policy Board at the Pentagon, was a member of its Board of Trustees. The US oil industry itself was represented by the Executive Vice President of ExxonMobil Exploration Co., the President of Conoco, the Vice President of Unocal International Energy Ventures, the 'General Manager for International Government Relations' of ChevronTexaco, the Vice President of Devon Energy and the Chairman of Montcrief Oil International. A further eight members of the Chamber were US businessmen or lawyers with oil and gas interests prominent among their portfolios.[21]

It would be difficult to imagine a more revealing testimony to the key role which the 'oil interest' was now playing in US foreign policy. Here we see key members of the US power elite – Brzezinski, former National Security Advisor to Democrat President Jimmy Carter; Scowcroft, a Republican 'realist' from the Bush Sr Administration; Perle the arch-ideologue of 'neo-conservativism' – all closely collaborating in an enterprise whose sole objective was the incorporation of Caspian oil into the commercial and political orbit of the USA.

One might have imagined that the US-Azerbaijan Chamber of Commerce would have something like equal representation of US and Azerbaijani citizens. In fact out of a total of 38 members only two were Azerbaijanis: one, Ilham Aliyev, the son of the President, and the other, Azerbaijan's Ambassador to the USA. This overwhelming American domination reflected its primary intention – the acquisition of privatised Azerbaijani assets by US companies. This intention was officially confirmed by the signing of a Bilateral Trade Agreement between the USA and Azerbaijan in 1997, similar to the 1989 US-Canadian FTA. According to the terms of the Agreement, whenever Azerbaijan privatises state assets it must not discriminate in favour of Azerbaijani citizens and against those of the USA. Similarly when the USA privatises its own state assets (for example in the sale of leases on federal oil lands) it must not discriminate in favour of US citizens and against those of Azerbaijan. Needless to say, the world is still waiting for Azerbaijani purchases of US publicly owned assets.

Meanwhile, at the northern end of the Caspian, in April 1993, Chevron had signed a 50/50 production-sharing agreement with Kazakhstan, and soon other multinational oil companies followed in the race to grab the hydrocarbon riches of the Caspian – from the USA, Exxon, Mobil, Halliburton, Texaco, Kerr-McGee, Oryx Energy, Devon Energy, Amerada Hess and Phillips Petroleum; from Italy, AGIP; from the UK, BG plc and Shell; and from France, TotalFinaElf – a roll call of Big Oil. Between June 1996 and June 2000, a further 35 production-sharing contracts were signed, including one for Shah Deniz, a giant gas field in Azerbaijani waters with 25–39 trillion cubic feet (Tcf) of gas; another at Karachaganak, onshore Kazakhstan, with an estimated 2.3 billion barrels of oil and condensate and 16 Tcf of gas; and potentially the biggest find of all, the offshore Kashagan oilfield, in Kazakh waters, whose total recoverable oil reserves have been estimated at 'up to ten billion barrels'.[22]

Although the geological prospectivity of the Caspian region looked remarkably promising, the financial and political risks which these companies were taking were considerable. While they could count on the political support of their own governments, nevertheless the general economic, political and social environment in which they were to work was challenging if not downright threatening. To understand why any oil company should want to risk its employees and its shareholders' capital by venturing into a region where, as yet, there were few guarantees of personal safety or that contracts would be respected and money invested protected from arbitrary seizure or expropriation, we must return to the concept of 'oil capitalism' which we introduced in Chapter One.

As we saw in the first chapter, in a capitalist economy, an oil company, unlike a manufacturing company, is driven by what we called a 'territorial imperative'. It must be continuously on the move, acquiring new reserves of oil to replace those which it is depleting as they are extracted and sold. Otherwise its share price will decline and its directors and managers will pay the price. Between 1985 and 1992, Chevron's worldwide oil reserves fell from 3,831 million barrels to 3,096 million. This was largely attributable to the fall in its US reserves which declined from 2,088 million barrels to 1,368 million over the same period. The company urgently needed to make a very large oil discovery or acquisition which would replenish its reserves. But as the company's annual report recorded in March 1994, 'opportunities to discover and develop major new reserves in the United States are limited due to regulatory barriers and drilling prohibitions.'[23] In other words, the few remaining areas of 'virgin' oil territory, like the Arctic National Wildlife Refuge in Alaska, were off-limits, mainly for environmental reasons (see Chapter Six). So it was vital that Chevron acquire oil reserves outside the USA. A continuous decline in reserves was not an option.

However, in 1994, with political and 'diplomatic' support from Condoleezza Rice, Richard Cheney and other conservative former US administration officials who descended on the Caspian region after the collapse of the Soviet Union, Chevron announced that during the previous year it had begun to develop what it described as 'the massive Tengiz oilfield' in Kazakhstan, henceforth to be called the Tengizchevroil project. Total investment requirements were $20 billion over a forty-year period to develop a total oil reserve estimated at 6 to 9 billion barrels.[24] The impact of this acquisition upon Chevron's worldwide oil reserves was immediately apparent from then on. By the end of 1993, Chevron's proved oil reserves had recovered to 4,185 million barrels, almost entirely due to the reserves attributable to Chevron's 50 per cent share in the Tengiz field – 1,102 million barrels of oil. Thereafter, Chevron's worldwide oil reserves increased further to 4,343 million by the end of 1995, by which time the company had pumped some US$717 million into developing Tengiz.

ENTER THE 82ND AIRBORNE

According to a survey by UK petroleum consultancy Wood Mackenzie, the remaining proven plus probable oil and gas reserves of the Caspian Sea region, as of January 2002, were 39.4 billion barrels of liquids (crude, NGL and condensate) and 207 trillion cubic feet of gas – a combined total of 75.8 billion barrels of oil equivalent (boe).[25] Twenty private-sector oil companies controlled 60 per cent (45.5 billion boe) of this total.[26] Depending upon certain 'risk factors' – exploration outcomes, availability of transportation infrastructure, development delays etc. – by 2020, these twenty companies will have invested between $237 billion and $314 billion in the Caspian oil and gas fields.[27] Four US companies (ChevronTexaco, ExxonMobil, Phillips Petroleum and Unocal) had the largest 'national' share of private-sector reserves – 36 per cent (16.2 billion boe). Calculating on a simple pro-rata basis, the US share of total Caspian oil and gas investment would therefore be between $85 billion and $113 billion. By far the largest single private-sector holder of Caspian oil and gas reserves was

ChevronTexaco with 11 per cent of the total oil and gas reserves (8.4 billion boe)[28] and a putative investment requirement of between $26 billion and $35 billion over the lifetime of its production-sharing contracts.

Such an important investment by US oil companies required the assurance of US military support. So, on 15 September 1997, 500 US parachutists from the 82nd Airborne Division, with the highly decorated General John Sheehan making the first jump, floated down into the Tien Shan mountains of southern Kazakhstan. The operation was codenamed CENTRAZBAT 97 and was ostensibly carried out as an exercise in providing support to Kazakhstan in the event of an attack by 'renegade forces' bent on disrupting a 'regional peace agreement'.[29] The most remarkable thing about the exercise was that it began with what security expert Michael Klare has called, 'the longest airborne operation in human history', entailing a flight of some 7,700 miles from Fort Bragg, North Carolina to the drop zone in Southern Kazakhstan.[30]

Three months later, setting the seal on this kind of 'forward' energy and national security strategy, a National Defense Panel report to the Secretary of Defense, co-authored by Richard Armitage warned that the USA faced new dangers threatening America's hegemony in the new world order. The report argued that America's national security apparatus should actively plan for a future in which the USA 'moulds the international environment rather than merely responds to it'. Military planners should be prepared to 'project military power and conduct operations into areas where we may not have forward-deployed forces or forward bases'. In particular the USA would need to 'be involved in regions that control scarce natural resources', and singled out the critical importance of 'the Middle East and the emerging Caspian Sea areas...as we try to hedge our own and our allies' resource dependencies'. Indeed, America's need to access Gulf and Caspian Sea oil was considered 'critical to global economic stability'.[31]

As if to confirm this new 'forward' energy security policy, the following year a second CENTRAZBAT exercise was carried out involving the transportation of several hundred US troops from Fort Drum, New York, to Tashkent, capital of Uzbekistan. And, in 1999, the US Army Training and Doctrine Command devised an elaborate computer model of the Caspian Basin for use in testing possible scenarios for military intervention in the area.[32] America's message then, was clear – any threat to the interests of US oil companies in the Caspian would be met by rapid military intervention, unimpeded by the great distance of the region from the USA.

KHANS AND CORRUPTION

In describing the current geopolitics of the Caspian and Central Asian region it has become customary to make some reference to the 'Great Game' – the nineteenth-century struggle between Great Britain and Tsarist Russia for control of the Khanates, the independent Muslim states which dominated the area until the late 1880s, ruled by men like the Emir of Bokhara and the Khan of Kiva. Today, it would seem that the rulers of the former Soviet republics have turned themselves into latter-day khans, reminiscent of those earlier times. But while the 'Great Game' led inexorably to the subjugation of these hitherto independent Muslim rulers, this time around it would appear that it is the new khans and their families who are gaining the greatest advantage from the competition to control the region's resources.

Kazakhstan provides a suitable example. In the years shortly before the country's independence, a certain James Giffen, a New York investment banker and President of the Mercator Corporation, became the confidant of Kazakhstan's Soviet ruler and today's President, Nursultan Nazarbayev. After independence Nazarbayev, helped by Giffen, set about energetically privatising large swathes of the Kazakh economy, which soon fell into the hands of either family friends or foreigners. Nazarbayev's rule, described as 'somewhere between Franco and Chile' by one enthusiastic western businessman, has been accompanied by massive nepotism and corruption.[33] In 1993, Giffen acted as one of Nazarbayev's key advisers in shaping the contract whereby Chevron gained access to the Tengiz field.[34] According to a report by Seymour Hersh, the investigative journalist, Giffen subsequently received from Chevron a 'success fee' of 7.5 cents per barrel of oil attributable to Chevron's share of the Tengiz project.[35]

In the summer of 2000, the US Justice Department's Organized Crime and Racketeering Section began an investigation into Giffen's activities, after allegations were made that he passed on bribes from certain US oil companies to senior Kazakh officials adjudicating the allocation of oil contracts. The companies named were Mobil, Amoco (since merged with BP) and Phillips Petroleum. According to the Justice Department, payments totalling $115 million flowed from the accounts of these oil companies to a private account in New York held by a Swiss Bank by way of several offshore locations. Justice Department investigators claim that Giffen transferred about $60 million to Swiss bank accounts controlled by President Nazarbayev, a former prime minister Akezhan Kazhegeldin, and Nursultan Balgimbayev, then head of the state oil company.[36] Two federal grand juries began investigating the bribery accusation and another related claim involving illegal oil swaps in which Griffen was alleged to be involved.

On 14 September 2001, news of a Swiss Justice Department investigation into the 'Giffen affair' reached the press. Its initial conclusions were particularly compromising for Nazarbayev and a former director of Mobil, J. Bryan Williams III. But coming only a few days after the terrorist attacks of 11 September, the story was given very limited media coverage. Taking advantage of the new climate of fear in Washington, an American attorney hired by Kazakhstan wrote to the Deputy Attorney General asking him to intervene to stop the investigation into oil company bribery in Kazakhstan which was now demanding the surrender of key Kazakh documents. 'I am deeply concerned,' wrote Kazakhstan's attorney, 'that foreign relations between the United States and the Republic of Kazakhstan – an important ally in the war on terrorism with significant oil and gas reserves in an unstable geographical region – will deteriorate if prosecutors maintain their pursuit of the documents in Kazakhstan and continue to aggressively investigate Kazakh government officials.'[37] The implication that Kazakhstan might, in the future, be less than helpful to American commercial and 'national security' interests in Nazarbayev's fiefdom was barely concealed.

A month later, two of Nazarbayev's aides met with Vice President Cheney to try to enlist his help in releasing $120 million in Swiss bank accounts belonging to Nazarbayev and the other two Kazakh officials and their families, which had been frozen by the Swiss authorities at the urging of the Justice Department. Although Cheney instructed aides to discuss the matter with Justice Department officials, it was evidently concluded that nothing could be done to halt the investigation. However Nazarbayev's aides were successful in setting up a meeting in Washington with President Bush on 21 December 2001.[38]

The joint statement issued by Bush and Nazarbayev after this meeting suggests that, in spite of the contretemps over Giffen and the Swiss bank accounts, the USA and Kazakhstan were, if anything, now closer than ever. The statement was full of references to cooperation between their two countries in the 'war against terrorism', to their intentions to 'strengthen joint activity in ensuring security and stability in Central Asia', to 'enhancing assistance programs to Kazakhstan to strengthen border security' and to increasing the 'defensive capabilities of the Armed Forces'. The two leaders also pledged their dedication to strengthening 'the rule of law, [and] reducing corruption'.[39]

Meanwhile, although Giffen was subsequently arrested and charged with violation of the Foreign Corrupt Practises Act, and the former Mobil executive J. Bryan Williams pleaded guilty to a bribery-related tax offence, Nazarbayev continued to exercise his khan-like powers, with his daughter controlling the national TV network and his son-in-law deputy chairman of Kazmunaigaz, the integrated state oil and gas company. State revenues from the taxation of foreign oil companies were squandered on grandiose projects, in particular the movement of the country's capital from Almaty to Astana where more than a billion dollars were spent on new construction projects including $50 million on a new presidential palace and parliament building.[40]

Things were much the same in the other Caspian and Central Asian 'Khanates'. In Azerbaijan, where state corruption is reputedly of monumental proportions, the gap between rich and poor is on a Latin American scale. And, in 2003, an Aliyev dynasty was created as a dying Heydar Aliyev was succeeded by his son Ilham in a presidential election widely regarded as fraudulent. Similarly, in Turkmenistan, President-for-life and 'Head of all the Turkmen', Saparmurat Niyazov, is accused by opposition leaders of running the country as 'Niyazov's private company',[41] while in Uzbekistan the USA's ally in the 'war on terror', President Islam Karimov, heads a regime which is accused of torturing to death suspected Islamist rebels.[42]

The overall consequences of the USA's 'oil and security' policy towards the Caspian and Central Asia was clearly to the detriment of overall political and economic development. Oil company agreements and top-level US government contacts with state governments 'entrenched ageing regional leaders and helped to transform governments into corrupt oligarchies that have enriched themselves with wealth generated through control of energy resources and suppressed opposition'.[43] Indeed, after 11 September 2001, the corrupt oligarchies of the Caspian became America's regional allies in the war against terror and, in effect, were given a free hand to continue the despoliation of their people's wealth in the knowledge that the USA would turn a blind eye.

PIPELINE POLITICS

The joint statement from Bush and Nazarbayev after their meeting of 21 December 2001, also included a statement backing 'multiple pipelines' for Caspian oil exports. The two leaders affirmed their 'desire to strengthen our energy partnership to diversify export options for Kazakhstan's oil and gas and to diversify global energy supplies'. They shared the view that 'a key element of this effort is development of multiple pipelines that will ensure delivery of Caspian energy to world markets, unfettered by monopolies or constrained by geographic chokepoints.'[44] Bush then made explicit reference to what has been a consistent theme in America's Caspian oil strategy since January 1995. He expressed the two leaders' 'support for development of the Aktau–Baku–Tbilisi–Ceyhan oil export route'. This was the long-favoured East-West 1,750 km pipeline from

Azerbaijan through Georgia to Turkey and, although other oil pipeline options were now available, the one which was closest to the hearts of Washington's energy security strategists.[45]

The concept of a Baku–Tbilisi–Ceyhan (BTC) oil pipeline (with or without the link to Aktau in Kazakhstan) appears to have first emerged at a meeting between the Turkish President Suleiman Demirel and President Aliyev of Azerbaijan in October 1994, shortly after the signing of the 'Contract of the Century'. It is quite possible though that the original proposal was put forward by the US Government, for, certainly by January 1995, the USA was fully supporting the idea.[46]

For the Americans, the proposal had several merits. Firstly, it would be particularly beneficial to its NATO ally Turkey which would earn a considerable income from the fees charged for oil in transit. Turkey also had concerns about the alternatives to the BTC pipeline, some of which involved shipping oil from Russia's Black Sea port of Novorossiysk, across the Black Sea and through the narrow Bosporos, with all the environmental dangers to Turkey's coastline which that entailed. A second reason for supporting BTC was that the principal alternatives would go either through Russia or Iran. That some oil would have to flow through Russia to the Black Sea was acknowledged, but it was not considered desirable for Russia to be the only export route. As for Iran, even apart from America's visceral hatred of the Islamic regime dating from the humiliating hostage crisis of 1979–1980, an export route terminating in the Gulf seemed manifestly counter-productive from the traditional energy security perspective. Thirdly, the construction of the BTC, at a total project cost of $3.6 billion would offer lucrative contracts for US companies, opportunities which would be unlikely to materialise if alternative major pipelines were built through Russia or Iran. Fourthly, the port of Ceyhan on Turkey's Mediterranean coast would not only be a 'safe' outlet for western oil supplies, but it was only 483 km by sea from the Israeli port of Haifa, providing a 'bonus' of secure oil supplies to America's Middle East ally. Finally, a major energy infrastructure (a gas pipeline from the Azeri Shah Deniz field was also envisaged in the 'corridor') which bonded two, or possibly three, former Soviet republics to a NATO ally in the West was believed to offer a promising geo-strategic platform on which to build further economic and political linkages to the East, as and when this was considered appropriate, while at the same time frustrating any tendency of Russia and Iran to form a North-South economic and political axis.[47]

Consequently, on 29 October 1998, choreographed by Bill Richardson, Clinton's Energy Secretary, the leaders of Turkey, Georgia, Kazakhstan, and Uzbekistan met in Ankara and together with the USA itself signed a formal declaration pledging support for the BTC oil pipeline. At the same time the US export credit agencies Eximbank, OPIC and the Trade Development Agency, promised $827 million in loans for the project.[48]

The project was controversial from the beginning. The oil companies who would have to fund part of its construction, especially BP, complained that it would be far too expensive, and in this they were supported by a number of US oil and energy economists and even the conservative, free-market CATO Institute. Moreover, in the meantime, Chevron had begun producing oil from its giant Tengiz field and realised that for the foreseeable future, the only realistic transportation route for its oil was through Russia, whether the US Government liked it or not. The Russians therefore easily persuaded Chevron that the only way it would get its Tengiz oil to market was by investing with them in the Caspian Pipeline Consortium (CPC), a new 1,580-km pipeline from Kazakhstan to their Black Sea port of Novorossiysk. And there were other pipeline projects · on the drawing board. Since 1997, the Chinese had been negotiating with Kazakhstan to build a 3,200-km pipeline from Aktobe, where the China National Petroleum Corporation had taken a majority share in a medium-sized oilfield, to north-west China. Another project was being promoted by Unocal, from Turkmenistan through Afghanistan to Pakistan's port of Gwadar – the Central Asia Oil Pipeline Project (CAOPP). The CAOPP would track Unocal's planned gas pipeline to Pakistan, CENTGAS, for which agreement had already been reached with Turkmenistan, Pakistan and Afghanistan's Taliban rulers.[49] There were also a number of 'combined' oil export routes under consideration involving shipment from Supsa on the coast of Georgia across the Black Sea to Bulgaria and Greece, or perhaps to the Ukraine.[50]

Nevertheless, the Clinton Administration persevered. On 18 November 1999, the leaders of Azerbaijan, Turkey, Georgia, Turkmenistan and Kazakhstan formally agreed with the USA that BTC should be the 'Main Export Pipeline for Caspian Oil'.[51] Subsequently, in October 2000, a further agreement was signed, in Baku, to establish the initial corporate structure of BTC, with BP as the project operator, initially with 25.4% ownership, later increased to 34.76%.[52]

In spite of the fact that Cheney had previously shown himself to be sceptical about the economics of the BTC, the incoming Bush-Cheney Administration took up the promotion of the project with equal vigour to that of their predecessors. Other former sceptics like BP's CEO John Browne now also fell into line. It is unclear why Browne reversed his former position. Part of the explanation may be that the opportunities for various forms of government financial subsidy were now looking more promising (Browne had earlier commented that to be viable BTC needed at least $400 million of what he called 'free money'). It is also possible that one of the conditions for US government approval of BP's 1999 merger with Amoco was that BP 'came on board' the BTC project.

But if there were still any lingering doubts about BTC, the events of 11 September 2001 swept them aside. Now, almost overnight, the building of the BTC became a key national security issue. The East-West energy corridor of which BTC was the critical component, now meshed perfectly with plans to integrate the USA's Caucasian, Caspian and Central Asian dependencies into a military alliance in the war against terror. Early in October, Bush promised military assistance to Georgia through which the BTC pipeline was to pass and, the following November, ten UH-1H Huey helicopters were sent to Tbilisi. On 27 February 2002, Washington announced that it would provide Georgia with $64 million in military aid and send 180 military advisers to train 2,000 Georgian troops, ostensibly to combat suspected al-Qaeda forces in the wild Pankrisi Gorge area bordering Chechnya.[53] However, on the same day, a Georgian Defence Ministry official told Radio Free Europe that the USA would train their rapid reaction force which would be guarding strategic sites in Georgia 'particularly oil pipelines'.[54]

Following this, on 28 March, US Deputy Assistant Defense Secretary, Mira Ricardel, announced that the US would also be providing military aid to Azerbaijan's navy as part of a $4.4 million aid package 'to counter threats such as terrorism...and to develop trade and transport corridors'.[55] Meanwhile, all the Central Asian States were prevailed upon to provide overflight facilities and base areas for US and allied forces attacking Afghanistan and the USA now reversed an earlier decision that it would not intervene militarily to halt incursions by 'Islamic terrorists', such as the Islamic Movement of Uzbekistan.

Reinforcing a strategic energy alliance which had already taken shape with BP's support for the BTC pipeline, in April 2002 Bush played host to Prime Minister Tony Blair at his Texas ranch, where a so-called 'US-UK energy dialogue' was initiated. The two leaders agreed that they had 'similar political, economic, social and energy objectives' and that they had noted the 'huge energy potential of Russia, Central Asia and the Caspian'. Furthermore, henceforth the two countries would weave together the 'separate strands' of their countries' energy and foreign policies in a 'frank sharing of strategic analysis and assessments'.[56]

CASPIAN OIL: FROM EUPHORIA TO REALITY

In spite of all the continuing declarations of support for the 'strategic' BTC pipeline, the project remained hobbled by continuing doubts about its economic viability. The final financial underpinning of the pipeline had split the cost between the pipeline's equity investors (the oil companies) and debt financing from private and international financial institutions, in a 30–70 per cent ratio. But in December 2002, the project's backers were forced to delay construction for a further six months because, according to BP, its operator, there had been 'difficulties in satisfying the requirements of financial institutions'.[57]

But there was a more fundamental underlying problem. The BTC pipeline would need a throughput of one million barrels per day to provide even a modest return on its owners' investment. It was originally expected that further substantial oil reserves would be discovered in the southern Caspian which would help fill the pipeline: these have not materialised. Feeding oil from Kazakhstan's oilfields in the northern Caspian would require an underwater pipeline from Aktau to Baku, but the possibility of this being built is remote. In any case, recoverable oil reserves in the northern sector of the Caspian have been revised down. Geological peculiarities of local oil deposits have led the operating companies to suspect that the quantities of oil to be produced from Kazakh offshore blocks will be less than expected: recovery costs will be higher and required export capacities lower than previously estimated.[58]

In spite of these obvious problems, Bush's Administration, firmly backed by the UK Government, decided to press on with the BTC pipeline. Although financial assistance from the World Bank's International Finance Corporation (IFC) and the European Bank for Reconstruction and Development (EBRD) had not yet been agreed, construction of the pipeline began in April 2003. Five months later, the IFC and ERBD dutifully produced the required loans. On 4 November 2003, the IFC handed over $125 million for its own account and a further $125 million in commercial syndication; and a week later, the ERBD made its own contribution in a loan of $250 million. With the backing of the IFC and the EBRD, it was now confidently expected that additional private-sector loan capital would be forthcoming.

Although the go-ahead for the BTC pipeline was a major strategic victory for the USA, the most revealing indication that the Caspian and Central Asia could fall a long way short of being a 'new Middle East', is provided by an examination of the US Energy Information Agency's (EIA) published data on Caspian oil reserves. Comparing the figures published for the four years 1998, 2001, 2002 and 2003, we observe that the data for 'total' oil reserves have fluctuated as follows – 218 billion barrels in 1998, 262 billion in 2001, 243 billion in 2002, but down to 211 billion in 2003. And the figures for proven reserves – those whose existence is known with a probability of more than 90 per cent – have fluctuated even more. They were put at 32.5 billion barrels in 1998, but reduced to 25.8 billion in 2001, then down even further to 10 billion in 2002, but then reviving to 25 billion in 2003 – but still well down on the 1998 figure.[59] And, as if to underline the possibility that the Caspian 'riches' might prove disappointing, on 10 April 2002, Gian Maria Gros-Pietro, Chairman of Italy's major oil company ENI, the operating company heading the consortium developing the Kashagan oil project, stated that the Caspian contained only 7.8 billion barrels of recoverable oil.[60]

Production costs for Caspian oil further underline the extent to which the region falls far short of any Middle East comparison. The fully built-up cost of a Caspian barrel of oil – the cost of getting a barrel to market including all the development, transportation, operating and overhead costs has been estimated at between $12 and $15 per barrel.[61] This is about three to four times the cost of producing and delivering oil from Saudi Arabia or Iraq. Moreover, the petroleum fiscal regime in Kazakhstan is one of the toughest in the world: about four fifths of the net profit is taken by Nazarbayev's Government.

Back in 1998, it will be remembered, the EIA was forecasting an oil production figure for the Caspian of 4.5 million barrels per day by 2010, rising to around 5.8 million b/d in 2015. But by 2003, the figure for 2010 had been reduced to a mid-point estimate of 4 million b/d.[62] However, according to the UK oil consultancy Wood Mackenzie, on the basis of what they describe as a 'realistic projection' employing various risk factors, Caspian oil might reach a peak of around 2.5–2.8 million barrels per day by 2010–2015, and then decline.[63] Confirming the reservations of the Wood Mackenzie study, it was reported in August 2003 that the development of the Kashagan field in Kazakhstan, upon which great hopes had been placed, was now expected to be delayed by two years. The first oil would not flow until 2007 at the earliest, compared with the original target date of 2005.[64] Downward revisions of reserves and production forecasts, souring relations between the oil companies and the Kazakhstan regime, high production costs and (in Kazakhstan) tough taxation – any idea that the Caspian would become a 'new Middle East' was now evaporating. At the most it might, for just a few years, produce only as much as the United Arab Emirates.

By late 2002, the hopes which the previous Administration and Cheney's energy policy report had done so much to cultivate – that the Caspian and Central Asia would make a major contribution to enhancing America's energy security – were clearly fading. Central Asia and the Caspian would still require American supervision because even modest amounts of additional oil would be helpful; and the War on Terror still required a US commitment to the region. But Bush, Rice and Cheney must have been increasingly inclined to agree with the advice from Energy Security Analysis Inc. (ESAI) of Boston: 'The trouble with diversifying outside the Middle East', ESAI told Reuters in September 2002, 'is that it is not where the oil is. One of the best things for our supply security would be to liberate Iraq.'[65]

9   America the Motorised

The car is the greatest modern symbol of American freedom ... cars are a powerful symbol of what makes America the greatest, and the freest, country in the World.

John Bragg, Center for the Moral Defense of Capitalism, 2001

While the developments in the world oil industry, described in the preceding chapters, were taking place, the economy of the USA experienced major changes. Between 1970 and 2000, the catalyst of the cold-war armaments and space race led to the birth of the computer industries and the so-called 'knowledge economy'. Older companies, like IBM, transformed themselves into new providers of desktop computers; new companies, like Microsoft, grew from humble beginnings to become mega-corporations; and California's Silicon Valley came to epitomise the 'asset-light, knowledge-heavy' world of information and telecommunications technology.

And yet the most remarkable aspect of this thirty-year period of economic transformation was the extent to which it left the cars-plus-oil economic base still broadly intact. Indeed, between 1991 and 1999, while public attention was focused on the rapid expansion of the 'new economy', US production of 'light' motor vehicles increased by a remarkable 48 per cent.[1]

In 1997, with the information technology and telecommunications boom in full spate, the three companies at the top of *Fortune Magazine*'s 500 largest US Corporations were still General Motors, Ford Motor Company and Exxon.[2] In 1999, the USA produced 13 million motor vehicles, a record production level which beat the previous record set in 1978 and comfortably exceeded the 9.9

million production level of its nearest rival, Japan.[3] According to a study carried out by the University of Michigan and commissioned by the Alliance of Automobile Manufacturers, 'The automotive industry is the largest manufacturing industry in the United States. No other single industry is linked to as much of US manufacturing or generates as much retail business and employment.'[4] The study was able to demonstrate 'the high level of indirect employment in the private non-manufacturing sector that is linked to automotive manufacturing', and cited 'business and professional services, wholesale trade, trucking, and finance' as examples of sectoral employment which is 'more linked to the supplier network for automotive manufacturing than is often recognised'.[5] It concluded that, when allowance is made for all the private-sector industrial and non-industrial (service) activities which provide inputs to the core motor manufacturing sector, and when the impact of the expenditure of automotive industry-generated incomes on other non-automotive sectors is taken into account, the total employment created was 6.6 million.[6]

Another report by the US National Research Council in 2003 stated that one in every six workers in the USA 'deals in some way with automobiles and trucks – making them, driving them professionally, insuring them, licensing them, and building and maintaining highways for them'.[7] It also argued that, 'The impact of the automotive industry on society is unlike that of any other industry. The automobile is not just a technology or mode of transportation; it is a fundamental determinant of the entire economy.'[8]

The extent to which the automotive industry has remained extremely important to the US economy can also be gauged by what happened between 1999 and 2002. As the millennium drew to a close, the hectic pace of the IT and telecommunications boom, and the general explosion of stock market prices which accompanied it, stalled and then began to collapse. It was then that the importance of the automotive industry once again became apparent. By reducing interests rates on vehicle finance deals – to zero in many cases – the automotive industry was able to sustain and even increase US consumer spending, with all the multiplier effects which have been described above.[9] US sales of motor vehicles in 1999, which at 17.4 million were already at record levels, continued to increase: to 17.8 million in 2000, remaining at slightly below that level (17.7 million) in 2001.[10]

Of course, the American car industry has itself changed since the early 1970s. About a third of light vehicles purchased in the USA are now produced by a foreign manufacturer, either directly imported or manufactured in a foreign-owned US branch plant. Competition is fierce and the profitability of car making has plummeted: General Motors now makes more money from finance than from manufacturing. However, in spite of the fact that imports of vehicles from Japan, Germany and South Korea rose substantially during the 1990s, on balance, these developments did not prevent the continued growth of the domestic US automobile industry, as we have observed.

WOULD JESUS DRIVE AN SUV?

However, one particular change in the US motor vehicle industry has also had important implications for the growth in US oil consumption. The share of 'light trucks' in total light vehicle sales – including the fashionable sports utility vehicle (SUV) category – has grown rapidly since the 1980s. In 2000, for the first time, US sales of 'light trucks' exceeded sales of standard automobiles.[11] SUVs and other types of light truck have lower fuel economy standards than automobiles. Until a very modest increase introduced in an April 2003 rulemaking decision by the National Highway Traffic and Safety Administration (NHTSA), an average fuel economy of 20.7 miles per US gallon was permitted for light trucks compared with 27.5 mpg for automobiles.[12] However, SUVs provide higher profit margins to both manufacturers and dealers than standard automobiles. For this reason, the corporate strategy of the so-called 'Big Three' of US motor vehicle manufacturing – General Motors, Ford and Chrysler (now Daimler-Chrysler) – has been to increase the share of light trucks in their total light vehicle output. Between 1985 and 2001, this share increased from 27 per cent to 63 per cent. In other words, the traditional core of the US motor vehicle industry has come to concentrate on the part of the market which contributes disproportionately to the USA's petroleum deficit.

In the aftermath of the 11 September terrorist attacks, the link between SUVs and America's dependence upon 'Arab oil', together with the vehicle's contribution to environmental pollution, led some Americans to begin to question the growing popularity of the SUV. In November 2002, General Motors' HQ was the scene of a lively demonstration by bishops, Jewish activists and evangelical Christians, who appealed to the company to 'take up the moral challenge' of building fewer of the gas-guzzling vehicles. One group of campaigners, the Evangelical Environmental Network based in Pennsylvania, launched their own TV advertising campaign against the SUV, asking, 'What would Jesus drive?'[13] The campaign's leader, the Revd Jim Ball, argued that vehicle pollution was having a damaging impact upon God's creation. 'We are spreading the word that to love our neighbours and care for creation, automakers and politicians need to build cars that reflect our moral values.' Other campaigners underlined the link between the SUV and rapidly growing oil imports from countries which they saw as harbouring terrorists.

However, Ball's message was rejected by other US evangelicals, many of whom are enthusiastic SUV drivers. The Revd Pat Robertson condemned the anti-SUV campaigners: 'I think the concept of linking Jesus to an anti-SUV campaign borders on blasphemy, and I regard it as a joke,' he declared. Joining the fray, the Sports Utility Vehicle Owners of America published a full page advert in USA Today, featuring an individual of Hispanic origin called Jesus Rivera standing proudly in front of his SUV and declaiming that *this* Jesus certainly loved his SUV. In similar vein, a spokesperson for the Alliance of Automobile Manufacturers, proclaimed that Jesus 'may well choose an SUV so that several of his apostles could travel with him'.[14]

AVERAGE AMERICANS AND THEIR CARS

Let us now pay a brief visit to Mr and Mrs Average America and their almost totally motorised way of life at the beginning of the twenty-first century. Together with their teenage daughter, the 'AAs' lived in the suburbs of a large US city. Since they were the average American household they owned two cars and, as such, they belonged to the 38.6 per cent of America's 104,700,000 households who did so, a proportion which had increased from 34 per cent in 1980.[15] However, since they would shortly be purchasing a car for their 16-year-old daughter, the AAs would soon stop being 'average' and form part of the 18.3 per cent of US households who owned three cars, a proportion which had increased from 17.5 per cent in 1980. Once acquired, their daughter's new car would be just one more to add to the 215,580,000 registered vehicles (cars, trucks and buses) owned by US drivers, a number which had increased from 155,796,000 in 1980.

In 2000, Mr and Mrs AA decided to take advantage of the low interest finance deals on offer to replace Mr AA's existing car and to buy a vehicle for Mrs AA. Both the AAs were working and between them they travelled 6,492 vehicle-miles to and from their places of employment each year. However this was only 26 per cent of the total 24,800 vehicle-miles per year which their family travelled, including shopping, family visits, holidays etc.

Mr AA had recently considered joining the 5.2 per cent of US employees who used the public transport system to travel to work (a proportion which had fallen from 6.4 per cent in 1980), but since the time spent travelling would have been about 42 minutes as opposed to the 20 minutes average by car, he had abandoned this idea. When told that in Western Europe 20 per cent of employees travel to work by public transport, Mr AA imagined it was because they are not wealthy enough to own a car. Mrs AA was previously one of the 11.2 per cent of US employees who got a lift to work with a friend (a proportion which had fallen from 19.7 per cent in 1980), but now that she could afford to have one she was going to purchase a car of her own.

Both the AAs liked the idea of supporting domestic manufacturing so they both bought Fords. Mr AA purchased a Ford Taurus sedan with a 3-litre, 6-cylinder engine, a city fuel economy of 20 miles-per-US-gallon and a highway mpg of 27. For Mrs AA they purchased a Ford Explorer sports utility vehicle (SUV) with a 4-litre, 6-cylinder engine, a city mpg of 14 and a highway mpg of 19. When answering a customer survey a couple of years previously, they were among the 50 per cent of consumers who said they were considering buying a SUV for their next vehicle purchase.[16] They were also among the 30 per cent of consumers who said that safety was the most important attribute when purchasing a new vehicle. The AAs were *not* among the mere 11 per cent of consumers who gave 'fuel economy' as their chief vehicle attribute preference. Their newly purchased SUV was just one of the 9.1 million 'light trucks' (SUVs, campers and pick-ups) sold in 2000 which, for the first time, outsold the number of standard automobiles purchased (8.9 million).[17] Light trucks had been steadily gaining market share since the early 1980s, when the minivan was introduced, but now SUVs were not only replacing cars but over the past few years were replacing other kinds of light truck as well.

The AAs prefer to drive large, powerful vehicles. In 2000, only 24.4 per cent out of a total of 17 million vehicles purchased were small cars, a proportion which had fallen from 38.5 per cent in 1991 and from 41 per cent in 1981. Indeed, according to AutoPacific, a California-based car industry consultancy, in a recent survey only 7 per cent of new-vehicle buyers said they would consider a small car for their next vehicle purchase.[18] Large sedans and SUVs are preferred because not only are they more spacious and comfortable than small cars but, in the opinion of most Americans, they are also safer. Sharing this belief, Mr AA is now trying to persuade his 16-year-old daughter against having a small car. She says she would like a little Chevrolet Cavalier but he'd rather put the same $10,000 to $12,000 into a three-year-old Mercury Grand Marquis, mainly for safety reasons.

His thoughts on this matter were strongly influenced by an article he read in the 2 July 1999 edition of *USA Today* called 'Death by the gallon'. Written by James Healey, the news magazine's motoring correspondent, the article claimed that the introduction of fuel economy standards for new vehicles in the aftermath of the 1973 oil crisis had caused thousands of deaths. In an analysis of crash data since 1975, when the Energy Policy and Conservation Act was passed, *USA Today*'s correspondent calculated that '46,000 people have died in crashes they would have survived in bigger, heavier cars.' Although the average miles per gallon of vehicles on US roads was now 20 mpg as compared with 14 mpg in 1975, the cost of this reduction 'has been roughly 7,700 deaths for every mile per gallon gained'. Small cars, it was claimed – those no bigger or heavier than Chevrolet Cavalier or Dodge Neon – comprised 18 per cent of all vehicles on the road yet they accounted for 37 per cent of vehicle deaths in 1997 – 12,144 people. 'That's about twice the death rate in big cars such as Dodge Intrepid, Chevrolet Impala, Ford Crown Victoria.' Healey supported this argument by quoting Mr Brian O'Neill, President of the Insurance Institute for Highway Safety, who says, 'We have a small-car problem. If you want to solve the safety puzzle, get rid of small cars.'[19]

Bill Lovejoy, General Motors group vice-president, clinched it for Mr AA when he said, 'When my kids were coming of age, I made sure they had big cars to drive. It's physics. When a large car meets a small car in an accident, the large car wins.'[20]

FUEL ECONOMY DECLINES, BUT SO DO MOTORING COSTS

The Corporate Average Fuel Economy (CAFE) standards introduced in 1975 required the average fuel economy of all new cars sold by a US car manufacturer to be at least 27.5 mpg: that is some of their cars could be above that as long as others are below. Automobile makers who fall short are fined. However, as we have already noted, until very recently (April 2003), new 'light trucks' were only required to have a fuel economy of 20.7 mpg. SUVs with their lower average fuel economy are classed as light trucks, not passenger cars, a loophole in the law which American lovers of big engines and big cars have been able to exploit. Even so, the CAFE standards have been under constant attack by US motor-industry executives and free-market ideologues, who reject what they see as government interference in business decisions and consumer choice. CAFE has been 'a bad mistake, one really bad mistake. It didn't meet any of the goals, it distorted the hell out of the new car market,' said Jim Johnston, fellow at the American Enterprise Institute and retired General Motors president who lobbied against the 1975 law.[21]

For many Americans, driving large cars is a basic right. Attempts to impose higher CAFE standards for SUVs have become the object of vitriolic attack by organisations like the Cato Institute, the Competitive Enterprise Institute and the Centre for the Moral Defence of Capitalism. John Bragg, a policy analyst with the last-named centre, pokes fun at the environmentalists' attack on SUVs asking, 'Why would anyone build these horrible engines of death?' answering 'They build them because SUVs have advantages in safety, cargo space and power that Americans demand.' According to Bragg, 'The minivan and the SUV gave America the powerful, spacious vehicles that they had demanded before regulations – they were our reply to Washington's attempts to force everyone into smaller cars.'[22]

Mr AA agrees; and he also agrees with the editorial he has read in his copy of the *Wall Street Journal*, that 'CAFE standards were the environmental lobby's attempt in the 1970s to force "gas-guzzling" Americans to abandon cars that were comfortable and safe in favour of motorised tin cans.' Americans responded 'by ignoring cars and buying SUVs'.[23]

Because of the growing popularity of SUVs and other light trucks, the average fuel economy of new light vehicles actually fell during the 1990s. Between 1973 and 1987 it improved from 14 mpg to 26.2 mpg as a result of the introduction of the CAFE standards. Since then, the fuel economy of new automobiles and light trucks remained more or less constant. But because light trucks increased their market share at the expense of standard automobiles, the fuel economy of the average light vehicle sold fell from 26.2 in 1987 to 24.7 mpg in 2000.[24]

Mr and Mrs AA spend 17.4 per cent of their family budget on motor vehicle transportation (capital as well as running costs), approximately the same as for an average European family. It is the second largest item of expenditure after housing. Their 'freedom' to drive cars and SUVs which are considerably larger and more powerful than European cars is therefore contingent upon the 'affordability' of the vehicles purchased and the availability of cheap fuel. Although the average real price of a new automobile increased between 1990 and 1999, from $19,753 to $21,420, the average rate of interest charged in car finance deals fell from 12.15 per cent to 7.96 per cent. Since wages and salaries also increased between 1990 and 1999, the Automobile Affordability Index (AAI), which expresses the full cost of an average automobile, including finance charges, in terms of weeks of salary, fell – from 29.4 weeks in 1990 to 23.8 weeks in 1999. Indeed, in 1999 the AAI was almost the same as it was in 1979 (23 weeks).

US gasoline prices are lower than in any other developed industrialised country and in 2000 were at about the same level as those in China ($1.47 in the USA, $1.44 in China). In fact, a gallon cost less than a large bottle of mineral water ($1.90).[25] After allowing for inflation, the 'real' price of a gallon of US gasoline in 2001 was only 3.6 per cent higher than in 1978 and between 1991 and 1999 it was substantially below the 1978 real price.[26]

The huge difference in price between the USA and the other industrialised countries is primarily due to the low level of tax on gasoline. In 1999 tax accounted for 33 per cent of the US price, whereas in Canada it was 49 per cent, Japan 59 per cent and the UK 76 per cent. Roughly the same differences also apply in the case of diesel fuel.[27] This difference in taxation also has an important implication. The lower proportion of tax in the final price of gasoline at the filling station in the USA means that the contribution of crude oil cost to the final price is proportionately larger. In turn, this means that the final price is more highly geared to the crude price in the USA than in other, more highly taxed countries. In this sense US motorists are more exposed to the vagaries of the world oil market than elsewhere and in such a highly motorised society they are especially sensitive to the fluctuations in the gasoline price which accompany those in the crude oil price. Furthermore, according to the president of the National Petrochemical and Refiners' Association, 'The gasoline price in America is probably the best known single price for any product or commodity because it is in on almost every street corner.'[28] It is also, therefore a highly 'political' price and although a higher gasoline tax would probably dampen its future volatility for the reasons explained above, proposing such a tax increase is a guaranteed vote-loser for most US politicians.

BUSH, ENERGY AND THE ENVIRONMENT

The USA is responsible for 44 per cent of all the energy-related carbon dioxide emissions from the industrialised, OECD nations.[29] Although Bush on the campaign trail had seemed to offer a constructive and even-handed approach to the thorny question of American compliance with the Kyoto protocols which limited worldwide emissions of carbon dioxide and other greenhouse gases, three months into his presidency, Bush swiftly abandoned his earlier position and in a letter replying to a group of senators vociferously opposed to Kyoto, he announced that 'he would oppose Kyoto because it exempted 80 per cent of the world, including China and India, and it was an unfair and ineffective means of addressing global climate change concerns.'[30] In the opinion of Paul O'Neil, then Bush's Treasury Secretary, Bush's decision showed all the signs of manipulation by Cheney, master of the political puppeteer's craft.[31] Bush's rejection of Kyoto won widespread approval from the large oil, gas and coal companies but it also reflected the reality of motorised America as a whole.

The combustion of motor gasoline in an internal combustion engine involves a reaction between the hydrocarbons in the fuel and oxygen, with vaporised water, carbon dioxide and heat energy being the products of combustion. For example, in the case of Pentane, one of the ingredients in petrol, about 3 kilograms of CO_2 are released for every kilogram of pentane consumed. One litre of pentane weighs about two thirds of a kilogram so an automobile releases 2 kilograms of CO_2 for every litre of motor fuel used. Now let us refer back to Mrs AA and her new Ford Explorer, who we met earlier in this chapter. The average fuel efficiency of her new vehicle is about 16.5 miles per US gallon (or 4.36 miles per litre). So if she travels an average of 10,000 miles per year her vehicle consumes 2,294 litres of fuel and releases over four and half tonnes of carbon dioxide into the atmosphere. In other words, to significantly reduce carbon dioxide emissions Bush would have had to clamp down not only on his corporate energy industry backers but on the motorised lifestyle of millions of ordinary Americans, a lifestyle which, as we have already noted, epitomises the very values of individualism and 'freedom' so lauded by conservative America and its political representatives.

However Bush did have one card to play in the environmental politics game. 'Today I am proposing $1.2 billion in research funding so that America can lead the world in developing clean, hydrogen-powered automobiles.' With these words, Bush's January 2003 State of the Union Address sought to portray his Administration as simultaneously pro-environment and 'doing something' about increasing dependence on foreign oil. According to some of the Administration's supporters this new apparent commitment to a non-gasoline automobile engine 'undermines the argument that Team Bush is the captive of oil interests'.[32] In fact the so-called 'FreedomCAR and Fuel Initiative', which would hand over $1.7 billion of US taxpayers' money to corporate America over a five-year period, did nothing of the sort. The prospect of a commercially viable fuel-cell-powered automobile is certainly one of the more remote alternative technologies currently under consideration. Currently hydrogen is four times as expensive to produce as gasoline and fuel cells are ten times more expensive than internal combustion engines. Even if research were to reduce these costs to equivalence with the conventional auto engine the problem of the slow market penetration rate (owing to the length of time owners retain their current vehicles) would place significant oil savings and environmental improvements decades ahead. This problem is compounded by the fact that Bush's programme lacks any mechanism to hold the automobile industry accountable for converting theoretical plans into real vehicles, or any economic or social mechanism to ensure a transition away from current gasoline-based technology.

'The president's announcement is encouraging,' said Ed Murphy, general manager of refining and marketing with the American Petroleum Institute, adding that, 'fuel cells are an exciting new technology that could figure prominently in America's energy future.' Energy *future* indeed. In the interim any serious attempt to deal with America's current problem of gas-guzzling, such as a really significant tightening of mandatory car manufacturers' average fuel efficiency standards, could be conveniently shelved. Indeed, the US environmental campaign group, the Natural Resources Defense Council, compared the oil savings from what they describe as an 'optimistic' fuel-cell engine scenario (100,000 fuel-cell vehicles per year by 2010 and 2.5 million by 2020) with their own fuel economy proposal (an average mandatory vehicle fuel consumption of 40 mpg by 2012 and 55 mpg by 2020), showing that potential oil savings between now and 2020 from their own programme are almost 25 times greater than those from the introduction of fuel-cell vehicles. Even in 2030, when fuel-cell vehicles would be more prevalent, savings from fuel-economy improvements would still be five times as great.[33] Far from indicating a new 'greener', less 'oily' Bush, the FreedomCAR and Fuel Initiative confirmed him as resolute friend of the oil industry and a generous contributor to US corporate welfare.

AMERICA'S MOTOR FUEL REQUIREMENTS 1999–2050

Let us return to Mr and Mrs Average America and multiply our data for this 'sample' household by all 104,700,000 US households to reach a figure for America's total motor fuel requirements. We know that the annual vehicle-miles travelled for a three-person household like the AA's is 24,800 miles. We will assume that the average fuel economy for both the AA's vehicles taken together and combining both city and highway use, is around 20 mpg; so the total volume of gasoline consumed by the AAs each year is 1,240 US gallons. On this basis, the total motor-vehicle fuel consumption of all US households would be 129,828 million gallons. Since there are 42 gallons to a barrel, we can calculate that US households consume 3,091 million barrels of transportation fuel per year, or 8.5 million barrels per day.[34]

Of course, this calculation is based on the assumption that the average fuel economy of all light vehicles on US roads today is the same as the combined average fuel economy of the AA household's two vehicles. It could be different: on the one hand, the total stock of cars is older than the AA's vehicles (which will therefore lower the average mpg); on the other hand, the total stock of light vehicles will also be considerably less 'weighted' by the presence of SUVs (which will therefore raise the average mpg). In fact, these factors appear to cancel each other out. The actual fuel economy of the average US light vehicle is indeed, 20 mpg, so our calculation of 8.5 million barrels per day for total US light vehicle fuel can stand. It is still an estimate, but one which compares quite well with the US Bureau of Transportation Statistics own figure of 8.2 million barrels per day.

To this we must add the motor fuel consumed by America's heavy trucks – those used for commercial road transport. The USA has 7,858,000 registered heavy trucks of which 2,154,000 are long-haul, so-called 'combination' trucks capable of pulling heavy trailers. In addition there are around 750,000 buses of different types. Heavy trucks and buses consume around 36,300 million gallons per year (2.4 million barrels of fuel per day). Adding the fuel consumption of heavy trucks and buses to the fuel consumed by light vehicles gives us a total motor-fuel consumption of 10.6 million barrels per day. To put this figure into perspective, it is roughly equivalent to the total daily petroleum consumption of South America, Africa and the former Soviet Union combined.

Looking to the future, the US Department of Energy's Energy Information Agency (EIA) forecasts that America's total oil requirements will continue to rise to around 26.7 million b/d in 2020, compared to 19.5 million b/d in 1999, an increase of 37 per cent. Demand for all transportation fuels will rise by over 40 per cent between 1999 and 2020.[35] Indeed, by 2020, demand for fuel from the transportation sector of the US economy alone (19.22 million b/d) will be about the same as the *total* US demand for petroleum in 1999 and most of this increase will be the due to higher demand from America's cars and trucks.

Looking even further into the future, the Department of Energy's Office of Transportation Technologies (OTT) examined a number of different scenarios for US transportation fuel demand until the year 2050. The 'base case' presented by the study is that total US petroleum demand increases from 19.5 million barrels per day in 1999 to 44 million b/d in 2050 and transportation demand increases to 30 million b/d, of which 21 million b/d is consumed by light and heavy highway vehicles.[36] This 'base case' assumes that light vehicle fuel economy does not improve over the next fifty years, because the increase in the oil price over this period would be modest. At the same time, the study notes that, by 2050, 'oil is assumed to be virtually 100 per cent imported.'[37]

In alternative scenarios, where different kinds of technological improvement (hybrid electric vehicles, fuel-cell-powered vehicles etc.) are factored in, there remains the problem that such technologies take a very long time to diffuse throughout the national vehicle stock. Due to relatively slow replacement rates, the inertia in the current stock of vehicles results in a substantial delay between the initial deployment in the market and realisation of the petroleum-saving benefits. For example, if the advanced vehicles followed a ten-year market penetration curve starting at 10 per cent of the market in 2001 and reaching 100 per cent by 2010, the on-road fuel economy of the stock would not double until about 2030. With a more realistic twenty-year penetration of the market, the stock fuel economy takes 38 years to double.

The intention of the OTT study was to show how essentially unrealistic is the 'base case' once two further constraints are added to the argument – the growing oil demand from the developing world and the possibility that conventional world oil production will peak around 2020. While the second of these two 'constraints' is arguably too pessimistic (see Chapter Ten), the OTT's concern that America would become increasingly vulnerable to oil price shocks unless measures are swiftly introduced to reduce highway consumption of petroleum was convincing. Their policy conclusion was that the government should be more prescriptive and interventionist in changing the public's existing preference for petroleum-fuelled motorisation. The OTT concluded that, to ensure an orderly transition from conventional fuels and stagnant fuel economy to new fuels and a more efficient fleet, there was a strong need for new policies 'at least some of which are likely to meet resistance from the general public and/or the auto industry'.[38] To date neither the auto industry nor the general public have anything to fear on this score.

FREEDOM'S JUGGERNAUT

At the end of Chapter One, we referred to the American motor vehicle as a 'juggernaut' – the ancient Hindu religious idol carried in procession by a huge wheeled vehicle under which the devotees of Krishna were supposed to throw themselves in adoring ecstasy. The religious metaphor may seem exaggerated, but it is nevertheless important to recognise the key ideological function which the automobile plays in the American value system. According to the Michigan University study of the US automotive industry to which we have already referred: 'Automobility facilitates individual determination, individual freedom of movement, self-directedness, privacy, choice of destination arrival time, and control over immediate environment. To many, automobility is the core of individualism in America.'[39] Indeed, in the words of the conservative policy analyst John Bragg: 'The car is the greatest modern symbol of American freedom… cars are a powerful symbol of what makes America the greatest, and the freest, country in the World.'[40]

Sentiments such as these formed part of the ideological bedrock of that small group of men and women who took control of the USA on 12 December

2000.[41] This new right-wing Republican Administration – an alliance between the corporate oil and energy interest represented by the 'Axis of Oil' and a group of extreme Reaganite ideologues dubbed 'neo-conservatives' by the media – would not fail to take whatever action was deemed necessary to safeguard America's completely motorised way of life. But as the new millennium dawned, and America's dependence on oil imports from the Gulf reached a new all-time high, there were grave warnings of an impending energy crisis of unprecedented severity; and although there were different views as to the precise nature of that crisis – as we shall see in the next chapter – there was general agreement among the different expert bodies of opinion that such a crisis was fast approaching.

10 The Looming Crisis

Oil is the lifeblood of America's Economy.

US Department of Energy website, 2001

In their relentless drive for energy security, and determination to protect 'the American Way', US leaders and legislators have an important resource at their disposal. With an annual budget of $75 million and over 600 highly educated and experienced full- and part-time functionaries, the US Department of Energy's Energy Information Administration (EIA) is undoubtedly the world's best source of statistical energy-related information. Since its creation in 1977, it has published thousands of detailed reports, analyses and forecasts to guide US policy-makers and corporate executives as they pursue the related objectives of secure energy supplies and profitable business opportunities.

On his arrival at the Department of Energy in January 2001, Bush's Energy Secretary, Spencer Abraham, would have been given an overview of the 'state of the Nation's energy' using the forecasts and analyses prepared for the latest versions of the EIA's *Annual* and *International, Energy Outlooks*, due to be published a few months later. For example, from the *Annual Energy Outlook* for 2001, he would have been able to see that over the next twenty years the USA's total energy consumption, already by far the highest in the world, was forecast to go on steadily rising, until by 2020 it would be nearly a third greater than in 1999.[1] And with respect to oil, the energy source which the website of Abraham's Department now proclaimed to be 'the lifeblood of the US Economy', the *Outlook* saw consumption rising from 19.4 million barrels per day in 1999 to around 26 million b/d in 2020.

At the same time, Abraham would have been able to observe the negative side of America's soaring energy consumption – a corresponding increase in

133

carbon dioxide emissions from 1,511 million metric tonnes of carbon equivalent in 1999 to 2,041 million by 2020. However, this would not have appeared unduly troublesome to a politician who had previously led the fight in the Senate against higher fuel-efficiency standards, who had campaigned vociferously in favour of drilling for oil in the Arctic National Wildlife Refuge and who was the third largest recipient of funding by oil and gas companies during the 2000 election cycle, receiving over a quarter of a million dollars from companies including Chevron, El Paso Energy, Coastal Corporation and Michigan Petroleum.[2] Not surprisingly, the environmental group Friends of the Earth denounced him as 'a big buddy of Big Oil'.[3]

Although, clearly an associate member of the 'Axis of Oil', Energy Secretary Abraham was also one of a group of right-wing Republicans who, for a number of years, had clustered around the mercurial figure of William Kristol. In 1990, Abraham had become deputy to Kristol who was then Vice President Dan Quayle's Chief of Staff. While Abraham was, by all accounts, something of a 'back-room boy', Kristol was an ideologically driven political activist who led the 'Project for the Republican Future', where he helped shape the strategy that produced the 1994 Republican congressional victory. After taking over the editorship of the influential journal *The Weekly Standard* the following year, Kristol was soon to become one of the leading neo-conservative propagandists, described by the website of the US Department of State as 'widely recognized as one of the nation's leading political analysts and commentators'.[4] According to the *Washington Post*, Energy Secretary Abraham was an 'acolyte' of Kristol, like many of the individuals who dominated the Bush Jr Administration.[5]

CHINA CHOOSES TO MOTORISE

Let us now return to the EIA's projections for future oil consumption and some numbers which might have caused Energy Secretary Abraham some cause for concern. For it was not only US consumption of oil that the EIA predicted would increase. The EIA was also forecasting that world oil consumption as a whole would increase, from 74.9 million barrels per day in 1999 to 119.6 million b/d in 2020, of which America would consume around 22 per cent,[6] At the same time, however, rising demand from the developing world would outpace the rich industrialised countries, and in the lead would be the People's Republic of China. Indeed, China would not only overtake Japan to become the world's second largest oil consumer in 2002 but would also more than double its oil consumption between 1999 and 2020, from 4.3 million b/d to 10 million b/d.

One of the main reasons for this was that China, with a population of 1.3 billion, was following the USA and the rest of the industrialised world down the primrose path of mass motorisation.

According to one expert on Chinese energy matters, the Chinese Government had faced the choice of whether to invest heavily in urban public transport systems or to encourage private car ownership since the late 1980s and 'with few exceptions central and city governments have taken the latter approach.'[7] In the new atmosphere of capitalist individualism encouraged by the post-Mao communist party leadership, there was certainly 'no talk of formulating a coherent policy to constrain private car ownership and thus oil imports.'[8] Indeed, private car ownership was soon to become official policy. In its eighth national five-year plan (1991–1995) the Chinese Government designated the automotive industry as a 'pillar industry' of the national economy.

In 1996, the country still only had 10 million motor vehicles (about 8 per thousand population) of which a mere 3.9 million were cars, all of which were produced by joint ventures with foreign companies. However, at the turn of the twenty-first century the Chinese Government took a further crucial decision – the country would restructure its fragmented national vehicle manufacturing industry into just two or three major enterprises with one key objective – the design, development and production of a Chinese family car at a price that would encourage mass ownership.[9] Commenting on the implications of this, Zhai Guangming, the retired director of the state-run China National Petroleum Corporation (CNPC) observed, 'If all our bicycles turn into our cars, that's a horrible figure...It would scare the world.'[10]

From the early 1990s, China's economy was booming, with annual increases in GDP of between 9 and 10 per cent. The official Chinese objective was for GDP to quadruple between 2001 and 2020, a compound growth rate of 7.2 per cent per year, and this was 'eminently achievable' according to the *Financial Times'* chief economics correspondent, Martin Wolf.[11] At the same time China was controlling its population growth so that GDP per head was rising rapidly, albeit with its distribution becoming more unequal. The Chinese vehicle market was experiencing a commensurately hectic growth. In 2002, a record 1.2 million passenger vehicles were sold in China of which General Motors sold 264,371. In 2003, Chinese car sales were 40 per cent higher than the previous year.[12] According to Rick Wagoner, General Motor's Chairman and Chief Executive, China is the world's fastest-growing car market. 'China is on course to become the world's third largest car market this year, surpassing Germany and eventually passing Japan as number two.'[13]

Chinese experts have predicted that the country's stock of automobiles will increase from 3.9 million in 1996 to 11.4 million by 2010 and to 28.5 million in

2020. Total motor vehicles would increase from 10 million in 1996 to 36 million in 2010 and to 77.8 million in 2020.[14] In other words within a mere 17 years, China would have as many motor vehicles on the road as the USA had in 1961. Indeed, some western sources expect China's motorisation rate to be much higher. According to a recent article in the *Wall Street Journal*, 'In the next decade, the number of cars on Chinese roads is expected to grow five-fold to 100 million, approaching half of the US total.'[15]

Meanwhile China was embarking on a massive programme of road construction to cope with the expected surge in car ownership. Between 1991 and 2001, the total length of China's expressway system increased from 552 km to 19,453 km, making the country second in the world, after Canada, in expressway length.[16] A trans-provincial expressway system comprising five major north-south roads and seven east-west roads was now under development, expected to take 30 years to complete. It will eventually comprise a 35,000 km network of major roads, linking Beijing with the capitals of all the other provincial capitals and autonomous regions. It will connect all large cities with a population of over one million inhabitants and 93 per cent of cities with a population of over 500,000. In total, the project will involve 200 cities covering a population of 600 million accounting for about half China's population. By the end of 2001, construction of the network was well under way with 21,576 km of national trunk roads completed, of which 13,533 km were expressways. Particular attention was being given to highway construction in the previously isolated western regions. In the major cities too, the construction of expressways was racing ahead, barely keeping up with the growth in traffic. Beijing had 300 km of expressways and plans to build two major ring-roads and eight radial expressways before 2005.[17] According to one recent western visitor to the city, it already 'feels like Los Angeles'.[18]

Needless to say, this had major implications for China's fuel consumption. In 2001, the EIA forecast that world demand for transportation-related oil would increase from 37.8 million b/d to 67.5 million b/d, an annual increase rate of 2.8 per cent. But China would easily outpace this rate of increase, with consumption of transportation oil surging from 1.5 million b/d in 1999 to 5.7 million b/d in 2020, an annual increase rate of 6.7 per cent. This means that two thirds of the expected increase in China's total oil consumption between 1999 and 2020 will be in the transportation sector whose share in total oil consumption will rise from a third in 1999 to just over half in 2020.[19] Already, according to a recent study, 'the rapid growth in the vehicle sector is the primary force driving China's rapid shift from being a net petroleum-exporting country to a net importer.'[20] In fact, China became a net importer of oil in 1993 and is expected to overtake Japan during the next decade as the world's second largest oil importer after the

USA.[21] Moreover, most of China's oil import requirements will be sourced from the Gulf: the 2002 version of the EIA's *International Energy Outlook* predicted that Gulf oil exports to China would rise from 0.7 million b/d in 2000 to 7.1 million b/d in 2020.[22]

The growing importance of China in world oil markets was also underlined by Lee Raymond, ExxonMobil's Chief Executive Officer, according to whom, 'The centre of gravity of our industry is inexorably moving to the Far East.' He added that the steady increase in demand from China, which will outstrip the rising production from international oil companies and non-OPEC producers, 'will put the Middle East in an even more dominant market position in supplying energy needs, and that has very, very significant geopolitical ramifications'.[23]

Like America, therefore, China was having to think seriously about the problem of the security of oil supplies. One strategic response was to make large investments via its state-owned oil companies in foreign oilfields – in Kazakhstan, Peru, Venezuela and Sudan. In 1997, China signed an agreement with Iraq to develop the Al Ahdab field and also began establishing closer relations with Saudi Arabia, raising the possibility that, 'Saudi Arabia could possibly begin looking to the Chinese for those economic, security and political needs it now garners from the US.'[24] So by the beginning of the twenty-first century one thing was becoming clear: China, too, wanted oil – and with the billions of dollars it was earning from its soaring manufacturing export trade it had the cash to pay for it.

'A CRISIS COULD ERUPT AT ANY TIME'

On 19 March 2001, Energy Secretary Abraham addressed a conference sponsored by the US Chamber of Commerce convened shortly before the special energy task force assembled by Vice President Dick Cheney was to make recommendations to President George W. Bush. Abraham warned that the USA was facing the most serious energy shortages since the 1970s. 'Without a solution…the energy crisis will threaten prosperity and national security and change the way Americans live.'[25]

One month later, in an independent report entitled *Strategic Energy Policy Challenges for the 21st Century*, the prestigious US Council on Foreign Relations and the James Baker III Institute for Public Policy came to an identical conclusion.[26] The executive summary of their report began in almost apocalyptic language:

> As the 21st century opens, the energy sector is in critical condition. A crisis
> could erupt at any time from a number of factors and would inevitably affect

every country in today's globalised world...it is clear that energy disruptions could have a potentially enormous impact on the US and the world economy, and would affect US national security and foreign policy in dramatic ways.[27]

The report made it clear that the most serious threat came from the oil sector:

Th world is currently precariously close to utilising all of its available global oil production capacity, raising the chances of an oil-supply crisis with more substantial consequences than seen in three decades.[28]

Meanwhile, the EIA was forecasting, in its '2001 reference case', that total world oil demand would grow at an annual rate of 2.25 per cent between 1999 and 2020. This was sharply up on the historical rate of increase during the preceding thirty years (1.6 per cent) and reflected the new demands upon world oil supplies from developing countries like China and India where motorisation programmes were rapidly taking off. America's own voracious appetite for oil was forecast to increase from 19.4 million b/d in 1999 to 26 million b/d in 2020, with its oil imports rising from 10.9 million b/d to 17.4 million b/d. The question many were now asking was 'Would there be enough oil to go around?'

A WORLD RUNNING OUT OF OIL?

Some authorities were now pointing to an imminent decline in world oil production resulting from what we might crudely term a 'geological shortage'. The idea is based partly on probability theory and the observation that since the geological conditions required for the formation of very large oil deposits are quite rare, it is probable that most of these have now been discovered and put into development. Consequently, as only smaller and smaller fields are discovered, there comes a point where the total oil resource base will no longer support the continuing rise in annual oil production that has characterised most of recent history. The geologists and economists who support this theory employ the 'Hubbert Peak' model which we briefly described in Chapter Six. The crucial conclusion of the theory, it will be remembered, is that oil production follows a bell-shaped pattern of increase and decline and the year of peak oil production occurs where approximately half of the original endowment of oil has been extracted.

These 'geological shortage' theorists (who, for convenience, we shall now refer to as the 'pessimists') argue as follows. If we assume that the original amount of world oil in place in the earth's crust – the amount before extraction began in 1859 – is around 6,000 billion barrels, then the maximum amount of oil recoverable from this original quantity is around 1,800–2000 billion barrels (between 30 and 33 per cent). The rest may never be recovered for technological and economic reasons. Thus if world oil consumption rises at about 2 per cent per year, the rate generally assumed by such authorities such the EIA, we will very soon have consumed half the world's oil resources at which point (the top of the bell-shaped curve) a decline in annual production and consumption must set in.[29]

For example, in 1998, the geologists Colin Campbell and Jean Laherrere forecast that the peak of world conventional oil supplies would be reached in the year 2004.[30] Similarly, the American geologist Kenneth Deffeyes argued that world production of conventional oil would peak about the year 2005. 'I'm not betting the farm that the actual year is 2005 and not 2003 or 2006,' he said; but he added, 'There is nothing plausible that could postpone the peak until 2009.'[31] R.W. Bentley, who heads an inter-disciplinary team of researchers at the UK's Reading University and at the London-based Oil Depletion Analysis Centre, placed the peak a little later, but nevertheless concluded that a date falling between 2010 and 2015 'looks pretty solid'.

If this theory is correct, especially the more pessimistic assessments of Campbell, Laherrere and Deffeyes, then the implications for the geopolitics of oil would be dramatic. Indeed, writing in early 2001, Deffeyes warned that:

> No initiative put in place starting today can have a substantial effect on the peak production year. No Caspian Sea exploration, no drilling in the South China Sea, no SUV replacements, no renewable energy projects can be brought on at a sufficient rate to avoid a bidding war for the remaining oil. At least let's hope that the war is waged with cash instead of with nuclear warheads.[32]

The EIA itself took a more relaxed view of this so-called depletion problem. In a discussion of the issue in 2002, it put the ultimately recoverable resource base at 3,003 billion barrels, basing this on a report from the US Geological Survey two years earlier. From this starting point, the EIA calculated that the year of peak world oil production – about 150 million barrels per day – would not arrive until the year 2037.[33] However, not everyone in the US Department of Energy agreed with the EIA's date for peak world oil production. The US Department of Energy's Office of Transportation Technologies (OTT), whose report of May 2001 adopted a slightly different methodology, saw world oil supplies peaking between 2016 and 2020 while demand for transportation oil continued to grow exponentially. Indeed, the bulk of their report was focused on the implications of this emerging 'oil gap' for US drivers.[34]

The 'geological shortage' theory is very plausible to those who genuinely fear that the modern industrial way of life is not sustainable.[35] Indeed, the idea that the world is shortly to face an insurmountable 'energy gap' arising from a physical shortage of oil, with all that that portends for the 'American way', was used by one British journalist to explain the Bush Administration's invasion of Iraq.[36] However, there are many oil experts – economists, geographers and geologists – who strongly disagree with the general theory and some even with the relatively optimistic version used by the US Geological Survey and the EIA.

The opponents of the 'geological shortage' theory, the 'optimists', bring some fairly powerful arguments into play. Firstly, they point out that some of the most vociferous pessimists have made predictions about the imminent peak before – and got it wrong.[37] Secondly, they underline the difficulty in correctly estimating the portion of the original world endowment of oil resources which is recoverable: an essential starting point if mathematical modelling is to correctly predict the year of peak world oil production. The 'optimists' argue that technology is constantly increasing that recoverable portion. This is called 'reserves revaluation'. For example, the oil expert Peter Odell pointed out that since 1970 over 1,200 billion barrels of oil have been added to the category of proven recoverable reserves and in only four individual years have additions to proven reserves been less than the volumes of oil extracted. More importantly, since 1970, 'the continuing upward revaluation of discovered reserves from known fields has been the more important component in enhancing reserves – compared to new discoveries.'[38] For example, what Odell called a 'backcast' from the year 1996 of the oil reserves declared available in the year 1955, shows that the original 1955 reserves figure has since been augmented by 105 per cent.

Thirdly, the optimists point out that there are large areas of the world where, for political or other reasons, oil exploration has barely begun.[39] The problem is that the pessimists frequently ignore these other impeding factors, and therefore ignore what might be achieved once these non-geological constraints are removed. As Michael Lynch has pointed out, 'forecasting oil supply is exceedingly difficult… geology, to the extent that it is known, only partly explains production trends… fiscal regimes, local infrastructure, and many other seemingly unrelated factors can also modify the underlying trends in exploration, discoveries and reserves.'[40]

This argument between the optimists and the pessimists is by no means settled and it is only fair to point out that the pessimists have their own replies to some of the optimists' criticisms.[41] Nevertheless, at the time of writing there appears scant evidence of any rapidly approaching 'geological' oil shortage. So was there any need for the incoming Bush Administration to worry about the availability of oil supplies and the threat, in Abraham's words, to 'prosperity and national security' and to 'the way Americans live'? Yes, for there was a threat – not, in fact, the threat of a geological oil shortage, but a grave threat just the same.

WHERE IS THE OIL GOING TO COME FROM?

Satisfied, for its part, that the world was nowhere near the much-feared peak of production, but having forecast that global demand for oil would increase rapidly between 1999 and 2020, the EIA had to work out exactly where the additional oil supplies were going to come from. Using their extensive and detailed database of oil industry information for the non-OPEC countries outside the former Soviet Union (FSSU), and assuming that the oil price would remain around $22–23 per barrel in real terms over the next two decades, they predicted that oil supplies from these non-OPEC, non-FSSU countries would rise from 37 million barrels per day to 45.2 million b/d. In the case of the former Soviet Union, there was much more uncertainty but the EIA took an optimistic view, forecasting that this region would increase output from 7.6 million b/d to 14.8 million b/d. So they believed total non-OPEC output would increase from 44.6 million b/d in 1999 to 60 million b/d in 2020.

That left 59.3 million b/d for OPEC to produce in order to meet the forecast world consumption level of 119.3 million b/d. Estimates about the probable contribution of the OPEC countries outside the Gulf totalled 17.8 million b/d, which left the Gulf OPEC producers having to account for the remaining 41.5 million b/d of forecast world demand in 2020. In other words, to meet the projected world oil demand by 2020 without a significant increase in oil prices, the Gulf OPEC producers – Saudi Arabia, Kuwait, Iraq, Iran, Qatar and the Emirates – were going to have to increase their production by a massive 108 per cent.

These assumptions appear even more demanding if we focus our attention on world oil trade (imports and exports) rather than on consumption and production. To meet the rapidly growing import requirements of the oil-consuming world, the EIA calculated that Venezuela and the former Soviet Union would expand their exports by 2.5 and 3.7 million b/d respectively between 2000 and 2020, increases which, for reasons explained in previous chapters, will probably turn out to be over-optimistic. OPEC members Nigeria, Libya and Algeria were to contribute an additional 2.3 million b/d, while Mexico and other non-OPEC producers were expected to account for an extra 2.1 million b/d. But the EIA believed that the oil exports of Indonesia and the North Sea would actually decline. This left the Gulf's oil exports having to increase by a remarkable 126 per cent (from 14.8 million b/d in 2000 to 33.5 million b/d in 2020), which would also involve the Gulf's share of world exports rising from 35 per cent to 47 per cent.[42] Needless to say, such staggering increases would require massive investments in additional oil-producing capacity in the Gulf states.

Indeed, according to the International Energy Agency (IEA), the body set up during the 1970s to further the interests of the oil-consuming Organisation of Economic Cooperation and Development (OECD), securing the required world oil supplies until 2030, would require $22 billion of investment in the Middle East every year for the next 28 years.[43] According to the IEA/OECD, these investment funds would have to come from the multinational oil companies. But why should the Gulf states go along with these plans? This thought appears to have occurred to the EIA, since it mentions, in passing, that, 'Some analysts suggest that OPEC might pursue significant price escalation through conservative capacity expansion decisions rather than undertake ambitious production expansion programs.'[44]

In fact, the International Energy Agency was already extremely concerned that the Gulf States, who have almost entirely excluded foreign oil companies from their upstream operations since the 1970s, might continue to do so. Its reaction was to lecture the Gulf states about the error of their ways. The IEA's Director General, Claude Mandil, told them, 'There is a very strong message to governments, a wake-up call,' and informed the governments of the Gulf states that they would have to 'pay attention to how to attract investment to energy. They have to ensure private equity will be happy to invest.'[45]

So, for the Gulf states, the issue was now clear. They had to allow the return of the multinational oil companies whose operations they had nationalised in the 1970s and to incentivise this return they should offer these companies highly attractive fiscal terms which would permit them to make the kind of profits they had made in earlier times. In return for these concessions, the oil companies and the governments of the rich oil-consuming nations would generously allow the Gulf states to deplete their oil reserves as quickly as possible.

That this was not a terribly attractive deal was recognised not only by the Gulf states themselves, but also by the American energy economist Dermot Gately, who argued that large oil-producing capacity expansions in the Gulf were implausible because they relied on supply behaviour by Gulf producers that was not in their own self-interest.[46] OPEC, and the Gulf OPEC members in particular, would receive higher total oil revenues by stabilising production capacity and enjoying higher prices than by opening the doors to foreign capital and maximising production. Moreover, as we shall explain in Chapter Eleven, by the mid-1990s there were other, religious and ideological considerations which the rulers of the Gulf states were having to confront, which certainly weighed heavily against any rapid depletion of their reserves in the interests of non-Muslim oil consumers.

Touching on these and other related concerns, the Saudi-born energy economist A.F. Alhajji drew a similar conclusion in an article in the July 2001 edition of *World Oil*. Asking the question, 'Will Gulf states double their collective oil capacity by 2020?' his answer was a resounding 'no'. This would require a capital investment programme of at least $100 billion. But Gulf states could not afford such a high level of investment. The EIA had realised this fact and suggested that these states embrace foreign investment. But in Alhajji's view, 'given various scenarios of Gulf geopolitics and economics, foreign investment in the oil sector will NOT take place in the next two decades – it just doesn't make sense.'[47] And according to Alhajji, the consequences of this failure to expand Gulf oil producing capacity were clear: if the EIA's demand projections were accurate – 'a crisis appears to be imminent'.

That there was nothing preordained about the Gulf states opening-up their oil industries to foreign investment was also recognised in the April 2001 report of the US Council for Foreign Relations, from which we have already quoted. It was now absolutely imperative, in the opinion of the Council, to ensure that 'political factors' do not 'block the development of new oil fields in the Gulf'. Therefore, the Department of State, together with the National Security Council, the Department of Energy, and the Department of Commerce should 'develop a strategic plan to encourage reopening to foreign investment in the important states of the Middle East Gulf.'[48]

But the Council also clearly recognised how difficult this was going to be and acknowledged that, 'while there is no question that this investment is vitally important to US interests, there is strong opposition to any such opening among key segments of the Saudi and Kuwaiti populations.'[49]

So the world now faced an immensely daunting energy future. Firstly, a motorisation-driven addiction to oil spreading like a pernicious virus to virtually every nation, rich or poor, with the USA and China in the lead. Secondly, American demands for pre-emption rights over an annual increment each year of around 110 million barrels coupled with Chinese claims for its own almost identical yearly increment of 106 million barrels. Meanwhile, the rest of the world would be ratcheting up its own consumption by a total of 561 million barrels per year. As for the available supply, on extremely optimistic assumptions, non-Gulf producers would be able to add about 413 million barrels of production each year leaving the remaining 364 million barrels of annual production increase to come from the Gulf itself. Yet all the evidence to date showed that oil-producing capacity in the Gulf was stagnating, if not actually declining. According to the EIA's own data, the total oil-producing capacity of the Gulf states in 1999 was 24 million b/d. In 2000, it was estimated to be 21.7 million and while it was believed to have recovered somewhat to 22.4 million b/d in 2001, by 2002 it was still put at 22.3 million b/d.[50] Hardly reassuring figures for those who expected

Gulf oil-producing capacity to reach 30.3 million b/d by 2010 and 44.5 million b/d by 2020.[51]

This then was the real threat to America's energy security. Not a world running out of oil, but a group of oil-producing states which, for a variety of reasons, were unwilling or unable to provide America, or the rest of the world for that matter, with an exponentially increasing supply to match their increasing demand. And if the Gulf refused to open up to western oil companies and continued to produce at around its current capacity, then the scene was set for a strategic contest between the major powers to 'lock-in' their desired share of supplies by fair means or foul.

In fact this was already happening, and Asia was already winning. According to the energy economist and former Shell executive Paul Tempest, China and other Asian states have made bilateral agreements with oil producers in the Gulf involving long-term trading, financing and economic cooperation arrangements and contracts 'which deliberately isolate them from the open market. The multinational oil companies and other carriers would not, therefore, be able to divert their cargoes to the West, whatever the price offered by the United States and Europe.'[52] But this in turn would put incredible demands on the oil producers outside the Gulf, leading inevitably to an oil-price explosion like that anticipated by the US Council on Foreign Relations, or perhaps much worse.

Meanwhile, there were those among Spencer Abraham's colleagues – those acolytes of Mr Kristol – who were already anticipating a major intensification of strategic rivalry between America and China, with all that that might imply for the struggle for oil supplies.

THE NEOCON PROJECT

In 1997, Kristol and Robert Kagan, a Reagan-era State Department official who had supported the Nicaraguan Contras, co-founded the 'Project for the New American Century', which was to become the intellectual launch pad for the 2000 Bush presidential campaign. In addition to Kristol and Kagan, the signatories of the Project's 'Statement of Principles' included future key members of George W. Bush's Administration – Dick Cheney, Donald Rumsfeld, Paul Wolfowitz, I. Lewis Libby, Elliott Abrams, Dov Zakheim, and Zalmay Khalilzad, along with Bush Jr's brother Jeb and a selection of conservative notables from the Nixon and Reagan eras. Prominent among these was Lewis E. Lehrman, a wealthy investment banker and sponsor of right-wing causes who had been an investor in George W. Bush's oil company Arbusto Energy during the early 1980s. This group also included Norman Podhoretz, a senior fellow with the neo-conservative Hudson Institute and former editor of the right-wing journal *Commentary*, which had advocated seizing the Gulf oilfields during the 1970s.

The essence of the Project was to 'rally support for American global leadership' by returning to a 'Reaganite policy of military strength and moral clarity'.[53] Its *magnum opus* was a manifesto published in 2000, and entitled *Rebuilding America's Defenses*. Its participating authors included Kristol, Robert Kagan and future administration officials Paul Wolfowitz, Dov Zakheim and I. Lewis Libby.[54] The report built upon the national defence and security strategy which had been outlined by Cheney's Defense Department in the waning days of the Bush Sr Administration and which had provided a blueprint for maintaining America's world dominance.

Rebuilding America's Defenses called for a significant increase in spending on the military to enable it 'to fight and decisively win multiple, simultaneous major theater wars',[55] while garrisoning the world's 'critical regions'. With regard to the latter objective, the report criticised the 'fiction' of the Clinton Administration that 'the operations of American forces in the Persian Gulf are merely temporary duties,' since nearly a decade after the Gulf War, US forces continued to protect what the report described as 'enduring American interests in the region'.[56]

While *Rebuilding America's Defenses* was primarily concerned with presenting the case for greater US spending on the armed forces, as part of its supporting argument its authors brought their attention to bear upon China, now unexpectedly metamorphosing into what could become America's major industrial rival and its potential future enemy. *Rebuilding America's Defenses* is replete with warnings of the threat posed by China to American interests. Indeed, with the exception of the Middle East, no other world region gets as much attention as China and its frequently used synonym, 'East Asia'. According to the report, there are 'increasing worries about the rise of China'. Since the end of the cold war with the Soviet Union, the new 'focus of strategic competition' has shifted from Europe to 'East Asia'. China is now a 'potential rival' for the USA. The USA must be prepared for what the report calls 'constabulary duties' in East Asia. East Asia is now a 'vital region'. A variety of new potential challenges can be detected, 'the Chinese military in particular', and 'the rise of Chinese military power' is of great concern. There is clear evidence of a 'Chinese challenge to American regional leadership' in Southeast Asia. The US Navy must be configured to meet 'the gradual shift in the focus of American strategic concerns towards East Asia' and the Marine Corp must 'turn its focus on the requirements for operations in East Asia' since China is now a 'potential adversary'.

However, the right-wing geo-strategists of the Project anticipated that relations with China would at worst be just another cold war. But something a little hotter was envisaged in the Middle East. In an 'Open Letter to the President' published on 19 February 1998, ten of the original signatories of the Project, and nine individuals who would later become officials of George W. Bush's Administration (John Bolton, Douglas Feith, Richard Perle, Elliott Abrams, Zalmay Khalilzad, Donald Rumsfeld, Paul Wolfowitz and Dov Zakheim), together with 24 former government officials, military men and academics, called upon President Clinton to launch a nine-point strategy to bring down Saddam Hussein and his regime. While ostensibly based on an 'insurrection' led by Ahmad Chalabi's Iraqi National Congress, the strategy called for the direct intervention of US ground troops 'to protect and assist the anti-Saddam forces'.[57]

The US Administration formed in January 2001 was firmly under the control of the Project's participants. Some of its members accepted the label of 'neo-conservatives' and others did not, but for practical purposes the distinction was soon to become meaningless.[58] Vice President Dick Cheney, the lynchpin of the Axis of Oil and a politician originally viewed as an 'assertive nationalist' rather than a neocon, was backed up by I. Lewis Libby as his Chief of Staff; Donald Rumsfeld as Secretary of Defense was flanked by Paul Wolfowitz as his Deputy and Douglas Feith as Under Secretary for Policy, both neocons closely associated with the far-right of Israeli politics.[59] Similarly, Dov Zakheim was appointed Under-Secretary in the Department of Defense and Pentagon Comptroller and Richard Perle, appointed to the Chair of the Defense Policy Board at the Pentagon, was, in effect, another key member of the Administration. Other leading lights in the Project, Elliott Abrams and Zalmay Khalilzad were ensconced in the National Security Council.

US OIL COMPANIES LOOK ABROAD – IN FRUSTRATION

Among the many energy-related issues which confronted the new Administration, some of which we have already referred to in previous chapters, there was one which was largely unknown and invisible to the general public. As we observed in Chapter One, the expulsion of the major US oil companies from the Middle East during the 1970s had compelled them to retrench in their home territory and other 'safe' oil provinces. But, by the 1990s, the increasingly poor prospects for finding sizeable new oil reserves in the USA was forcing its oil companies to look abroad once again. Cheney's energy policy report had continued to advocate the established strategy of seeking out new opportunities of US oil companies outside the Gulf, ostensibly for energy security reasons. But as we saw in chapters Six, Seven and Eight, progress on this front had been far from satisfactory. True, there had been some useful reserve acquisitions in Canada and in West Africa,[60] but the North Sea had failed to offer them any new large oilfield discoveries for several years. US oil companies had been unable to break into Mexico; their brief entry into Venezuela had been checked; the Southern Caspian sea had proved disappointingly short of oil and the Northern Caspian costly, heavily taxed and as yet, accessible only via Russian pipelines. In Russia itself, Putin's government, pressured by public opinion, was beginning to make threatening moves against the country's private-sector oil barons and creating anxiety among potential foreign investors in Russian oilfields. Even in America itself, Alaska's Wildlife Refuge was still off-limits and, in any case, might also prove to be too expensive to develop, unless oil prices remained so high that they were themselves damaging to the US economy. Indeed, in recognition of these difficulties, Cheney's energy policy report had rather inconsistently also included the recommendation that the Administration should support 'initiatives by Saudi Arabia, Kuwait, Algeria, Qatar, the UAE and other suppliers to open up areas of their energy sectors to foreign investment'.

But herein lay the strategic problem for the US oil companies and the government which so closely represented their interests. What small 'initiatives' had so far been taken by the countries to which Cheney's report referred had been almost entirely related to gas rather than oil and, by 2001, even these looked like being reversed. But as we have already emphasised, by far the most profitable oil reserves, the world's remaining giant and super-giant fields both developed and undeveloped, are in the Gulf. Both capital and operating costs for the Gulf are a fraction of those in the 'mature' oil producing regions like the USA, North Sea, Canada and Indonesia. According to the EIA, the average capital cost of bringing into production a medium-sized oilfield (50–200 million barrels) in the typical geological 'plays' of the Gulf is $2,784 per daily barrel of production capacity and the operating cost is a mere dollar per barrel.[61] In comparison, a medium-sized field in Alaska would have capital and operating costs at least four times as high.[62]

Not surprisingly therefore, in a speech in California in 1998, Kenneth Derr, Chief Executive of ChevronTexaco stated, 'Iraq possesses huge reserves of oil and gas – reserves I'd love Chevron to have access to,'[63] and a few years later, Archie Dunham, Chairman of the newly merged US oil multinational ConocoPhillips, was echoing these words.[64] But unfortunately for the US oil majors – not to mention a growing number of larger US independents which were also moving abroad in search of higher profits – Saudi Arabia and Kuwait, were stubbornly refusing to give them access to their upstream oil resources while Iraq and Iran were completely off-limits to US companies for political reasons.

Yet there was a further twist to this tale of frustrated oil-industry objectives. In Iraq, with oil reserves which potentially might rival even the hydrocarbon riches of Saudi Arabia, a crafty Saddam Hussein was beginning to offer some of the choicest oil prospects to non-US oil companies. According to the US Department of Energy, prior to the invasion of Iraq, 'the country reportedly had signed several multi-billion dollar deals with foreign oil companies mainly from China, France and Russia.'[65] As we noted earlier, in 1997 Iraq had signed a contract with the Chinese for the development of the al-Ahdab field; in the same year a contract had also been signed for the development of the giant West Qurna field with the Russian oil company Lukoil; other companies – Australia's BHP, Italy's ENI/AGIP, Spain's Repsol, a consortium involving Shell, Malaysia's Petronas and Canada's CanOxy and many others – were all showing keen interest in developing or redeveloping a considerable number of Iraqi fields.[66]

These developments must have infuriated Cheney and his oil-industry colleagues. Here were America's 'strategic rivals' unscrupulously stealing a march on America's own oil companies: something had to be done. That the Administration took these developments extremely seriously is revealed by an intriguing passage in Ron Suskind's account of Paul O'Neill's days in the Administration. O'Neill is said to have had sight of 'documents... being prepared by the Defense Intelligence Agency, Rumsfeld's intelligence arm, mapping Iraq's oilfields and exploration areas.' One document was apparently headed 'Foreign suitors for Iraqi Oilfield Contracts' and listed companies from thirty countries including France, Germany and Russia.[67] An attached document had maps of Iraq with markings for 'supergiant oilfield', 'other oilfield' and a field 'earmarked for production sharing'. But then, rather oddly, O'Neill (or perhaps Suskind himself) refers to these oilfields as being identified for development by these 'foreign suitors' *after* the US invasion and the intelligence agency's comments as referring to 'plans for how the world's second largest oil reserve might be divided up among the world's contractors', once the USA was in control.[68]

But none of this makes any sense at all. Why on earth should the US Administration have wanted to hand out Iraq's oil riches to companies from Russia, Germany and France? It seems fairly obvious that the reason why the Defense Intelligence Agency was so interested in this subject was because the 'foreign suitors for Iraqi oil' they referred to were *already* paying court to Saddam Hussein and indeed had already done deals such as the one for the field 'earmarked for production sharing'.

While the incursions of America's strategic rivals into the oilfields of Iraq were being so assiduously studied, Cheney remained deeply concerned about the USA's precarious dependence on foreign oil. Indeed, it seems that he was even coming round to the idea that the country might have to reactivate a major programme of nuclear power.[69] He must have recognised, however, that even if it became possible to overcome the lingering fears of Americans for an energy technology which had produced the near-disaster of Three Mile Island it would be many years before such an oil-saving energy programme could be implemented. In the meantime, according to the US Council on Foreign Relations and various independent energy experts, America was now under threat from a widening gap between world oil demand and available supplies which could cause a severe increase in the price of oil. So what might that mean for the US economy and for an Administration which itself was closely identified with the oil industry?

THE ECONOMIC IMPACT OF AN OIL-PRICE CRISIS

In 1996, the US General Accounting Office (GAO) commissioned a panel of expert energy economists to quantify the benefits to the US economy of continuing to import large quantities of 'cheap' foreign oil ('cheap' compared to the high marginal cost of domestic alternatives) and compare these benefits with the costs of occasional, though severe, supply disruptions and the attendant oil-price crises.[70] The GAO's experts made their own calculations as to the benefits of oil imports but with respect to the economic damage caused by oil-price shocks they referred to existing studies on this topic. One such study cited calculated that the 1973–1974 oil shock cost the developed oil-consuming countries 2.9 per cent of their combined GDP. Another estimated that a similar oil shock would mean a loss of $209 billion to the US economy in a 'shock year'. However, the GAO economists reasoned that 'because shocks do not occur every year, the annual cost, averaged over time, would be smaller.'[71] They also referred to a third study carried out in 1993, which had estimated that oil shocks may have cost the US economy $73 billion per year on average, between 1972 and 1991.

As far as future oil shocks were concerned, the GAO cited a 1990 study which had estimated that three hypothetical oil shocks between then and 2020 might cost the USA about $22 billion per year on average. On the basis of this evidence, and especially the last-mentioned study, the GAO economists concluded that by most estimates, 'the day-to-day benefits for the United States of relying on low-cost foreign oil substantially exceed the occasional, but severe, costs of disruptions to the world oil supply.'[72]

In October 1996, after studying the GAO's report, Mark Chupka, the Department of Energy's Assistant Secretary for Policy, wrote to the GAO stating that, 'in our view the analysis that motivates your conclusion regarding the benefits of imported oil is seriously flawed.'[73] He added that, 'the attempted comparison between the economic benefits of imported oil and the potential economic costs of vulnerability to oil shocks yields no insight into the overall consequences of imports,' and that 'we strongly disagree with the GAO analysis and observations GAO draws from it.' In the more detailed critique of the GAO report which accompanied Chupka's letter, the Department of Energy singled out what it considered the 'unlikely scenarios' which it had used.

In May 2000, economists at the Department of Energy's Oak Ridge National Laboratory carried out their own study of the costs of foreign oil dependence, focusing on the damaging consequences of long-term oil dependence rather than simply on the effect of occasional price shocks. In this study, the 'reference case' was one where the USA purchased all of its oil requirements at a free-market price, estimated at between at between $10.85 and $11.27 per barrel. In addition to calculating the loss of potential GDP and GDP adjustment losses they also included the cost of the wealth transfer between the USA and the oil-exporting countries when the former pays higher than free-market prices to the latter. On this basis, the Oak Ridge Laboratory calculated that between 1970 and 2000 the costs to the US economy had totalled around $3.5 trillion, or $113 billion per year on average.[74]

However, it is doubtful whether this new research by the Department of Energy's own economists would have made much impression on the GAO's panel of experts. For example, Douglas Bohi, one of the GAO's experts argued elsewhere that the economic damage caused by oil-price shocks cannot be very serious because the oil cost share of GDP was now only about 3 per cent. So even an economic loss of $113 billion per year is a only small fraction of total US GDP per year ($9,825 billion in 2000).

PANIC!

Yet Americans did worry about dependence on oil imports and their vulnerability to oil shocks – and for a very good reason. The economic damage caused by such shocks – regardless of the figure put upon them – is not thinly spread across the whole US economy, as comparisons made with the total GDP figure suggest. In fact, the damage would be almost entirely concentrated in just one sector of the economy – motor-vehicle transportation, the sector where currently there were absolutely no substitutes for petroleum fuel and none likely for many years to come. Indeed, because motor-vehicle transportation plays such a critical role in the life of almost all American citizens, the damage would be as much social and political as 'economic', as we may observe by recalling the history of previous major oil shocks.

Writing in 1965, the historian of the US automobile industry, John Rae, observed that 'For good or ill, the contemporary American metropolis is now so constituted that it could not live, if movement by motor vehicle were to cease for any reason whatsoever.'[75] Twenty-five years later, this point was echoed by Michael Prowse, the *Financial Times'* US correspondent, who pointed out that while in Britain or Germany it was still possible to walk the streets in search of shops or amusement, 'In the urban sprawl of much of the US the pedestrian is helpless…Outside frequently rundown city centres there is virtually no public transport. A car – and cheap petrol – is thus a prerequisite for functioning as a normal consumer, if not as a normal human being.'[76]

In the oil shocks of 1973 and 1979, the American metropolis did indeed, come perilously close to paralysis. Suddenly Americans realised precisely how dependent they were on an uninterrupted flow of motor gasoline. The pattern was at first one of rapidly rising prices. In December 1973, with 5 million barrels per day of Arab oil withdrawn from the world market, gasoline prices soared by 40 per cent. As Daniel Yergin describes it, the effect on the public was dramatic because 'no other price change has such visible, immediate and visceral effects as that of gasoline.'[77] The next stage was real, physical shortage culminating in the 'gas lines' – angry Americans actually reduced to queuing for gasoline! 'Incipient signs of panic' were reported to George Schultz, President Nixon's Treasury Secretary and immediately forwarded to the President himself. The public mood was described as one of 'mistrust, confusion and fear'.[78] Even more worrying, in spite of the fact that the oil embargo had been imposed by the Arab nations, the public began to look for scapegoats at home.

There were two favourite targets – the major oil companies, widely suspected of profiteering, and the Administration, believed by many to be far too close to big business and especially to 'Big Oil'. In 1975, this pervasive mistrust of the oil companies led Congress to pass legislation requiring the 27 largest US oil companies to disclose far more detailed financial and operating data to the Department of Energy than was then disclosed to stockholders. Congress also laid the groundwork for new accounting standards to be applied exclusively to oil companies.[79]

For a time the crisis passed but, in December 1978, with the cessation of Iranian exports during the Iranian Revolution, the dreaded cycle of price increases, shortages and gas lines began once again. Daniel Yergin's account of these days relates how much of the nation was in the grip of the gasoline shortage: 58 per cent of service stations nationwide were closed on Saturday 23 June and 70 per cent were closed on Sunday 24 June, leaving Americans with very little gasoline on the first weekend of the summer. Meanwhile, independent truckers were conducting a rowdy, violent nationwide strike, now three weeks old, to protest fuel shortages and rising prices.[80]

According to Yergin, 'to the American public, the re-emergence of gas lines, which snaked for blocks around gasoline stations, became the embodiment of the panic!'[81] Moreover, as the gas lines spread across the country, 'the oil companies were once again public enemy number one.'[82] President Jimmy Carter's Administration tottered under the growing pressure from America's motorised citizens. Even before the crisis of the US hostages in Iran, opinion polls showed that Carter's approval ratings had fallen to a mere 25 per cent. The frustration and anger even spread to senior members of the Administration itself. Stuart Eizenstat, Carter's principal domestic policy adviser, confessed to Yergin that, on the way to the White House one morning, he had sat for forty-five minutes in a gas line at his local Amoco station on Connecticut Avenue, and he had found himself 'seized by the same almost uncontrollable rage that was afflicting his fellow citizens from one end of the country to the other'. And the target of the national fury was not merely hapless station operators and the oil companies, but the Administration itself. 'It was a black, dark period,' Eizenstat later said.[83]

OIL PRICE CRISIS: DIFFERENT NEXT TIME?

The oil crises of 1973 and 1978–1979 burned deep into the American psyche and it is the collective memory of these events which underlies the continuing intense anxiety among Americans about vulnerability to oil shocks. And if the general public still fears a sudden loss of cheap gasoline supplies, how much more foreboding must there be in the ranks of the nation's politicians and oil company executives. Little wonder that the Bush Administration – a government even more closely associated in the public mind with the corporate interests of the oil and energy companies – should consider the removal of any potential threats to the smooth functioning of the nation's transportation system, a strategic priority.

Of course, lessons had been learned since the 1970s. In particular, the creation of the national Strategic Petroleum Reserve (SPR) provided a temporary cushion against new supply disruptions. The SPR reserves are held in a group of about 500 salt cavities along the coast of the Gulf of Mexico and have the capacity to hold a maximum of 700 million barrels of crude.[84] The principal problem associated with the SPR is the difficulty of deciding exactly when to release oil supplies from it. A certain amount of controversy surrounded the use of the SPR during the 1990–1991 Gulf War, when world oil prices briefly spiked at around $40 per barrel in October 1990. The following January, President George Bush Sr authorised the release of 33.75 million barrels from the SPR. In the event, only 17.5 million barrels were released and sold to 13 companies because, in the meantime, world oil supply and demand had stabilised. However, some observers criticised the President for not authorising the SPR deliveries sooner.[85]

However, the utility of the SPR during situations of more serious, long-term supply disruptions and sustained price increases has remained extremely doubtful. Since the creation of the SPR, the relentlessly increasing motorisation of American society raised the nation's daily petroleum consumption from 16 million barrels per day to 19.6 million in 2001 and its net imports of crude and petroleum products from 5.8 million b/d to 10.6 million b/d. In other words, whereas an SPR with a typical content of 600 million barrels would have covered 103 days of oil imports when it was first conceived, in 2001 it covered only 57 days import supply. According to one of the GAO's experts, 'the SPR is not large enough to play a significant role in large or long-term disruptions because such disruptions would greatly exceed the capacity of the reserve to affect the world oil market.'[86]

These considerations lead to an important conclusion. The existence of the SPR does not remove the vulnerability of the USA to serious and long-term threats to its oil supply – and hence, to the 'way of life' of its motorised citizens. It could not banish those lingering fears, both in the White House and in oil company boardrooms, that another major curtailment of motor gasoline supplies would bring down upon their heads the sort of execration experienced by Presidents Nixon and Carter. The existence of the SPR does not therefore in any way diminish the possibility that the USA might feel it necessary to strike pre-emptively to avert a long-term threat to the everyday life of the American metropolis. But it does give the Administration an extremely useful cushion against the much briefer supply disruption and rise in oil prices that might be expected during a short and successful war against a Middle East adversary. Moreover, in such a war, patriotic Americans might bear any short-term financial loss from higher gasoline prices without complaint and largely absolve the country's leaders from any blame in the matter.

GAO'S REPORT – A KEY CONCLUSION

As we have repeatedly observed, among politicians, government officials and the press, the share of US oil consumption supplied by foreign producers has been used as a measure of America's diminishing energy security more than any other indicator. The GAO, however, questioned the usefulness of this indicator and focused instead on what had become an even less tractable energy security problem.

According to the GAO's experts, it wasn't the high percentage of oil imports which threatened America's energy security, but the nation's dependence *on oil itself*. The GAO recognised that, 'because the world's lowest-cost oil reserves are currently concentrated in the Middle East, especially in the Persian Gulf, the United States and other oil importing countries will rely more on this historically unstable region.'[87] But they also argued that reducing the nation's reliance on foreign oil by increasing domestic production would probably do little to decrease the economic cost of disruptions because it would not substantially reduce their likelihood or cost. It was *dependence on oil itself* – as distinct from dependence on oil imports – coupled with participation in the world oil market, which would cause the US economy to bear the consequences of disruptions. Regardless of the level of imports, the US economy could suffer economic harm from a disruption, particularly if the disruption were severe or long-lasting.[88]

This is because oil is a highly 'fungible' commodity. At any one moment there are hundreds of oil tankers at sea, many waiting to be despatched to wherever the price for their particular quality of crude is highest. Even if the USA were to produce *all* of the oil it consumes, as long as the US economy is integrated into the world economy and oil prices are set in the global marketplace, oil-supply disruptions anywhere in the world will have a substantial effect upon the US economy. For example, an America self-sufficient in oil would not initially be affected by a major supply disruption in the Middle East. But this disruption would immediately push up prices in European oil markets. Sooner or latter this would inevitably attract oil supplies from the USA (or its hemispheric suppliers) as traders sought to benefit from the higher European prices and this, in turn, would require US refiners to bid up the price of US domestic oil supplies to a level comparable with those in Europe, net of shipping costs. As the GAO report explained, the integration of the US oil market into the world oil market meant that the USA could not isolate itself from the effects of oil-supply disruptions:

> As long as oil prices are set in the marketplace, oil price changes in one part of the world affect oil prices everywhere, including the United States...Unless the United States were to shift fundamentally away from a market-based economy and ban all oil imports and exports, reducing oil imports could not substantially reduce the effects of oil supply disruptions on the US economy.[89]

THE IMPACT OF 9/11: ENERGY POLICY
VERSUS AIRCRAFT CARRIERS

As one might imagine, the devastating impact of the terrorist attacks on New York and Washington on 11 September 2001 added a horrifying new dimension to the ongoing debate about US energy security. All those 'what if' scenarios about oil-supply disruptions emanating from the Middle East now took on a dire and disturbing relevance.

One month after the attacks, George L. Perry, an eminent US economist, former government economic adviser and now a senior fellow at the Brookings Institute, published a paper in which he argued that, 'The terrorist attack of 11 September raised important questions about what may lie ahead for the world oil market and what it could mean for the US economy.'[90] Perry shared the GAO's conclusion that the 'fungibility' of the world oil market meant that oil import reductions would be unable to shield America from events in the Middle East, and he emphasised that 'the risk to the US economy comes down to how events affect the world supply-demand balance for oil.'

Firstly, Perry presented a brief analysis of world oil supplies showing that in 2000, the Arab oil producers in OAPEC (Organisation of Arab Oil Exporting Countries – which included some Arab countries that were not members of OPEC) supplied 28.2 per cent of total world oil supplies. This was the supply source which, he said, was now directly threatened by 'religious extremists'. He presented three scenarios involving increasing degrees of Islamist control over OAPEC supplies. Perry hoped that, 'The war on terrorism may some day bring lasting stability to the oil producing states of the Persian Gulf' but, in the meantime, he urged consideration of these three 'bad-to-worst case' scenarios. He acknowledged that at the present time they might seem 'unlikely and will inevitably have an air of unreality about them', but added reasonably enough, that 'so did the September terrorist attack on the United States.'[91]

Perry then pointed out that what economists call the *price elasticity of demand* for oil is, in the short term, very low ('inelastic'): about -0.05. 'Elasticity' is defined for any commodity as the percentage change in quantity divided by the percentage change in price. An 'elasticity' of only -0.05 means that a 1.0 per cent *increase* in the oil price results in only a 0.05 per cent *fall* in demand. This is because the demand for oil cannot adjust very much to an oil-price increase because, in the short term, there are very few energy substitutes for oil. But it is when we turn this formula on its head that we see the real implications: if *supply* is reduced by 1.0 per cent then the price will *rise* by 20 per cent (1.0 divided by 0.05), similarly a 10 per cent reduction in supply is followed by 200 per cent increase in price, and so on.

In the first of Perry's scenarios, 7 million b/d of Arab oil is withdrawn from world supplies by Gulf and North African producers who are assumed to be under control of the *Jihadis;* but Saudi Arabia and Kuwait are unaffected, and increases in 'friendly' Arab production combined with a draw-down of the Strategic Petroleum Reserve reduces the net withdrawal to around 1 million b/d. This scenario only produces relatively minor damage to the US economy. However, Perry's remaining two scenarios, 'worse case' and 'worst case', present a much more pessimistic outlook.

In the second scenario, the Saudi government fails to make up any of the oil-supply shortfall emanating from the Islamist states which results in a net reduction in world oil supplies of 4.5 million b/d, the oil price rises to $75 per barrel, the motor gasoline price rises to $2.78 per gallon, nearly 75 per cent higher than the pre-crisis level and there is a fall in US real GDP of 2.69 per cent in the first year. Such a fall in GDP would 'cause or deepen recessions in the United States and throughout the world'.[92]

In the final scenario, things are even worse. Here it is assumed that radical Islamists take over most of the Middle East and North Africa and bring about production cuts amounting to a net 7.5 million b/d, the oil price rises to $161 per barrel, the motor gasoline price rises to $4.84 per gallon, three times its pre-crisis level, and GDP falls by 4.6 per cent initiating a recession which 'is the steepest and deepest of the post-war period'. For Perry, an even more disturbing aspect of these hypothetical events would be that the *oil revenues* would pass into the hands of governments now violently opposed to the USA. Even after their production cuts, the first and second scenarios would, respectively, place $13 and $30 billion into the hands of the extremists, while the third 'armageddon' scenario would provide the *Jihadis* with $689 billion per year.[93]

In the end, however, it was not so much the accuracy of his quantitative calculations that gave Perry's argument its true significance – economists of a different school could argue that this or that particular number is inaccurate or misleading, or that a different economic model would give different results (maybe worse as well as better). Rather it was the brooding, intense anxiety of the piece which was of interest – and this not from the pen of one of 'the usual suspects' in the neo-conservative American Enterprise Institute or the Hudson Institute, but from a moderate think tank of a impeccably scholarly reputation. Moreover, in spite of this background, Perry was driven to conclude, albeit in a resigned rather than sabre-rattling manner, that US military intervention in the Middle East was now very much an option. Considering the possibility that Islamists might 'overthrow the Saudi monarchy and other dynastic rulers in the region' his response was that 'the United States would be expected to use military force to prevent it,' and elsewhere he commented that if Islamists seize control of oil production in the Gulf, 'we would no doubt resist a disruption with force.'[94]

A fortnight after Perry's paper was published, on 1 November 2001, one of the GAO panel of experts, Irwin Stelzer, returned to the subject of its investigation in an article in the neo-conservative *Weekly Standard*. Stelzer concluded that if reducing oil imports from the Gulf would fail to protect America against major supply disruptions from that source, then only one possibility remained – the USA must take whatever measures are necessary to ensure that such disruptions do not occur in the first place, or if they do occur, they are immediately suppressed by the most vigorous military action. Observing that, 'we are... dependent not only on those countries from which we buy oil directly,' because 'oil is a fungible product,' he concluded that 'a shutdown of production in any country, even one from which we buy little oil, will affect the price we pay for our own supplies.' Saudi Arabia would inevitably remain the kingpin of the oil world, able to pump enough oil to satisfy America's thirst if it chose. But should the Saudi regime come to believe that its survival required unsheathing the oil weapon, or should a regime less wedded to cash flow come to power, supplies might be cut off. In the latter case, 'analysts would suddenly find themselves following the words of a bin Laden oil minister more closely than those of Alan Greenspan when they prepare their forecasts of the course of the American economy.' According to Stelzer: 'This leaves us with very few options...Asked some years ago what our energy policy is, I replied "aircraft carriers". That is as good a description as any of our present predicament. And it is about all we have to rely on at the moment.'[95]

11   Oil and Islamism

How would the Islamists influence the depletion policy?...It is likely that the Islamists would prefer leaving more oil in the ground.

Muhammad Karim, 2001

In 1991, a few months after the end of the Gulf War, a professor from the Norwegian School of Management, named Oystein Noreng, embarked on an academic research project whose real relevance would only become apparent ten years later. The project was to investigate the significance for the world oil industry of 'Islamism': the emergence – or perhaps one should say re-emergence – of Islam as a *political* mass movement on a world scale. Linking 'oil' with 'Islam', Noreng's project was not an individual endeavour; it was backed by the state-sponsored Research Council of Norway under a special programme called 'PETRO', administered by a committee of representatives drawn from the Norwegian oil ministry, state and private oil companies and the academic research community.

The Norwegians had very good reasons for enquiring into such a subject. Anything which might have a significant impact upon the development of the world oil market was of particular interest to that country, which, by 1991, was well on the way to becoming a world petro-power itself. With a daily production from its North Sea oilfields of 1.96 million barrels per day, it had now overtaken not only the UK, but also OPEC members Indonesia, Nigeria and Algeria. By 1991, the contribution of Norway's oil and gas industry to the country's National Income (GDP) had already reached 16 per cent (and would rise to 27 per cent by 2000). The share of oil and gas in total export revenues had reached 30 per cent (45 per cent by 2000),[1] while the earnings of its state oil company, Statoil, and the taxation of foreign oil companies ensured a net cash flow of around $5 billion per year into the Norwegian Government's coffers.[2] Perhaps most important of all, Norway was on track to becoming the second largest oil exporting country in the world after Saudi Arabia (a position it would briefly achieve before the end of the decade).[3] It is hardly surprising therefore, that, 'realizing the importance of petroleum to Norwegian society', the Norwegian authorities had acknowledged 'the need for academic research to guide long term decisions',[4] which was just what the PETRO programme was designed to do. It was nevertheless particularly prescient to focus on the emerging challenge of Islamism at a moment in history when the existing Muslim oil-producing nations, already accounting for 70 per cent of proven world oil reserves, were about to be joined by four oil-producing Muslim nations that had newly won independence from the former Soviet Union.[5]

ISLAM AS A POLITICAL PROJECT

Islamism, the explicit foundation of political practice upon references to Islam's holy texts, the *Quran* and the *Sunna*, emerged as a major world phenomenon with the Iranian Revolution in 1978 (although some would locate its origins in the Egyptian Muslim Brotherhood founded in the 1920s). 'Islamist' is not synonymous with 'Muslim'. An Islamist is not just a convinced believer or a religious teacher but a political activist and social critic, using religion as a means of gaining support, influence and power. While it would be a mistake to assume that Islamism is necessarily an insurrectionary or violent force, some of its manifestations have clearly had those characteristics during the last twenty-five years. For example, the seizure of the Grand Mosque at Mecca in November 1979, by a group of three hundred armed men led by Juhayman Muhammad Utteibi, a *Wahhabi* extremist, was an Islamist attempt to replace the 'corrupt' House of Saud with a regime modelled on the *Ikhwan* of the 1920s, and as such it may be regarded as the precursor to a number of movements of the *Jihadi* variety, which began to recruit from alienated young Sunni Muslims during the 1980s and 1990s. Similarly, the bloodthirsty terrorism of the groups that took up arms in response to the Algerian Government's cancellation of the second round of parliamentary elections in 1992 may also be categorised as a form of Islamism. Clearly, the sequence of events since 11 September 2001 has also confirmed in the minds of many westerners an image of Islamism as a fanatical and violent force.

On the other hand, many millions of ordinary Muslims have adopted a completely peaceful turn towards Islam as a source of political reference; indeed, the Algerian FIS party which was denied its electoral victory in 1992 might well be viewed in such a light. We must also recognise that while the term 'Islamism' may be a convenient 'shorthand' way of characterising contemporary political movements based on Islam, it is also an extremely crude one, in that it cannot capture the different traditions, tendencies and sects to which contemporary Islamists adhere, most notably the schism between the Sunni and Shia versions of Islam.

Noreng's three-year investigation into the relationship between oil and Islam culminated in a report to PETRO in 1996, followed a year later by the publication of the report as the book *Oil and Islam*. Noreng observed that the social and economic context within which Islam had originated – the Hedjazi region of Saudi Arabia – was a mercantile economy which had served as an entrepôt between the Byzantine empire to the north and the producers of exotic 'consumer goods' to the south and east. However, this society of urban merchant families was surrounded by a periphery of nomadic Bedouin herdsmen, a tribal society which was at the same time both conservative and egalitarian. According to Noreng, Muhammad's genius, was to provide a set of integrated religious and political ideas which welded these two social groups together, laying the foundation for the amazing sweep of Arab conquests which were to follow during the seventh and eighth centuries AD. He argued that, 'A monotheistic religion was an efficient way to ideologically unite different factions of a complex society, split into clans and tribes, in the cities and in the countryside.' The new religion essentially expressed the ideas and interests of the urban Hedjazi merchant class, amidst whom it arose but it also had sufficient flexibility to take the Bedouin interests and points of view into account. 'It could thus serve as an ideological instrument to make the Bedouins submit to the authority of the new state.'[6] As a consequence, the movement had, from the outset, certain clear economic and social implications. On the one hand, Islam was a capitalist religion, with its emphasis on individual responsibility, private property, and the private accumulation of wealth through trade and productive work. To this extent, it represented the interests of the urban merchant class. At the same time, 'Islam also, however, emphasises social justice, the sharing of wealth and welfare with the poorer parts of society. Compassion for the poor is a central element in the faith. In this way it also represents the interests of the Bedouins and the poorer urban strata.'[7]

Noreng also emphasised the extent to which Islam had developed as a practical, political religion which prescribed in detail modes of behaviour for everyday life and personal relations. It did not recognise any separation of the worldly from the godly. 'Islam is more than a religion: it is a political project aiming to shape society.'[8] Indeed, Muhammad himself was as much a statesman as a prophet. Consequently, following his death in 632 AD, the precepts of his religion became progressively codified into an all-embracing system of law known as the *sharia*.

Although there are significant differences between the various manifestations of contemporary Islamism it is a defining characteristic of all these movements that, like the Muslims of the seventh century AD, they do not recognise any distinction between secular and religious spheres of social activity: they are 'unified in their demand for the implementation of *sharia* or Islamic law'.[9] Consequently they seek to overturn and replace the modern Muslim states, all of which have – in varying degrees – incorporated non-*sharia* principles into their juridical systems or replaced *sharia* principles by secular, western-inspired ones. It is customary in the West to associate the *sharia* with various archaic forms of punishment – and little else. Less well known are its social and economic precepts. Two of these are of particular relevance to the challenges posed to Muslim societies by the enormous influx of oil wealth which began in the 1950s: *israf* and *riba*.

ISRAF – THE AVOIDANCE OF WASTE AND LUXURY

Israf – wasteful consumption or profligacy – is prohibited by Islam as a key element in the 'pact' between rich and poor whereby the former do not exploit their advantage through the consumption of luxuries so long as the latter still lack the basic necessities of life. Since it recognises and accepts the existence of rich individuals in society the prohibition of *israf* is not a socialist principle, but it is clearly an ethical one. It is also, in part, the justification for the Islamic wealth tax, the *zakat* (typically 2.5 per cent of annual cash balances) which intends a certain amount of redistribution but is also a partial 'remedy' for *israf*. Despite this, *israf* has been an almost continuous feature of the modern Muslim oil-producing states since the money began pouring in. By pointing to the unparalleled luxury consumption of some of the rulers of these states, especially since the huge rise in oil prices in 1973 and 1979, the Islamists have successfully appealed to many idealistic and socially conscious young people in those countries.

The uncontrolled consumption of luxuries became a feature of Saudi rule almost as soon as the kingdom received its first influx of oil wealth. David Howarth, who wrote an otherwise sympathetic biography of Ibn Saud in 1964, described how the spartan life of this 'Desert King' and his 42 sons was utterly transformed by the vast sums which flowed into his country after the

Second World War. 'No social system, no ruler and no people, could have been much less fitted for the deluge of wealth that the western world would suddenly thrust upon them, poured over them and drowned them in: wealth beyond all need, beyond all dreams, and beyond all reason.'[10]

By 1950, Ibn Saud had received $120 million – 'and that was before the big money started'. Treating this revenue as his own personal income, he had little idea what to do with it except to give it away to family and friends. Unfortunately his family's first taste of riches coincided with their first glimpse of western luxuries. When a group of his princely sons was despatched on a diplomatic mission to San Francisco in 1945, the thing which one of them later said had impressed him most was an underwater restaurant where he had been able to watch scantily clad girls swimming by, while eating his lunch. As Howarth sadly observed, 'that was a fair enough measure of the taste and comprehension of a good many of them.'[11]

But this was only a trivial example because the King and his sons had no overall concept of economic or social development. 'It seemed never to occur to Ibn Saud that his overflowing wealth laid any duty on him to give his people the amenities they lacked.'[12] Not a penny of the $600 million paid to the King by the US oil companies between 1946 and 1953 was spent in this way.

Ibn Saud died in 1953 to be succeeded by his son Saud Ibn Abdul Aziz. Under Saud, extravagant and self-indulgent as he was simple-minded, oil revenues had increased from $170 million to $334 million by the end of the decade. The royal family appropriated half of this, while their entourage of government officials, advisers and merchants accounted for most of the rest.[13] *Israf* was now unleashed with escalating frivolity and foolishness. A royal yacht, which nobody knew how to sail, was bought for $3 million and then sold for a quarter of its price. Ten opulent palaces were built; for each of them the catering bill alone was $7.5 million per year. On desert safari with his tribal friends, Saud never moved with fewer than fifty vehicles and he held court in a special travelling palace tent, large enough for a circus ring. His personal US-made safari trailer, equipped with a pale green drawing room with gilt armchairs, a bathroom with gold fittings and a bedroom with a king-sized velvet bed placed beneath wall-to-wall mirrors, reputedly cost $400,000.[14] Meanwhile, in July 1956, in the oilfields of the eastern al-Hasa region, a wave of popular opposition to ARAMCO and the House of Saud, involving strikes, demonstrations and demands for the legalisation of political parties and trade unions, was ruthlessly crushed and its leaders arrested, tortured and executed.[15]

Saud was deposed in 1964. But from then on – through the reigns of his kinsmen successors, Feisal, Khalid and Fahd, the extravagance, corruption and waste continued undiminished. During the early 1990s, according to Said Aburish, the House of Saud's annual budget fluctuated between $4 billion and $7 billion, most years still around 15 per cent of the national income. But it was no longer a budget – it was closer to a rake-off. 'The greater part ... is paid to King Fahd from the oil income before it is recorded as national income.'[16]

Said Aburish's admittedly hostile account is confirmed by an IMF study of the Saudi economy. According to the report, in 2000, total oil-export receipts were estimated by western economists to be $72 billion, but the published Saudi budget only acknowledged receipts of $57 billion. The difference is accounted for by off-balance-sheet expenses of the state oil company made up of 'generous stipends to the 7,000-member royal family'.[17] Little wonder that a Saudi taxi driver should complain bitterly to Said Aburish that 'It's not their oil, it's my oil, and I don't get a single barrel.'[18]

Radical Islamists and *Jihadis* quickly exploited this genuine sense of grievance. For example, the behaviour of King Fahd's favourite son, Abdul Aziz ibn Fahd, is singled out by one Islamist website, denouncing his 'recent trip to the Spanish seaside, accompanied by his large flotilla of servants, and aeroplanes which specialise in bringing the meals prepared in Parisian kitchens, and "other needs"'. For the Islamists this is nothing less than 'the theft of the Muslim community's funds' at the hands of 'thousands of princes belonging to the ruling family who draw tremendous salaries'.[19]

At the same time, the radical Islamists characteristically linked this appeal to social justice with their own fundamentalist pronouncements, condemning the House of Saud for abandoning the 'pure' Islam of the *Wahhabis* and the *Ikhwan*. The Saudi regime, they proclaimed, had 'lost the most important card which it uses to take advantage of to maintain its existence ... the card of Islam'. The claims of applying *sharia* and defence of Islam had become empty, and 'no longer have any connection with the real situation'.[20]

There is another aspect of *israf* which has been the equal of luxury consumption in its deleterious impact upon the Saudi economy and society. In the mid-1950s, a quarter of the royal income was spent importing military equipment, much of which the unschooled Saudi military did not know how to use and some of which was never unpacked from its crates.[21] By 1990, military spending accounted for an astonishing 17.7 per cent of the country's gross national product compared with an average 5.2 per cent for the industrialised western nations.[22] Oystein Noreng calculated that between 1973 and 1992, Saudi Arabia exported 6.2 billion tonnes of oil whose value in real (US$ 1992) dollars was $1,378.4 billion. Over the same period Saudi Arabia spent $418.8 billion on imported military equipment out of a total government expenditure of $739.6 billion. This military expenditure therefore represented 30 per cent of the country's petroleum export revenues and accounted for 57 per cent of total government spending.

The two-stage £20 billion (US$30 billion) Al-Yamama arms deal between Saudi Arabia and the UK's Thatcher government in 1986 and 1988, is a classic example of this type of *israf*. It was the largest UK arms deal ever conducted and may ultimately cost Saudi Arabia £50 billion when all the various additional service contracts are included.[23] According to a UK academic who has studied the deal, it was accompanied by 'unprecedented levels of bribery'.[24] Not surprisingly, many Saudi citizens, not just the Islamists, but liberals and democrats seeking reforms, questioned the Al-Yamama deal and others like it. According to one website of secular Saudi oppositionists, 'Saudi citizens... see Saudi Arabia being used as a dumping ground for weapons the Saudis cannot use or do not need, only so the royal family and weapons companies can line their pockets.'[25]

Both the Saudis themselves and their western arms suppliers maintained that these huge military expenditures reflected the needs of national self-defence. However, there are good reasons to question whether there was any real security gain, given that the country did not have the skilled military manpower or the technical expertise to effectively operate this vast and complex arsenal. Moreover there is a more convincing explanation for why the disproportionately huge quantities of military hardware were acquired. Arms contracts provided one of the largest and most easily concealed source of income for another 'army' – the ever-multiplying host of corrupt princelings and their hangers-on – whose sumptuous living conditions were funded from the huge pay-offs made by western arms companies to those who facilitate the deals: and the bigger the deal, the bigger the pay-off.

RIBA – INTEREST RATES AND DISCOUNTING THE FUTURE

The Arabic word *riba* has often been translated as 'usury';[26] but today most Islamic authorities define it simply as 'interest' – that is the charging of *any* fixed amount of money over and above the capital sum loaned (except, perhaps, for an allowance for price inflation). The prohibition of this form of income is consistent with that strand of socio-economic thought in Islam which accepts the accumulation of wealth through personal effort while rejecting a purely *rentier* type of economic activity.

However, In western economics the role of interest in the functioning of the capitalist system is not simply as a source of income. It is also held to reflect society's 'time preference'. It is at this point that the Islamic prohibition of *riba* starts to have specific practical implications for oil-industry policy, implications which, as we shall see, led Oystein Noreng's study to draw a particularly sharp-edged conclusion.

Oil reserves are a non-renewable energy resource. The problem of how rapidly this non-renewable resource should be used up (depleted) has been troubling economists since the early 1930s. There is a sharp divide among economists and geologists as to the seriousness of the 'dilemma' about how fast the oil resource should be depleted. However there is no denying the fact that, for a given country, there is a finite time horizon for the life of its oil reserves, even if that time horizon is, as yet, far into the distant future. Consequently, extracting and consuming (or selling) the oil today is to deny the benefit of doing so to future generations. Noreng outlined the reasons why this problem of 'inter-generational welfare' might be particularly acute for Islamists.

Strict adherence to Islam's prohibition of *riba* (interest) would rule out the use of 'discounting' when making choices about present versus future consumption. Discounting is part of the tool-kit of every western economist or businessman. In everyday conversation we often talk of 'discounting' some future event, meaning we attach a lower value to it. Economists do the same, but they quantify this discounting by applying an interest rate.

In a western capitalist economy where individuals can place their wealth on deposit in the banking system and receive interest payments on it, a dollar received in one year's time is worth less than a dollar received today. This is simply because I can place today's dollar in a bank and end the year with a sum which is larger than that future dollar received on the same date. By the same reasoning, the 'present value' of that future dollar is, today, worth *less than* one dollar: this is what economists mean by 'discounting'.

Since Islam prohibits *riba*, i.e. charging interest, such a discounting procedure would be forbidden in a strict and literal interpretation of Islam, with the result that an Islamist economic regime which was comparing a future sum of wealth with the same sum today would, in effect, use a zero discount (interest) rate. Which is to say that, contrary to western economics, Muslims should put exactly the same value on future wealth as on present wealth, provided of course that both are measured in 'real' terms – after allowing for anticipated price inflation.

The relevance of this to oil depletion policy is as follows. Essentially, an oil producer has two basic options: to extract the oil now or to preserve the oil for future extraction. For the western economist or oilman, who discounts the future oil sales with a rate of interest, it will usually be preferable to extract the oil earlier rather than later. Muslims, on the other hand, should be indifferent about when the extraction takes place.

Moreover, if they choose immediate, value-maximising extraction, this would probably lead to wealth creation well beyond the basic needs of the society and thus, inevitably, to *israf*, wasteful expenditure on luxuries or useless armaments. In the 1980s, even Sheikh Yamani had been forced to admit that a Saudi production level of just 3.5 million b/d was sufficient to ensure the normal functioning of the economy at a time when the country's actual production level was running at more than twice that level.[27] It follows that in many circumstances the strict application of Islamic principles to oil depletion policy should dictate, at the very least, a slower rate of extraction than has historically been applied by Saudi Arabia and many other Muslim countries.

All this led Noreng to conclude that 'because oil represents the major national asset, oil policy is likely to be strongly affected by any Islamist access to power in the Middle East.'[28] And if any such regime did come to power, he added, 'because Islam rejects the concept of interest', an Islamist state would be 'indifferent to the time value of money', and as a result concern for future members of the *umma*, the timeless Islamic nation, would incline such a state towards 'keeping more oil in the ground than would otherwise have been the case'.[29]

Noreng's views on the likely consequences for oil policy under an Islamist regime are shared by Muhammad Karim, a Pakistani student of Islam and petroleum law, who has argued that 'In an Islamic outlook, oil is a commodity jointly owned by the Muslim community,' and that 'hence a consideration must be made for the future generations while producing this exhaustible resource.' 'How,' he asked, 'would the Islamists influence the depletion policy?' Like Noreng, he concluded that 'it is likely that the Islamists would prefer...leaving more oil in the ground.'[30]

Noreng and Karim therefore argued that, in power, Islamists would reject an oil policy which pumps out oil at a rate higher than is consistent with the principle of intergenerational equity. This is certainly how Islamists would characterise an oil policy which resulted in abundant supplies to the West at low prices. For example, the radical Islamist Jihad Abdel-Muntasir attacked the Saudi Government for 'the failed policies which led to a slide in the value of oil...'[31] In identical vein was bin Laden's 1998 declaration that the 'correct' price of oil should be $144 per barrel, about twelve times the actual level for that year.

Some cynical western observers might argue that all this fine analysis of Islamic thought would be washed away by reality once an Islamist state actually came to power. The day-to-day requirements of satisfying the demands of a growing population and of military defence would surely require the abandonment of a depletion policy and a rapid return to maximising oil production. But this argument simply ignores the fact that restricting current oil production is not necessarily detrimental to current welfare: it may be quite the opposite if the consequence is a substantial rise in oil prices.

In this respect, Islamists like Jihad Abdel-Muntasir, from whom we have quoted, were particularly critical of the oil policy initiated by Saudi Arabia in 1986 and followed by the other OAPEC countries at that time. Between 1985 and 1986, the Middle Eastern and North African OAPEC countries increased oil output from 9.96 million to 12.4 million b/d. As a result, the price of the Gulf oil export blend (Dubai Light) immediately fell from $27.53/b to $12.95. During the 1990s, they continued to increase oil output, from 15.7 million b/d in 1990 to 19.2 million in 1998; Saudi production rose from 7.1 million b/d to 9.2 million b/d over the same period. When Venezuela too increased production in 1998, there was another sudden collapse in the price of the Gulf oil export blend to $12.16/b in 1998. Moreover, over the years, general price inflation had drastically eroded the nominal per-barrel value, so that the 'real' value per barrel in 1998 was approximately the same as in 1972, before all the achievements of the 'OPEC Revolution'.

It was against this background that the Islamists (and not only the Islamists) called for a change in oil policy that would raise prices once more. As we saw in the previous chapter, a policy which 'leaves more oil in the ground' would automatically have a substantial impact on the world oil price. To this extent, therefore, there is no inconsistency between a desire to leave more oil in the ground for future generations and one seeking a major increase in the oil price (and current welfare). The only problem with such a policy is that, over time, a very high oil price might encourage the development of substitutes for petroleum, but Islamists and others favouring 'leaving more oil in the ground' might reasonably conclude that there are few signs that the world's rapidly proliferating motorists are showing any interest in abandoning the gasoline- or diesel-powered internal combustion engine and if they eventually do, it will take decades for this to have any serious impact on the demand for oil.

OIL REVENUES, POPULATION GROWTH AND SOCIAL UNREST

The Gulf states have some of the highest rates of population growth in the world. Saudi Arabia, for example had an annual rate of 4.74 per cent between 1970 and 1994,[32] and in 2003 the rate was still 3.3 per cent (compared with the USA's 0.9 per cent).[33] This means that when we compare the real (inflation-adjusted) oil-export revenues of the Gulf states per capita in 2003 with their value in former years we discover that the oil revenue per head today is on average lower than it was in 1972 – $1,046 per head in 2003 compared with $1,287 in 1972. In Saudi Arabia it has fallen from $3,357 per head to $2,700, a drop of around 20 per cent.[34]

This is not to suggest that Saudi Arabia and the other oil-producing countries are now poorer than in 1972. Although a huge amount of the oil wealth flowing into these countries since 1972 was dissipated through *israf*, enough trickled down to support economic growth and some diversification. In particular, some of the traditional merchant middle classes saw their incomes increase dramatically as they positioned themselves in the interstices of the rapidly expanding state apparatus, exercising their traditional role of deal makers and intermediaries – but now on a much grander scale than hitherto. In Saudi Arabia, trading families unrelated to the House of Saud, such as the Mahfouz, the bin Laden and the Oloyan grew incredibly rich in the import business, construction industry and the burgeoning service sector. Similarly the number of state employees grew rapidly: in 1970 there were ten Saudi ministries with 120,000 employees; ten years later the number of ministries and similar government agencies had doubled and they now employed more than 300,000 people.[35] The urban population also benefited from state expenditure on education, health and housing.

The main problem, however, was that an economy not only based on *rentier* income from oil but with a built-in traditional social model of clientelism failed to produce a dynamic capitalist bourgeoisie that might generate a self-sustaining industrial and manufacturing base and a potential source of opposition to the corrupting and debilitating rule of the House of Saud. The high technological level and capital-intensive character of modern industry were serious obstacles to a middle class which frequently lacked the relevant knowledge, assets and scientific education. Moreover, 'local capital was reluctant to engage in sophisticated enterprises, since commerce, financial deals and land speculation already yielded large profits.'[36] Another factor discouraging any widespread demand for a more representative government was the absence of any system of income taxation. By funding all public expenditure from the oil revenues, the House of Saud prevented the emergence of a tax-paying bourgeoisie demanding 'no taxation without representation'.

Civilian government expenditure per capita in the Gulf states increased from $302 in 1970 to $1,038 in 1980, an increase of 244 per cent. However, the general decline in world oil prices which set-in after 1980, culminating in the dramatic collapse of oil-export revenues in early 1986, placed intense strains upon the national budgets of Saudi Arabia and the other Middle East oil producers.

Between 1980 and 1985, the overall picture became one of virtually stagnant government expenditure per head, while the years between 1985 and 1990, saw a marked decline, from $1,081 per head to $920. In the case of Saudi Arabia, civilian government expenditure per head which had risen from a mere $252 in 1970 to $1,628 in 1985, fell back to $1,345 in 1990.[37] The decline would have been much sharper had not the governments in question begun to run budget deficits and to borrow heavily. In the Saudi case, this amounted to a government debt of $168 billion by 2001, approximately the same size as the country's GDP.

Social dissatisfaction and unrest are rarely the result of absolute poverty. Much more conducive is a situation in which rising expectations are suddenly frustrated. For the generation of young people born in the Gulf and North Africa during the 1980s, the 1990s must have seemed a depressing and demoralising period. Their parents had done well out of the oil boom, but now they were facing a far less promising future. The apparatus of state-owned industries and agencies built up during the oil boom years was closing its doors to new recruits; unemployment and the lack of self-esteem which goes with it, was growing daily. Yet the ruling elites still continued in their corrupt and greedy ways. When young people looked abroad, the situation was equally depressing. Instead of fighting to restore the rights of the Palestinians, Islamic countries were fighting among themselves. In Palestine itself, the secular leadership of FATAH seemed to care more about lucrative business opportunities than restoring Jerusalem to Islam. Only in the mountains of Afghanistan could a young Muslim see some vindication of his religious and cultural values, as the atheistic communists and their Soviet backers went down in defeat before the victorious *Mujahidin*.

Between 1982 and 1992 around 35,000 Islamic radicals from 43 countries went to fight with the Afghan *Mujahidin*.[38] Tens of thousands more came to study in the *madrasas*, the religious schools funded by Pakistan's General Zia, along the Afghan-Pakistani border. There they learnt a deformed version of a particular school of Islamic thought called Deobandism, which had originated in nineteenth-century India. Deobandism and Wahhabism shared a similar outlook on the world and were both equally susceptible to extremist interpretations demanding violence – not only against non-Muslims but also against other expressions of Islam, in particular the Shia. Eventually more than 100,000 Islamists were to have direct contact with Afghanistan and become indoctrinated in the spirit of the *Jihad*. Afterwards, many returned home bursting with tales of heroic endeavour and a burning desire to restore their countries to the *Sirat al mustaqim*, the straight path – the path of righteousness.

AMERICA AWAKES TO A NIGHTMARE

For years, America had made use of Islamic fundamentalism for its own ends, as part of its worldwide struggle against communism, including national liberation movements to which the Soviets had lent support. For example, in 1976, the USA had prevailed upon Saudi Arabia's *Wahhabi* rulers to give one of its client dictators, General Mobutu of Zaire, $50 million to help him try to crush the Marxist-orientated MPLA independence movement in Angola. In the 1980s, Saudi Arabia was also used by Reagan's Administration to bank-roll the Nicaraguan Contras. At the same time, in what the American historian Douglas Little describes as 'one of the cruellest ironies of the Cold War', the USA also 'helped stoke the fires of radical Islam among bin Laden and the Afghan mujahidin', providing them with billions of dollars in cash and armaments. So until the emergence of bin Laden's anti-American terrorism, 'freedom-loving' America and Islamic fundamentalism were the very best of friends.

Then, suddenly, around 1993, the Frankenstein's monster which America had casually assembled for the war against the old Soviet enemy, began to take on a life of its own. In that year, Afghan-trained radical Islamists blew up the World Trade Center in New York, killing six people and wounding hundreds. Islamic fundamentalism was mutating into new and more vicious forms, with its own demands and priorities. It found the presence of US troops in Saudi Arabia, land of the two holy places, totally unacceptable. In its rising anger against the continued Israeli occupation of the West Bank and Gaza, it no longer distinguished between the fanatical armed Jewish settler and the secular third-generation inhabitant of Haifa who would happily trade 'land for peace'. Soon it was randomly killing both Arab intellectuals in Algeria and western tourists in Egypt. Most seriously for America, it even formed governments in Afghanistan and Sudan, governments which began to make the Iranian regime look positively moderate.

In November 1995, a car bomb killed five US citizens in Saudi Arabia. A similar incident followed in June 1996, and the following year Osama bin Laden demanded the removal of all US military and civilian personnel from Saudi territory. Even then, the USA thought it could coexist with some radical Islamists. As Ahmed Rashid has extensively documented, between 1994 and 1997 America was openly 'romancing' the Taliban to further its geo-strategic objectives and in pursuit of its Central Asian energy strategy. 'The USA supported the Taliban politically through its allies Pakistan and Saudi Arabia, essentially because Washington viewed the Taliban as anti-Iranian, anti-Shia and pro-Western.' The USA conveniently ignored the Taliban's own Islamic fundamentalist agenda, including its suppression of women. And, according to Rashid, between 1995 and 1997 US support was 'even more driven' because of the US Government's support for the oil and gas pipeline project under negotiation between the Taliban and UNOCAL, a major US oil and gas company.[39]

Eventually, however, after the Taliban's principal Arab guest had organised the bombing of America's embassies in Kenya and Tanzania in August 1998, the USA finally broke with them. Two weeks after the bombings, 70 cruise missiles rained down upon bin Laden's camps around Khost and Jalalabad, killing 20 Afghans, 7 Pakistanis, 6 Arabs and 1 Turk. In apparent retaliation, three years later, 19 *Jihadis* of whom 15 were Saudi citizens, immolated themselves together with 3,019 innocent civilians in New York and Washington.

SAUDI ARABIA – KEY ALLY OR KERNEL OF EVIL?

The UK Government has long waxed lyrical about its 'special relationship' with the USA since the end of the Second World War. From the American perspective, however, a similar 'special relationship' has existed, for exactly the same duration, with the Kingdom of Saudi Arabia. Indeed, from a strategic point of view, one could argue that although the USA-UK relationship has been of symbolic and ideological importance to the USA, the USA-Saudi relationship has been of greater material significance. This latter relationship has been aptly and concisely defined by Charles W. Freeman, US Ambassador to Saudi Arabia, during the Gulf War: 'The basic bargain of Saudi-American relations was thus simple: in return for preferred access to Saudi oil, the United States undertook to protect the Kingdom against foreign threats.'

However, in the immediate aftermath of the 9/11 atrocities, this 'basic bargain' came under fierce attack in the pages of the neo-conservative *Weekly Standard*. In an article by the influential Irwin Stelzer, of the Hudson Institute, Americans were told, 'So now we know: the Saudi Arabian regime is no friend of ours.' In a lengthy diatribe he accused the Saudi Government of 'playing a double game'. Even as the Saudi regime had accepted American protection and nurtured its long-standing relationship with Washington, 'it has also been playing footsie with the organizations that murdered thousands of Americans in the World Trade Center and the Pentagon.'[40] At the same time, Stelzer asked the question, 'Can we do without Saudi Oil?' and answered, very clearly, 'No.' He rightly dismissed any notion that the USA could reduce its oil consumption in a timely fashion or source sufficient replacement volumes from other countries.

On this point, at least, Stelzer was in agreement with the views of ex-Ambassador Freeman, now President of the Washington-based Middle East

Policy Council (MEPC), whose board of directors includes former Defense Secretary, Frank Carlucci, now Chairman of the Carlyle Group and Fuad Rihani, Research Director of the Saudi Bin Laden Group of companies. In December 2001, the MEPC, along with similarly minded Washington-based think tanks, the Middle East Institute (MEI) and the Atlantic Council, issued the first of a series of jointly sponsored congressional staff briefings, in response to the attacks of Stelzer and other neo-conservatives upon the traditional Saudi-US alliance. Having robustly denied that there was 'any credible evidence to support the allegations of some commentators that the government of Saudi Arabia has directly funded terror organizations', the briefing proceeded to remind its audience that 'the most important of the Saudi state's distinctive assets is its oil, and Saudi oil policy is thus of key concern to the United States.'[41]

In another *Policy Brief,* issued in May 2002, the MEPC, MEI and Atlantic Council stressed that over the years the Saudis had acted in a manner consistent with western and US interests in setting their oil policies. In exchange, the USA had provided Saudi Arabia with military equipment and acted militarily with its own forces to provide the Saudi regime with a measure of protection.[42] And in answering the fundamental question – 'What can be done to assure US energy security?' – the *Policy Brief* was forthright: 'Protect the Saudi Government. From an energy security standpoint, a friendly Saudi Arabia serves the interests of the United States as well as any alternative that seems plausible.' This implied that 'the United States should continue to provide a troop presence (so long as they are welcome) and to sell US weapons to Saudi Arabia.'[43]

The organisations which had jointly sponsored these *Policy Briefs* represented a wide range of US political luminaries, spanning both Republican and Democratic parties. Ambassador Freeman and Defense Secretary Carlucci we have already mentioned. But the Atlantic Council, the largest, and perhaps the most prestigious of these organisations also numbered among its directors and honorary directors Henry Kissinger, Brent Scowcroft, James Baker, Warren Christopher, Alexander Haig, Robert McNamara, Wesley Clark and many long-standing veterans of US policy-making. Such an assembly of notables ensured that the *Policy Briefs* represented a solid reaffirmation of the traditional relationship between the USA and Saudi Arabia, at a time when both countries were in a state of shock over the identification of 15 Saudi citizens among the 9/11 terrorists.

Nevertheless, a mere two months later, on 10 July 2002, at a classified and closed meeting of the Pentagon's Defense Policy Board, a Rand Corporation analyst named Laurent Murawiec presented a PowerPoint presentation in which he claimed that 'Saudi Arabia supports our enemies and attacks our allies', and that the Kingdom was 'the kernel of evil, the prime mover, the most dangerous opponent'.[44] According to an article in the *Washington Post*, to which the details of the Defense Policy Board seminar had apparently been leaked, Murawiec also argued that Riyadh should 'stop funding fundamentalist Islamic outlets around the world, stop all anti-US and anti-Israeli statements' and 'prosecute or isolate those involved in the terror chain, including the Saudi intelligence services'. If the Saudis refused to cooperate, 'Saudi oilfields and overseas financial assets should be targeted.'

According to the *Washington Post*, 'The briefing did not represent the views of the Board or official government policy.' Yet the *Post* believed that it represented a point of view that had growing currency within the Bush Administration – especially on the staff of Vice President Cheney and the Pentagon's civilian leadership – and among neo-conservative writers and thinkers closely allied with administration policy-makers.[45]

Indeed, Murawiec's vitriolic attack and its suggestions of 'targeting' Saudi oilfields, was not that different from Irwin Stelzer's earlier criticism of the Saudis in the *Weekly Standard*. There, Stelzer had concluded that although there was actually very little the USA could do at the time to influence the existing Saudi regime, it had 'one overriding strategic imperative': the USA must make clear that 'in the event of an upheaval in Saudi Arabia, we will take control of, protect, and run the kingdom's oil fields, which American oil companies originally developed after paying substantial sums for the right to do so.'[46]

Unsurprisingly, the leaked news of Murawiec's PowerPoint presentation caused some disarray in Bush's Administration and the Rand Corporation itself. The seminar had been organised by Richard Perle, the Defense Policy Board's Chairman, and reflected the strong influence of another Defense Policy Board associate, Daniel Pipes, son of the cold-war ideologue Richard Pipes. A former academic 'Middle East expert' and supporter of the far-right of Israeli politics, Pipes views the Arab world as a new 'Evil Empire'.[47] Like Murawiec, Pipes considered the Saudis to be 'the number one funders of terrorism'.

Murawiec's presentation was later given support by other neo-conservative members of the Board. The only voice raised against Murawiec's thesis during the seminar was that of Henry Kissinger. However, in the succeeding weeks, Administration spokespersons were at pains to distance Bush from the affair and it appears that on this issue the more extreme neo-conservatives had gone too far. By early November, Bush's Administration had clearly decided that, for the time being at least, it would be prudent to play down the Saudi-terror link allegations and on 1 November they duly wheeled out Richard Boucher, the State Department spokesman, to praise Saudi cooperation in the war on terror.[48]

Two weeks later, the need to dissociate the Administration from the Defense Policy Board's seminar became even more urgent. On 15 November Bush, Cheney and Rice hosted Prince Bandar bin Sultan, the Saudi Ambassador and close friend of the Bushs, at a meeting in the Oval Office where the Ambassador delivered a personal letter to the President from Crown Prince Abdullah, the Kingdom's de facto ruler. Bandar reminded Bush that since 1994 the Saudis had supported joint Saudi-US covert action to overthrow Saddam Hussein, but now he seemed to call into question American willingness to take the necessary measures. Bandar clearly wanted assurances from the President that this time, America was serious. He pointed out to Bush that being seen as an ally of the USA in a further struggle with Saddam Hussein would 'create a lot of difficulties' for the House of Saud, and that the situation in the Arabic and Islamic world was 'quite fluid in a way that it could hurt or threaten our interests and your interests'.[49] Nevertheless, provided he could report back to the Crown Prince that the USA was absolutely serious about using its full military might against Hussein, that Saudi Arabia would 'play a major role in shaping the regime that will emerge not only in Iraq but in the region' after Hussein's fall, and that the USA was genuinely committed to an equitable and lasting Palestinian-Israeli peace process, the House of Saud would give its full (albeit secret) support to an invasion of Iraq.[50] Bandar also reassured the President that he didn't need to worry about a shortfall in world oil supplies in the aftermath of another Gulf War because 'the Saudis hoped to fine-tune oil prices over 10 months to prime the economy for 2004' and Bush's re-election campaign.[51]

In the aftermath of the Defense Policy Board affair Murawiec departed the Rand Corporation and became resident at the Hudson Institute along with Irwin Stelzer. However, in the remaining months preceding the invasion of Iraq there was little sign that the neo-conservatives had suffered anything more than superficial wounds in the minor melee over Murawiec. On the face of it, there would appear to be a sharp divide between the policy positions of the neo-conservatives and those of the politicians and academics who constitute the membership of organisations like the Atlantic Council and the Middle East Policy Council. And yet it is worthwhile going behind the rhetoric and examining the substantive content of their approaches toward Saudi Arabia and its oil wealth. Both sides emphasised the crucial importance of Saudi oil supplies to America; and both threatened punishment for those who might seek to replace the existing Saudi regime with another – Islamist or otherwise – which would be inclined to pursue a more radical oil policy. This is explicit in the case of Stelzer – but also implicit in views of the Atlantic Council and the MEPC whose third *Policy Brief* stated unambiguously that the USA can only preserve its energy security if it is ready to 'protect the Saudi Government'. Clearly, in the event of a serious political crisis in the country which threatened to remove the House of Saud, the only way in which the USA could 'protect the Saudi Government' and its oilfields would be by the use of force against the House of Saud's domestic enemies.

Writing in 2001, Michael Klare, Director of Peace and World Security Studies at Hampshire College, Massachusetts, drew precisely the same conclusion about the likely US response to an anti-Saud insurgency. He argued that ultimately the USA was prepared to intervene with its own forces to defend the Saudi regime against internal attack and while it was impossible to predict the exact nature of the US response to any particular threat to the regime, 'it is likely to be swift, muscular and lethal'.[52]

Nevertheless, even the neo-conservatives would have to admit that taking such drastic measures against what might appear to the world as a popular uprising – and in a country which housed the most sacred Islamic shrines – might be a very risky business. Indeed, it might even lead to a wider conflagration, prejudicing American interests throughout the whole Islamic world. But might there not be some other way of protecting America's crucial energy interests in Saudi Arabia and the Gulf?

'IRAQ IS MORE IMPORTANT THAN SAUDI ARABIA'

In 1997, a report prepared by a team of US national security experts had spoken of the need to 'continue to be involved in regions that control scarce resources' and to 'hedge our own and our allies' resource dependencies' in the Middle East and the Caspian.[53] What better way to 'hedge' against the possibility that Saudi Arabia might sooner or later fall to the Islamists – or to any political force hostile to the USA – than to take control of an adjacent Gulf country, so richly endowed with oil resources that it might one day rival Saudi Arabia itself. And if such a strategy simultaneously opened hugely profitable Gulf oilfields to American capital, gave intense satisfaction to the Israelis, could legitimately be portrayed worldwide as the removal of cruel tyrant, and at the same time taught the militant Islamists a serious lesson about the true reach of American power, then so much the better. As it happened there was just the plan already on the drawing board – the nine-point strategy to 'bring down Saddam and his regime' placed before Clinton in February 1998 by members of the Project for the New American Century. Of course it needed to be converted from concept to operational and logistical practicality, but the Pentagon had been working on that since January 2001.

That 'regime change' in Baghdad would also bring about a fundamental change in the balance of world oil power was explicitly stated by one of the plan's leading supporters. William Kristol, editor of the *Weekly Standard* and co-founder of the Project for the New American Century, placed the 'hedging Saudi oil' strategy at the forefront of the growing campaign to invade Iraq. In April 2002, the Project's website carried a 'Memorandum to Opinion Leaders' in which Kristol, announced that 'Removing Saddam Hussein's regime from power in Baghdad will reduce the Saudis' leverage' and that 'returning Iraqi oil fully to market can only reduce the Saudis' ability to set oil prices, and make the US bases there superfluous.'[54] And in testimony to a hearing of the House Subcommittee on Middle East and South Asia on 22 May 2002, he expanded on this theme, arguing that the USA 'should develop strategic alternatives to reliance on Riyadh'. Noting that even under the existing Saudi regime, the country might use the oil weapon against US policies in the Middle East, Kristol argued that removing the regime of Saddam Hussein would be a 'tremendous step toward reducing Saudi leverage', that 'bringing Iraqi oil fully into world markets would improve energy economics' and that 'from a military and strategic perspective, Iraq is more important than Saudi Arabia.'[55]

It would be fascinating to know how these kind of public remarks, made by a prominent neo-conservative known to be highly influential with the Bush Administration, were received by the House of Saud. Ambassador Bandar and the Crown Prince were still, privately, offering support to the President – even to the point of promising Energy Secretary Abraham that they would 'cover for any loss of oil from Iraq by upping production to 10.5 million b/d for thirty days',[56] an extraordinary pledge given that their current production level was only 8 million b/d. To the outside world, however, a different message was being broadcast. Even while the Saudi Ambassador to the USA was still offering Bush this kind of support, Prince Turki Al Faisal, his counterpart in London, was appearing on UK television criticising the coming invasion.

By Autumn 2002, events were moving rapidly towards war. On 17 September, Bush released his Administration's National Security Strategy, enshrining many of the fundamental principles outlined five years earlier by the Project for a New American Century. In defiance of the foundations of international law, it called for a war of pre-emptive strikes against America's perceived enemies throughout the world and pledged that the USA would never allow its military supremacy to be challenged as it had been during the cold war. On 10 October, in an atmosphere of growing militaristic hysteria, Congress adopted a joint resolution authorising the use of force against Iraq and giving Bush *carte blanche* to take pre-emptive and unilateral military action against Iraq whenever he deemed it necessary. Although UN weapons inspections in Iraq resumed on 27 November, US preparations for war continued unabated and, on 21 December, Bush approved the deployment of US troops to the Gulf region. Then, on 28 January 2003, he declared that he was ready to attack Iraq without a UN mandate.

Although opposition from UN security council members France, Russia and China remained unswerving, as did Germany's, Bush was able to buttress his existing support from the British Government with pledges of military aid from a number of former East European Soviet satellites, including Poland whose foreign minister, Wlodzimierz Cimoszewitz was later to display few reservations about the real motive behind the invasion of Iraq. 'We have never hidden our desire for Polish oil companies to finally have access to sources of commodities,' he announced, adding that access to Iraqi oilfields 'is our ultimate objective'.[57]

Although the UN weapons inspection team announced considerable progress in gaining Iraq's cooperation on 14 February, and the following day eight million people worldwide demonstrated against the impending war, the build-up to the invasion continued. On 17 March, the UK's ambassador to the UN declared that the diplomatic process on Iraq had now come to an end and the UN weapons inspection teams were to withdraw. Two days later, starting with massive air attacks, the war on Iraq began.

The objective was simple: an Iraq free from Saddam Hussein and under a pro-American government that would open up Iraqi oil reserves for the benefit of both US companies and US consumers. In the event of any trouble from Saudi Arabia, these oil reserves could be used to undercut any Saudi moves to slash production and hike oil prices. No longer would the oil weapon hang over America like the Sword of Damocles and the USA would be free at last to pursue her wider military and political objectives throughout the Middle East and the world at large, not the least of which was the desire to impose upon the Palestinians a 'peace' acceptable to the neo-conservatives' Israeli allies, Sharon and the Likud. But as the unfolding events were to reveal, it was not long before the central objective – gaining control over Iraq's potentially vast oil resources – began to prove immensely more complex and difficult than anyone had fore-seen. Or as one oil company executive was to put it four months after the invasion began, the outcome was 'all a lot more complicated than anyone had expected'.[58]

12   A War for Oil

Iraqi exiles have approached us saying, you can have our oil if we can get back in there.

R. Gerald Bailey, former president, Arabian Gulf Operations,
Exxon Corporation 2002

As the build-up to invasion began, the State Department set about organising a number of meetings with Iraqi exiles, Administration officials and invited corporate executives and consultants, to plan for a post-invasion Iraq. These gatherings were to be known as the 'Future of Iraq Project' working groups. In September 2002, a State Department spokesperson claimed that the Future of Iraq Project 'does not have oil on its list of issues'.[1] Nevertheless, a preliminary meeting to discuss the future of Iraq's oil did in fact, take place the following month. It involved Cheney's staff, senior representatives of ExxonMobil, ChevronTexaco, ConocoPhillips and Halliburton, together with the Iraqi National Congress (INC) leader, Ahmad Chalabi, the Pentagon's favourite to lead a post-Saddam government.[2] The fact that the meeting had been held, and that it had been attended by major US oil companies was later confirmed to journalists by an INC spokesperson who also acknowledged that 'the oil people are naturally nervous. We've had discussions with them, but they're not going around talking about them.'[3] Other INC officials were at pains to stress that although a meeting with the oil companies had taken place, 'There have not been any substantive discussions or negotiations. No one is able to commit the natural resources of Iraq except an Iraqi government legitimately elected by the people.'[4]

JOCKEYING FOR POSITION IN IRAQ'S OILFIELDS

But this was not the message being received by the oil companies. That something more than an exchange of pleasantries was taking place in their meetings with the INC was revealed by R. Gerald Bailey, a former president of Exxon's Arabian Gulf operations and now Chairman of Houston-based Bailey Petroleum. According to Bailey, Iraqi exiles had been lobbying the executives of major US oil companies, promising 'you can have our oil if we can get back in there.' Bailey also revealed that 'all the major American companies' had met with the exiles in Paris, London and other major European cities and that the majors were 'all jockeying for position' in Iraq. These meetings and discussions had to be held in secret, Bailey admitted, but, for fear of missing out, no company could afford to 'wait till it gets too far along'.[5]

Indeed, fearing that US oil companies might win out in the Iraqi oil grab, BP's Chief Executive, John Browne, was compelled to publicly express his anxieties on this score by declaring that, 'we have let it be known that the thing we would like to make sure, if Iraq changes regime, is that there should be a level playing field for the selection of oil companies to go in there.'[6]

George W. Bush's speech-writer, David Frum, would later deny that the invasion of Iraq had anything to do with oil. 'The United States is not fighting for oil in Iraq,' he declared. 'The United States covets nobody's wealth, if only because it is far too rich to be susceptible to covetousness.'[7] But Frum had made an unfortunate choice of words. A few months later, referring to Iraq, the Chairman of ConocoPhillips frankly stated, 'We know where the best reserves are [and] we covet the opportunity to get those some day.'[8]

R. Gerald Bailey's remarks on the meeting with Iraqi exiles is therefore highly significant and adds yet another piece to the jigsaw; because now we know not only that the US oil companies were urgently seeking access to Iraq's oilfields, but also that a significant group of Iraqi exiles was virtually offering them as an inducement to have themselves hoisted into power in a post-Saddam Iraq. In fact, it was not long before Ahmad Chalabi was openly promising that, after Saddam's overthrow, 'American oil companies will have a big shot at Iraqi oil.'[9] As the planned invasion drew nearer, oil came back onto the Future of Iraq Project's agenda. The State Department and Vice President Cheney's staff formally convened two 'Oil and Energy Working Group Meetings' in Washington, the first on 20–21 December 2002 and the second on 31 January–1 February 2003. According to a State Department press release announcing the first of these meetings, the Department's Bureau of Near Eastern Affairs was planning to host approximately fifteen 'Free Iraqis' for discussions regarding the current state of

Iraq's oil and energy sectors, scenarios for the restoration and modernisation of Iraq's oilfields and other essential energy infrastructure; and 'management of the energy sector to meet the needs of the Iraqi people in the post-Saddam era'.[10]

The meetings were closed to the press but from subsequent leaks we can get a fair idea of both the participants and the main themes under discussion. One of the key Iraqi participants was Fadhil Chalabi, the cousin of INC leader Ahmad Chalabi. Fadhil Chalabi is the Executive Director of the London-based Centre for Global Energy Studies, an energy 'think tank' established by the former Saudi oil minister Sheikh Yamani. In earlier years, Chalabi had been Iraq's Under-Secretary at the Oil Ministry and, for a time, OPEC's Deputy Secretary General; now he took a generally anti-OPEC position and was a strong supporter of oil industry privatisation. He was also, reputedly, the Pentagon's favourite to take over the oil ministry in a post-Saddam Iraqi government.[11]

Another strong supporter of privatisation attending the meetings was Ibrahim Bahr al-Uloum, a US-educated petroleum engineer whose father was a leading Shia cleric. Muhammad-Ali Zainy, another analyst with the Centre for Global Energy Studies, was also present at the talks. Zainy had also been an official at the Iraqi Oil Ministry, before leaving to work as a petroleum engineer in the USA. Although Zainy recognised Iraq's need for foreign technical and financial assistance, it appears that he was more sceptical about privatisation than Fadhil Chalabi or Ibrahim Bahr al-Uloum.[12]

As for the American participants, in addition to State Department and Vice President Cheney's staff, we know that one of those in attendance was Robert Ebel, Director of Energy Programs at the Washington-based Center for Strategic and International Studies, which also includes former head of Venezuela's PDVSA Luis Giusti among its leading experts. Ebel was previously Vice President for International Affairs at the major US diversified energy company, Enserch Corporation, and an employee of the CIA. US oil companies represented at the meetings again included ExxonMobil, ChevronTexaco, ConocoPhillips and Halliburton.[13]

Behind the bland official agenda for the Oil and Energy Working Group meetings, three major issues confronted the participants:

(1) How should the USA deal with the existing Iraqi oil industry in the immediate aftermath of the invasion, given that it was anticipated that the industry might suffer widespread sabotage by Iraqi forces.

(2) How should the ownership of the industry be restructured so as to provide the necessary conditions for US oil companies to move in?

(3) How should the post-invasion Iraqi oil industry relate to OPEC?

At the time of the invasion, Iraq's oil industry, with proven reserves of 112 billion barrels, contained 80 known fields of which only 17 had actually been developed for production. The country's daily oil output had reached a maximum of 3.7 million b/d in 1979 and then peaked again at 3.5 million b/d in July 1990, shortly before the outbreak of the Gulf War. After collapsing almost completely during the Gulf War, it had slowly recovered to 0.6 million b/d in 1996, and then, with the introduction of the UN 'oil-for-food' programme, it further recovered to 2.2 million b/d in 1998 rising to around 2.5 million b/d just before the invasion.[14]

SEIZING THE OILFIELDS

The first task of the invading forces was to safeguard this current production capacity. In fact the solution had already been decided on by the Pentagon. The US military had drawn up a detailed plan for the US-UK coalition forces to seize the oilfields in the opening stages of the invasion. The State Department agreed that this was 'issue number one'.[15] It also seems probable that similar plans had been made for the seizure of the Oil Ministry building once Baghdad had been subdued. The Ministry contained valuable geological databases which could prove invaluable to US oil companies once pacification of the country allowed the occupation forces to move forward with the second important task – raising Iraq's productive oil capacity. That controlling the Oil Ministry building was given the utmost importance was later confirmed by the fact that it was the only major public building given heavy US army protection in the tumultuous days of rioting following the capture of Baghdad.

With regard to any necessary emergency repair work in the oilfields, the meeting was presented with a fait accompli: Halliburton, the oil services company formerly run by Cheney, would do the work. In December 2001, anticipating the coming invasion, Kellogg Brown and Root, a subsidiary of Halliburton, had signed a contract with the US Defense Department called the Logistics Civil Augmentation Program (LOGCAP) according to the terms of which the company would 'put out oil well fires and assess the facilities, clean up oil spills or other environmental dangers at the sites, repair or reconstruct damaged infrastructure and operate facilities and distribute products'. In fact, the terms of this vague and open-ended contract 'would allow Halliburton to profit from virtually every phase of the war in Iraq' according to the California Democrat

Representative Henry Waxman.[16] The cost-plus contract (with a guaranteed 7 per cent profit margin) was initially estimated at around US$1 billion, but would eventually grow to over US$1.7 billion by December 2003.[17]

As far as the revenues from Iraq's current oil production was concerned, these would continued to be administered by the UN-supervised oil-for-food programme until such time as the occupying powers could redirect them into some other vehicle under their control, but still primarily dedicated to continuing the work of relief and/or reconstruction. In this manner, the USA could maintain the façade that it had no designs on Iraqi oil revenues, while avoiding, as much as possible, public discussion of what would happen to the future revenues which would flow from the new large scale oilfield developments that would follow the installation of a new regime, friendly to the USA.

PRIVATISATION

The second major subject of deliberation among the participants at the State Department-sponsored meetings concerned the manner in which the ownership structure of the Iraqi oil industry was to be changed. There was also the related problem of what to do about the existing oil contracts which had been agreed between Saddam's regime and the Russian, Chinese and European oil companies already in the country. The official US position was that 'the US would not prejudice future Iraqi government decisions concerning the oil sector' meaning that 'they would not meddle with existing...oil contracts.'[18] However, they would have had every expectation that these would, in fact, be cancelled by a post-invasion Iraqi regime. The Russian, Chinese and European companies which had signed deals with Saddam Hussein had indubitably aided and abetted his regime and in almost anybody's estimation had little moral claim to the country's oil. The exiles would need little encouragement to scrap them.

With regard to the future structure of Iraq's state-owned oil industry many of the participants in the State Department's meetings appear to have been in favour of some form of privatisation and on this issue some of the participants would have been supported by a formidable ideological position then circulating among right-wing economists and politicians.

The ownership of oil brings with it great wealth. This wealth, which economists usually refer to as 'economic rent' is essentially a gift of nature. Even without the intervention of monopoly control, the market value of a barrel of oil far transcends the necessary cost of finding and extracting it in most oil-producing regions, and in those countries whose geology has favoured exceptionally large deposits – the giant, super-giant and mega-giant oilfields which are every oilman's dream – the economic rent or super-profit exceeds the cost of production by a huge margin. Observing that in most oil-producing and other mineral resource-rich states this enormous super-profit has been appropriated by the state, and that this state-ownership of the mineral wealth has not infrequently been associated with an absence of democracy, corruption, and a huge expenditure on armaments, the supporters of privatisation concluded that they would be doing a great favour to the unfortunate citizens of these nations by rapidly de-nationalising their oil resources. Thus, for example, the American neo-conservative writer Amity Shlaes, writing in the *Financial Times*, criticised the notion that Iraq's oil 'belongs to the Iraqi people' because 'belonging to the people tends to translate into belonging to the government.' According to Shlaes, even a democratic Iraq couldn't be trusted with oil wealth, because 'control of the oil bounty could corrupt any new Iraqi political leader within a few years.'[19] Shlaes alternative was simple: 'The single most important thing that the US and Britain can do to facilitate stability is to privatise Iraq's reserves...even if it means being accused of creating a "Texas on the Tigris".'[20]

Yet another proponent of radical privatisation was Deepak Lal, Professor of International Development Studies at the University of California. He too wished to 'lift the curse of natural resources' from the benighted citizens of these unfortunate mineral-rich nations. Under Lal's proposals the oil and other mineral resources of 'failed states' could be taken over by the World Bank and then leased to the oil companies. Further than this, he even advocated a full return to colonial or semi-colonial domination. Pondering how it might be possible to prevent what he called 'predators' from attacking the oil companies' newly acquired assets, Lal stressed the need to harness 'the prowess of an imperial power or a coalition of such powers' proposing that 'such a power could follow the example of China during the inter-war period by leasing foreign companies territory that they could protect with their own police forces.'[21]

The participants in the State Department's oil conferences do not seem to have gone quite this far. Most informed observers inferred that the majority viewpoint on oil privatisation favoured a more moderate and realistic alternative to the explicitly neo-colonial 'oil concession' model admired by Shlaes, Lal and others.

PRODUCTION-SHARING AGREEMENTS AND PROFITABILITY

According to Robert Ebel, a key US participant in the oil conferences, the most acceptable form of privatisation was a regime of production-sharing agreements (PSAs). Ebel stated that PSAs are 'the standard approach around the world', adding 'I know the Iraqis are looking at that very closely.'[22] PSAs originated in Indonesia in the 1960s and they were later adopted by both OPEC and non-OPEC countries including Libya Algeria, Qatar, Kazakhstan, Angola, Egypt, Oman, Yemen and Malaysia. There are large number of variations in these contracts, but all share the same broad features.[23]

Firstly, the PSA is a contract between the private-sector oil company and the state oil company of the host country. In other words, the complete privatisation of the industry is not necessary for a PSA to function. Indeed, the pre-existence of a state oil company 'partner' is usually required for the PSA to take place, although in many cases the state oil company is not itself an active explorer and oil producer but more of a revenue-collecting agency. When an oil company signs a PSA, the company does not acquire legal title to any of the *in situ* oil reserves. This is a crucial political feature of the PSA which enables the host country to maintain the principle of national sovereignty over its petroleum resources. At the same time, however, the regulations and accounting principles of the oil companies' countries of origin allow the companies to 'book' the share of oil reserves to which they will eventually become entitled as they extract the oil. This is particularly important to the companies, given the propensity of the stock markets to value them according to the size of their proven reserves.

Secondly, the oil in a particular field is divided into 'cost oil' and 'profit oil'. As the oil company begins to develop the field, spending money on drilling wells, building infrastructure, paying out operating costs, etc., it is remunerated for these costs out of the 'cost oil', which is valued at the going market price. The oil company receives the cost oil and sells it on the open market – or perhaps back to the state oil company.[24] When all the costs have been recovered, the amount of oil left in the field, which is the 'profit oil', is divided between the oil company and the state company according to an agreed proportion, for example 40 per cent to the company and 60 per cent to the state oil company. But if the field is a particularly large one with great economies of scale, the amount of 'profit oil' remaining might be huge. In such cases, the company will normally have to accept a much lower share of the profit oil, in some cases as little as 20 per cent.

However, this in no way implies that the company's rate of profit would be unacceptably low. Let us consider an example using a fairly straightforward PSA model – that of the Gulf state of Oman, a relatively small oil producer which is not a member of OPEC. As with most PSAs, the basic contract includes a 'signature bonus' paid to the state oil company on concluding the contract, after which the company recovers all its capital investment and operating costs as the initial oil is extracted and sold, up to an annual cap of 40 per cent of the gross revenues realised.[25] Once all the costs are recovered, the 'profit oil' remaining is divided between the state company and the oil company in a ratio of 80:20.

On the face of it this seems fairly tough on the company, but given the highly favourable geology of the region, the PSA can still translate into a very attractive company rate of profit. For example, if the Oman field falls into the 'giant' category with say, proven reserves of 750 million barrels and a capital investment cost per barrel of reserves of only $1.5 (as a result of the huge economies of scale), with a market price of $23/b, the 80:20 profit oil split in favour of the state company still yields a rate of profit for its private-sector partner of 31 per cent – a highly attractive rate compared with most oil companies' target rates of profit of 12–15 per cent.[26]

Let us now return to the case of Iraq. A medium-sized field of 300 million barrels in the Zagros Mezozoic formation, for example, would have a capital cost per barrel of reserves of only $0.41, while a giant field of 1,000 million barrels in the Arabian Mezozoic formation would be even lower, at $0.39/b.[27] Clearly, with a capital cost almost a quarter of that in the Oman example and market prices currently well in excess of the $23/b, a 'state take' of 80 per cent in an Iraqi PSA would leave the oil company with a truly enormous rate of return on capital. My own calculation is that applying the Omani PSA terms to a 300-million-barrel field in the Zagros Mezozoic 'play' would provide a 59 per cent rate of return with a $25/b price and a 66 per cent return with a $30/b price.[28]

PSAs, in other words, while seemingly equitable to the host country may still generate huge profits for the foreign oil company. Everything depends on how strong a negotiating position the government or state oil company feels it has as it begins talks. If the country in question is not obligated in any way to the foreign oil company's own government, then it will come to the bargaining table in a much more independent frame of mind and the PSA terms finally agreed will be tough. But if the government of the host country is almost entirely beholden for its very existence to the oil company's government, then common sense suggests that it will probably have to adopt a much more accommodating negotiating stance. The relevance of this for the Iraq case is obvious: prior to the invasion American oilmen and politicians would have had every reason to believe that they would soon be negotiating PSAs with just such a dependent and pliable regime.

WHAT TO DO ABOUT OPEC?

As we have already seen, Fadhil Chalabi, Washington's preferred choice to head the Iraqi oil industry, had become disenchanted with OPEC since the days when he helped to run it. He was also in favour of privatisation, although in exactly what form remained unclear. His recommendation for Iraq's post-invasion oil policy was that it should aim, with the assistance of foreign investment, to raise output as quickly as possible to around 7 million b/d – more than twice its previous all-time peak – and to do this it would probably have to leave OPEC. 'I would choose maximising the revenue through oil, with or without OPEC,' Fadhil Chalabi stated. 'If it is within OPEC it would be better, but it may not be possible.' According to Chalabi, Iraq was going to need a lot of money in the next five years, up to $300 billion. 'Privatization or partial privatization is the way to secure this investment,' he believed, adding that 'The nationalised oil industry has led to the shrinkage of the share of Middle Eastern OPEC countries in the world market to the benefit of non-OPEC producers – the growth of the oil industry outside the Gulf.'[29]

Now, it is undeniably true that, by restricting their own output to raise or protect prices, the OPEC countries' market share, especially that of Saudi Arabia, fell during the 1970s and early 1980s and that the most recent toughening of OPEC's stance, in 1999, has also given some leeway for non-OPEC producers to expand. But in suggesting that Iraq should ignore any OPEC quota and ramp up its productive capacity to 7 million b/d as soon as possible, Fadhil Chalabi seemed to have forgotten that, faced with such a challenge, other OPEC producers such as Venezuela and Saudi Arabia might feel they had to do likewise. Strategies to increase market share can rarely be pursued in isolation. For if every other large player in the market joins in, the result can only be the sort of price collapse and near ruination of major parts of the world oil industry that we witnessed in 1998–1999. In other words, a strategy of OPEC-busting would almost certainly be self-defeating for Iraq.

In the event, it seems that the only decision taken at the State Department meetings on Iraq's future relationship with OPEC was a largely meaningless one – that 'Iraq should remain a member of OPEC but be exempt from quota restrictions.'[30] However, there was probably little to gain at this stage from making unnecessarily provocative public gestures which might confirm the suspicions of some of those hostile to the US and UK who felt that the Americans wanted to 'bust OPEC' and that this indeed was the real motive behind the threatened invasion. As a matter of fact, since the 1980s, the USA has never wanted to 'bust OPEC' because of the dependence of its own oil industry on prices significantly higher than free-market levels.[31] Rather, America's objective – as the world's third largest oil producer – has been to control OPEC to set an upper limit on oil prices (an objective which might well have been achieved had its war for oil succeeded).

THE INVASION – INITIAL OPTIMISM

At 1.00pm on 19 March 2003, US special forces entered Iraq. The invasion had begun. Although US troops encountered some spirited local resistance along their rapid push to Baghdad, especially at Nasariya, their armoured spearheads quickly overwhelmed the regular Iraqi forces and by 24 March they were within 60 miles of the capital. Thereafter, the Iraqi forces appear to have just melted away and on 9 April US troops advanced into the centre of Baghdad. Meanwhile, Kurdish troops supported by US special forces took control of the northern cities of Kirkuk and Mosul. At the same time, fearful of enemy sabotage, Coalition forces made the Iraqi oilfields one of their main objectives but in the event, only seven out of 1,500 wells were set on fire and by 14 April the last of these had been extinguished.

A fortnight later, Defense Secretary Donald Rumsfeld was able to announce that, by the end of the summer, virtually all US military personnel currently stationed in Saudi Arabia would be withdrawn, as the overthrow of Saddam Hussein meant that their presence in the Kingdom was no longer necessary. As the *Financial Times* explained, 'The move signals a reduced US reliance [on Saudi Arabia], now that Iraq, with its second largest reserves, is under American control.'[32] This was also the judgement of Francis Brooke, an American oil consultant and long-time friend of the INC Leader Ahmed Chalabi. 'We have a new ally in the Middle East – one that is secular, modern and pro free market… It's time to replace the Saudis with the Iraqis.'[33]

On 1 May, George W. Bush, dressed in a flying suit, on the deck of the US aircraft carrier *Abraham Lincoln*, announced the end of major combat operations. Altogether, somewhere between 4,900 and 6,400 Iraqi soldiers had been killed and between 7,800 and 9,600 civilians had lost their lives in the massive campaign of bombing and shelling, as against a mere 114 US troops killed in combat and 22 dead in non-combat incidents.[34]

Meanwhile, while combat operations had still been going on, two further State Department-sponsored meetings to determine the future of Iraqi oil had taken place. Once again, there were calls for the rapid introduction of foreign oil companies and a general agreement that production-sharing agreements should be the vehicle through which privatisation would take place.[35] Furthermore, the US Administration now appointed a Texan oilman, Philip Caroll, formerly head of Shell's US operations, as the American 'Oil Czar', to head a team of experts who would run Iraq's oil industry. It had been expected that Fadhil Chalabi would be one such expert, but he appears to have decided that conditions were not yet propitious for his return.

However, on 26 April, his colleague, Muhammad-Ali Zainy, did arrive in Baghdad, full of enthusiasm and expecting to play a major part in the reconstruction of Iraq's oil industry. At first the signs were encouraging. Although daily oil production had collapsed to a mere 800,000 barrels and the rioting and looting which followed the initial collapse of the Baath regime had devastated many government offices, the Oil Ministry, now ringed by US tanks, had survived intact and by the third week of April employees had begun to drift back to work.

One such employee was Thamir Ghadhban, previously a top official in Iraq's Southern Oil Company, who, on 4 May, was appointed by the US-controlled Office of Reconstruction and Humanitarian Assistance (ORHA) to act as Chief Executive of an interim management team for the Iraqi oil sector. Ghadhban's immediate concerns were to try to get production back to something like pre-war levels. 'We must focus on immediate issues,' he said, at an extraordinary meeting of the World Economic Forum in June. He also moved swiftly to settle the matter of the pre-invasion oil contracts with Russian and Chinese companies and these were either terminated or frozen.

However, Ghadhban was sceptical about privatisation of the state oil company. 'Privatization does not ring a bell inside of Iraq. The economy and people's livelihoods revolve around the oil industry. Privatization is not only premature, it is unacceptable.'[36] Ghadhban also struck a somewhat discordant note when asked by a fellow conference delegate whether he thought the war in Iraq had been fought 'for oil'. He replied that it was a 'difficult question' and that while 'it was not totally about oil...I cannot say oil was not involved.'[37]

Muhammad-Ali Zainy found himself equally out of tune with some of the developments taking place in his native country. Despite his desire to help his country recover from the horrors of Saddam, invasion and war, his initial enthusiasm, was quickly dented. When he had been initially recruited, 'we were told that we would be advisers in a position to reconstitute and restructure the ministries, and to oversee the reconstruction of the damaged infrastructure.' But when Zainy arrived in Baghdad it soon became clear to him that in spite of his professional expertise he would have no such role. 'There was already an American team that was established...helping restructure the Ministry of Oil.

The American Department of Defense took it upon themselves to repair the damaged infrastructure due to the war.' Zainy quickly realised that he had no authority or influence at all: he was just being used as 'a go-between to convey American orders to the Ministry'.[38]

He, too, was becoming dubious about US motives. Although he still did not believe that the USA wanted to take permanent control of the Iraqi oil industry and hoped that 'eventually the Iraqi Ministry of Oil will take control,' he also suspected that the Americans 'wanted to open up an important Iraqi oil province as a secure source of oil for the world, and of course for themselves'.[39] As far as privatisation was concerned, Zainy thought that this should be restricted to the downstream sector, 'building refineries and so on'.[40] Eventually, on 4 September, dissatisfied with the subordinate role which he had been allocated, and deeply concerned about the escalating violence and insecurity in the country, Zainy resigned and returned to England.[41]

A DIPLOMATIC COUP FOR THE USA

On 22 May, although the security situation in Iraq was beginning to deteriorate rapidly, America managed to pull off a diplomatic coup when it persuaded the UN Security Council to recognise the USA and UK as occupying powers and to end UN sanctions on Iraq. It also won the UN's approval for the transfer of 95 per cent of all the revenues of the existing Iraqi oil industry into a so-called Iraq Development Fund, an opaque financial instrument which could be deployed by the USA in any manner it considered appropriate, under the general heading of 'reconstruction'. In order to encourage the flow of oil revenues into the Development Fund the UN Security Council was also persuaded to declare that Iraqi oil and gas, and those companies producing them, would be immune from all legal proceedings until 31 December 2007. The intent was to immunise the oil and gas only 'until title passes to the initial purchaser' and did not encompass liability for environmental damage. But the same day that the UN adopted resolution 1483 setting up the Development Fund, the Bush Administration went much further by issuing Executive Order 13303 which placed US oil companies completely above the law for any activities they carried out 'relating to' Iraqi oil, either in Iraq or in the USA. The legal concept of corporate responsibility was thereby abolished in relation to Iraqi oil products that are 'in the United States, hereafter come within the United States, or that are or hereafter come within the possession or control of United States persons.' In the judgement of some US legal experts, Executive Order 13303 meant that if US oil companies established separate subsidiaries to handle Iraqi oil they might be able to escape liability entirely and, in the words of Jim Vallette, Senior Researcher with the US Institute for Policy Studies, 'This order reveals the true motivation for the present occupation: absolute power for US corporate interests over Iraqi oil.'[42] Certainly, during the summer of 2003, there was ample evidence that, in the words of the American historian Douglas Little, 'US policymakers and oil executives seemed to be working as closely together … as they had sixty years earlier.'[43]

However, the big question now was whether there would be any significant oil revenues to deploy. Before the invasion, Cheney had confidently forecast that by the end of the year Iraqi oil production would be running at 3 million barrels per day. But by mid-August, amid growing chaos and sabotage, daily oil output was still only 1 million barrels, of which 200–300,000 b/d were having to be re-injected into northern oilfields due to serious constraints on both domestic processing facilities and export outlets – oil which the US Energy Information Agency considered 'may be lost forever'.[44] Then, on 15 and 17 August, the newly opened oil export pipeline from Kirkuk to the Turkish port of Ceyhan was seriously damaged by Iraqi resistance fighters.

Meanwhile, an event of singular importance had occurred outside Iraq. For nearly five years Saudi Arabia had been in negotiations with an ExxonMobil-led consortium hoping to gain access to its upstream gas industry, The Saudi Gas Initiative (SGI) had been heralded as a major breakthrough in which, for the first time since nationalisation in the 1970s, multinational oil companies were to be allowed back into Saudi Arabia's upstream hydrocarbon sector. But on 5 June 2003, negotiations were terminated.[45] The Saudis refused to allow the consortium access to the quantity of gas reserves which the companies said they required in order to make a satisfactory return on capital. The collapse of the project was a major blow to the hopes of the oil companies and although a much smaller gas project, which excluded the upstream production stage, was eventually agreed with Shell and Total in mid-June, in comparison with the SGI it was insignificant. This meant that the task of securing Iraq's oil reserves for development by US companies was now even more pressing. However, in late July a number of top oil executives warned the US Administration that they couldn't make any significant investments in Iraq until the security situation had markedly improved and the country had returned to some kind of internationally accepted legitimacy.[46]

Some steps towards providing at least a façade of legitimacy were being taken. On 13 July, the Coalition Provisional Authority appointed an Interim Governing Council. This would have the power to name ministers and help draw up a new constitution. Subsequently, on 1 September it was announced that the Governing Council had chosen, what was officially described as 'the first post-Saddam Hussein cabinet', dividing 25 ministries between the country's feuding religious and ethnic groups, but giving the majority Shia group the largest share of posts. Nevertheless, for all practical purposes the Governing Council and its ministerial cabinet remained subject to the ultimate authority of the CPA's Administrator, Paul Bremer. All this fell a long way short of a sovereign democratic Iraqi state.

THE OIL MINISTER IS APPOINTED

Given his solid work struggling to rehabilitate the national oil industry, it had been expected that Thamir Ghadhban would be appointed Iraqi Oil Minister in the new post-Saddam cabinet. Only three days before the ministerial posts were to be announced, the *Financial Times* considered him the likely successful candidate for the post, lauding him as 'a technocrat whose 30-year experience in the state-run sector would help meet the challenges of long-term under-investment and recent sabotage'. But instead, it was the exile, Ibrahim Bahr Al-Uloum, the 49-year-old, US-educated son of Governing Council member and Shia notable Muhammad Bahr Al-Uloum, who got the top oil industry job.

With Thamir Ghadhban having to accept merely an advisory role, Bahr Al-Uloum swiftly put privatisation back at the top of the agenda. Three days after his appointment, the new Oil Minister informed the *Financial Times* that Iraq was now preparing plans for privatisation, although he acknowledged that he would have to proceed cautiously: 'The Iraqi oil sector needs privatization, but it's a cultural issue. People lived for the last 30 to 40 years with this idea of nationalism,'[47] a habit which it would obviously take some time to change. Then, throwing caution to the winds, Bahr Al-Uloum announced that 'priority for involvement in the oil sector would be given to US oil companies.'[48] So it was to be Texas on the Tigris after all – or at least that was the plan.

But on 21 September, the issue suddenly became clouded by an announcement from the new Finance Minister, Kamil Mubdir Al-Gailani, that henceforth Iraq was to be thrown open to foreign investors, with 100 per cent foreign ownership permissible 'in all sectors except natural resources'. This announcement initially caused some confusion, with some US neo-conservative commentators, like Amity Shlaes, criticising the Minister's timidity in apparently banning foreign investment in the oil sector. Indeed, one anonymous Arab finance minister was quoted as saying that the 'ban' was a good thing, 'because it sends the message that America was not only after Iraq's oil'.[49]

In reality, the Finance Minister's announcement did nothing of the sort. The reaction of some observers displayed ignorance of the form of upstream oil privatisation which was now customary throughout the world and was apparently favoured at the State Department-sponsored meetings we have already described. In fact, the oil companies neither needed nor wanted 100 per cent ownership of Iraq's oil reserves: what they wanted was production-sharing agreements. As we have already explained, PSAs provide the political and ideological gloss that the oil *in situ* remains wholly the property of the state, while at the same time allowing the private sector-oil company to extract and sell a proportion of it – a proportion which, depending on the specific details of the PSA contract – could yield massive profits.

All was made clear only three days later. On 24 September, Bahr Al-Uloum, attending his first OPEC ministerial meeting, enthusiastically reaffirmed that foreign oil companies were welcome in his country, while his Deputy, Nabil Ahmad Al-Musawi, promised not only that US oil companies were 'likely to receive preferential treatment',[50] but also that, with regard to this issue, there was no need to wait for a constitution to be drawn up. 'Baghdad need not wait for Washington to hand over power,' he declared. At the same time, however, Bahr Al-Uloum tacitly acknowledged the current difficulties arising from the continuing insurgency by stating that it was unlikely that Iraqi oil production would recover to its pre-invasion level until early 2004 – although he hoped to lift output to 3.5–4 million b/d by the end of 2005 and to 6 million b/d by 2010.

A CONFERENCE IS ANNOUNCED

In the meantime, however, the problems of restoring Iraqi oil production in the middle of what was rapidly becoming a significant low-intensity war had apparently become too much for Iraq's first American 'Oil Czar', Philip Carroll, who quit the job in September. According to Robin West, Chairman of the US energy consultancy PFC Energy, Carroll 'tried to do his best…to bring order from chaos, but there were forces there beyond his control – or anybody else's frankly'.[51] In October, he was replaced by Robert McKee III, Chairman of Houston-based Enventure Global Technology, a company owned jointly by Halliburton and Shell. McKee had recently retired as Executive Vice President for Exploration and Production with ConocoPhillips but had suddenly 'received a phone call from an unnamed but high-level Bush administration official'.[52] Three months earlier, after a meeting with the State

Department, Archie Dunham, ConocoPhillips's Chairman, had offered what he described as 'the technical capability of our company' to the Coalition Provisional Authority, McKee's appointment was the Administration's response to Dunham's offer to 'lend a hand in both in the upstream and downstream sectors'.[53]

American officials were still busy promoting Iraq as a golden opportunity for US oil companies. McKee declared that Iraq had 'outstanding potential for companies like my old company ... Oilmen and oil women would drool to come into an environment like this'.[54] Indeed, in early October it was announced that a major conference would be held in Baghdad in December, to which 60 foreign oil companies would be invited. According to the petroleum news service, *Alexander's Gas and Oil Connections*, it would be, 'A brain-storming session for companies hungry for investment opportunities and for Iraqi oil officials eager to acquaint themselves with key players and technologies long denied them under UN sanctions.' The December conference would 'focus on the upstream part of Iraq's oil industry – production at existing fields and exploration for and development of new fields'.[55]

However, there was an increasing note of caution in the language being employed by some US officials. McKee himself admitted there was still 'relative instability' and it was too early for major American companies to begin making large investments there. That was certainly true. On 29 October, Coalition forces passed a grim milestone. With total US casualties now reaching 358, more Americans had died since Bush announced the end of major combat operations than during the combat operations themselves.[56]

In January 2004, McKee announced that he now favoured 'the formation of a state-run petroleum company'.[57] Given the fact that Iraq already had a state-run petroleum industry (although not a state 'company' as such, like PDVSA or Saudi ARAMCO) it was understandably difficult for observers to draw any meaningful conclusion from McKee's announcement, other than that it was intended to allay 'widespread concerns that the American-led invasion was an oil grab'. But as we have already explained, neither the USA nor its oil companies had ever contemplated an 'oil grab' in the sense of transferring the ownership of Iraq's oil resources and existing producing oilfields to US citizens; since McKee's statement about a state oil company was coupled with another claiming that 'such a model can attract the massive foreign investment the industry needs,'[58] it soon became clear that he was simply adding a political gloss to the by now long-established preference for production-sharing agreements. The primary function of the putative new 'state petroleum company' would be to sign those agreements and to receive Iraq's share of the oil production.

But it takes two to share and unfortunately the requisite December conference in Baghdad, with its 60 eager foreign oil companies in attendance, never took place.[59] The party had been announced, the invitations had gone out – but the guests had politely declined.

And who could blame them? Nobody wants to go to work wearing body armour, yet the security situation was deteriorating day by day. After a few days of much-trumpeted successes against the Iraqi insurgents, the second week of January 2004 witnessed the shooting down of a Blackhawk helicopter that killed all its nine US occupants, a missile attack on a US military transport aircraft departing Baghdad airport and a mortar attack on a US logistics base that killed one US soldier and wounded 32.[60]

A SOVEREIGN IRAQ?

Meanwhile, on 15 November, the Coalition Provisional Authority and the Governing Council announced that the occupation would end the following June and a 'sovereign Iraqi government' would take power. However, any illusion that this might mean a withdrawal of US forces was quickly dashed by the Coalition officials, who clarified that there would be a 'security agreement' with the new government which would provide for US troops to remain in the country 'to provide for the safety and security of the Iraqi people'.[61] At the same time, plans were being made for a huge new US Embassy in Baghdad – with 4,000 staff the largest ever run by any country – to be based in Saddam Hussein's palace, currently the site of the CPA's headquarters.[62] This new centre of US vice-regal authority, which would replace the dissolved CPA, would then continue to exercise control over Iraq and ultimately, so it was hoped, over a new 'reformed' Middle East.

While many observers drew the reasonable conclusion that the announcement of an 'end to the occupation' reflected the desire of the Bush Administration to undercut growing domestic opposition to the continuing hostilities in a year in which they would be standing for re-election, there was another equally strong motive for this new political initiative. The oil companies were now making it absolutely clear that even if the security situation did improve markedly, they were unwilling to commit themselves to large-scale investment in Iraqi oil without the establishment of an Iraqi government which had considerably greater international legitimacy than the existing Governing Council and its cabinet. Without this legitimacy, there remained a strong possibility that any oil deals they might make could be deemed illegal by some future Iraqi government, and their assets in Iraq subject to expropriation.

The Bush Administration was now on the horns of a formidable dilemma. On the one hand, to ensure that US oil companies gained access to Iraqi oil reserves and US consumers and taxpayers benefited from the recovery and growth of Iraqi oil production, it was essential that those ministers friendly to the Americans should remain in power. On the other hand, if a truly sovereign Iraqi government were to be formed via an electoral process which conferred undisputed legitimacy on the new regime, it was almost certain that America's friends would be swept aside: in which case, there was no guarantee that those who replaced them would deliver the promised oil deals. Worse still, elections might result in a fractured state dominated by a combination of Shia Islamists and Sunni Arab nationalists which could further undermine any possibility of establishing a stable US oil protectorate in the Gulf. On this point Bush, Cheney and Rice may well have harkened back to the advice offered by the Administration's favourite 'arabist', Daniel Pipes, who had long argued that the remoulding of the Middle East might well be a lengthy process. Pipes took the view that the USA should 'be very careful about pushing for elections' in countries where the threat of Islamism loomed. Indeed, 'to hold premature elections... is in no one's interests.' and, as far as timing is concerned, 'It requires 10, 20, 30 years of evolution before fully fledged democracy can come into existence.'[63]

LOSING THE WAR FOR OIL

As the winter months of 2004 slipped by and the US occupation forces now faced a second appallingly hot Iraqi summer, the insurgency spread to almost all parts of the country. With mounting casualties among both coalition troops and private-sector contractors and an almost total breakdown in security outside a few fortress-like US-controlled enclaves, another much heralded major conference of foreign oil companies, planned for Basra in April, had to be cancelled. By May 2004, it was beginning to look as though the Bush Administration had launched a war for oil in the Middle East – and lost it. For the demoralised US forces and their leaders, now badly weakened by the revelations of torture in the Abu Ghraib prison, the best that could now be hoped for was an orderly withdrawal of US forces after elections in 2005 in which a regime not wholly antagonistic to America might – just might – take power.

The indications were not good, however. Even among the appointees of the new 'sovereign' government installed on 30 June, voices were now being raised which were not exactly in tune with the invasion's original objectives. One particularly significant indication that the ambitious plans of the US neo-conservatives for the creation of a pliable Iraqi oil protectorate were fading was the reinstatement of Thamir Ghadhban to the post of Oil Minister, a decision which appears to have been made at the instigation of the UN emissary, Lakhdar Brahimi, who had frequently stressed Iraq's need for experienced technocrats and to whom the Americans were now having to make concessions in return for UN approval of the new 'sovereign' government. Ghadhban, it will be recalled, was a veteran of the Baathist oil industry and an opponent of privatising the national industry. Although he appears to have had no particular objections to production-sharing agreements, in his first interview since his appointment he pointedly referred to the possibility of utilising only 'Arab and foreign investment' to supplement the operations of a new state oil company based on 'the old healthy management of the 1970s'. He also struck a strongly nationalist pose by declaring that 'when sovereignty is regained it means there will be no more US advisors in the oil ministry.'[64]

If America had lost the war for oil – that is, if it were to leave Iraq with its tail between its legs, or remain bogged-down fighting a vicious and debilitating low-level insurgency for many years to come – without any of the benefits of expanded Iraqi oil production which had been originally anticipated for both its companies and its consumers – then the implications would be far-reaching.

'I kind of think,' said Mr Blair to President Bush on the morning of 20 March 2003, 'that the decisions taken in the next few weeks will determine the rest of the world for years to come.'[65] Undoubtedly true. Two major consequences, closely linked together, can be identified: the political impact on Saudi Arabia and the probable trajectory of the world oil price.

CONCLUSION

We shall conclude by examining these possible consequences of America's losing her war for oil, but to put them in context let us first revisit the central arguments of the book. We began by emphasising the remarkable physical properties of oil as an energy source and how these properties came into their element when utilised in Large Independent Mobile Machines, of which the modern motor vehicle was the outstanding example. It was upon the mass manufacture of such vehicles that America's thriving capitalist economy became established in the first decades of the twentieth century and, in the furtherance of its development, viable existing public transport alternatives were ruthlessly dismantled. The subsequent construction of a vast network of transcontinental roads and radial urban motorways and the accompanying development of US suburbia in which almost all alternatives to motor-vehicle transportation were foreclosed left millions of US citizens entirely dependent on their cars to a degree which far outweighed similar developments in older, European societies. In turn, these fundamental economic and social developments created an emanant system of ideology and aspirations. In the words of the essayist Clarence Page, 'We drive our cars and our cars drive our culture.'[66]

Although America's interest in Middle East oil was originally led by military considerations, by the 1960s these had largely taken second place to the ever-increasing demands of the USA's domestic economy, almost every facet of which, and especially its transportation sector, was heavily oil dependent. However, the growing conflict between US oil companies and their Middle East host countries over the division of the oil rent culminating in the 'OPEC revolution' of the early 1970s, together with rising Arab and Iranian anger against America's military and diplomatic support for Israel, eventually convinced American geo-strategists that the USA must strive to become less dependent on Gulf oil.

While this seemed possible for a time during the late 1980s and early 1990s, as the USA successfully diversified its electricity generation away from oil in general and Middle East oil in particular, the ever-increasing motorisation of American society culminated in an inevitable return to reliance on Gulf oil which, by 2001, had reached an all-time maximum as a proportion of total US supplies.

The possibility of freeing itself from this dependence now seemed as remote as ever and, as if to emphasise the intractability of America's energy security problem, some economists were now arguing that, in a global oil market, even if a reduction in dependence on the Gulf could be achieved, it would not protect American consumers from the impact of a major oil-price shock emanating from the Middle East. The logical conclusion was that America would have to prevent such a shock happening in the first place and that meant dominating and controlling the Middle East.

The inauguration of the Bush Administration in January 2001 signified the arrival of a government more heavily dominated by oil and energy corporate interests than ever before in the nation's history and at a time when competition for the world's oil reserves had been intensified by significant changes in the corporate structure of the world oil industry. As we observed in Chapter One, 'everyone now wanted to become a multinational oil company.'

For a few months after its installation, the Bush Administration continued to advocate the, by now, traditional policy of trying to diversify oil imports away from the Gulf. But largely thwarted in these attempts in Venezuela, Mexico and Alaska and with evidence mounting that the much-hyped Caspian oilfields might fail to live up to earlier extremely optimistic expectations, Bush, Cheney and Rice were soon thrown back on the realisation that the prosperity of their citizens, indeed the normal functioning of everyday life in the hyper-motorised USA, remained fatefully tied to events in the Gulf, which Cheney's own Energy Policy report was predicting would have to provide between 54 and 67 per cent of the world's oil supplies by 2020.

But here was the crucial problem: if these much-needed oil supplies were to be forthcoming, the Gulf states – and Saudi Arabia in particular – would have to open up to foreign investment. This, also, was what America's oil companies desired in order to restock their reserve inventories with the lowest cost oil resources in the world. Yet, Saudi Arabia and Kuwait remained unwilling to proffer the necessary invitations, while Iraq and Iran remained off-limits for reasons of state. Meanwhile, the US Council on Foreign Relations had independently published a devastating report anticipating an imminent world oil-price shock, reinforcing the message that, to avoid such a crisis, the Gulf states must somehow be persuaded to open up to western oil capital.

And then, at the very moment that the Bush Administration was engaged with these critical energy policy issues, America was cruelly awakened to the realities of Gulf geopolitics. The terrorist attacks of 9/11 harshly illuminated a different, more sinister Saudi Arabia: no longer a friendly, reliable oil supplier with inconveniently archaic and despotic domestic policies but now, at best, a devious and double-dealing breeding-ground for fanatical Islamic fundamentalists and at worst a potential theocracy under the command of Osama bin Laden.

At this juncture, the invasion and occupation of Iraq appeared to offer the Bush Administration and its attendant neo-conservative ideologues a bold solution which could satisfy both the energy security needs of America's citizens and the business requirements of America's energy companies. In particular it would create a hedge against Saudi Arabia's market power by establishing a rival Gulf oil 'powerhouse' in Iraq. Effective control over an expanding Iraqi oil industry would provide the means to undermine any future Saudi moves to increase oil prices beyond the tolerance levels of US consumers or make use of the oil weapon in support of the Palestinians.

But the 'hedge' would only work if America has something to hedge with. So long as the insecurity and violence in Iraq continue, American attempts to restore and expand Iraq's oil industry are doomed to failure, with or without the participation of its own oil companies. As if to underline this sobering lesson to America and its political leaders, in June 2004 Iraq's oil ministry acknowledged that production in May had been only 1.8 million b/d, lower than in previous months and still below pre-invasion levels.

So America and the world remained dependent on Saudi oil. On the other hand, Saudi Arabia's need for support from the USA had diminished considerably with Saddam Hussein's overthrow. There was still the internal threat, from Islamist *Jihadis*, but this seemed to be focused more on western expatriates.

In any case, the House of Saud must now surely have had grave doubts about whether American troops could be counted on to put down a serious uprising, especially if it meant a more or less permanent US military presence in the country. Could a future US government of any political hue seriously consider an endless, debilitating counter-insurgency war against Islamists in both Iraq and Saudi Arabia?

We can only speculate about the likely Saudi response to these considerations, but one serious possibility is a reassessment of the utility of the historic alliance with America. Before the invasion of Iraq, such a reassessment was being made by the USA; but now it is more likely being made by the Saudis themselves: but the USA still remains dependent on Saudi oil. In this respect, strategic bargaining power may have shifted from the Americans to the House of Saud. It remains to be seen whether the House of Saud uses that bargaining power, but it is not inconceivable that if the Israelis continue their oppressive policies against the Palestinians, the Saudis may decide that the best way to undermine the internal Islamist threat is to adopt a much more combative stance against America's continuing support for Israel. One way of doing this would be by threatening not to renew contracts with American refineries as they expired, in the knowledge that, if the Americans failed to respond, the oil could be sold into the rapidly expanding Chinese market instead.

Returning, finally, to the fundamental question of oil prices, three uncomfortable conclusions can be drawn, all of which point to a continuation of relatively high prices at best and, at worst, a major oil-price shock within the next ten years.

Quite apart from the possibility that the Saudis might one day cut off supplies of oil to the USA in support of the Palestinians, there are three further factors pointing to a continuation of high oil prices.

Firstly, there is the persistent anxiety in the oil markets that Saudi Arabia's production might be seriously damaged by sabotage from an internal Islamist opposition, emboldened by America's fiasco in Iraq. Indeed, in June 2004, just such a reaction pushed world oil prices to their highest (nominal) level since 1991. Secondly, there is the probability that Saudi Arabia itself now favours prices considerably higher than those prevailing before the invasion of Iraq because it now feels considerably less beholden to the USA, as we suggested above. Moreover, higher prices will provide the House of Saud with the resources to spend on economic development and public welfare, thereby undermining support for the violent Islamist opposition. Thirdly, and most importantly, there remains the impact upon the world oil price of America's failure to forcibly open up the Gulf to US and western oil capital. It will be recalled that, in their 2001 report, *Strategic Energy Policy Challenges for the 21st Century*, the US Council on Foreign Relations stressed that the prospects for meeting future world oil demand, while preserving moderate oil prices, was crucially dependent on opening up the Gulf oilfields to the massive foreign investment required to commensurately increase oil production capacity. It is now very unlikely that this will happen. Indeed, in February 2004, Saudi ARAMCO published a '50 Year Crude Oil Supply Scenario' in which it clearly stated that, whatever the world market conditions, Saudi Arabia did not have either the intention or the ability to increase its current 10 million b/d crude production capacity until well after 2010. Even then its 'maximum sustainable capacity' would be a modest 12 million b/d and this would not be achieved until 2016.[67] It is implicit in this forecast that there will be no significant recourse to foreign investment in the country's oilfields.

Apart from a major world economic recession, there remains one possible mitigating factor which might significantly reduce pressure on oil prices – a major reduction in demand resulting from a serious and sustained American initiative to curb and reduce its rampant motorisation. A nation with the enormous technological resources and human ingenuity to be planning inter-planetary travel could surely make a massive transition to energy-efficient public transport if the political will were there.

Unfortunately there are no signs of this occurring. In 2003, the top three light vehicles sold in the USA were in the high-fuel-consumption, 'light-truck' category and half of the top ten light vehicles were light trucks. As a proportion of total light vehicle sales in 2003, light trucks – SUVs, pickups and minivans – accounted for 54.2 per cent, rising from 51.8 per cent the previous year and from 50.7 per cent in 2000. Nearly 30 per cent of light vehicles sold in 2003 had gas-guzzling eight-cylinder engines; indeed, the share of vehicles with the larger, V-8 engines has increased year on year since 2000. Not surprisingly, in 2003, America's oil consumption hit a record 20 million barrels per day with net imports climbing to 11.2 million b/d. The EIA was now forecasting that US oil consumption would rise to 22.7 million b/d by 2010 with net oil imports increasing to 13.2 million b/d.[68]

Unveiling the first of the new models with which Ford hoped to win back market share from its Asian rivals, in January 2004 the company announced that this would be 'The Year of the Car'. But while the reference to 'car' meant 'passenger car' as opposed to SUV, there was clearly no intention of trying to wean Americans away from their love affair with vehicle size. Ford's own consumer research was showing that American consumers expected their new cars to be equipped with many of the features found in SUVs, such as higher driving positions and extra storage space.[69] Similarly, Chrysler's new Dodge Magnum was proclaimed to be 'a cross between a car and a sporty estate, reflecting the growing trend towards cross-over vehicles that combine the characteristics of a car and an SUV'.

Even the surge in gasoline prices in the spring of 2004 appeared to have had little impact on sales of SUVs. According to press reports, 'large sport/utility models held their own...in the face of record gasoline prices.'[70] The major US manufacturers reported that overall there was no evidence of falling demand for vehicles with a higher fuel consumption and, in June, General Motors' Vice President for US Sales concluded that 'consumers are...voting their preferences by purchasing record numbers of pickups and SUVs.'[71]

For nearly a century, motorisation was the driving force behind the US economy. More than any other single factor, it shaped American society and moulded the American psyche. In 2003, motorisation had ultimately driven America to war; but America was just carrying on driving. Addicted to oil, it remained unrepentantly the car country, rejoicing with the Pulitzer Prize-winning essayist Clarence Page that 'Cars are us in this big-car nation, and we are our cars...Cleaner Air? Fuel Efficiency? Maybe next century.'[72]

Notes

PREFACE TO THE PAPERBACK EDITION

1   US Department of Energy, EIA, *Annual Energy Review 2004*, p.127, updated to 2005 by EIA Petroleum Navigator, US Crude and Petroleum Product Supplied, online: available http://tonto.eia.gov/dnav/pet/hist/mttupus2m.htm,(2/2/06) (11 months data for 2005 annualised).

2   Ibid.

3   Ibid.

4   US Department of Energy, EIA, *Annual Energy Review 2004*, p.154

5   US Department of Transportation, Bureau of Transportation Statistics, Motor Vehicle Fuel Consumption and Travel, online: available http://www.bis.gov/publications/national_transportation_statistics/2005/html/table_04_09.html (2/2/06)

6   Ibid.

7   US Department of Transportation, Bureau of Transportation Statistics, Average Fuel Efficiency of US Passenger Cars and Light Trucks, online: available http://www.bts.gov/national_transportation_statistics/2005/html/table_04_23.html (6/2/06)

8   US Department of Transportation, Bureau of Transportation Statistics, Principal Means of Transportation to Work, online: available http://www.bts.gov/publications/national_transportation_statistics/2005/html/table_01_38.html (6/2/06)

9   US Department of Transportation, Bureau of Transportation Statistics, World Motor Vehicle Production, Selected Countries, online: available http://www.bts.gov/publications/national_transportation_statistics/2005/html/table_01_22.html (6/2/06)

10   Senate Fiscal Agency, Michigan, online: available http://www.senate.michigan.gov/sfa/Economics/RetailAutosales.PDF (6/2/06)

11   See for example, Jeremy Grant, 'Efficiency drive a worry for SUV market', *Financial Times*, 1 June 2004 and Bernard Simon, 'Carmakers suffer as drivers downsize', Financial Times, 12 May 2005

12   Walter S. McManus, *The Effects of Higher Gasoline Prices on US Light Vehicle Sales, Prices and Variable Profit by Segment and Manufacturing Group, 2001 to 2004*, Office for the Study of Automotive Transportation, University of Michigan Transportation Research Institute, 23 May 2005, p.3

13   Warren Brown, 'Despite all the hype, the sky isn't falling on the SUV market, *Washington Post*, 31 December 2005

14   US Department of Energy, EIA, Total energy supply and disposition in the AEO 2006 reference case, 2003-2030, online: available http://www.eia.doe.gov/oiaf/aeo/table1.html (2/2/06)

15   President Bush's speech quoted in the *Guardian* 1 February 2006

16   US Department of Energy, Office of Transportation Technologies (OTT), *Future US Highway Energy Use: a Fifty Year Perspective*, (Washington, May 2001)

17   US General Accounting Office (GAO), *Energy Security: Evaluating US Vulnerability to Oil Supply Disruptions and Options for Mitigating their Effects*, Report to the Chairman on the Budget, House of Representatives (Washington, December 1996)

18   US Department of Energy (EIA), *International Energy Outlook 2005*, (Washington, 2005) p.34

19   Carola Hoyos, Mideast oil to play bigger role in global growth, *Financial Times*, 14 February 2006

20   US Department of Energy (EIA), *International Energy Outlook 2005*, (Washington, 2005) p.34

21   Carola Hoyos, 'Oil spike gives BP room to return up to $65bn', *Financial Times*, 8 February 2006

22   Richard Cheney et al., *Report of the National Energy Policy Development Group*, May 2001, online: available http://www.whitehouse.gov/energy/ 1 December 2002 p.8:5

23   See, for example, Carola Hoyos, 'Iraq's oilfields slip backwards since departure of Saddam', *Financial Times*, 7 December 2005

24   The proposal by the ruling Al-Sabah family, supported by the Kuwait Oil Company, that Kuwait should allow foreign oil companies to develop four northern oilfields under a type of service contract (the so-called 'Project Kuwait') has still not been ratified by Kuwait's Parliament even though it has been under discussion for many years. Even if it is eventually approved the project will be of only limited advantage to foreign oil companies because under the contractual terms in question they will be unable to 'book' their Kuwaiti oil as 'reserves' under US accounting rules.

25   *Oil and Gas Journal*, 6 February 2006 p.5

26   Abdulaziz Sager, 'Saudi-Chinese Relations: Energy First, but not Last', *Arab News*, online: available http://arabnews.com/?page=7&section=0&article=76692&d=23& m=1&y=2006 (16/2/06)

27   Andrew Yeh, 'Chinese in energy deal with Saudis', *Financial Times* 24 February 2006

28   Martin Feldstein, 'America will fall harder if oil prices rise again', *Financial Times* (3/2/06)

29   See, for example, James Howard Kunstler, *The Long Emergency: Surviving the Converging Catastrophes of the Twenty-First Century*, Atlantic Books (London, 2005)

30   Andrew Ward, 'Global thirst for bottled water attacked', *Financial Times*, 13 February 2006

31   Richard McGregor, Jo Johnson and Carola Hoyos, 'China and India forge alliance on oil with aim of ending mindless rivalry', *Financial Times* 13 January 2006

32   Quoted in Victor Mallet, Power hungry: Asia's surging energy demand reverberates around the World', *Financial Times*, 12 May 2004

PREFACE

1   The academic literature on this subject is voluminous. The following works are therefore only a sample, most of which are referred to in the main body of the book: Stivers, William, *Supremacy and Oil: Iraq, Turkey and the Anglo-American World Order, 1918–1930,* Cornell University Press (Ithaca and London, 1982). Anderson, Irvine H., *Aramco, the United States and Saudi Arabia: A Study of the Dynamics of Foreign Policy, 1933–1950,* Princeton University Press (Princeton, 1981); Conant, Melvin A., *The Oil Factor in US Foreign Policy, 1980–1990,* Lexington Books (Lexington Mass.,1982); Hartshorn, J.E., *Oil Companies and Governments*, Faber and Faber (London, 1962); Klare, Michael T., *Resource Wars: The New Landscape of Global Conflict*, Metropolitan Books (New York, 2001); Painter, David S., *Private Power and Public Policy: Multinational Oil Companies and US Foreign Policy 1941–1954,* I. B. Tauris (London, 1986); DeNovo, John, 'The Movement for an Aggressive American Oil Policy Abroad, 1918–1920', *American Historical Review*, Vol.61, No.4, 1956; Finlayson, Jock A. and Hagland, David G., 'Oil Politics and Canada-United States Relations', *Political Science Quarterly*, Vol.99, No.2, 1984; Kaufman, Burton I., 'Mideast Multinational Oil, US Foreign Policy and Antitrust: The 1950s', *Journal of American History*, Vol.63, No.4, 1977; Krasner, Stephen D., 'A Statist Interpretation of American Oil Policy Toward the Middle East', *Political Science Quarterly*, Vol.94, No.1,1979; Volman, Daniel, 'The Bush Administration and African Oil: The Security Implications of US Energy Policy', *Review of African Political Economy*, Vol.30, No.28, December 2003.

2   Charles A. Kohlhaas, 'War in Iraq': 'Not a "War for Oil"' *In the National Interest*, 5 March 2003. The general line of argument of most of those who denied an oil motive is a kind of crude cost-benefit analysis according to which the estimated financial cost of the war to the USA was set against the value of the oil revenues which would accrue to the USA from seizing the existing Iraqi oil production facilities. (See also,

for example, Tatom, John, 'Iraqi Oil is not America's Objective', *Financial Times*, 13 February 2003; and Frum, David, 'Myth 2: America Wants War with Saddam because of Oil', *Daily Telegraph*, 22 October 2002.) Apart from the fact that this kind of argument completely ignores the whole issue of energy security policy which is central to my own book, as well as making the fallacious assumption that it was current, existing oil production facilities which were of interest to the USA (as opposed to the vast potential of future Iraqi oil developments) any cost-benefit analysis which compares the costs of the invasion and war with the benefits to the US oil companies simply ignores the fact that whereas the latter would be a *private* benefit, accruing to the corporate backers of the Bush Administration, the former are a *social cost* paid by the US taxpayer.

3   See Berger, Peter L. and Luckman, Thomas, *The Social Construction of Reality*, Alan Lane The Penguin Press (London 1967), p.141.

4   Harding, James, 'Bush Speaks for Cause of Freedom in Middle East', *Financial Times*, 7 November 2003.

5   Woodward, Bob, *Bush at War*, Simon and Schuster (New York, 2003), p.341.

6   Carr, Edward Hallet, *What is History?* (2nd edition) Penguin Books (Harmondsworth, 1987), p.48.

7   *Rebuilding America's Defenses: Strategy, Forces and Resources for a New Century*, Project for the New American Century (Washington, September 2000), p.14.

CHAPTER 1

1   Klare, Michael T., *Resource Wars: The New Landscape of Global Conflict*, Metropolitan Books (New York, 2001), p.27.

2   The exception is the USA, which still measures energy in British Thermal Units (BTUs). 1 BTU = 1,055.1 joules.

3   The material included in this and subsequent paragraphs draws heavily upon the following article: Reynolds, Douglas B., 'The Value of Oil', *Oxford Energy Forum*, Oxford Institute for Energy Studies (Oxford, August 2000), pp.9–10. Reynolds actually distinguishes *four* energy grades. Here, we have simplified matters by omitting the 'area grade', which in our view is less important than the other three.

4   As stated in the introductory notes, 'oil' refers to both crude oil and natural gas liquids (NGLs). The latter have a higher weight-grade than crude oil, so the figure of 43 MJ/kg given for 'oil' is intended to represent a rough average for crude oil-plus-NGLs.

5   MPa (Megapascal) is a measure of pressure, meaning one million Pascals, equal to 200 Bar.

6   The significance of the word 'Independent' in this phrase is that it denotes the capacity for movement unaided by external motive power (e.g. as with electric trolley buses) and unrestricted by fixed tracks (as with steam or electric railways).

7   Reynolds: 'The Value of Oil', p.10.

8   See Sampson, Anthony, *The Seven Sisters: The Great Oil Companies and the World They Made*, Hodder & Stoughton (London, 1975).

9   See Mommer, Bernard, *Global Oil and the Nation State*, Oxford Institute for Energy Studies, Oxford University Press (Oxford, 2002), pp.1–8.

10   Those unfamiliar with the concepts of 'present value' and 'discounting' might wish to consult one of the many treatments of this subject included in standard texts on business economics. The author's preference would be David Whigham's *Managerial Economics Using Excel*, Thomson Learning (London, 2001), pp.235–55.

11   US Department of Energy, EIA, *Oil and Gas Development in the United States in the Early 1990s: An Expanded Role for Independent Producers* (Washington, 1995), p.v.

12   US Department of Energy, EIA, *Performance Profiles of Major Energy Producers 2002*, 1998 (Washington). The Department of Energy annually designates around 30 oil companies as 'majors' but about a third of these are refining or marketing companies with little or no oil-producing operations. Also, the Department's definition of a 'major' is somewhat broader than the one used in this book, which I believe corresponds more closely to the everyday notion of a 'major oil company'. Throughout this book 'major US oil company' refers to the top ten companies operating in the USA (but not necessarily US-controlled), ranked according to the size of their total assets. In 2000, this list included (in descending order) ExxonMobil, Chevron, BP Amoco, Shell Oil, Texaco, Phillips Petroleum, Occidental Petroleum, Conoco, Anadarko Petroleum and USX-Marathon. This approach is broadly consistent with that used by the *Oil and Gas Journal* in its annual oil company rankings.

13   Corzine, Robert, 'From Minor to Major: Formerly Monolithic Oil Companies are Challenging the Western Majors on Their Home Turf', *Financial Times*, 19 August 1997.

14   An 'independent' is an oil company operating exclusively in the upstream sector – oil and gas exploration and production, i.e. without any refining or marketing operations.

15   *Oil and Gas Journal*, 1 October 2001. The total number of companies surveyed was 197, from which we have deducted the top ten major US oil and gas companies all of which were multinationals (see also note 12 above).

16   Petroconsultants, *Annual Review of Petroleum Fiscal Regimes* (Geneva, 1995), Ranking Tables, p.8.

17   See Antill, Nick and Arnott, Robert, *Oil Company Crisis: Managing Structure, Profitability and Growth*, Oxford Institute for Energy Studies (Oxford, 2002), pp.74–5.

18   Quoted by Hoyos, Carola, 'Oil Groups Lose Money on UK Energy Fields', *Financial Times*, 7 April 2003.

19   See US Department of Energy, EIA, *Oil Production Capacity Expansion Costs For the Persian Gulf* (Washington, January 1996).

20   See for example, Painter, David S., *Private Power and Public Policy: Multinational Oil Companies and US Foreign Policy 1941–1954*, I. B. Tauris (London, 1986).

21   I use the concept of 'Oil Capitalism' to refer to companies which are not only involved in oil production but are also active in many other energy sectors. This is because, today, only the smaller so-called 'independent' oil companies actually specialise exclusively in the upstream, oil exploration and production business. The major oil companies are increasingly diversified energy companies with interests in natural gas production, gas pipelines and processing (natural gas liquids), gas and electricity marketing, electric power generation, solar power, etc. However since many energy products are substitutes for one another (for example both fuel oil and natural gas

can be used in many industrial boilers), over time, their prices generally tend to move in the same direction. To this extent, it is reasonable to think of oil itself – the most valuable and widely traded energy commodity – as being the ultimate energy market driver.

22 Harris, Anthony, 'A Head-in the-Sand Approach to Oil', *Financial Times*, 13 August 1990.

23 Oil consumption is defined as total petroleum products supplied to US consumers and for export. In 2000, this was 19.701 million barrels per day. See US Department of Energy, Energy Information Administration (EIA), *Annual Energy Review 2001*, Washington, p.127. There are between 7 and 8 barrels of oil to a metric tonne of oil, depending on the specific gravity of the oil. 1 barrel of oil = 42 US gallons. NGLs, which are lighter than crude oil, have a higher conversion factor, typically around 11 barrels per tonne.

24 For an account of the crisis, see for example, Daniel Yergin, *The Prize: the Epic Quest for Oil, Money and Power*, Simon and Schuster (London, 1991), Chapters 29–30, and Anthony Sampson, *The Seven Sisters*, Chapters 11–13. For more recent discussion and analysis of this crucial period see Francisco Parra, *A Modern History of Petroleum*, I.B. Tauris (London, 2003) and Douglas Little, *American Orientalism: The United States and the Middle East since 1945*, I.B. Tauris (London, 2004).

25 Conant, Melvin, *The Oil Factor in US Foreign Policy 1980–1990*, Lexington Books (Lexington Mass. 1982), p.3.

26 US Department of Energy, EIA, *Annual Energy Review 2001*, 'Gross' imports were 11.6 million barrels per day (b/d); 'Net' imports are gross imports minus exports of 0.98 million b/d., the latter being mainly petroleum products and crude exported from the USA to Eastern Canada.

27 US Department of Energy, EIA, *Monthly Energy Review*, online: available http://www.eia.doe.gov/emeu/mer/txt/mer1–8 (7 September 2002).

28 World Resources Institute, 'Resource Consumption', *Earth Trends: The Environmental Portal*, online: available http://earthtrends.wri.org (10 May 2004).

29 Ibid.

30 Fulton, George A., Grimes, Donald R., Schmidt, Lucie G., McAlinden, Sean P. and Richardson, Barbara C., *Contribution of the Automotive Industry to the US Economy in 1998*, Institute of Labour & Industrial Relations, Office for the Study of Automotive Transportation, University of Michigan and Center for Automotive Research, Environmental Research Institute of Michigan (Winter 2001), p.49.

31 Quoted in *The Observer*, 25 August 2002, by Jonathon Porritt who was present at the 1992 Earth Summit.

32 Competitive Enterprise Institute, 'Statement on the National Energy Policy Security Act of 2001', 16 February 2001, online: available http://www.cei.org/utils/printer.cfm?AID=2506 (9 February 2003).

33 The subject of 'Islamism' (as opposed to Islam) is discussed in Chapter 11. However, as a short, general definition of the term we use that offered by Fred Halliday, 'Term used as an alternative to "fundamentalist" and the French *integriste*, to denote a movement that used a return to a supposedly traditional Islam as the basis for a radical political programme. Examples would include the Iranian Revolution, the Muslim Brotherhood, Deobandism and the Taliban'. See Halliday,

Fred, *Two Hours that Shook the World, September 11 2001: Causes and Consequences*, Saqi Books (London, 2002), p.15.

34   Since this book was written, I have come across an important article in the *British Medical Journal* by Ian Roberts, Professor of Public Health at the London School of Hygiene and Tropical Medicine, which encapsulates many of the ideas contained in *Addicted to Oil*. See Roberts, Ian, 'The Second Gasoline War and How We Can Prevent the Third', *British Medical Journal*, Vol.326, No.171, 18 January 2003.

CHAPTER 2

1   US Department of Energy, Energy Efficiency and Renewable Energy, *Fact of the Week: Vehicles Per Thousand People: An International Comparison*, 15 September 2003, online: available http://www.eere.energy.gov/vehiclesandfuels/facts/2003/fcvt_fotw285.shtml (12 June 2004). Data are for the year 2001.

2   Bardou, Jean-Pierre, Chanaron, Jean-Jacques, Fridenson, Patrick and Laux, James M., *The Automobile Revolution: The Impact of an Industry*, University of North Carolina Press (Chapel Hill, 1982), p.74.

3   Ibid. pp.112,117.

4   Ibid. p.113.

5   Ibid. p.120.

6   American sources tend to use the term 'transit' or 'mass transportation', where UK ones would use 'public transport'. Henceforth we shall use the UK term, although the US alternatives may appear when quotations from US sources are used.

7   Bardou et al., *The Automobile Revolution: The Impact of an Industry*, p.198. The authors note the 'relative under-motorisation' of European metropolises 'encouraged by the existence of public transit systems'.

8   Jerome B. Wiesner, quoted in St. Clair, David J., *The Motorisation of American Cities*, Praeger (New York, 1986), p.25.

9   St Clair, *The Motorisation of American Cities*, p.82.

10   Schurr, Sam H. and Netschert, Bruce C., *Energy in the American Economy 1850–1975*, Johns Hopkins Press (Baltimore, 1960), pp. 93,117.

11   Production of crude oil did not increase in the same proportion as gasoline consumption because technological advances in refining raised the fraction of gasoline in the total of refined products.

12   Studebaker Corporation: a medium-sized US automobile manufacturing company, merged into Studebaker-Packard Corporation in 1954.

13   Hoffman, Paul, *New York Times*, 7 January 1934, quoted in St Clair, *The Motorisation of American Cities*, p.134.

14   St Clair, *The Motorisation of American Cities*, p.58.

15   Ibid. p.60.

16   See, for example, articles published, online by the Modern Transit Society at http://www.trainweb.org and St Clair, *The Motorisation of American Cities*.

17   Szoboszlay, Akos, *The Desired Result: Drive People to Drive*, Modern Transit Society, online: available http://www.trainweb.org/mts/ctc/ctc05.html (14 December 2002).

18   St Clair, *The Motorisation of American Cities*, p.177.

19   Szoboszlay, *The Desired Result: Drive People to Drive.*
20   Rae, John B., *The American Automobile: A Brief History*, University of Chicago Press (Chicago, 1965), p.220.
21   Quoted in St Clair, *The Motorisation of American Cities*, p.122.
22   Ibid. p.160.
23   Rae, *The American Automobile: A Brief History*, p.175.
24   *Fortune Magazine*, July 1961, p.168.
25   US Department of Energy, OTT, Oak Ridge National Laboratory, *Transportation Energy Data Book: Edition 21* (Tennessee, 2001), p.11–15.
26   Rae, *The American Automobile: A Brief History*, p.219.
27   American Petroleum Institute, *Basic Petroleum Data Book*, Vol.XVIII, No.1, 1998.

CHAPTER 3

1   This brief geological sketch is based on the geology of the Arabian-Iranian petroleum province and draws particularly on Nawwab, Ismail, Speers, Peter and Hoye, Paul (eds), *Saudi Aramco and its World*, Saudi Aramco (Dharan, 1995), pp.195–7. In other parts of the Gulf region, the geological 'history' would be different in detail.
2   Data on oilfield size and distribution is taken from World Resources Institute, *Global Topic: Size Distribution of Oil Fields*, online: available http://www.wri.org/wri/climate/jm_oil_006.html (29 September 2002), updated to allow for more recent discoveries.
3   DeNovo, John, 'The Movement for an Aggressive American Oil Policy Abroad 1918–20', *American Historical Review*, Vol.61, No.4, 1956, pp.854–76.
4   Yergin, *The Prize: The Epic Quest for Oil, Money and Power*, p.14.
5   Schurr and Netschert, *Energy in the American Economy 1850–1975*, p.117.
6   DeNovo, 'The Movement for an Aggressive American Oil Policy Abroad, 1918–20', p.857.
7   Quoted in Ibid. p.869.
8   Ibid. p.860.
9   Ibid. p.868.
10   Hamilton, Charles, *Americans and Oil in the Middle East*, Gulf Publishing Co (Houston, 1962), p.83.
11   Yergin, *The Prize*, p.196.
12   See Hamilton, *Americans and Oil in the Middle East*, p.128.
13   Ibid.
14   Aburish, Said, *The Rise, Corruption and Coming Fall of the House of Saud*, Bloomsbury Publishing (London, 1995), p.288.
15   Mommer, *Global Oil and the Nation State*, p.120.
16   The term 'Wahhabism' is used by historians (but not by *Wahhabis* themselves) to refer to the religious reform movement founded by Muhammad Ibn Abd al-Wahhab (1703–92). The movement was 'fundamentalist' in that it called for a return to a pure form of Islam unadulterated by the various accretions which had been added over the centuries – in particular the worship of Muslim saints and holy places. Such practices were condemned and their practitioners classed as unbelievers who

could legitimately be killed. The movement was especially hostile towards Sufism, the predominant strand of Islam among the Ottoman Turks who controlled Arabia. The movement therefore had a primitive 'nationalist' or 'anti-colonial' aspect. For an excellent analysis of the social, economic and religious origins of Wahhabism, see Vassiliev, Alexei, *The History of Saudi Arabia*, Saqi Books (London, 2000), pp.29–82.

17 Quoted in Hamilton, *Americans and Oil in the Middle East*, p.152.

18 Quoted in Vietor, Richard H.K., *Energy Policy in America since 1945*, Cambridge University Press (Cambridge, 1984), p.29.

19 The phrase is that of Michael T. Klare, Professor of Peace and World Security Studies at Hampshire College, Amhurst Mass. See Klare, Michael T., *The Geopolitics of War*, online: available http://www.geocities.com/hal9000report/hal.3.html (9 November 2003).

20 Vietor, *Energy Policy in America since 1945*, p.30.

21 Painter David, S., *Private Power and Public Policy: Multinational Oil Companies and US Foreign Policy 1941–1954*, I. B. Tauris (London, 1986), p.95.

22 US Senate Foreign Relations Committee Subcommittee on Multinational Corporations, *Multinational Corporations and US Foreign Policy*, 1976, quoted in Holden, David and Johns, Richard, *The House of Saud*, Sidgwick & Jackson (London, 1981), p.314.

23 McCarthy, Justin, *The Population of Palestine*, Columbia University Press (New York, 1990).

24 Holden and Johns, *The House of Saud*, p.137.

25 The phrase quoted is that of Abdulaziz Hussein Al-Sowayegh, formerly Assistant Deputy Minister for Foreign Information, Kingdom of Saudi Arabia, writing in the early 1980s. See Al-Sowayegh, Abdulaziz Hussein, *Arab Petro-Politics*, Croom Helm (Beckenham, 1984), p.53.

26 Ali, Tariq, *Bush in Babylon: The Recolonisation of Iraq*, Verso (London, 2003), p.113.

27 Hamilton: *Americans and Oil in the Middle East*, p.65.

28 Our treatment of this crucial episode in Middle East oil history is necessarily cursory in a monograph of this nature. For an excellent narrative of the events before and after the Iranian coup see Elm, Mostafa, *Oil Power and Principle: Iran's Oil Nationalization and its Aftermath*, Syracuse University Press (Syracuse, New York, 1992).

29 Tanzer, Michael, *The Political Economy of International Oil and the Underdeveloped Countries*, Temple Smith (London, 1969), p.326.

30 See Kaufman, Burton I., 'Mideast Multinational Oil, US Foreign Policy and Antitrust: The 1950s', *Journal of American History*, Vol.63, No.4, 1977, pp 937–59; see also Krasner, Stephen D., 'A Statist Interpretation of American Oil Policy Toward the Middle East', *Political Science Quarterly*, Vol. 94, No.1, 1979, pp.77–96.

31 Hamilton, *Americans and Oil in the Middle East*, p.270.

32 De Chazeau, Melvin G. and Kahn, Alfred E., *Integration and Competition in the Petroleum Industry*, Yale University Press (New Haven, 1959), p.8n; and Jenkins, Gilbert, 'World Oil Reserves reporting 1948–96: Political, Economic and Subjective Influences', *OPEC Review*, Vol.XXI, No.2, 1997.

33   Quoted from an essay by Clarence Page of the *Chicago Tribune*, 'Century of Cars', Online NewsHour, 6 October 2003, online: available http://www.pbs.org/newshour/essays/july-dec03/page_10–06.html (8 June 2004).

CHAPTER 4

1   Vietor, *Energy Policy in America since 1945*, p.92.
2   Later to become the Interstate Oil & Gas Compact Commission (IOGCC).
3   Ali Rodriguez Araque, OPEC Secretary General, 'OPEC and the New-Oil Realities', speech delivered to the Venezuelan-American Association of the United States (VAAUS) at the Harvard Club, New York City, 4 February 2002.
4   Bohi, Douglas and Russel, Milton, *Limiting Oil Imports: An Economic History and Analysis*, Johns Hopkins University Press (Baltimore, 1978), p.26.
5   Vietor, *Energy Policy in America since 1945*, p.92.
6   Quoted in Ibid. p.94.
7   Quoted in Ibid. p.96.
8   Quoted in Ibid. p.99.
9   See Lubell, Harold, *Middle East Oil Crisis and Western Europe's Energy Supplies*, Rand Corporation and Johns Hopkins Press (Baltimore, 1963).
10   Ibid. p.3.
11   Data relating to the size and duration of Middle East oil supply disruptions, cited here, and elsewhere in the book are derived from US Department of Energy, EIA, *Global Oil Supply Disruptions Since 1951*, online: available http://www.eia.doe.gov/emeu/security/distable.html (8 September 2002).
12   For a brilliant dissection of America's pervasive and deep-rooted cultural and racial prejudices against the people of the Middle East, see Little, Douglas, *American Orientalism: The United States and the Middle East since 1945*, I.B.Tauris (London, 2004).
13   Kissinger, Henry, *Years of Renewal*, Wiedenfeld & Nicolson (London, 1999), p.665.
14   Mikdashi, Zuhayr, *A Financial Analysis of Middle Eastern Oil Concessions, 1901–65*, Praeger (New York, 1966), The figure of 35 per cent is based on data in the two tables on pp.106 and 275.
15   Mikdashi, *A Financial Analysis of Middle East Oil Concessions*, pp.135–45. See also Hartshorn, J.E. *Oil Companies and Governments*, Faber and Faber (London, 1962), pp.175–81.
16   Mikdashi calculated the internal rate of return (cashflow profit rate) for the Persian oil consortium between 1954 and 1964 at 69 per cent. See Mikdashi, *Financial Analysis of Middle Eastern Oil Concessions, 1901–65*. See also Halliday, *Arabia Without Sultans*, Penguin Books (Harmondsworth,1974), p.412, where rates of 61 per cent and 72 per cent are given for the periods 1948–1949 and 1958–1960 respectively; and Adelman, Morris, *The Genie Out of the Bottle: World Oil Since 1970*, MIT Press (Cambridge Mass., 1995), p.36, who calculates the post-tax internal rate of return for a new oilfield development by ARAMCO to be 106 per cent.
17   Halliday, *Arabia Without Sultans*, p.412

18 Khadduri, Majid, *Republican Iraq: A Study in Iraqi Politics since the Revolution of 1958*, Oxford University Press (London, 1969), pp.65–6.

19 See Ali, *Bush in Babylon: The Recolonisation of Iraq*, pp.87–8, and Khadduri, *Republican Iraq*, pp.189–99.

20 The 'posted' price of oil was the reference price for calculating taxes and royalties. Originally it had been the price at which the oil companies had sold oil to third parties as opposed to 'internal' sales (i.e. sales at notional transfer prices) to their own affiliated refineries. The posted price was, of course, higher than the transfer price. During the 1950s and 1960s, the oil-producing countries negotiated successfully for the posted price to become the reference price for calculating royalties and petroleum taxes.

21 Yergin, *The Prize*, p.580.

22 Ibid. p.591.

23 See Akins, James, 'The Oil Crisis: This Time the Wolf is Here', *Foreign Affairs*, April 1973, pp.462–90.

24 Harvie, Christopher, *Fool's Gold: The Story of North Sea Oil*, Hamish Hamilton (London, 1994), p.92.

25 The increase in the posted price of Saudi light crude between January 1973 ($2.591/b) and January 1974 ($11.651/b).

26 Kissinger, *Years of Renewal*, pp.665–7.

27 Ibid.

28 Jaggi, Rohit, 'Britain Feared Oil Crisis Could Spark US Military Retaliation', *Financial Times*, 6 January 2004.

29 Conant, *The Oil Factor in US Foreign Policy, 1980–90*.

30 Ibid. p.107.

31 Ibid. p.111.

32 Yergin, *The Prize*, p.770.

CHAPTER 5

1 Freedman, Lawrence and Karsh, Efraim, *The Gulf Conflict 1990–91: Diplomacy and War in the New World Order*, Faber and Faber (London, 1993), p.74.

2 Little, *American Orientalism: The United States and the Middle East since 1945*, p.256.

3 Freedman and Karsh, *The Gulf Conflict 1990–91*, p.76.

4 Quoted in Yergin, *The Prize*, p.773.

5 Yergin, *The Prize*, p.773.

6 Yergin, *The Prize*, p.774.

7 See Suskind, Ron, *The Price of Loyalty: George W. Bush, The White House and the Education of Paul O'Neill*, Simon and Schuster (New York, 2004), pp. 70–2, 258.

8 Ibid. p.72.

9 Woodward, Bob, *Bush at War*, Simon and Schuster (New York, 2003), p.49.

10 Woodward, *Bush at War*, p.83.

11 According to Woodward, Condoleezza Rice was the first to be told by Bush of his decision to instruct Rumsfeld to begin work on the war plans, on 21 November 2001. However, it seems highly probable that Bush had already been in discussion with

Cheney before this. Woodward tells us that Bush 'could not recall' if he had talked to Vice President Cheney on that morning, although 'he was certainly aware of Cheney's own position'. Indeed, since Woodward also tells us that 'on the long walk-up to war in Iraq, Dick Cheney was "a powerful steamrolling force"', we might reasonably choose to ignore Bush's 'forgetfulness' and infer that the two men had indeed discussed the war on Iraq either on 21 November 2001 or before and that the proposal to prepare the Iraq battle plans probably originated with Cheney himself. See Woodward, Bob, *Plan of Attack*, Simon and Schuster (New York, 2004), p.4.

12   Lardner Jr, George and Romano, Lois, 'Bush Name Helps Fuel Oil Dealings', *Washington Post*, 30 July 1999.

13   Yergin, *The Prize*, p.756.

14   US Department of Energy, EIA, *Oil and Gas Development in the United States in the Early 1990s: An Expanded Role for Independent Producers* (Washington, October 1995), p.11.

15   This very abbreviated account of the Harken affair is based on the following sources: Lardner Jr, George and Romano, Lois, 'Bush Name Helps Fuel Oil Dealings'; 'Right on the Money: the George Bush Profile', *Center for Public Integrity*, online. available http://www.publici.org/dtaweb/report.asp?ReportID=431&LI=10&L2=10&L3=0 &L4=0&L5=0 (14 November 2002); Flocco, Tom, 'Harken Energy – Bush's No Good Trade', *WorldNet Daily*, 18 February 2000, republished online: available http://www.scoop.co.nz/mason/stories/HL0207/S00047.htm (9 November 2002); Tran, Mark, 'Bush and Harken Energy', *Guardian Unlimited*, 10 July 2002, online: available http://www.guardian.co.uk/theissues/article/0,6512,752705,00.html (9 November 2002); New York State Society of Certified Public Accountants, 'Bush's Harken Past Becoming Clearer', online: available http://www.nysscpa.org/home/2002/ 702/3week/article19.htm (24 October 2002).

16   For a description of production sharing agreements, see Chapter Twelve.

17   The information that 'Yousuf Shirawi already had a link to the administration dating to the days when George Bush was Vice-President,' was unintentionally revealed in an article in the *Washington Post* attempting to defend Bush Jr. See Lardner Jr, George, 'The Harken-Bahrain Deal: A Baseless Suspicion', *Washington Post*, 30 July 1999, republished online: available http://www.washingtonpost.com/wp-srv/politics/ campaigns/wh2000/stories/bushside073099.htm (10 November 2002).

18   Woodward, *Plan of Attack*, pp.264–5.

19   Interstate Oil and Gas Compact Commission, *A Battle for Survival? The Real Story Behind Low Oil Prices* (Oklahoma City, April 1999), p.5.

20   According to the Texas Independent Producers and Royalty Owners Association (TIPRO), about 3 million individuals are owners of royalty interests in the state of Texas. However, not all of these are residents of Texas. We have therefore reduced the 3 million figure to 2.5 million to account for this, although this is obviously only a rough estimate. (Original information from Mr M. Fleming, Public Affairs Director, TIPRO.)

21   Interstate Oil and Gas Compact Commission, *A Battle for Survival? The Real Story Behind Low Oil Prices*, p.15.

22   Ibid. p.7.

23   See Corn, David, 'W.'s First Enron Connection', *The Nation*, 4 March 2002, online: available http://www.thenation.com/capitalgames/index.mhtm1?bid-3&pid=21 (14 November 2002).

24   The term 'BTU mega-marketer' is the term more commonly encountered in the US energy industry press; 'BTU' stands for 'British Thermal Units' and is the measure of energy used by the Americans in preference to the Joule: 'energy mega-marketer' conveys the same idea.

25   Texans for Public Justice, 'Pioneer Profiles: George W. Bush's $1000,000 Club, Name Kenneth Lay', online: available http://tpj.org/pioneers/kenneth_lay.html (14 November 2002).

26   See Perry, Sam, 'Bush Did Try to Save Enron', *Consortiumnews.com*, online: available http://www.consortiumnews.com/2002/05902a.html (24 October 2002).

27   Center for Responsible Politics, online: available http://opensecrets.org/industries/ (17 November 2002).

28   Texans for Public Justice, 'George W. Bush's $100,000 Club', online: available http://tpj.org/pioneers (17 November 2002). Of 221 'pioneers' identified by July 2001, the single largest group were 'lawyers and lobbyists' whose clients include a variety of different business interests (some of them energy-related). Excluding this amorphous group, 'Finance' was the largest industry source of 'pioneers' and 'Energy & Natural Resources' was the second largest.

29   For example, Sanchez-O'Brien Oil & Gas, Pruet Drilling, McCutchin Drilling, Vaughan Petroleum, Permian Exploration, Lee M.Bass Inc., Pickens Companies.

30   According to the *Oil and Gas Journal*, 15 June 1998, a study of 65 US 'independents' and 16 US 'Majors' showed that the average finding and development cost for the former was $5.77 per barrel of oil and oil equivalent gas compared with $3.69 per barrel for the Majors. (Note that these costs refer to exploration and capital costs, whereas the figure of $9–10 dollars per barrel for the smaller independents quoted earlier in this chapter refers to operating cost.)

31   *Oil and Gas Journal*, 16 March 2001, p.19.

32   *Financial Times*, 27 July 2001.

33   Harding, James, 'Schultz is Still Making his Voice Heard After 50 Years at the Top', *Financial Times*, 21 November 2002.

34   Martin, Patrick, 'Oil Company Adviser Named US Representative to Afghanistan', Afghan Information Center, 3 January 2002, online: available http://www.afghan-info.com//Politics/Khalilzad_Nomination.htm (21 November 2002). After Clinton's missile attack on the bin Laden camps, it became absolutely clear that, for the time being, Unocal's trans-Afghanistan pipeline projects were no longer politically feasible. At this point, Khalilzad metamorphosed into an opponent of the Taliban and started to favour switching support to the Northern Alliance. For the detailed story of the Unocal-Taliban connection, see Rashid, Ahmed, *Taliban: Islam, Oil and the New Great Game in Central Asia*, I. B. Tauris (London, 2000).

35   Khalilzad later became special envoy to Afghanistan and his place was taken by Elliott Abrams, previously in charge of Central American affairs under Reagan and a notorious participant in the Iran-Contra affair for which he was found guilty of criminal actions, only to be pardoned later by George Bush Sr.

36 Williams, Garry, 'Dick Cheney Ain't Studying War No More', *Business Week*, 2 March 1998, online: available http://www.businessweek.com/1998/09/b3567127.htm (18 November 2002).

37 Rohloff, Greg, 'Cheney's Experience Pays off as a CEO', *Amarillo Business Journal*, 13 June 1998, online: available http://businessjournal.net/stories/061398/ABJ_pays.html (21 November 2002).

38 Quoted in Williams: 'Dick Cheney Ain't Studying War No More'.

39 Halliburton Company, *Annual Report on Form 10-K 2001* (2002).

40 Quoted by Madson, Wayne, 'Cheney at Helm', *The Progressive*, online: available http://www.progressive.org/wm0900.htm (24 October 2002).

41 Quoted in Ibid.

42 Halliburton Company, *Annual Report on Form 10-K 1994* (1995) and *Annual Report on Form 10-K 2001* (2002).

43 Martinson, Jane, 'Cheney Linked to Oil Loans', *The Guardian*, 5 August 2000, republished online: available http://search.ft.com:80/search/artciles.html (18 November 2002).

44 Cheney, Richard, 'Defending Liberty in a Global Economy', *Collateral Damage Conference*, Cato Institute, 23 June 1998, online: available http://www.cato.org/speeches/sp-dc062398.html (14 January 2003).

45 See, for example, Holstein, Lisa, 'Cheney's Oil Days: Iran Stance Raises Concern among Jews', *Jewish Bulletin News*, online: available http://www.jewishsf.com/bk000804/uscheney.shtml (24 October 2002).

46 Quoted in AFX Europe, 'Halliburton Reportedly Dealt with Iraq While Cheney Was CEO', *AFX Europe*, 24 June 2001, online: available http://search.ft.com:80/search/articles.html (18 November 2002).

47 Hoyos, Carola, 'A Discreet Way of Doing Business', F.T.Com, 3 November 2000, online: available http://search.ft.com:80/search/artciles.html (18 November 2002); other sources give a higher value for the Iraq deals: e.g. both Farah, Joseph, 'Why Cheney is Compromised', *Jerusalem Post*, 13 July 2001, same electronic document, and 'Halliburton Reportedly Dealt with Iraq while Cheney Was CEO', *AFX Europe*, 24 June 2001, same electronic document, state that the contracts were worth $73 million. With regard to Halliburton's ownership stakes in Dresser-Rand (51 per cent) and Ingersoll-Dresser-Pump (49 per cent), a 51 per cent ownership means the former company would be a fully consolidated subsidiary of Halliburton, whereas the 49 per cent equity in Ingersoll-Dresser-Rand, while falling short of the criteria for a 'subsidiary', would have been comfortably sufficient to guarantee effective management control.

48 Woodward, *Plan of Attack*, p.9.

49 Associated Press, 'Cheney, Oil Executives Raise $8 Million for GOP', 28 September 2000, online: available http://quest.conline.com/stories/092800/gen_ 0928006149.shtml (24 October 2002).

50 Lay met with Cheney in his capacity as head of the Energy Policy Task Force a total of six times, four of these being before the Report was published; see Dizikes, Peter, 'Cheney: We Met With Enron Execs', abcnews.com, 9 January 2002, online: available http://abcnews.go.com/sections/business/DailyNews/enron_cheneyletter020109.html (20 November 2002).

51 Cheney, Richard et al., *Report of the National Energy Policy Group*, May 2001, online: available http://www.whitehouse.gov/energy/ (1 December 2002).

52 Enron's Indian interests consisted of its new Dabhol gas-fired power station and offshore oil and gas reserves operated by Enron Oil & Gas Company.

CHAPTER 6

1 Cheney, Richard et al., *Report of the National Energy Policy Group*, p.8:1.

2 US Department of the Interior, 'First Alaska Offshore Energy Flows Today,' *News Release*, 1 November 2001.

3 US Fish and Wildlife Service, *Potential Impacts of Proposed Oil and Gas Development on the Arctic Refuge's Coastal Plain: Historical Overview and Issues of Concern*, online: available http://www.fws.gov/issues1.html (4 February 2003).

4 Natural Resources Defense Council, *Oil and the Arctic National Wildlife Refuge*, online: available http://www.nrdc.org/land/wilderness/artic.asp (5 February 2003).

5 Miller, Pamela A., *The Impact of Oil Development on Prudhoe Bay*, online: available http://arcticcircle.uconn.edu/ANWR/arcticconnections.htm (11 February 2003).

6 US Fish and Wildlife Service, *Potential Impacts of Proposed Oil and Gas Development*.

7 Ibid.

8 Ibid.

9 Hubbert, M. King, 'Nuclear Energy and the Fossil Fuels', in American Petroleum Institute (eds), *Drilling and Production Practice*, API (New York, 1956).

10 In fact, Hubbert produced two forecasts for peak US oil production, based on different estimates of the initial endowment of ultimately recoverable oil, one of 150 billion barrels and the other of 200 billion. It was the second estimate which produced the 1972 peak forecast.

11 It should be noted however, that Hubbert's forecast of the actual size of US oil production 'at the peak' (using his 'best' estimate of about 7 million barrels per day) was about 1.6 million b/d lower than the out-turn. See Deming, David, 'Are We Running Out of Oil?', National Center for Policy Analysis, 29 January 2003, online: available http://www.ncpa.org/pub/bg/bg159/index.html (6 February 2003). It also now seems probable that Hubbert's accurate prediction of the date of the 'peak' was more fortuitous than he would have liked to believe. See Kaufmann, Robert K. and Cleveland, Cutler J., 'Oil Production in the Lower 48 States: Economic, Geological and Institutional Determinants', *The Energy Journal*, Vol. 22, No.1, 2001.

12 Quoted in, *Alexander's Gas and Oil Connections*, 'National Security Act of 2001', Vol.6, Issue 11, 18 June 2001, online: available http://www.gasandoil.com/goc/news/ntn12531.htm (9 February 2003).

13 Quoted in Rosenbaum, David E., 'Two Sides Push on Arctic Oil, but Proposal Lacks Votes', *New York Times*, 18 April 2002.

14 ANWR, 'Top 10 Reasons to Support Development in ANWR', online: available http://www.anwr.org/topten.htm (4 February 2002).

15 US Geological Survey, *Arctic National Wildlife Refuge, 1002 Area, Petroleum Assessment 1998, Including Economic Analysis*, online: available http://pubs.usgs.gov/fs/fs-0028-01/fs-0028-01.htm (11 February 2002).

16 'At prices less than $13 per barrel, no commercial oil is estimated' (US Geological Survey). Note that Cheney's report berates OPEC for 'efforts…to maintain oil prices above levels dictated by market forces' (*Report of the National Energy Policy Group:* p.8:6.)

17 Dunne, Nancy, 'Iraq Oil Ban Mooted to Win Support for Arctic Drilling', *Financial Times*, 16 April 2002.

18 Besser, James D., 'Arctic Drillers Cozying Up to Jews', *The Jewish Week*, 16 November 2001.

19 McNulty, Sheila, 'BP Quits Campaign on Alaskan Drilling', *Financial Times*, 27 November 2002.

20 Ragsdale, Rose, 'Liberty Called Tip of Offshore Oil, Gas Riches', *Alaska Oil and Gas Reporter*, 5 February 2002, online: available http://www.oilandgasreporter.com/ stories/020502/nor_liberty_hopeful.shtml (15 February 2002).

21 David Rosenbaum, 'Two Sides Push on Arctic Oil, but Proposal Lacks Votes'.

22 Hebert, H.Joseph, 'Oil Companies Largely Silent on Alaska', Associated Press, 17 April 2002, online: available http://www.anwr.org/features/oil-silent.htm (11 February 2003).

23 US Department of the Interior, 'First Alaska Offshore Energy Flows Today', *News Release*, 1 November 2001.

24 World Resources Institute, 'Database', *Earth Trends: The Environmental Portal*, online: available http://earthtrends.wri.org.

CHAPTER 7

1   Cheney, Richard et al., *Report of the National Energy Policy Group*, pp.8:9–8:10.

2   US Department of Energy, Energy Information Administration (EIA), *Privatization and the Globalization of Energy Markets* (Washington, 1996).

3   Venezuela already had a small state oil company but it had limited powers. Petroleos de Venezuela SA (PDVSA), the new state company formed in 1976, absorbed the old one at the same time as the existing foreign oil operations in Venezuela were nationalised. Mexico's oil industry had already been nationalised in 1938.

4   In fact the British experience was rather complicated by the intrusion of a separate 'Scottish' oil nationalism, see Harvie, Christopher, *Fool's Gold: The Story of North Sea Oil*, Hamish Hamilton (London, 1994).

5   Finlayson, Jock A. and Hagland, David G., 'Oil Politics and Canada-United States Relations', *Political Science Quarterly*, Vol.99, No.2, 1984, p.273.

6   Weir, Erin M.K., *NEP to FTA: The Political Economy of Canadian Petroleum Policy in the 1980s* (University of Regina, 2001), p.2, online: available http://www.web.net/ ~pef/eweir.pdf (1 April 2003).

7   Ibid. p.2

8   Finlayson and Hagland, 'Oil Politics and Canada-United States Relations', p.278.

9   Weir, *NEP to FTA*, p.8.

10 *Canada-USA Free Trade Agreement*, Chapter Nine, online: available http:// wehner.tamu.edu/mgmt.www/nafta/fta/9.htm (5 January 2003).

11 The official was Ann Hughes. See: Barlow, Maude (Council of Canadians), 'US Tops up with Canadian Oil', *Toronto Globe and Mail*, 26 September 2000, online: available http://www.hartford-hwp.com/archives/44/100.htm (5 January 2003).

12 BP plc, *BP Statistical Review of World Energy 2001* (London, 2002), pp.6, 18–19. The numbers have been rounded and adjusted slightly to allow for balancing items not identified in the BP study.

13 Simon, Bernard, 'Canada Oil Group to be Privatised', *Financial Times*, 14 May 1991.

14 Park, Gary, 'Conoco's C\$9.8 billion Offer for Gulf Canada Jolts Calgary Boardrooms', *Petroleum News Alaska*, 25 June 2001, online: available http://www.petroleumnewsalaska.com/pmarch/010625-51.html (3 January 2003).

15 Clouser, Gary, 'Crossborder M&A: Keeping it Fair, and Canadian', *Oil and Gas Investor*, online: available http://www.oilandgasinvestor.com/reports/crossborder/crossborder03.htm (3 January 2003).

16 Editorial, 'U.S. interest in Canadian Mergers Not a Cause for Concern, Analysts Say', *Oil and Gas Investor*, online: available http://www.oilandgasinvestor.com/comment/994111170.html (3 January 2003).

17 Park, 'Conoco's C\$9.8 billion Offer for Gulf Canada Jolts Calgary Boardrooms'.

18 Brown, Jonathon C., 'Why Foreign Oil Companies Shifted Their Production from Mexico to Venezuela during the 1920s', *American Historical Review*, Vol.90, No.2, 1985, pp.362–85.

19 See Espinasa, Ramon and Mommer, Bernard, 'Venezuelan Oil Policy in the Long Run', in Dorian, J.P. and Fesharaki, F., *International Issues in Energy Policy, Development and Economics*, Westview Press (Boulder, 1992).

20 Mommer, Bernard, *The Political Role of National Oil Companies in Exporting Countries: The Venezuelan Case*, Oxford Institute for Energy Studies (Oxford, 1994), p.21.

21 See, e.g., Mora Contreras, Jesus, *Reparto de Ingresos Petroleros Extraordinarios y Proceso de Apertura Petrolera en Venezuela*, Instituto de Investigaciones Economicas y Sociales, Universidad de Los Andes (Merida, n.d.), and Mommer, *The Political Role of National Oil Companies in Exporting Countries: The Venezuelan Case*.

22 *Oil and Gas Journal*, 4 January 1999, p.28.

23 Center for Strategic and International Studies (CSIS), online: available http://www.csis.org/sei/event991208bioGiusti.html (7 September 2002). In 1999, the CSIS reported that Giusti was currently serving as a 'Senior Adviser' to the organisation.

24 During the 1980s, PDVSA bought into a number of refining companies outside Venezuela, of which the most significant was the acquisition of CITGO Petroleum in the USA.

25 Mora Contreras, *Reparto de Ingresos Petroleros*, p.22.

26 See for example, Odell, Peter, *Oil and Gas: Crises and Controversies, 1961–2000*, Vol.1, Multi-Science Publishing Company (Brentwood, 2001), p.424.

27 US National Security Council, *A National Security Strategy for a New Century* (Washington, October 1998), quoted in Klare, *Resource Wars*, p.46.

28 See Crow, Patrick, 'Seeking Scapegoats', *Oil and Gas Journal*, 1 March 1999, p.34.

29 American Petroleum Institute (API), Policy Analysis and Planning Department, *Economic State of the US Oil and Natural Gas Exploration and Production Industry: Long Term Trends and Recent Events*, 30 April 1999, p.14.

30 Independent Petroleum Association of America (IPAA), Information Services, *1998 Profile of Independent Producers* (no place of publication given, 1999).

31 Rutledge, Ian, 'Profitability and Supply Price in the US Domestic Oil Industry: Implications for the Political Economy of Oil in the 21st Century', *Cambridge Journal of Economics*, Vol.27, No.1, 2003, p.14.

32 Independent Petroleum Association of America (IPAA), *1998 Profile of Independent Producers.*

33 Ibid. p.16.

34 *Save Domestic Oil*, online: available http://www.savedomesticoil.com/hhammdoc.htm (12 January 2002).

35 Ibid.

36 *Oil and Gas Journal*, 21 December 1998, p.33.

37 Rodriguez, Ali, 'Comentario, Regimenes Fiscales en Economias Petroleras', *Segundo Encuentro International de Economia*, Banco Central de Venezuela, March 1999, p.310.

38 'Quien es Quien: Luis Giusti', Veneconomia.com, online: available http://www.veneconomia.com/esp/aldia/resumenQuien.asp?pub=141 (7 September 2002).

39 *Oil and Gas Journal*, 29 March 1999.

40 Independent Petroleum Association of America, *Press Release* 30 June 1999, online: available http://www.ipaa.org.departments/communications/PR1999/PRO6301999.htm (26 February 2001).

41 Mabro, Robert, 'Some Fundamental OPEC Issues', *Oxford Energy Forum*, August 2000, Oxford Institute for Energy Studies, p.7.

42 *Oil and Gas Journal*, 8 March 1999, p.37.

43 *Oil and Gas Journal*, 21 December 1998, p.32.

44 Mommer, Bernard, 'Venezuelan Oil Politics at the Crossroads', *Monthly Comment*, March 2001, Oxford Institute for Energy Studies, online: available http://www.oxfordenergy.org/13mar01.html (16 April 2002).

45 See Boué, Juan Carlos, *The Political Control of State Oil Companies: A Case Study of the Vertical Integration Programme of Petroleos de Venezuela, 1982–95*, Oxford, D.Phil. thesis, 1998; *Venezuela: The Political Economy of Oil*, Oxford University Press (Oxford, 1994).

46 Mommer, Bernard, 'Subversive Oil' in Ellner, Steve and Hellinger, Daniel (eds), *Venezuelan Politics in the Chavez Era: Polarization and Social Conflict*, Lynne Rienner (Boulder, Colo., 2002).

47 See Crossette, Barbara, 'A Different Kind of Rogue: When Democracy Runs off the Rails', *New York Times*, 4 June 2000. Crossette quotes Susan Kaufman Purcell, President of the Americas Society in New York, to the effect that Chavez's government qualifies as a 'rogue democracy', although Purcell apparently prefers the term 'imperfect democracy'.

48 See Borger, Julian and Bellos, Alex, 'US 'Gave the Nod' to Venezuelan Coup', *The Guardian*, 17 April 2002. See also Wolffe, Richard and Webb-Vidal, Andy, 'US Insists it Rebuffed Approaches by Anti-Chavez Opposition', *Financial Times*, 17 April 2002. In spite of the title to the latter piece, the content of the article broadly confirms the analysis of the *Guardian* article.

49   Monaldi, Francisco, 'Capitalismo Popular', *Escritos de Francisco Monaldi Mas*, online: available http://www.fmonaldi.com/fmmas/art05.htm (17 April 2002).

50   Monaldi, Francisco, 'Capitalism Popular',*Escritos de Francisco Monaldi Mas*, online: available http://www.fmonaldi.com/fmmas/art07.htm (17 April 2002).

51   Andres Sosa Pietri quoted in *El Universal*, 11 June 2002, online: available http://archivo.eluniversal.com/2002/07/11/11204DD.html (8 September 2002).

52   Horsnell, Paul, 'Oil Market: Why Venezuela Matters', *Global Energy Research*, 16 December 2002, JP Morgan Securities Inc., online: available http://morganmarkets.jpmorgan.com (31 January 2003).

53   Ibid.

54   Ibid.

55   See Mommer, *Global Oil and the Nation State*, pp.70–81.

56   Brown, 'Why Foreign Oil Companies Shifted their Production from Mexico to Venezuela during the 1920s', pp.364, 367, 384.

57   Ibid.

58   BP, op. cit. p.4.

59   Johns, Richard, 'Mexico Applauds Iraq's Belligerence', *Financial Times*, 26 July 1990.

60   See Claes, Dag Harald, *The Politics of Oil-Producer Cooperation*, Westview Press (Boulder, 2001), pp.281–95.

61   Alberro, Jose, *The Politics of Petroleum: Outline of Remarks by Jose Alberro*, September 2002, Center for Latin American Studies, University of California, Berkeley, online: available http://ist-socrates.berkeley.edu:7001/Events/fall2002/09-12-02-Alberroetal/alberroremarks.html (7 January 2003).

62   Morse, Edward L. (Chair) and Jaffe, Amy Myers (Project Director), *Strategic Energy Policy Challenges for the 21st Century*, Report of an Independent Task Force, sponsored by the James Baker III Institute for Public Policy of Rice University and the Council on Foreign Relations, April 2001, p.69.

63   Ibid.

64   Quoted in Vaicius, Ingrid and Isacson, Adam, 'The War on Drugs Meets the War on Terror', *International Policy Report*, February 2003, Colombia Project, Center for International Policy, online: available http://www.ciponline.org/colombia/0302ipr.htm (12 October 2003).

65   McDermott, Jeremy, 'Green Berets Move into Colombia's Oilfields', *Daily Telegraph*, 12 October 2002.

CHAPTER 8

1   See Medvedev, Zhores, 'The War for Caspian Oil', *European Labour Forum*, Summer 1995, pp.27–30.

2   See Rashid, Ahmed, *Taliban* Chapter 13, I. B. Tauris (London, 2000).

3   Nichol, Jim, *Central Asia's New States: Political Developments and Implications for US Interests – Issue Brief for Congress*, Congressional Research Service, Library of Congress (Washington, November 2002), p.4. The per capita GDP figure for the Central Asian states only was put at $705. GDP per capita for Azerbaijan was estimated even lower at $525 for 2000 ('Azerbaijan Survey', *Financial Times*, 22 November 2000).

4   Hill, Fiona, 'Areas for Future Cooperation or Conflict in Central Asia and the Caucasus', paper presented at the Yale University Conference, *The Silk Road in the 21st Century*, 19 September 2002, online: available http://www.brook.edu/views/speeches/hillf/20020919.htm (14 January 2003).

5   *Christian Science Monitor*, 25 October 2001, online: available http://www.csmonitor.com/2001/1025/p8s1-comv.html (14 January 2003).

6   US Department of Energy, Energy Information Administration (EIA), *International Energy Outlook* 1998 (Washington,1998), p.34.

7   The reserves terminology used by the EIA in its Caspian reports has been notably opaque and confusing. In 1998, it used the terms 'proven reserves' and 'potential resources'. By 2002, the latter had been replaced by 'possible reserves' but to confuse matters further a footnote to that term explains that 'possible reserves' are those which are 'considered 50 per cent probable'. The simplest and clearest terminology, which we use and which is the general convention in oil and gas studies, is to distinguish between 'proven' and 'probable' reserves. 'Proven reserves' are those whose probability of extraction with current prices and technology is more than 90 per cent, while in the case of 'probable' reserves the probability is only 50–90 per cent. Much of the confusion and disagreement over the amounts of oil and gas in the Caspian has been caused by a failure to make clear which particular definition of reserves is being used. Further confusion has been caused on occasion by failing to specify whether Russia's Caspian region reserves are included or not (they are included in the EIA data we have cited).

8   US Department of Energy, EIA, *International Energy Outlook, 1998*, p.34. The EIA states that 'Only the USA and Saudi Arabia are thought to have more ultimately recoverable, conventional oil resources' than the Caspian.

9   Ibid. These figures include estimates of both Russian and Iranian production from their respective Caspian regions.

10   Hill, Fiona, 'A Not-So-Grand Strategy: United States Policy in the Caucasus and Central Asia since 1991', *Politique Etrangere*, February 2001; reprinted by Brookings Institution, online: available http://www.brook.edu/dybdocroot/views/articles/fhill/2001politique.htm (14 January 2003).

11   Ibid.

12   Quoted by Nelan, Bruce W., 'The Rush for Caspian Oil', *Time Magazine*, 4 May 1998, online: available http://www.time.com/time/magazine/1998/dom/980504/world.the_rush_for_caspi6.html (2 January 2002).

13   Ibid.

14   Armenia and Azerbaijan remain in a state of suspended hostilities since the Nagorno Karabakh war of 1988–1994 when Azerbaijan lost over a fifth of its territory to Armenia. Commercial relations between the two countries are therefore impossible for the time being, and it is for this reason that oil and gas from Azerbaijan must pass through Georgia rather than Armenia. Armenia is therefore excluded from the US strategic plan for the region.

15   Hassman, Heinrich, *Oil in the Soviet Union*, Princeton University Press (Princeton, 1953), pp.45, 50.

16   Ibid. p.142.

17   Campbell, Robert W., *The Economics of Soviet Oil and Gas*, Johns Hopkins University Press (Baltimore,1968), p.124.

18   Bahgat, Gawdat, 'The Caspian Sea Geopolitical Game: Prospects for the Millennium', *OPEC Review*, Vol.XXIII, No.3, 1999, p.202–3; see also Dekmeijian R. Hrair and Simonian, Hovann H., *Troubled Waters: The Geopolitics of the Caspian Region*, I.B.Tauris (London, 2003).

19   *BP Statistical Review of World Energy 2001*, BP plc, 2002, p.6.

20   US Department of Energy, EIA, *Azerbaijan: Production Sharing Agreements*, online: available http://www.eia.doe.gov/emeu/cabs/azerproj.html (16 January 2003).

21   Information derived from Cooperativeresearch.org, online: available http://www.cooperativeresearch.org/organizations/corporate/usacc.htm (3 March 2003).

22   The EIA muddies the waters by using the term 'recoverable' without any clear explanation as to what this means. The EIA states that Kashagan has 'approximately 40 billion barrels – up to 10 billion of which are thought to be recoverable'. This suggests that 'recoverable' means 'proven' but this is inconsistent with the total proven reserves which the EIA elsewhere attributes to the whole of Kazakhstan (5.4 billion at July 2002).

23   Chevron Corporation, *Annual Report on Form 10-K for 1993* (1994), p.2.

24   US Department of Energy, EIA, *Kazakhstan: Major Oil and Natural Gas Projects*, online: available http://www.eia.doe.gov/emeu/cabs/kazaproj.html (16 January 2003).

25   The Wood Mackenzie consultants use the term 'remaining reserves' in their December 2001 *Oil and Gas Journal* articles. This term is synonymous with the term 'proven plus probable' according to Wood Mackenzie's Edinburgh office (telephone enquiry by author on 27/1/03). The Wood Mackenzie figures are therefore more or less compatible with the individual production-sharing contract data, the most significant of which are quoted from the EIA (see above) but they are much larger than the 'proven' reserve figures also published by the EIA at a country level. See, for example, US Department of Energy, EIA, *Caspian Sea Region Oil and Natural Gas Reserves*, July 2002, online: available http://www.eia.doe.gov/emeu/cabs/caspgrph.html (25 January 2003) or those published in BP's *Statistical Review of World Energy*.

26   McCutcheon, Hilary and Osbon, Richard, 'Discoveries Alter Caspian Region Energy Potential', *Oil and Gas Journal*, 17 December 2001, pp.18–25.

27   McCutcheon, Hilary and Osbon, Richard, 'Risks Temper Caspian Rewards Potential', *Oil and Gas Journal*, 24 December 2001, p.26. The figures include Capex and Opex. 'Capex' means Capital Expenditure (Exploration plus Development costs). 'Opex' means operating expenditures/costs, sometimes also referred to as 'lifting costs'. It should also be noted, however, that in the case of the Caspian, both capex and opex figures include estimates of expenditure upon transportation infrastructure.

28   McCutcheon and Osbon, 'Discoveries Alter Caspian Region Energy Potential', p.22.

29   Klare, *Resource Wars*, p.1.

30   Ibid. p.2.

31   Armitage, Richard L., et al., *Transforming Defense and National Security in the 21st Century*, National Defense Panel (Arlington, December 1997), covering letter and pp.ii, 6, 7.

32   Klare, *Resource Wars*, p. 5

33   Clover, Charles and Corzine, Robert, 'Politics: A Worrying Emphasis on Re-Centralisation', and 'Guarded Optimism over Oil Revenues' in 'Kazakhstan Survey', *Financial Times*, 23 July 1997.

34   Corzine, Robert, 'Strange, Shadowy World of President's Advisor', in 'Kazakhstan Survey', *Financial Times*, 11 December 2000.

35   Hersh, Seymour, 'The Price of Oil: What was Mobil up to in Kazakhstan and Russia', *New Yorker*, 9 July 2001.

36   'Kazakhstan: US Investigates Possible Payments to Government Officials from Oil Firm Funds', *Wall Street Journal*, 30 June 2000. For this and other aspects of the 'Giffen affair', see also: Center for Strategic and International Studies (CSIS), 'Crude Business: Corruption and Caspian Oil', 1 September 2000, online: available http:// www.csis.org/turkey/CEU000901.htm (15 January 2003); Chin, Larry, 'Big Oil, the United States and Corruption in Kazakhstan', online: available www.onlinejournal.com (16 May 2002); 'What was Mobil up to in Kazakhstan', online: available http:// www. whatreallyhappened.com/mobil.html (17 January 2003); Gerth, Jeff, 'Bribery Inquiry Involves Kazakh Chief, and He's Unhappy', *New York Times*, 12 November 2002.

37   Quoted in Ibid.

38   Ibid.

39   Joint Statement by President Bush and President Nursultan Nazarbayev on the New Kazakhstan-American Relationship, Office of the Press Secretary, 21 December 2001, online: available http://www.whitehouse.gov/news/releases/2001/12/ 20011221-10.html (17 January 2003).

40   For a vivid impression of Nazarbayev's new capital, see Kleveman, Lutz, *The New Great Game: Blood and Oil in Central Asia*, Atlantic Books (London, 2003), pp.87–8.

41   See the report on a visit to Washington by former Turkmen political leaders Nazar Soyunov and Avdi Kuliev, online: available http://www.eisenhowerinstitute.org/ presscenter/release16-02.htm (19 January 2003).

42   Paton, Nick, 'US Looks Away as New Ally Tortures Islamists', *The Guardian*, 26 May 2003.

43   Hill, Fiona, 'A Not-So-Grand Strategy: United States Policy in the Caucasus and Central Asia since 1991'.

44   Joint Statement by President Bush and Kazakhstan President Nursultan Nazarbayev on the New Kazakhstan-American Relationship (full reference already given).

45   Bush's addition of 'Aktau' as the first link in the energy chain was to bring Kazakhstan into the frame. Aktau, in Kazakhstan, is on the eastern shore of the Caspian and the addition of this link would require an undersea trans-Caspian pipeline. To date there are no signs whatsoever of this pipeline being seriously considered and the inclusion of Aktau must have been for diplomatic reasons.

46   According to the US Center for Strategic and International Studies; see Aliriza, Bulent, 'US Caspian Pipeline Policy: Substance or Spin?', Center for Strategic and International Studies, 24 August 2000, online: available http://www.csis.org/turkey/ CEU00824.htm (15 January 2003).

47   See Hill, 'A Not-so-Grand Strategy: United States Policy in the Caucasus and Central Asia since 1991'.

48 Muttitt, Greg and Marriott, James, *Some Common Concerns: Imagining BP's Azerbaijan-Georgia-Turkey Pipelines System*, PLATFORM (London, 2002), p.TL3.

49 See Rashid, *Taliban*. Both CENTGAS and CAOPP died when Clinton's missiles hit al Qaeda's training camps in Afghanistan and the US Government 'gave up' on the Taliban.

50 See Barnes, Joe and Siligo, Ronald, 'Baku–Ceyhan Pipeline: Bad Economics, Bad Politics, Bad Idea', *Oil and Gas Journal*, 26 October 1998; and Delay, Jennifer, 'Georgia Tries to Maximise its Pipeline Options', *Alexander's Gas and Oil Connections*, Vol.4, Issue 9, 11 May 1999.

51 Muttitt and Marriott, *Some Common Concerns*, p.30.

52 Ibid. pp.TL5, 54.

53 According to Kleveman, *The New Great Game: Blood and Oil in Central Asia*, p.3, in May 2002, the Pentagon stationed 500 green berets in Georgia.

54 Georgian, Armen, 'US Eyes Caspian Oil in "War on Terror"', Armenian National Committee, 1 May 2002, online: available http://www.ancsf.org/essays_analyses/caspian_oil.htm (14 January 2003).

55 Ibid. and Muttitt and Marriott, *Some Common Concerns*, p.TL13.

56 See Evans, Rob and Hencke, David, 'UK and US in Joint Effort to Secure African Oil', *The Guardian*, 14 November 2003.

57 *Baku Ceyhan Campaign News*, January 2003. The pipeline eventually won the support of the International Finance Corporation and the European Bank for Reconstruction and Development in November 2003.

58 See e.g. Rusenergy.com, 'AGIP KCP Revises Valuation of Northern Caspian Reserves under Kazakh pressure', 19 July 2002, online: available http://www.rusenergy.com/eng/caspian.htm (19 January 2003).

59 US Department of Energy, EIA, *International Energy Outlook 1998*, p.34; US Department of Energy, EIA, *Caspian Sea Region Oil and Natural Gas Reserves*, July 2001 online: available http://www.eia.doe.gov/emeu/cabs/caspgrph.html (13 January 2002); US Department of Energy, EIA, *Caspian Sea Region: Reserves and Pipelines Tables*, July 2002, online: available http://www.eia.doe.gov/emeu/cabs/caspgrph.html (25 January 2003); and US Department of Energy, EIA, *Caspian Sea Region, Key Oil and Gas Statistics*, August 2003, online: available http://www.eia.doe.gov/emeu/cabs/caspstats.html (5 January 2004). The figure for 2001 is the mid-point in a range 17.5 – 34 billion barrels, and the figure for 2003 is the mid-point in a range 17.2 – 32.8 billion barrels In fact, the use of a range of numbers for 'proven' reserves is itself self-contradictory, given that proven reserves numbers are defined as having a probability of 90 per cent.

60 Michael Lelyveld, 'Caspian Sea's Oil Reserves Estimate Revised Downwards', *Radio Free Europe*, online: available File://C:\DOCUME~1\trade\LOCALS~1\Temp\CGB501UV.htm.

61 Salameh, Mamdouh G., 'Caspian Sea Is No Middle East', *Newsletter of the International Association for Energy Economics*, Third Quarter 2002, p.15.

62 US Department of Energy: EIA, *Caspian Sea Region, Key Oil and Gas Statistics*.

63 McCutcheon and Osborn, 'Risks Temper Caspian Rewards Potential', p.26.

64 See Hoyos, Carola, '$20 Billion Kazak Oil Project Faces Two-Year Delay', *Financial Times*, 20 August 2003.

65   Emerson, Sarah, Energy Security Analysis Inc., quoted by Reuters, 21 September 2002 and reported in 'US Oil Diversity Drive Comes Back to Middle East, *New Zealand Herald*, 22 September 2002.

CHAPTER 9

1   Fulton et al., *Contribution of the Automotive Industry to the US Economy in 1998*, p.3.
2   *Fortune Magazine*, 26 April 1999.
3   Fulton et al., *Contribution of the Automotive Industry to the US Economy in 1998*, pp. 4–5.
4   Ibid. p.1. The term 'automotive industry' is used by the authors of the report to describe the complete network of companies, including new vehicle dealers and car-purchase-related financial services, which are involved in the production and sale of motor vehicles.
5   Ibid. p.24.
6   Ibid. p.37.
7   Chinese Academy of Engineering and National Research Council, *Personal Cars and China*, National Academies Press (Washington, 2003), p.7.
8   Ibid.
9   See Despeignes, Peronet, 'Detroit Boosts US Industrial Output', *Financial Times*, 16 August 2002. According to another article in the *Financial Times* (Grant, Jeremy, 'GM and Ford Head to Head on SUV Incentives', *Financial Times*, 31 January 2003), financial incentives to boost US automobile and SUV sales were 'aimed at stimulating the US economy', in the wake of the terrorist attacks of 11 September 2001.
10   US Senate, *US Automobile and Truck Retail Sales 1970–2002*, online: available http://www.senate.state.mi.us/sfe/Economics/RetailAutosales.pdf.
11   US Department of Energy, Office of Transportation Technologies, *Fact of the Week: US Light Truck Sales Exceed Car Sales*, 21 January 2002, online: available http://www.ott.doe.gov/facts/archives/fotw200.shtml (10 July 2002). See also Durbin, Dee-Ann, 'Light Trucks Beat Car Sales in All but Four States', *Autoinsider*, 24 April 2004, online: available, http://detnews.com/2004/autoinsider/0404/ 24/autos-132375.htm (19 June 2004). However, there are some discrepancies between the different sources as to exact proportions of light trucks and cars in total light vehicle sales. The data cited above are drawn from the industry source Wards Communications. However some other sources put the figure for light truck sales in 2000 as 48.1 per cent, only exceeding 50 per cent in 2002.
12   The US gallon is equal to 0.833 of an imperial (UK) gallon. The US mpg figures quoted in this chapter and elsewhere should therefore be increased by 20 per cent to make a fair comparison with the UK mpg. The April 2003 rule-making decision by the NHTSA requires manufacturers to increase the mpg of 'light trucks' (including SUVs) from 20.7 in 2003 to 21.0 in 2005, 21.6 in 2006 and 22.7 in 2007. These very modest changes mean that the fuel economy of all new US light vehicles (including cars) will only have been improved by 0.8 mpg by the year 2025, according to the US Department of Energy, EIA, *Annual Energy Outlook* 2004, Washington.

13 Grant, Jeremy and Sevastopulo, Demetri, 'Holy Wrath Descends upon Gas Guzzlers', *Financial Times*, 21 November 2002.

14 'A Divine Driver', *ABCNews.com*, online: available http://abcnews.go.com/sections/ GMA/GoodMorningAmerica?GMA021121Jesusu_drive.html (1 August 2003).

15 US Department of Energy, *Transportation Energy Data Book: Edition 21*, p.11:5. 33.79% owned one vehicle and 9.35% no vehicles.

16 US Department of Energy, OTT, *Fact of the Week: Per Cent of Vehicle Buyers Who Are Considering an SUV for Their Next Vehicle Purchase*, 8 June 1999, online: available at http://www.ott.doe.gov/facts/archives/fotw92.shtml (7 October 2002).

17 Durbin, 'Light Trucks Beat Car Sales in All but Four States'.

18 Healey, James R., 'Death by the Gallon' *USA Today*, 2 July 1999.

19 Quoted in Ibid.

20 Quoted in Healey, James R., 'Fuel efficiency Fires Renewed Public Debate', *USA Today*, 27 July 2001.

21 Ibid.

22 Bragg, John, 'See the USA in your SUV', Campaign in Defence of Industry and Technology, Center for the Moral Defence of Capitalism, 2001, online: available http://www.moraldefense.com/ProTech/Philosophy/Essays/suv.htm (30 June 2002).

23 'CAFE Society', *Wall Street Journal*, 28 February 2002, reproduced in the Competitive Enterprise Institute NewsCenter, online: available http:// www.cei.org/gencon/003,02417.cfm (10 July 2002).

24 US Department of Energy, *Transportation Energy Data Book: Edition 21*, p. 7:19; US Department of Energy, OTT, *Fact of the Week: New Vehicle Fuel Cost Per Mile, 1978–99*, 28 August 2000, online: available http://www.ott.doe.gov/facts/archives/ fotw141supp.shtml (10 July 2002).

25 Burt, Tim, 'Alternative Fuels Still Outpaced by Petrol', *Financial Times*, 14 September 2000.

26 US Department of Energy, EIA, *Retail Motor Gasoline and On-Highway Diesel Fuel Prices 1949–2001*, online: available http://www.eia.doe.gov/emeu/aer/txt/ ptb0522.html (11 December 2002).

27 US Department of Energy, *Transportation Energy Data Book: Edition 21*, pp.5:3, 5:5.

28 Sevastopulo, Demetri, 'Bush and Kerry Clash on Surging Fuel Price', *Financial Times*, 25 March 2004.

29 International Energy Agency (IEA), *Coal Information 1998*, IEA/OECD (Paris, 1998), p.1.228.

30 See Suskind, *The Price of Loyalty*, p.121.

31 Ibid. p.120.

32 See e.g. Shlaes, Amity, 'Team Bush Polishes its Green Credentials', *Financial Times*, 15 September 2003.

33 Natural Resource Defense Council, 'The Bush Administration's Fuel Cell Fake-out', online: available http://www.nrdc.org/air/transportation/ffuelcell.asp (11 October 2003). According to the NRDC, the fuel economy scenario would make a cumulative reduction of 13.2 billion barrels by 2020 compared to 0.55 billion barrels for the fuel-cell scenario. For the year 2030, the equivalent figures would be 37.1 billion barrels and 7.7 billion respectively.

34 US Bureau of Transportation Statistics, *National Transportation Statistics 2002*, series of electronic documents, online: available http://www.bts.gov (11 October 2003).

35 US Department of Energy, EIA, *Annual Energy Outlook 2002* (Washington, 2003).

36 US Department of Energy, OTT, *Future US Highway Energy Use: A Fifty Year Perspective*, 3 May 2001, p.7.

37 Ibid. p.17.

38 Ibid. p.31.

39 Fulton et al., *Contribution of the Automotive Industry to the US Economy in 1998*, p.49.

40 Bragg, 'See the USA in your SUV'.

41 12 December 2000 was the day on which a conservative dominated US Supreme Court ruled against further recounts in the US Presidential election and handed power to what Gore Vidal has named the 'Cheney-Bush Junta'. See Vidal, Gore, *Dreaming War: Blood for Oil and the Cheney-Bush Junta*, Thunder's Mouth Press/Nation Books (New York, 2002), pp.3–8.

CHAPTER 10

1 US Department of Energy, Energy Information Administration (EIA), *Energy Plug: Annual Energy Outlook 2001, Early Release*, online: available http://www.eia.doe.gov/emeu/plugs/plaeo01e.html (25 November 2003).

2 Opensecrets.org, 'Oil and Gas Top 20 Recipients', online: available. http://www.opensecrets.org/industries/recips.asp?Ind=E01&Cycle=2000&recipdetail=A&mem=N&sortorder=U (14 February 2004); also Associated Press, 'Abraham to Lead Department He Wanted Shut', 3 January 2001, online: available http://quest.cjonline.com/stories/010301/gen_013017592.shtml (25 November 2003).

3 ABC News, 'Spencer Abraham, Friend to Oil and Immigrants', 3 January 2001, online: available http://abcnews.go.com/sections/politics/Daily News/Abraham_ profile.html (25 January 2003).

4 US Department Of State, online: available http://www.state.gov/s/p/of/ca/23927.htm (30 November 2003).

5 Milbank, Dana, 'Bush's Blunder' May be Kristol's Inside Influence', *Washington Post*, 19 March 2002, online: available http://www.washingtonpost.com/ac2/wp-dyn/A46994-20002Mar18?language=printer (30 November 2003).

6 US Department of Energy, EIA, *International Energy Outlook 2001*, p.27.

7 Andrews-Speed, Philip, 'China's Future Energy Policy', *Oxford Energy Forum*, Oxford Institute for Energy Studies (Oxford, May 2003), p.6.

8 Ibid.

9 Chinese Academy of Engineering and the National Research Council, *Personal Cars and China*, National Academy of Sciences (Washington, 2003), p.8.

10 Quoted in Wonacott, Peter, Whalen, Jeanne and Bahree, Bhushan, 'China's Growing Thirst for Oil Remakes the World Market', *Wall Street Journal*, 3 December 2003.

11 Wolf, Martin, 'The Long March to Prosperity: Why China Can Maintain its Explosive Rate of Growth for Another Two Decades', *Financial Times*, 9 December 2003.

12   Associated Press, 'GM to Launch Chevrolet Mini-Car in China', *AP Biz Wire*, 1 December 2003, online: available http://seatlepi.nwsource.com/business/apbiz_story.asp?category=1310&slug=China%20GM (6 December 2003).

13   Wagoner, Rick, 'Carmakers Are Vying to Meet China's Needs', *Financial Times*, 7 November 2003.

14   Chinese Academy of Engineering and the National Research Council, *Personal Cars and China*, p.24.

15   Wonacott et al., 'China's Growing Thirst for Oil Remakes the World Market'.

16   Pi, Lu, 'Expressway Construction in High Swing', *Beijing Review*, 18 July 2002, p.19.

17   Ibid. p.21.

18   Hutton, Will, 'Confucius Goes to Market', *The Observer*, 21 September 2003.

19   US Department of Energy, EIA, *International Energy Outlook 2001*, p.29.

20   Chinese Academy of Engineering and National Research Council, *Personal Cars and China*, p.114.

21   Rahman, Bayan and Jack, Andrew, 'Japan Lures Russia with $7bn Offer on Pipeline', *Financial Times*, 14 October 2003.

22   US Department of Energy, EIA, *International Energy Outlook 2002*, p.39.

23   Lee Raymond quoted in Hoyos, Carola, 'OPEC is Creating a Tidal Wave of Crude That Cannot All Be Absorbed. A Production Cut May Be Unavoidable', *Financial Times*, 9 April 2003.

24   Wonacott et.al., 'China's Growing Thirst for Oil Remakes the World Market'.

25   Associated Press, 'Abraham Sees Nation Threatened by Energy Crisis', *Arizona Daily Wildcat*, 9 March 2001, online: available http://wildcat.arizona.edu/papers/94/118/01_93_m.html (8 December 2003).

26   Morse, Edward L. (Chair) and Jaffe, Amy Myers (Project Director), *Strategic Energy Policy Challenges for the 21st Century*, Report of an Independent Task Force, Council on Foreign Relations and James A. Baker III Institute for Public Policy of Rice University (New York, April 2001).

27   Ibid. p.8.

28   Ibid. p.4.

29   This is only a very crude sketch of the 'geological shortage' argument; for a fuller and exceptionally well-explained version of the methodology used, see Deffeyes, Kenneth S., *Hubbert's Peak: The Impending World Oil Shortage*, Princeton University Press (Princeton, 2001).

30   Campbell, Colin and Laherrere, Jean, 'The End of Cheap Oil?' *Scientific American*, March 1998.

31   Deffeyes, *Hubbert's Peak*, p.158.

32   Ibid. p.149.

33   US Department of Energy, EIA, *Energy Plug: Long-Term World Oil Supply – A Resource Base/Production Path Analysis*, online: available http://www.eia.doe.gov/emeu/plugs/plworld.html (20 July 2002).

34   See US Department of Energy, Office of Transportation Technologies (OTT), *Future US Highway Energy Use: A Fifty Year Perspective* (May 2001), p.2; the OTT states, 'the more traditional exhaustion pattern used in this report is the 2 per year decline, which results in a peak in 2016.'

35 See, for example, Heinberg, Richard, *The Party's Over: Oil, War and the Fate of Industrial Societies*, Clairview Books (Forrest Row, 2003).

36 See Monbiot, George, 'The World is Running Out of Oil – So Why Do Politicians Refuse to Talk About It?', *The Guardian*, 2 December 2003.

37 See the criticism of C.J. Campbell by Lynch, Michael C., 'Farce this Time: Renewed Pessimism About Oil Supply', *Geopolitics of Energy*, December 1998/January 1999, pp.9–10', also David Deming's criticism in Deming, David, 'Are We Running Out of Oil?', *Policy Backgrounder*, No.159, 29 January 2003, National Center for Policy Analysis, online: available http://www.ncpa.org/pub/bg/bg159/index.html (6 February 2003).

38 Odell, Peter, 'Oil and Gas Reserves: Retrospect and Prospect', *Geopolitics of Energy*, December 1998/January 1999, p.15.

39 Ibid.

40 Lynch, 'Farce this Time', p.10.

41 See for example, Bentley, R.J., *Perspectives on the Future of Oil*, Department of Cybernetics, University of Reading (Reading, 30 May 1999).

42 US Department of Energy, EIA, *International Energy Outlook 2002*, p.38.

43 Hoyos, Carola, 'Middle East Oil Industry Will Need Big Investment', *Financial Times*, 5 November 2003. According to the IEA, a total of $3,100 billion of investment will be required for the oil and gas industry worldwide between now and 2030, of which one fifth will need to be invested in the Middle East.

44 US Department of Energy, EIA, *International Energy Outlook 2001*, p.33.

45 Quoted in *Middle East International*, 21 November 2003.

46 Gately, Dermot, 'How Plausible is the Consensus Projection of Oil below $25 and Persian Gulf Oil Capacity and Output Doubling by 2020?', *The Energy Journal*, Vol.22, 2001, p.1.

47 AlHajji, A.F., 'Will Gulf States Live Up to EIA and IEA Projections? *World Oil*, June 2001.

48 Morse and Jaffe; *Strategic Energy Policy Challenges for the 21st Century*, p.71.

49 Ibid.

50 The figures for Gulf states oil-producing capacity are larger than those for actual production because of OPEC quotas. The capacity data for 1999–2001 referred to here are taken from the Appendix Table D1 of the EIA's *International Energy Outlook, 2001, 2002* and *2003*. The figure for 2002 is taken from EIA, *Persian Gulf Oil and Gas Exports Fact Sheet*, April 2003, online: available http://www.eia.doe.gov/emeu/cabs/pgulf.html#oil (15 December 2003): 'At the end of 2002, Persian Gulf countries maintained about 22.3 million b/d of oil production capacity.'

51 It is worth noting that in its latest (2004) *Annual Energy Outlook*, the EIA has substantially reduced its forecast for Gulf oil production in 2010 and later. The 'gap' is now apparently going to be made up by a massive increase in Russian and Caspian oil production. Certainly their Caspian figure looks too optimistic.

52 Tempest, Paul, 'Energy Security in an Insecure World', *Newsletter of the International Association for Energy Economics*, 1st Quarter 2004, p.20.

53 *Statement of Principles*, Project for the New American Century, 3 June 1997, online: available http://www.newamericancentury.org/statementofprinciples.htm (12 December 2003).

54 Project for the New American Century, *Rebuilding America's Defenses: Strategy, Forces and Resources for a New Century* (Washington, September 2000).

55 Ibid. p.iv.

56 Ibid. p.4.

57 *Open Letter to the President,* 19 February 1998, online: available http://www.cooperativeresearch.org/archive/1990s/openletter021998.htm (24 December 2003).

58 See Fidler, Stephen and Baker, Gerard, 'America's Democratic Imperialists: Humility to Empire in Two Years', *Financial Times,* 6 March 2003. The article provides a useful account of the rather fine points of distinction between 'neo-conservatives' (or 'democratic imperialists') and 'assertive nationalists'. However, according to the article, after 11 September 2001, those members of the Administration described as 'assertive nationalists' began to move closer to a 'neocon world view'. 'After 9–11, you don't see a lot of daylight between the democratic imperialists and the assertive nationalists.'

59 In 1996, Douglas Feith, Daniel Perle and David Wurmser were members of the Study Group on a New Israeli Strategy Toward 2000 at the Institute for Advanced Strategic and Political Studies, which published a report entitled, *A Clean Break: A New Strategy for Securing the Realm.* The report advocated that Israel should adopt a raft of extremist policies involving attacks on Palestinian towns, Lebanon and Syria and the demand that the Palestinians accept unconditionally the Israeli occupation.

60 On the role of West African oil in the US energy security strategy and its political implications see Volman, Daniel, 'The Bush Administration and African Oil: The Security Implications of US Energy Policy', *Review of African Political Economy,* Vol.30, No.28, December 2003.

61 US Department of Energy, EIA, *Oil Production Capacity Expansion Costs For the Persian Gulf* (Washington, January 1996), p.3.

62 See Rutledge, 'Profitability and Supply Price in the US Domestic Oil Industry', pp.9–11.

63 Quoted in 'Iraq is a Field of Dreams for Big Oil Firms', *Alexander's Oil and Gas Connections,* 1 May 2003, online: available http://www.gasandoil.com/goc/company/cm31821.htm (18 December 2003).

64 Hoyos, Carola, 'Big players Rub Hands in Anticipation of Iraq's Return to the Fold', *Financial Times,* 21 February 2003.

65 US Department of Energy (EIA), *Country Analysis Briefs: Iraq,* August, 2003. online: available http://www.eia.doe.gov/emeu/cabs/iraq.html (31 December 2003).

66 Ibid.

67 Suskind, *The Price of Loyalty,* p.96. These are presumably the same documents referred to by Scott Thompson in 'Dick Cheney Has Long Planned to Loot Iraqi Oil', *Executive Intelligence Review,* 1 August 2003.

68 Suskind, *The Price of Loyalty,* p.96.

69 Ibid. p.47.

70 US General Accounting Office (GAO), *Energy Security: Evaluating US Vulnerability to Oil Supply Disruptions and Options for Mitigating their Effects,* Report to the Chairman on the Budget, House of Representatives (Washington, December 1996).

71 Ibid. p.33.

72 Ibid. p.19.

73 Letter from Mark Chupka, Acting Assistant Secretary for Policy and International Affairs, Department of Energy, to Victor S. Rezendes, Director, Energy, Resources and Science Issues, General Accounting Office, Washington DC, 18 October 1996.

74 Greene, David L. and Tishchishnya, Nataliya I., *Costs of Oil Dependence: A 2000 Update*, US Department of Energy, Oak Ridge National Laboratory (Tennessee, May 2000), pp.1–46.

75 Rae, *The American Automobile: A Brief History*, p.221.

76 Prowse, Michael, 'The Fat Man Refuses to Follow a Diet', *Financial Times*, 25 February 1991.

77 Yergin, *The Prize*, p.616.

78 Ibid. p.618.

79 See Rutledge, Ian and Wright, Philip, 'Companies as Sources for Upstream Oil and Gas Information'. *Journal of Energy Literature*, Vol.V, No.1, 1999.

80 Yergin, *The Prize*, p.694.

81 Ibid. p.691.

82 Ibid. p.692.

83 Ibid. p.695.

84 US Department of Energy, *Profile of the Strategic Petroleum Reserve*, Fossil Energy.gov, online: available http://www.fe.doe.gov/spr/ (25 February 2003).

85 See for example, GAO, *Energy Security*, p.60.

86 Ibid. p.62.

87 Ibid. p.14.

88 Ibid. p.19.

89 Ibid. p.34.

90 Perry, George L., 'The War on Terrorism, the World Oil Market and the US Economy', *Analysis Paper 7*, 28 November 2001, Brookings Institute, p.1, online: available http://www.brookings.edu/views/papers/perry/20011024.htm (12 November 2003).

91 Ibid. p.5.

92 Ibid. p.8.

93 Ibid. p.10.

94 Ibid. pp.5, 6.

95 Stelzer, Irwin M., 'Can We Do Without Saudi Oil?', *Weekly Standard*, 19 November 2001, online: available http://www.weeklystandard.com/content/public/articles/000/000/525pggsa.asp (9 August 2002).

CHAPTER 11

1 Fjell, Olav, *Norway, the Petro-Nation: Today and in Ten Years Time*, Statoil, March 2001.

2 Royal Norwegian Ministry of Finance – data supplied directly to author.

3 It was, however, to lose this position to Russia after the turn of the century.

4 See the Preface to Noreng, Oystein, *Oil and Islam: Social and Economic Issues*, Research Council of Norway and John Wiley and Sons (Chichester, 1997).

5   In 1990, the existing Muslim oil producers were: Abu Dhabi, Dubai & Northern Emirates, Iran, Iraq, Kuwait, Oman, Qatar, Saudi Arabia, Syria, Yemen, Algeria, Egypt, Libya, Tunisia, Brunei, Indonesia and Malaysia. Together they accounted for 704 billion barrels of proved oil reserves out of a world total of 1,000 (BP data). They were shortly to be joined by: Azerbaijan, Kazakhstan, Turkmenistan and Uzbekistan with an additional 16 billion barrels (according to BP).

6   Noreng, *Oil and Islam*, p.32.

7   Ibid.

8   Ibid. p.5.

9   Karim, Muhammad S., *Oil, Islamism and the International Petroleum Industry: Legal, Economic, Political and Cultural Issues*, LL.M. Dissertation, Centre for Energy, Petroleum and Mineral Law and Policy, University of Dundee (Dundee, 2001), p.8.

10   Howarth, David, *The Desert King*, Collins (London, 1964), pp.211–12.

11   Ibid. p.213.

12   Ibid. p.225.

13   Vassiliev, Alexei, *The History of Saudi Arabia*, Saqi Books (London, 2000), pp. 401–2.

14   Holden, David and Johns, Richard, *The House of Saud*, Sidgwick & Jackson (London, 1981), p.183.

15   Vassiliev, *The History of Saudi Arabia*, pp.336–37.

16   Aburish, *The Rise, Corruption and Coming Fall of the House of Saud*, pp.294–95.

17   Khalaf, Roula, 'Saudi Arabia Urged to Speed up Economic Reform', *Financial Times*, 23 October 2002.

18   Aburish, *The Rise, Corruption and Coming Fall of the House of Saud*, p.301.

19   Abdel-Muntasir, Jihad, 'The Saudi Regime its Legality and Achievements', *Nidaul Islam*, 1995, online: available http://www.islam.org.au/articles/10/SAUD.HTM (9 August 2002). *Nidaul Islam* (the Proclamation of Islam) is an openly *Jihadi* publication and website based in Australia. Its perspective has been strongly criticised by the orthodox *Wahhabi* publication *The Wahhabi Myth: Dispelling Prevalent Fallacies and the Fictitious Link with Bin Laden*, online: available http://www.thewahhabymyth.com (9 August 2002).

20   Ibid.

21   Aburish, *The Rise, Corruption and Coming Fall of the House of Saud*, p.182.

22   Noreng, *Oil and Islam*, p.174.

23   Odell, Mark, 'Courting Controversy in the Desert', *Financial Times*, 12 September 2003.

24   UK Academic Mark Phythian, quoted in the *Financial Times*, 12 September 2003.

25   *Al-Yamamah Scandal*, online: available http://www.saudhouse.com/saudi_al_Al-Yamamah_scandal.htm (25 November 2003). Of course, Saudi Arabia is not the only culprit as far as arms purchasing is concerned. Between 1973 and 1992, the combined military spending of the seven major Gulf and North African oil producers (Algeria, Iran, Iraq, Kuwait, Libya, Saudi Arabia and the UAE) amounted to nearly $1,000 billion.

26 The most widely used Arabic-English dictionary translates *riba* ambiguously as 'interest; usurious interest; usury.' See Cowan, J.M., *The Hans Wehr Dictionary of Modern Written Arabic*, Spoken Language Services Inc. (Ithaca, 1994) p.375.

27 Vassiliev, *The History of Saudi Arabia*, p.453.

28 Noreng, *Oil and Islam*, p.289.

29 Ibid. p.307.

30 Karim, *Oil, Islamism and the International Petroleum Industry*.

31 Abdel-Muntasir, Jihad, 'The Saudi Regime its Legality and Achievements'.

32 Noreng, *Oil and Islam*, p.152. The population data for Saudi Arabia, Kuwait, Libya and the UAE are complicated by the fact that they include substantial numbers of migrant workers. Estimates of the latter are available but throughout this chapter we have used the gross figures, making sure that we always compare 'like with like'.

33 Central Intelligence Agency, *CIA Fact Book 2003*, online: available http://www.cia.gov/cia/publications/factbook (12 December 2003).

34 Data for real oil-export revenues are taken from US Department of Energy, EIA, *OPEC Revenues Fact Sheet*, online: available http://www.eia.doe.gov/emeu/cabs/opecrev.html (12 December 2003) population data are taken from Noreng: *Oil and Islam* and the *2003 CIA Fact book*.

35 Vassiliev, *The History of Saudi Arabia*, p.462.

36 Ibid. p.461.

37 Figures are based on Noreng, *Oil and Islam*, pp. 152, 158. For reasons which are unclear, our own calculations of the pre-capita data in some cases differ slightly from those calculated by Noreng himself (see p.159).

38 Little, *American Orientalism: The United States and the Middle East since 1945*, p.316.

39 Rashid, *Taliban*, p.176.

40 Stelzer, Irwin, 'Can We Do Without Saudi Oil – Alas no.' *The Weekly Standard*, 19 November 2001.

41 Atlantic Council of the United States et al., 'US Challenges and Choices in the Gulf: Saudi Arabia', *Policy Brief 1*, Atlantic Council of the United States, Middle East Institute, Middle East Policy Council, and Stanley Foundation (Washington, 2001), p.3.

42 Atlantic Council of the United States et al., 'US Challenges and Choices in the Gulf: Energy Security', *Policy Brief 3*, Atlantic Council of the United States, The Middle East Institute, Middle East Policy Council and Stanley Foundation (Washington, 2002), p.3.

43 Ibid.

44 Quoted by Ricks, Thomas E., 'Briefing Depicted Saudis as Enemies', *Washington Post*, 2 August 2002.

45 Ibid.

46 Stelzer, 'Can We Do Without Saudi Oil – Alas no.'

47 See Daniel Pipes's interview with John Lloyd, 'Radical Islam Sees Itself just as Communism Did – in a Battle with a Hostile World,' *Financial Times*, 12 January 2003

48 Daniel, Caroline, 'US Backs Saudi Stance on Terrorism', *Financial Times*, 2 November 2002.

49   Woodward, *Plan of Attack*, p.230.

50   Ibid. p.231.

51   Ibid. p.324.

52   Klare, *Resource Wars: The New Landscape of Global Conflict*, p.78.

53   Armitage, Richard L. et al., *Transforming Defense and National Security in the 21st Century*, National Defense Panel (Arlington, December 1997), p.6.

54   Kristol, William, 'Memorandum to Opinion Leaders', Project for the New American Century, 25 April 2002, online: available http://www.newamericancentury.org/saudi-042502.htm (16 February 2003).

55   Kristol, William, 'A New Approach to the Middle East', *The Daily Standard*, 22 May 2002, online: available http://www.weeklystandard.com/content/public/articles/000/000/001/273awdje.asp (9 August 2002). The view that 'hedging Saudi oil supplies' lay at the heart of the Bush Administration's invasion of Iraq was shared by a number of observers opposed to the war, including the former UK cabinet minister, Mo Mowlem, the distinguished US economist Jeffrey Sachs, Francisco Parra, Former Secretary General of OPEC and the author and journalist Anthony Sampson. See Mowlem, Mo, 'The Real Goal is the Seizure of Saudi Oil', *The Guardian*, 5 September 2002; Sachs, Jeffrey, 'The Real Target of the War in Iraq was Saudi Arabia', *Financial Times*, 13 August 2003; Sampson, Anthony, 'West's Greed for Oil Fuels Saddam Fever', *The Observer*, 11 August 2002, and Parra, Francisco, *Oil Politics, a Modern History* (Epilogue) I. B. Tauris (London, 2004).

56   Woodward, *Plan of Attack*, p.381.

57   BBC News, World Edition, 'Poland Seeks Iraqi Oil Stake', 3 July 2003, online: available, http://news.bbc.co.uk/2/hi/europe/3043330.stm (17 June 2004).

58   Quoted in Clover, Charles and Hoyos, Carola, 'Expectations Weigh Heavy on Man Who Must Get Oil Flowing', *Financial Times*, 18 July 2003.

CHAPTER 12

1   Morgan, Dan and Ottaway, David B., 'In Iraqi War Scenario, Oil is Key Issue', *Washington Post*, 15 September 2002.

2   Paton, Nick, Borger, Julian, Macalister, Terry and MacAskill, Ewen, 'US Begins Secret Talks to Secure Iraq's Oilfields', *The Guardian*, 23 January 2003; the presence of Ahmad Chalabi was confirmed by an spokesperson to Beaumont, Peter and Islam, Feisal, 'Carve-up of Oil Riches Begins', *The Observer*, 3 November 2002.

3   Beaumont and Islam, 'Carve-up of Oil Riches Begins'.

4   Buck, Tobias and Clover, Charles, 'Oil Groups Poised to Pick over the Spoils of Iraqi Battlefield', *Financial Times*, 2 November 2002.

5   Dr Gerald Bailey quoted in, Platts, *The Future of Iraq's Oil*, Platts.com, online: available http://www.platts.com/features/oilprices/iraqoutlook.sthml (14 January 2003).

6   McAlister, Terry, 'BP Chief Fears US Will Carve up Iraqi Oil Riches', *The Guardian*, 30 October 2002.

7   Frum, David, 'The Curse of Oil Dependence', *Jerusalem Post*, 20 December 2002.

8   Quoted by Hoyos, Carola, 'Big Players Rub Hands in Anticipation of Iraq's Return to the Fold', *Financial Times*, 21 February 2003.

9 Ibid.

10 US Department of State, Press Release, 19 December 2002.

11 See Morgan, Oliver, 'Iraq May Have to Quit OPEC', *The Observer*, 27 April 2003.

12 See Morgan, Oliver, 'US Struggles to Unlock Iraq's Black Gold,' *The Observer*, 4 May 2003; and Morgan, Oliver, 'Fields of Dreams Turned to Ashes,' *The Observer*, 2 September 2003.

13 Islam, Faisal and Paton, Nick, 'US Buys up Iraqi Oil to Stave off Crisis', *The Observer*, 26 January 2003.

14 US Department of Energy, EIA, *Country Analysis Briefs: Iraq*, August 2003, online: available http://www.eia.doe.gov/emeu/cabs/iraq.html (31 December 2003).

15 Paton, Borger, Macalister and MacAskill, 'US Begins Secret Talks to Secure Iraq's Oilfields.'

16 'Halliburton Iraq Contract Queried', BBC News/Business, 30 May 2003, online: available http://www.bbc.co.uk/2/low/business/2950154.stm (21 January 2004).

17 Morgan, Oliver, 'Iraq Delay Hands Cheney Firm $1bn', *The Observer*, 7 December 2003.

18 Woodward, *Plan of Attack*, p.323.

19 Shlaes, Amity, 'Oil Must be Seized from the Hands of the State', *Financial Times*, 26 March 2003.

20 Ibid.

21 Lal, Deepak, 'A Force to Lift the Curse of Natural Resources', *Financial Times*, 3 October 2003.

22 Robert Ebel quoted in: Tully, Andrew F., 'Iraq: After Hussein, How Will Iraqis Assert Control Over Their Oil?', *Radio Free Europe*, 28 April 2003, online: available http://www.rferl.org/nca/features/2003/04/28042003151159.asp (26 September 2003); Simon Wardell, senior analyst at the World Markets Research Centre (London), is reported as concluding that 'the Iraqi government will sign a series of production-sharing agreements that give Western partners as share in profits...a straightforward privatization would be a denial of Iraq's modern history'. quoted in 'Iraq is a Field of Dreams for Big Oil Firms', *Alexander's Gas and Oil Connections*, online: available http://www.gasandoil.com/goc/company/cnm31821.htm (18 December 2003). Also, while commenting on the obvious problems of privatisation in the unexpectedly turbulent and bloody months following the end of the regular phase of the invasion and war, the authoritative oil and gas news service *Platts* stated, 'in the medium to long term, however, the issue of Production Sharing Agreements (PSAs), will almost certainly become a dominant theme'. See Platts.com, online: available http://www.platts.com/features/oilprices/iraqoutlook.sthml (14 January 2003).

23 For a more detailed study of PSAs see Bindemann, Kirsten, *Production Sharing Agreements: An Economic Analysis*, Oxford Institute for Energy Studies (Oxford 1999); and Johnston, Daniel, *International Petroleum Fiscal Regimes and Production Sharing Contracts*, Penwell (Tulsa, 1994).

24 There is usually a cap on the annual amount of 'cost oil' that can recovered out of gross annual revenues (e.g. 40 per cent of total annual production). If there is such a 'cap', the amount of cost which exceeds the cap is carried over into the next financial year and added to that year's annual costs.

25   The 'cost cap' is a limit on the annual amount of 'cost oil' that can be recovered by the company out of gross annual production. It allows the government to receive some 'profit oil' earlier than would otherwise be the case.

26   These data are derived from Petroconsultants, *Annual Review of Petroleum Fiscal Regimes, 1995*, Petroconsultants (Geneva, 1996). The 'company return on capital' cited is the economists' 'Internal Rate of Return' (or 'cash flow profit rate') which may differ from the accounting rate of return on capital calculated on an accruals basis from the profit and loss account and the balance sheet.

27   US Department of Energy, EIA, *Oil Production Capacity Expansion Costs For the Persian Gulf* (Washington, January 1996), p.3.

28   Using a spreadsheet model similar to that of Bindemann (1999). Operating and technical data for the Iraq Zagros Mezozoic taken from EIA, *Oil Production Capacity Expansion Costs For the Persian Gulf*. Oman PSA terms from Petroconsultants (1996). I have assumed it takes two years to complete capital expenditure before production begins.

29   Dr Fadhil Chalabi quoted in: Morgan, Oliver, 'Iraq May Have to Quit OPEC', *The Observer*, 27 April 2003.

30   Hoyos, Carola, 'Exiles Call for Iraq to Let in Big Oil Companies', *Financial Times*, 7 April 2003.

31   See Rutledge, 'Profitability and Supply Price in the US Domestic Oil Industry: Implications for the Political Economy of Oil in the 21st Century'.

32   Khalaf, Roula and Dinmore, Guy, 'Bombs in Riyadh, Disorder in Iraq, Opposition to the Road Map: Bush's Vision Confronts reality', *Financial Times*, 15 May 2003. (My parentheses – 'the oil-rich nation' in original.)

33   Quoted in Little, *American Orientalism*, p.321.

34   Casualties as calculated by the US Department of Defense, published in the *Financial Times*, 30 October 2003. A substantial number of the Iraqi civilians may have been killed after 1 May.

35   Hoyos, Carola, 'Exiles Call for Iraq to Let in Big Oil Companies', *Financial Times*, 7 April 2003: 'participants said many in the group favoured production sharing agreements with oil companies.'

36   Dr Thamir Ghadhban quoted in World Economic Forum, *The Geopolitics of Oil*, Extraordinary Meeting, 21 June 2003, online: available http://www.weforum.org /site/knowledgenavigator.nsf/The%20geopolitics%20oc%20Oil_2003?open&event _id (1 January 2004).

37   Ibid.

38   Dr Muhammad-Ali Zainy, quoted in: Morgan, Oliver, 'Fields of Dreams Turned to Ashes', *The Observer*, 21 September 2003.

39   Ibid.

40   Ibid.

41   Ibid.

42   Quoted in Institute for Policy Studies, SEEN Project, *Press Release*, 23 July 2003, online: available http://www.seen.org/BushEO.shtml (5 June 2004).

43   Little, *American Orientalism*, p.321.

44   US Department of Energy, EIA, *Country Analysis Briefs: Iraq* (Washington, August 2003), p.3.

45   See Khalaf, Roula and Hoyos, Carola, 'Setback for Saudi Gas Initiative as Project is Scrapped', *Financial Times*, 6 June 2003; and Khalaf, Roula and Hoyos, Carola, 'Collapse of Saudi Gas Talks Reveals Gap in Understanding', *Financial Times*, 7 June 2003.

46   Hoyos, Carola, 'Oil Groups Snub US on Iraq Investment', *Financial Times*, 25 July 2003. In January 2004, Saudi Arabia announced deals with China's Sinopec, Russia's Lukoil, Italy's ENI and Spain's Repsol to explore for gas in Saudi Arabia. No US companies were involved and the ban on foreign involvement in the oil sector continued.

47   Pelham, Nicolas, 'Minister Sets out Timetable for Iraqi Oil Privatization', *Financial Times*, 5 September 2003.

48   In what sounds like a diplomatic afterthought, Bahr Al-Uloum added, 'and European companies, probably'.

49   Quoted in Somerville, Glenn, 'Iraq to Allow Full Foreign Ownership Outside Oil', *Reuters*, 21 September 2003, online: available http://biz.yahoo.com/rf/030921/group_iraq_5.html (26 September 2003).

50   'Iraq Seeks Quick Infusion of Foreign Oil Money', Reuters News Service, 24 September 2003, online: available at http://www.chron.com/cs/CDA/ssistory.mpl/business/2117622 (26 September 2003).

51   Robin West quoted in Ivanovich, David, 'Houston Exec Gets Top Iraq Energy Post', *Houston Chronicle*, 23 September 2003.

52   Hedges, Michael, 'As Nation Recovers, US Oil Czar Focuses on Production Levels', *Houston Chronicle*, 18 October 2003.

53   'US-Iran Standoff Over Nuclear Policy Disappoints Conoco', Reuters, 22 June 2003, online: available http://www.iranexpert.com/2003/usiranstandoff22june.htm (30 September 2003).

54   Hedges, 'As Nation Recovers, US Oil Czar Focuses on Production Levels'.

55   'Iraq to Invite 60 Foreign Companies to First-Ever Oil Conference', *Alexander's Gas and Oil Connections*, online: available http://www.gasandoil.com/goc/news/ntm34438.htm (10 January 2004).

56   Drummond, James and Speigel, Peter, 'US Post-War Iraq Deaths Exceed Those of Invasion', *Financial Times*, 30 October 2003.

57   Cummins, Chip, 'Iraq/State-Run Oil Co: US Advisers Support Move', *Wall Street Journal*, 7 January 2004, republished in press release from HSBC Bank, online: available at http://marketinfo.hsbc.com.au/public/story.asp?storyID=DCYHDTD (9 January 2004).

58   Ibid.

59   Hoyos, Carola and Catan, Thomas, 'Security Fears Force Oil Conference Postponement', *Financial Times*, 22 October 2003.

60   Clover, Charles, 'Nine Die as US Helicopter Crashes in Iraq', *Financial Times*, 9 January 2004.

61   Chmaytelli, Maher, 'Coalition Troops to Stay in Iraq after Power Handover: Officials', *Agence France-Presse*, 16 November 2003, online: available http://quickstart.clari.net/qs_se/webnews/wed/av/Qirag-us-politics-troops.Rbn6_DNG.html (17 January 2004).

62   Krane, Jim, 'Saddam's Palace May be New US Embassy', *Boston.com News*, 12 December 2003, online: available http://www.boston.com/news/world/middleeast/articles/2003/12/12/saddams_palace_may_be_new_us_embassy/ (3 May 2004).

63   Pipes, Daniel, 'Distinguishing between Islam and Islamism', Center for Strategic and International Studies, 30 June 1998, online: available http://www.danielpipes.org/article/954 (27 October 2003).

64   Nicholas Pelham, 'Iraqi Minister Unveils Proposal to Control Oil', *Financial Times*, 10 June 2004.

65   Woodward, *Plan of Attack*, p.399.

66   Page, *Century of Cars*, p.1.

67   Baqi, Mahmoud M. Abdul and Saleri, Nansen G., *Fifty-Year Crude Oil Supply Scenarios: Saudi Aramco's Perspective*, Center for Strategic and International Studies, Washington D.C., 24 February 2004.

68   US Department of Energy, EIA, *Annual Energy Outlook 2004* (Washington 2004), Table A11.

69   Grant, Jeremy and Mackintosh, James, 'Year of the Car: How the Big Three Are Battling to Regain the Lead in One of Their Most Crucial Markets', *Financial Times*, 5 January 2004.

70   CNN Money, 'Gas Doesn't Bite SUV Sales', online: available http://money.cnn.com/2004/06/02/pf/autos/suv_sales/ (12 June 2004).

71   Karush, Sarah, 'Automakers Report SUV Sales Unaffected by Higher Fuel Prices', *Naperville Sun Business*, online: available http://www.suburbanchicagonews.com/sunpub/naper/business/n0603cars.htm (12 June 2004).

72   Page, Clarence, 'Century of Cars', Online NewsHour, 6 October 2003, online: available http://www.pbs.org/newshour/essays/july-dec03/page_10-06.html (8 June 2004).

Bibliography

BOOKS AND MAJOR NON-GOVERNMENTAL REPORTS

Aburish, Said, *The Rise, Corruption and Coming Fall of the House of Saud*, Bloomsbury Publishing (London, 1995)

Adelman, Morris, *The Genie out of the Bottle: World Oil since 1970*, MIT Press (Cambridge Mass., 1995)

Ali, Tariq, *Bush in Babylon: The Recolonisation of Iraq*, Verso (London, 2003)

Al-Sowayegh, Abdulaziz Hussein, *Arab Petro-Politics*, Croom Helm (Beckenham, 1984)

American Petroleum Institute (API), *Basic Petroleum Data Book*, Vol.XVIII, No.1 (Washington, 1998)

American Petroleum Institute (API), Policy Analysis and Planning Department, *Economic State of the US Oil and Natural Gas Exploration and Production Industry: Long Term Trends and Recent Events* (Washington, 30 April 1999)

Anderson, Irvine H., *Aramco, the United States and Saudi Arabia: A Study of the Dynamics of Foreign Policy, 1933–50*, Princeton University Press (Princeton, 1981)

Antill, Nick and Arnott, Robert, *Oil Company Crisis: Managing Structure, Profitability and Growth*, Oxford Institute for Energy Studies (Oxford, 2002)

Bardou, Jean-Pierre, Chanaron, Jean-Jacques, Fridenson, Patrick and Laux, James M., *The Automobile Revolution: The Impact of an Industry*, University of North Carolina Press (Chapel Hill, 1982)

Bentley, R.J., *Perspectives on the Future of Oil*, Department of Cybernetics, University of Reading (Reading, 30 May 1999)

Berger, Peter L. and Luckman, Thomas, *The Social Construction of Reality*, Alan Lane The Penguin Press (London, 1967)

Bindemann, Kirsten, *Production Sharing Agreements: An Economic Analysis*, Oxford Institute for Energy Studies (Oxford, 1999)

Bohi, Douglas and Russel, Milton, *Limiting Oil Imports: An Economic History and Analysis*, Johns Hopkins University Press (Baltimore, 1978)

Boué, Juan Carlos, *The Political Control of State Oil Companies: A Case Study of the Vertical Integration Programme of Petroleos de Venezuela 1982–95*, D.Phil. thesis (Oxford, 1998)

Boué, Juan Carlos, *Venezuela: The Political Economy of Oil*, Oxford University Press (Oxford, 1994)

BP, *Statistical Review of World Energy 2001*, BP plc (London, 2002)

Campbell, Robert W., *The Economics of Soviet Oil and Gas*, Johns Hopkins University Press (Baltimore, 1968)

Carr, Edward Hallet, *What is History?* (2nd Edition) Penguin Books (Harmondsworth, 1987)

Chinese Academy of Engineering and the National Research Council, *Personal Cars and China*, National Academy of Sciences (Washington, 2003)

Claes, Dag Harald, *The Politics of Oil-Producer Cooperation*, Westview Press (Boulder, 2001)

Conant, Melvin A., *The Oil Factor in US Foreign Policy, 1980–1990*, Lexington Books (Lexington Mass., 1982)

Cowan, J.M., *The Hans Wehr Dictionary of Modern Written Arabic*, Spoken Language Services Inc. (Ithaca, 1994)

De Chazeau, Melvin G., and Kahn, Alfred A., *Integration and Competition in the Petroleum Industry*, Yale University Press (New Haven, 1959)

Deffeyes, Kenneth S., *Hubbert's Peak: The Impending World Oil Shortage*, Princeton University Press (Princeton, New Jersey, 2001)

Dekmeijian R. Hrair and Simonian, Hovann H., *Troubled Waters: The Geopolitics of the Caspian Region*, I. B. Tauris (London, 2003)

Elm, Mostafa, *Oil Power and Principle: Iran's Oil Nationalisation and its Aftermath*, Syracuse University Press (Syracuse, New York, 1992)

Freedman, Lawrence and Karsh, Efraim, *The Gulf Conflict 1990–91: Diplomacy and War in the New World Order*, Faber and Faber (London, 1993)

Fulton, George A., Grimes, Donald R., Schmidt, Lucie G., McAlinden, Sean P. and Richardson, Barbara C., *Contribution of the Automotive Industry to the US Economy in 1998*, Institute of Labour and Industrial Relations, Office for the Study of Automotive Transportation, University of Michigan and Center for Automotive Research, Environmental Research Institute of Michigan (Winter 2001)

Halliday, Fred, *Arabia Without Sultans*, Penguin Books (Harmondsworth, 1974)

Halliday, Fred, *Two Hours that Shook the World, September 11 2001: Causes and Consequences*, Saqi Books (London, 2002)

Hamilton, Charles, *Americans and Oil in the Middle East*, Gulf Publishing Co (Houston, 1962)

Hartshorn, J.E., *Oil Companies and Governments*, Faber and Faber (London, 1962)

Harvie, Christopher, *Fool's Gold: The Story of North Sea Oil*, Hamish Hamilton (London, 1994)

Hassman, Heinrich, *Oil in the Soviet Union*, Princeton University Press (Princeton, 1953)

Heinberg, Richard, *The Party's Over: Oil, War and the Fate of Industrial Societies*, Clairview Books (Forrest Row, 2003)

Holden, David and Johns, Richard, *The House of Saud*, Sidgwick & Jackson (London, 1981)

Howarth, David, *The Desert King,* Collins (London, 1964)

Johnston, Daniel, *International Petroleum Fiscal Regimes and Production Sharing Contracts,* Penwell Books (Tulsa, Oklahoma 1994)

Karim, Muhammad S., *Oil, Islamism and the International Petroleum Industry: Legal, Economic, Political and Cultural Issues,* LL.M. Dissertation, Centre for Energy, Petroleum and Mineral Law and Policy, University of Dundee (Dundee, 2001)

Khadduri, Majid, *Republican Iraq: A Study in Iraqi Politics since the Revolution of 1958,* Oxford University Press (London, 1969)

Kissinger, Henry, *Years of Renewal,* Wiedenfeld & Nicolson (London, 1999)

Klare, Michael T., *Resource Wars: The New Landscape of Global Conflict,* Metropolitan Books (New York, 2001)

Kleveman, Lutz, *The New Great Game: Blood and Oil in Central Asia,* Atlantic Books (London, 2003)

Little, Douglas, *American Orientalism: The United States and the Middle East since 1945,* I. B. Tauris (London, 2004)

Lubell, Harold, *Middle East Oil Crisis and Western Europe's Energy Supplies,* Rand Corporation and Johns Hopkins Press (Baltimore, 1963)

McCarthy, Justin, *The Population of Palestine,* Columbia University Press (New York, 1990)

Mikdashi, Zuhayr, *Financial Analysis of Middle Eastern Oil Concessions, 1901–65,* Praeger (New York, 1966)

Mommer, Bernard, *The Political Role of National Oil Companies in Exporting Countries: The Venezuelan Case,* Oxford Institute for Energy Studies (Oxford, 1994)

Mommer, Bernard, *Global Oil and the Nation State,* Oxford Institute for Energy Studies, Oxford University Press (Oxford, 2002)

Mora Contreras, Jesus, *Reparto de Ingresos Petroleros Extraordinarios y Proceso de Apertura Petrolera en Venezuela,* Instituto de Investigaciones Economicas y Sociales, Universidad de Los Andes (Merida, n.d.)

Morse, Edward L. (Chair) and Jaffe, Amy Myers (Project Director), *Strategic Energy Policy Challenges for the 21st Century,* Report of an Independent Task Force, Council on Foreign Relations and James A. Baker III Institute for Public Policy of Rice University (New York, April 2001)

Muttitt, Greg and Marriott, James, *Some Common Concerns: Imagining BP's Azerbaijan-Georgia-Turkey Pipelines System,* PLATFORM (London, 2002)

Nawwab, Ismail, Speers, Peter and Hoye, Paul (eds), *Saudi Aramco and its World,* Saudi Aramco (Dharan, 1995)

Noreng, Oystein, *Oil and Islam: Social and Economic Issues,* Research Council of Norway and John Wiley and Sons (Chichester, 1997)

Odell, Peter, *Oil and Gas: Crises and Controversies 1961–2000,* Vol.1, Multi-Science Publishing Company (Brentwood London, 2001)

Painter, David S., *Private Power and Public Policy: Multinational Oil Companies and US Foreign Policy 1941–54,* I. B. Tauris (London, 1986)

Parra, Francisco, *Oil Politics: A Modern History of Petroleum,* I. B. Tauris (London, 2004)

Petroconsultants, *Annual Review of Petroleum Fiscal Regimes,* 1995, Petroconsultants (Geneva, 1996)

Rae, John B., *The American Automobile: A Brief History*, University of Chicago Press (Chicago, 1965)

Rashid, Ahmed, *Taliban: Islam, Oil and the New Great Game in Central Asia*, I.B.Tauris (London, 2000)

St. Clair, David J., *The Motorisation of American Cities*, Praeger (New York, 1986)

Sampson, Anthony, *The Seven Sisters: The Great Oil Companies and the World They Made*, Hodder & Stoughton (London, 1975)

Schurr, Sam H.and Netschert, Bruce C., *Energy in the American Economy 1850–1975*, Johns Hopkins Press (Baltimore, 1960)

Suskind, Ron, *The Price of Loyalty: George W. Bush, The White House and the Education of Paul O'Neill*, Simon and Schuster (New York, 2004)

Tanzer, Michael, *The Political Economy of International Oil and the Underdeveloped Countries*, Temple Smith (London, 1969)

Vassiliev, Alexei, *The History of Saudi Arabia*, Saqi Books (London, 2000)

Vidal, Gore, *Dreaming War: Blood for Oil and the Cheney-Bush Junta*, Thunder's Mouth Press/Nation Books (New York, 2002)

Vietor, Richard H.K., *Energy Policy in America since 1945*, Cambridge University Press (Cambridge, 1984)

Weir, Erin M.K., *NEP to FTA: The Political Economy of Canadian Petroleum Policy in the 1980s* (University of Regina 2001), online: available http://www.web.net/~pef/eweir.pdf (2 July 2003)

Whigham, David, *Managerial Economics Using Excel*, Thomson Learning (London, 2001)

Woodward, Bob, *Bush at War*, Simon and Schuster (New York, 2003)

Woodward, Bob, *Plan of Attack*, Simon and Schuster (New York, 2004)

Yergin, Daniel, *The Prize: The Epic Quest for Oil, Money and Power*, Simon and Schuster (London, 1991)

ACADEMIC JOURNALS, ARTICLES IN BOOKS AND AUTHORED ONLINE ARTICLES

Akins, James, 'The Oil Crisis: This Time the Wolf is Here', *Foreign Affairs*, April 1973

Alberro, Jose, 'The Politics of Petroleum: Outline of Remarks by Jose Alberro', September 2002, *Center for Latin American Studies*, University of California, Berkeley, online: available http://ist-socrates.berkeley.edu:7001/Events/fall2002/09-12-02-Alberroetal/alberroremarks.html (7 January 2003)

AlHajji, A.F., ' Will Gulf States Live Up to EIA and IEA Projections?', *World Oil*, June 2001

Aliriza, Bulent, 'US Caspian Pipeline Policy: Substance or Spin?' Center for Strategic and International Studies, 24 August 2000, online: available http://www.csis.org (2 July 2003)

Ali Rodriguez Araque, 'OPEC and the New-Oil Realities', speech delivered to the Venezuelan-American Association of the United States (VAAUS) at the Harvard Club, New York City, 4 February 2002.

Andrews-Speed, Philip, 'China's Future Energy Policy', *Oxford Energy Forum*, Oxford Institute for Energy Studies (Oxford, May 2003)

Bahgat, Gawdat, 'The Caspian Sea Geopolitical Game: Prospects for the Millennium', *OPEC Review*, Vol.XXIII, No.3, 1999

Baqi, Mahmoud M. Abdul and Saleri, Nansen G., *Fifty-Year Crude Oil Supply Scenarios: Saudi Aramco's Perspective*, Center for Strategic and International Studies, Washington D.C., 24 February 2004

Brown, Jonathan, 'Why Foreign Oil Companies Shifted Their Production from Mexico to Venezuela During the 1920s', *American Historical Review*, Vol.90, No.2, 1985

Campbell, Colin and Laherrere, Jean, 'The End of Cheap Oil?', *Scientific American*, March 1998

Cheney, Richard, 'Defending Liberty in a Global Economy', *Collateral Damage Conference*, Cato Institute, 23 June 1998, online: available http://www.cato.org/speeches/sp-dc062398.html (14 January 2003)

Deming, David, 'Are We Running out of Oil?', *Policy Backgrounder*, No.159, 29 January 2003, National Center for Policy Analysis, online: available http://www.ncpa.org/pub/bg/bg159/index.html (6 February 2003)

DeNovo, John, 'The Movement for an Aggressive American Oil Policy Abroad, 1918–20', *American Historical Review*, Vol.61, No.4, 1956

Espinasa, Ramon and Mommer, Bernard, 'Venezuelan Oil Policy in the Long Run', in Dorian, J.P. and Fesharaki, F., *International Issues in Energy Policy, Development and Economics*, Westview Press (Boulder, 1992)

Finlayson, Jock A. and Hagland, David G., 'Oil Politics and Canada-United States Relations', *Political Science Quarterly*, Vol.99, No.2, 1984

Fjell, Olav, *Norway, the Petro-Nation: Today and in Ten Years Time*, Statoil, March 2001

Gately, Dermot, 'How Plausible is the Consensus Projection of Oil Below $25 and Persian Gulf Oil Capacity and Output Doubling by 2020?', *Energy Journal*, Vol.22, 2001

Hill, Fiona, 'A Not-So-Grand Strategy: United States Policy in the Caucasus and Central Asia since 1991', *Politique Etrangere*, February 2001; reprinted by Brookings Institution, online: available http://www.brook.edu/dybdocroot/views/articles/fhill/2001politique.htm (14 January 2003)

Hill, Fiona, 'Areas for Future Cooperation or Conflict in Central Asia and the Caucasus', paper presented at the Yale University Conference, *The Silk Road in the 21st Century*, 19 September 2002, online: available http://www.brook.edu/views/speeches/hillf/20020919.htm (14 January 2003)

Horsnell, Paul, 'Oil Market: Why Venezuela Matters', *Global Energy Research*, 16 December 2002, JP Morgan Securities Inc., online: available http://morganmarkets.jpmorgan.com (31 January 2003)

Hubbert, M. King, 'Nuclear Energy and the Fossil Fuels', in American Petroleum Institute (eds), *Drilling and Production Practice* (New York, 1956)

Jenkins, Gilbert, 'World Oil Reserves Reporting, 1948–96: Political, Economic and Subjective Influences', *OPEC Review*, Vol.XXI, No.2, 1997

Kaufman, Burton I., 'Mideast Multinational Oil, US Foreign Policy and Antitrust: The 1950s', *Journal of American History*, Vol.63, No.4, 1977

Kaufmann, Robert K. and Cleveland, Cutler J., 'Oil production in the Lower 48 States: Economic, Geological and Institutional Determinants', *Energy Journal*, Vol.22, No.1, 2001

Klare, Michael T., *Washington's Oil Politik*, online: available http://greatchange.org/ov-klare,oilpolitik.html (9 November 2003)

Klare, Michael T., *The Geopolitics of War*, online: available http://www.geocities.com/
hal9000report/hal.3.html (9 November 2003)

Krasner, Stephen D., 'A Statist Interpretation of American Oil Policy Toward the Middle
East', *Political Science Quarterly*, Vol.94, No.1, 1979

Lynch, Michael C., 'Farce this Time: Renewed Pessimism About Oil Supply', *Geopolitics
of Energy*, December 1998/January 1999

Mabro, Robert, 'Some Fundamental OPEC Issues', *Oxford Energy Forum*, August 2000,
Oxford Institute for Energy Studies

Medvedev, Zhores, 'The War for Caspian Oil', *European Labour Forum*, Summer 1995

Miller, Pamela A., *The Impact of Oil Development on Prudhoe Bay*, online: available
http://arcticcircle.uconn.edu/ANWR/arcticconnections.htm (11 February 2003)

Mommer, Bernard, 'Venezuelan Oil Politics at the Crossroads', *Monthly Comment*, March
2001, Oxford Institute for Energy Studies, online: available http://www.oxfordenergy.org

Mommer, Bernard, 'Subversive Oil', in Ellner, Steve and Hellinger, Daniel (eds), *Venezuelan
Politics in the Chavez Era: Polarization and Social Conflict*, Lynne Rienner (Boulder,
Colorado, 2002)

Odell, Peter, 'Oil and Gas Reserves: Retrospect and Prospect', *Geopolitics of Energy*,
December 1998/January 1999

Perry, George L., 'The War on Terrorism, the World Oil Market and the US Economy',
Analysis Paper 7, 28 November 2001, Brookings Institute, online: available http://
www.brookings.edu/views/papers/perry/20011024.htm (12 November 2003)

Pipes, Daniel, *Distinguishing between Islam and Islamism*, Center for Strategic and
International Studies, 30 June 1998, online: available http://www.danielpipes.org/
article/954 (27 October 2003)

Platts, *The Future of Iraq's Oil*, online: available http://www.platts.com/features/
oilprices/iraqoutlook.shtml (14 October 2003)

Reynolds, Douglas B., 'The Value of Oil', *Oxford Energy Forum*, Oxford Institute for
Energy Studies, August 2000

Roberts, Ian, 'The Second Gasoline War and How We Can Prevent the Third', *British
Medical Journal*, Vol.326, No.171, 18 January 2003

Rodriguez, Ali, 'Comentario, Regimenes Fiscales en Economias Petroleras', *Segundo
Encuentro International de Economia*, Banco Central de Venezuela (Caracas, March 1999)

Rutledge, Ian, 'Profitability and Supply Price in the US Domestic Oil Industry:
Implications for the Political Economy of Oil in the 21st Century', *Cambridge
Journal of Economics*, Vol.27, No.1, 2003

Rutledge, Ian and Wright, Philip, 'Companies as Sources for Upstream Oil and Gas
Information', *Journal of Energy Literature*, Vol.V, No.1, 1999

Salameh, Mamdouh G., 'Caspian Sea Is No Middle East', *Newsletter of the International
Association for Energy Economics*, Third Quarter 2002

Szoboszlay, Akos, *The Desired Result: Drive People to Drive*, Modern Transit Society,
online: available http://www.trainweb.org/mts/ctc/ctc05.html (14 December 2002)

Tempest, Paul, 'Energy Security in an Insecure World', *Newsletter of the International
Association for Energy Economics*, 1st Quarter 2004

Vaicius, Ingrid and Isacson, Adam, 'The War on Drugs Meets the War on Terror',
International Policy Report, February 2003, Colombia Project, Center for

International Policy, online: available http://www.ciponline.org/colombia/ 0302ipr.htm (12 October 2003)

Volman, Daniel, 'The Bush Administration and African Oil: The Security Implications of US Energy Policy', *Review of African Political Economy*, Vol.30, No.28, December 2003

Weir, Erin M.K., *NEP to FTA: the Political Economy of Canadian Petroleum Policy in the 1980s* (University of Regina, 2001), online: available http://www.web.net/~pef/ eweir.pdf (1 April 2003)

GOVERNMENT AND OTHER OFFICIAL REPORTS

Armitage, Richard L. et al., *Transforming Defense and National Security in the 21st Century*, National Defense Panel (Arlington, December 1997)

Canada-USA Free Trade Agreement, Chapter Nine, online: available http:// wehner.tamu.edu/mgmt.www/nafta/fta/9.htm (5 January 2003)

Central Intelligence Agency, *CIA Fact Book 2003*, online: available http://www.cia.gov/ cia/publications/factbook (12 December 2003)

Cheney, Richard et al., *Report of the National Energy Development Group*, May 2001, online: available http://www.whitehouse.gov/energy/ (1 December 2002)

Greene, David L. and Tishchishnya, Nataliya I., *Costs of Oil Dependence: A 2000 Update*, US Department of Energy, Oak Ridge National Laboratory (Tennessee, May 2000)

International Energy Agency (IEA), *Coal Information 1998*, IEA/OECD (Paris, 1998)

Joint Statement by President Bush and President Nursultan Nazarbayev on the New Kazakhstan-American Relationship, online: available http://www.whitehouse.gov/ news/releases/2001/12/20011221–10.html (17 January 2003)

Kumins, Lawrence, *Iraq Oil: Reserves, Production and Potential Revenues*, Congressional Research Service, Library of Congress (Washington, 29 September 2003)

Nichol, Jim, *Central Asia's New States: Political Developments and Implications for US Interests – Issue Brief for Congress*, Congressional Research Service, Library of Congress (Washington, November 2002)

US Bureau of Transportation Statistics, *National Transportation Statistics 2002*, series of electronic documents, online: available http://www.bts.gov (11 October 2003)

US Department of Energy, Energy Efficiency and Renewable Energy, *Fact of the Week: Vehicles Per Thousand People: An International Comparison*, 15 September 2003, online: available http://www.eere.energy.gov/vehiclesandfuels/facts/2003/ fcvt_fotw285.shtml

US Department of Energy, Energy Information Administration (EIA), *Annual Energy Outlook 1996* (Washington 1996), also online: available http://www.eia.doe.gov

US Department of Energy, EIA, *Annual Energy Outlook 2001* (Washington 2001), also online: available http://www.eia.doe.gov

US Department of Energy, EIA, *Annual Energy Outlook 2002* (Washington 2002), also online: available http://www.eia.doe.gov

US Department of Energy, EIA, *Annual Energy Outlook 2004* (Washington 2004), also online: available http://www.eia.doe.gov

US Department of Energy,EIA, *Annual Energy Review 1999* (Washington 2000), also online: available http://www.eia.doe.gov

US Department of Energy, EIA, *Annual Energy Review 2001* (Washington 2002), also online: available http://www.eia.doe.gov

US Department of Energy, EIA, *Azerbaijan: Production Sharing Agreements*, June 2002, online: available http://www.eia.doe.gov/emeu/cabs/azerproj.html (16 January 2003)

US Department of Energy, EIA, *Caspian Sea Region Oil and Natural Gas Reserves*, July 2001, online: available http://www.eia.doe.gov/emeu/cabs/caspgrph.html (13 January 2002)

US Department of Energy, EIA, *Caspian Sea Region Oil and Natural Gas Reserves*, July 2002, online: available http://www.eia.doe.gov/emeu/cabs/caspgrph.html (25 January 2003)

US Department of Energy, EIA, *Caspian Sea Region: Reserves and Pipelines Tables*, July 2002, online: available http://www.eia.doe.gov/emeu/cabs/caspgrph.html (25 January 2003)

US Department of Energy: EIA, *Caspian Sea Region, Key Oil and Gas Statistics*, August 2003, online: available http://www.eia.doe.gov/emeu/cabs/caspstats.html (5 January 2004)

US Department of Energy, EIA, *Country Analysis Briefs: Iraq*, August 2003, online: available http://www.eia.doe.gov/emeu/cabs/iraq.html (31 December 2003)

US Department of Energy, EIA, *Country Analysis Briefs: Kazakhstan*, July 2002, online: available http://www.eia.doe.gov/emeu/cabs/kazak.html (1 August 2002)

US Department of Energy, EIA, *Country Analysis Briefs: Venezuela*, online: available Available http://www.eia.doe.gov/emeu/cabs/venez.html (17 April 2002)

US Department of Energy, EIA, *Energy Plug: Annual Energy Outlook 2001, Early Release*, online: available http://www.eia.doe.gov (1 January 2001)

US Department of Energy, EIA, *Energy Plug: Long-Term World Oil Supply – A Resource Base/Production Path Analysis*, online: available http://www.eia.doe.gov/emeu/plugs/plworld.html (20 July 2002)

US Department of Energy, EIA, *Global Oil Supply Disruptions Since 1951*, online: available http://www.eia.doe.gov/emeu/security/distable.html (8 September 2002)

US Department of Energy, EIA, *International Energy Outlook 1995* (Washington 1995), also online: available http://www.eia.doe.gov

US Department of Energy, EIA, *International Energy Outlook 1998* (Washington 1998), also online: available http://www.eia.doe.gov

US Department of Energy, EIA, *International Energy Outlook 2001* (Washington 2001), also online: available http://www.eia.doe.gov

US Department of Energy, EIA, *International Energy Outlook 2002* (Washington 2002), also online: available http://www.eia.doe.gov

US Department of Energy, EIA, *International Petroleum Information 2002* (Washington 2003), also online: available http://www.eia.doe.gov

US Department of Energy, EIA, *Kazakhstan: Major Oil and Natural Gas Projects*, online: available http://www.eia.doe.gov/emeu/cabs/kazaproj.html (16 January 2003)

US Department of Energy, EIA, *Monthly Energy Review*, online: available http://www.eia.doe.gov/emeu/mer/txt/mer1–8 (7 September 2002)

US Department of Energy, EIA, *Oil and Gas Development in the United States in the Early 1990s: An Expanded Role for Independent Producers* (Washington, October 1995), also online: available http://www.eia.doe.gov

US Department of Energy, EIA, *Oil Production Capacity Expansion Costs For the Persian Gulf* (Washington D.C., January 1996)

US Department of Energy, EIA, *OPEC Revenues Fact Sheet*, December 2003, online: available http://www.eia.doe.gov/emeu/cabs/opecrev.html (12 December 2003)

US Department of Energy, EIA, *Performance Profiles of Major Energy Producers 1999*, online: available http://www.eia.doe.gov/emeu/perfpro/index.html (3 January 2003)

US Department of Energy, EIA, *Performance Profiles of Major Energy Producers 2000*, online: available http://www.eia.doe.gov/emeu/perfpro/index.html (3 January 2003)

US Department of Energy, EIA, *Persian Gulf Oil and Gas Exports Fact Sheet*, April 2003, online: available http://www.eia.doe.gov/emeu/cabs/pgulf.html#oil (15 December 2003)

US Department of Energy, EIA, *Petroleum Marketing Monthly*, April 2000, online: available http://www.eia.doe.gov (7 June 2003)

US Department of Energy, EIA, *Petroleum Supply Annual 2001* (Washington 2002), also online: available http://www.eia.doe.gov

US Department of Energy, EIA, *Privatization and the Globalization of Energy Markets* (Washington, 1996)

US Department of Energy, EIA, *Profile of the Strategic Petroleum Reserve*, online: available http://www.fe.doe.gov/spr

US Department of Energy, EIA, *Retail Motor Gasoline and On-Highway Diesel Fuel Prices 1949–2001*, online: available http://www.eia.doe.gov/emeu/aer/txt/ptb0522.html (11 December 2002)

US Department of Energy, EIA, *World Energy 'Areas to Watch'*, August 2002, online: available http://www.eia.doe.gov (7 August 2003)

US Department of Energy, Office of Transportation Technologies (OTT), *Fact of the Week: Per Cent of Vehicle Buyers Who Are Considering an SUV for Their Next Vehicle Purchase*, 8 June 1999, online: available http://www.ott.doe.gov/facts/archives/fotw92.shtml (7 October 2002)

US Department of Energy, OTT, *Fact of the Week: Dealer Profits by Market Segment*, October 1999, online: available http://www.oft.doe.gov/facts/archives/fotw111.shtml (7 October 2002)

US Department of Energy, OTT, *Fact of the Week: Automobile Affordability, 1979–99*, 20 March 2000, online: available http://www.ott.doe.gov/facts/archives/fotw121.shtml (7 October 2002)

US Department of Energy, OTT, *Fact of the Week: International Vehicle Ownership in 1998 Compared to the US, from 1990–98*, 7 August 2000, online: available http://www.ott.doe.gov/facts/archives/fotw139supp.shtml (10 July 2002)

US Department of Energy, OTT, *Fact of the Week: Historical US Vehicles/1000 People Compared to 1998 Vehicles/1000 People around the World*, online: available http://www.ott.doe.gov/facts/archives/fotw233.shtml (14 December 2002)

US Department of Energy, OTT, *Fact of the Week: Trends in New Vehicle Attribute Preference*, 13 August 2001, online: available http://www.ott.doe.gov/facts/archives/fotw178supp.shtml (7 October 2002)

US Department of Energy, OTT, *Fact of the Week: US Light Truck Sales Exceed Car Sales*, 21 January 2002, online: available http://www.ott.doe.gov/facts/archives/fotw200.shtml (7 October 2002)

US Department of Energy, OTT, *Fact of the Week: New Light Vehicle Sales Shares by Size Class 1976–2001*, 5 August 2002, online: available http://www.ott.doe.gov/facts/archives/fotw228supp.shtml (14 December 2002)

US Department of Energy, OTT, *Fact of the Week: Vehicles Per Thousand People: USA Compared to Other Countries*, 9 September 2002, online: available http://www.ott.doe.gov/facts/archives/fotw233.shtml (14 December 2002)

US Department of Energy, OTT, *Future US Highway Energy Use: A Fifty Year Perspective* (Washington, May 2001)

US Department of Energy, OTT, Oak Ridge National Laboratory, *Transportation Energy Data Book: Edition 21* (Tennessee, 2001)

US Department of the Interior, 'First Alaska Offshore Energy Flows Today', *News Release*, 1 November 2001

US Department of State, online: available http://www.state.gov/s/p/of/ca/23927.htm (30 November 2003)

US Department of State, Press Release, 19 December 2002

US Fish and Wildlife Service, *Potential Impacts of Proposed Oil and Gas Development on the Arctic Refuge's Coastal Plain: Historical Overview and Issues of Concern*, online: available http://www.fws.gov/issues1.html (4 February 2003)

US General Accounting Office (GAO), *Energy Security: Evaluating US Vulnerability to Oil Supply Disruptions and Options for Mitigating their Effects*, Report to the Chairman on the Budget, House of Representatives (Washington, December 1996)

US Geological Survey, *Arctic National Wildlife Refuge, 1002 Area, Petroleum Assessment 1998, Including Economic Analysis*, online: available http://pubs.usgs.gov/fs/fs-0028-01/fs-0028-01.htm (11 February 2002)

US International Trade Commission, *Industry and Trade Summary: Motor Vehicles*, USITC Publication 3545 (Washington, September 2002)

US National Security Council, *A National Security Strategy for a New Century*, Washington, October 1998, online: available http://clinton2.nara.gov/WH/EOP/NSC/html/documents/nssr.pdf (3 November 2003)

US Senate, *US Automobile and Truck Retail Sales 1970–2002*, online: available http://www.senate.state.mi.us/sfe/Economics/RetailAutosales.pdf (1 July 2003)

AUTHORED ARTICLES IN NEWSPAPERS, OTHER PRESS AND 'THINK TANKS' (INCLUDING ONLINE)

Abdel-Muntasir, Jihad, 'The Saudi Regime, its Legality and Achievements', *Nidaul Islam*, 1995, online: available http://www.islam.org.au/articles/10/SAUD.HTM (9 August 2002)

Barlow, Maude (Council of Canadians), *Toronto Globe and Mail*, 26 September 2000, online: available http://www.hartford-hwp.com/archives/44/100.htm (5 January 2003)

Barnes, Joe and Siligo, Ronald, 'Baku–Ceyhan Pipeline: Bad Economics, Bad Politics, Bad Idea', *Oil and Gas Journal*, 26 October 1998

Beattie, Alan, 'American Companies to Gain from US Outlay', *Financial Times*, 18/19 October 2003

Beaumont, Peter and Islam, Feisal, 'Carve-up of Oil Riches Begins', *The Observer*, 3 November 2002

Besser, James D., 'Arctic Drillers Cozying Up to Jews', *Jewish Week*, 16 November 2001

Borger, Julian and Bellos, Alex, 'US "Gave the Nod" to Venezuelan Coup', *The Guardian*, 17 April 2002.

Bragg, John, 'See the USA in your SUV', Campaign in Defence of Industry and Technology, Center for the Moral Defence of Capitalism, 2001, online: available http://www.moraldefense.com/ProTech/Philosophy/Essays/su.htm (30 June 2002)

Bremmer, Ian and Morse, Edward, 'Caspian Energy Hype Begins Running Low', *St Petersburg Times*, 14 January 2003

Buck, Tobias and Clover, Charles, 'Oil Groups Poised to Pick Over the Spoils of Iraqi Battlefield', *Financial Times*, 2 November 2002

Burt, Tim, 'Alternative Fuels Still Outpaced by Petrol', *Financial Times*, 14 September 2000

Chin, Larry, 'Big Oil, the United States and Corruption in Kazakhstan', online: available www.onlinejournal.com (16 May 2002);

Chmaytelli, Maher, 'Coalition Troops to Stay in Iraq after Power Handover: Officials', *Agence France-Presse*, 16 November 2003, online: available http://quickstart.clari.net/ qs_se/webnews/wed/av/Qirag-us-politics-troops.Rbn6_DNG.html (17 January 2004)

Clouser, Gary, 'Crossborder M&A: Keeping it Fair, and Canadian', *Oil and Gas Investor*, online: available http://www.oilandgasinvestor.com/reports/crossborder/ crossborder03.htm (3 January 2003)

Clover, Charles, 'Nine Die as US Helicopter Crashes in Iraq', *Financial Times*, 9 January 2004

Clover, Charles and Corzine, Robert, 'Politics: A Worrying Emphasis on Re-Centralisation', and 'Guarded Optimism over Oil Revenues' in 'Kazakhstan Survey', *Financial Times*, 23 July 1997

Clover, Charles and Hoyos, Carola, 'Expectations Weigh Heavy on Man who Must Get Oil Flowing', *Financial Times*, 18 July 2003

Corn, David, 'W.'s First Enron Connection', *The Nation*, 4 March 2002, online: available http://www.thenation.com/capitalgames/index.mhtm1?bid-3&pid=21 (14 November 2002)

Corzine, Robert, 'From Minor to Major: Formerly Monolithic Oil Companies are Challenging the Western Majors on Their Home Turf', *Financial Times*, 19 August 1997

Corzine, Robert, 'Strange, Shadowy World of President's Advisor', in 'Kazakhstan Survey', *Financial Times*, 11 December 2000

Crossette, Barbara, 'A Different Kind of Rogue: When Democracy Runs off the Rails', *New York Times*, 4 June 2000

Crow, Patrick, 'Seeking Scapegoats', *Oil and Gas Journal*, 1 March 1999

Cummins, Chip, 'Iraq/State-run Oil Co: US Advisers Support Move', *Wall Street Journal*, 7 January 2004, republished in press release from HSBC Bank, online: available http:// marketinfo.hsbc.com.au/public/story.asp?storyID=DCYHDTD (9 January 2004)

Daniel, Caroline, 'US Backs Saudi Stance on Terrorism', *Financial Times*, 2 November 2002

Delay, Jennifer, 'Georgia Tries to Maximise its Pipeline Options', *Alexander's Gas and Oil Connections*, Vol.4, Issue 9, 2003

Despeignes, Peronet, 'Detroit Boosts US Industrial Output', *Financial Times*, 16 August 2002

Drummond, James and Speigel, Peter, 'US Post-War Iraq Deaths Exceed Those of Invasion', *Financial Times*, 30 October 2003

Dunne, Nancy, 'Iraq Oil Ban Mooted to Win Support for Arctic Drilling', *Financial Times*, 16 April 2002

Durbin, Dee-Ann, 'Light Trucks Beat Car Sales in All but Four States', *Autoinsider*, 24 April 2004, online: available, http://detnews.com/2004/autoinsider/0404/24/autos-132375.htm (19 June 2004)

Elliott, Larry and Stewart, Heather, 'World Counts Cost of War's Siren Call', *The Guardian*, 20 September 2002

Evans, Rob and Hencke, David, 'UK and US in Joint Effort to Secure African Oil', *The Guardian*, 14 November 2003

Fidler, Stephen and Baker, Gerard, 'America's Democratic Imperialists: Humility to Empire in Two Years', *Financial Times*, 6 March 2003

Flocco, Tom, 'Harken Energy – Bush's No Good Trade', *WorldNet Daily*, 18 February 2000, online: available http://www.scoop.co.nz/mason/stories/HL0207/S00047.htm (9 November 2002)

Friedman, Lisa, 'President's "Green Car" Called a Ruse', *Oakland Tribune*, 30 January 2003

Frum, David, 'Myth 2: America Wants War with Saddam because of Oil', *Daily Telegraph*, 22 October 2002

Frum, David, 'The Curse of Oil Dependence', *Jerusalem Post*, 20 December 2002

Georgian, Armen, 'US Eyes Caspian Oil in "War on Terror"', Armenian National Committee, 1 May 2002, online: available http://www.ancsf.org/essays_analyses/caspian_oil.htm(14 January 2003)

Gerth, Jeff, 'Bribery Inquiry Involves Kazakh Chief, and He's Unhappy', *New York Times*, 12 November 2002

Grant, Jeremy, 'GM and Ford Head to Head on SUV Incentives', *Financial Times*, 31 January 2003

Grant, Jeremy and Mackintosh, James, 'Year of the Car: How the Big Three Are Battling to Regain the Lead in One of Their Most Crucial Markets', *Financial Times*, 5 January 2004

Grant, Jeremy and Sevastopulo, Demetri, 'Holy Wrath Descends upon Gas Guzzlers', *Financial Times*, 21 November 2002

Harding, James, 'Schultz is Still Making his Voice Heard After 50 Years at the Top', *Financial Times*, 21 November 2002

Harding, James, 'Bush Speaks for Cause of Freedom in Middle East', *Financial Times*, 7 November 2003

Harris, Anthony, 'A Head-in the-Sand Approach to Oil', *Financial Times*, 13 August 1990

Healey, James R.,'Death by the Gallon', *USA Today*, 2 July 1999

Healey, James R., 'Fuel Efficiency Fires Renewed Public Debate', *USA Today*, 27 July 2001

Hebert, H. Joseph, 'Oil Companies Largely Silent on Alaska', *Associated Press*, 17 April 2002, online: available http://www.anwr.org/features/oil-silent.htm (11 February 2003)

Hedges, Michael, 'As Nation Recovers, US Oil Czar Focuses on Production Levels', *Houston Chronicle*, 18 October 2003

Hersh, Seymour, 'The Price of Oil: What was Mobil up to in Kazakhstan and Russia', *New Yorker*, 9 July 2001

Holstein, Lisa, 'Cheney's Oil Days: Iran Stance Raises Concern Among Jews', *Jewish Bulletin News*, online: available http://www.jewishsf.com/bk000804/uscheney.shtml (24 October 2002)

Hoyos, Carola, 'A Discreet Way of Doing Business', 3 November 2000, online: available http://search.ft.com:80/search/artciles.html (18 November 2002)

Hoyos, Carola, 'Big Players Rub Hands in Anticipation of Iraq's Return to the Fold', *Financial Times*, 21 February 2003

Hoyos, Carola, 'Oil Groups Lose Money on UK Energy Fields', *Financial Times*, 7 April 2003

Hoyos, Carola, 'Exiles Call for Iraq to Let in Big Oil Companies', *Financial Times*, 7 April 2003

Hoyos, Carola, 'OPEC is Creating a Tidal Wave of Crude That Cannot All Be Absorbed. A Production Cut May Be Unavoidable', *Financial Times*, 9 April 2003

Hoyos, Carola, 'Iran Raises the Stakes with Oilfield Find', *Financial Times*, 16 July 2003

Hoyos, Carola, 'Oil Groups Snub US on Iraq Investment', *Financial Times*, 25 July 2003

Hoyos, Carola, '$20 Billion Kazak Oil Project Faces Two-Year Delay', *Financial Times*, 20 August 2003

Hoyos, Carola, 'Middle East Oil Industry Will Need Big Investment', *Financial Times*, 5 November 2003

Hoyos, Carola and Catan, Thomas, 'Security Fears Force Oil Conference Postponement', *Financial Times*, 22 October 2003

Hutton, Will, 'Confucius Goes to Market', *The Observer*, 21 September 2003

Islam, Faisal and Paton, Nick, 'US Buys up Iraqi Oil to Stave off Crisis, *The Observer*, 26 January 2003

Ivanovich, David, 'Houston Exec Gets Top Iraq Energy Post', *Houston Chronicle*, 23 September 2003

Jaggi, Rohit, 'Britain Feared Oil Crisis Could Spark US Military Retaliation', *Financial Times*, 6 January 2004

Johns, Richard, 'Mexico Applauds Iraq's Belligerence', *Financial Times*, 26 July 1990

Karush, Sarah, 'Automakers Report SUV Sales Unaffected by Higher Fuel Prices', *Naperville Sun Business*, online: available http://www.suburbanchicagonews.com/sunpub/naper/business/n0603cars.htm (12 June 2004)

Kettle, Martin, 'Hidden Powerhouse of the US Presidency', *The Guardian*, 28 April 2001

Khalaf, Roula, 'Saudi Arabia Urged to Speed up Economic Reform', *Financial Times*, 23 October 2002

Khalaf, Roula and Dinmore, Guy, 'Bombs in Riyadh, Disorder in Iraq, Opposition to the Road Map: Bush's Vision Confronts Reality', *Financial Times*, 15 May 2003

Khalaf, Roula and Hoyos, Carola, 'Setback for Saudi Gas Initiative as Project is Scrapped', *Financial Times*, 6 June 2003

Khalaf, Roula and Hoyos, Carola, 'Collapse of Saudi Gas Talks Reveals Gap in Understanding', *Financial Times*, 7 June 2003

Kohlhaas, Charles A., 'War in Iraq: Not a "War for Oil"', *In the National Interest*, online: available http://www.inthenationalinterest.com/Articles/Vol2Issue9/vol2issue9kohlaas.html (26 September 2002)

Krane, Jim, 'Saddam's Palace May Be New US Embassy', *Boston.com News*, 12 December 2003, online: available http://www.boston.com/news/world/middleeast/articles/2003/12/12/saddams_palace_may_be_new_us_embassy/ (3 May 2004)

Kristol, William, 'Memorandum to Opinion Leaders', Project for the New American Century, 25 April 2002, online: available http://www.newamericancentury.org/saudi-042502.htm (16 February 2003)

Kristol, William, 'A New Approach to the Middle East', *The Daily Standard*, 22 May 2002, online: available http://www.weeklystandard.com/content/public/articles/000/000/001/273awdje.asp (9 August 2002)

Kynge, James, 'Concerns Grow over Chinese Overheating', *Financial Times*, 18 October 2002

Lal, Deepak, 'A Force to Lift the Curse of Natural Resources', *Financial Times*, 3 October 2003

Lardner Jr, George, 'The Harken-Bahrain Deal: A Baseless Suspicion', *Washington Post*, 30 July 1999, online: available http://www.washingtonpost.com/wp-srv/politics/campaigns/wh2000/stories/bushside073099.htm (10 November 2002)

Lardner Jr, George and Romano, Lois, 'Bush Name Helps Fuel Oil Dealings', *Washington Post*, 30 July 1999

Lloyd, John, 'Radical Islam Sees Itself just as Communism Did – in a Battle with a Hostile World', *Financial Times*, 12 January 2003

Madson, Wayne, 'Cheney at Helm', *The Progressive*, online: available http://www.progressive.org/wm0900.htm (24 October 2002)

Martin, Patrick, 'Oil Company Adviser Named US Representative to Afghanistan', Afghan Information Center, 3 January 2002, online: available http://www.afghan-info.com//Politics/Khalilzad_Nomination.htm (21 November 2002)

Martinson, Jane, 'Cheney Linked to Oil Loans', *The Guardian*, 5 August 2000, online: available http://search.ft.com:80/search/artciles.html (18 November 2002)

McAlister, Terry, 'BP Chief Fears US Will Carve up Iraqi Oil Riches', *The Guardian*, 30 October 2002

McCutcheon, Hilary and Osbon, Richard, 'Discoveries Alter Caspian Region Energy Potential', *Oil and Gas Journal*, 17 December 2001

McCutcheon, Hilary and Osbon, Richard, 'Risks Temper Caspian Rewards Potential', *Oil and Gas Journal*, 24 December 2001

McDermott, Jeremy, 'Green Berets Move into Colombia's Oilfields', *Daily Telegraph*, 12 October 2002

McNulty, Sheila, 'BP Quits Campaign on Alaskan Drilling', *Financial Times*, 27 November 2002

Milbank, Dana, 'Bush's Blunder May be Kristol's Inside Influence', *Washington Post*, 19 March 2002, online: available http://www.washingtonpost.com/ac2/wp-dyn/A46994-20002Mar18?language=printer (30 November 2003)

Monaldi, Francisco, 'Capitalism Popular', Escritos de Francisco Monaldi Mas, online: available http://www.fmonaldi.com/fmmas/art07.htm (17 April 2002)

Monbiot, George, 'The World is Running Out of Oil – So Why Do Politicians Refuse to Talk About It?', *The Guardian*, 2 December 2003

Morgan, Dan and Ottaway, David B., 'In Iraqi War Scenario, Oil is Key Issue', *Washington Post*, 15 September 2002

Morgan, Oliver, 'Iraq May Have to Quit OPEC', *The Observer*, 27 April 2003

Morgan, Oliver, 'US Struggles to Unlock Iraq's Black Gold', *The Observer*, 4 May 2003

Morgan, Oliver, 'Fields of Dreams Turned to Ashes', *The Observer*, 2 September 2003

Morgan, Oliver, 'Iraq Delay Hands Cheney Firm $1bn', *The Observer*, 7 December 2003

Mowlem, Mo, 'The Real Goal is the Seizure of Saudi Oil', *The Guardian*, 5 September 2002

Nelan, Bruce W., 'The Rush for Caspian Oil', *Time*, 4 May 1998, online: available http://www.time.com/time/magazine/1998/dom/980504/world.the_rush_for_caspi6.html (2 January 2002)

Odell, Mark, 'Courting Controversy in the Desert', *Financial Times*, 12 September 2003

Page, Clarence, 'Century of Cars', Online News Hour, 6 October 2003, online: available http://www.pbs.org/newshour/essays/july–dec03/page_10-06.html (8 June 2004)

Park, Gary, 'Conoco's C$9.8 Billion Offer for Gulf Canada Jolts Calgary Boardrooms', *Petroleum News Alaska*, 25 June 2001, online: available http://www.petroleumnewsalaska.com/pmarch/010625-51.html (3 January 2003)

Paton, Nick, 'US Looks Away as New Ally Tortures Islamists', *The Guardian*, 26 May 2003

Paton, Nick, Borger, Julian, Macalister, Terry and MacAskill, Ewen, 'US Begins Secret Talks to Secure Iraq's Oilfields', *The Guardian*, 23 January 2003

Pelham, Nicolas, 'Minister Sets out Timetable for Iraqi Oil Privatization', *Financial Times*, 5 September 2003

Perry, Sam, 'Bush Did Try to Save Enron', *Consortiumnews.com*, online: available http://www.consortiumnews.com/2002/05902a.html (24 October 2002)

Pi, Lu, 'Expressway Construction in High Swing', *Beijing Review*, 18 July 2002

Prowse, Michael, 'The Fat Man Refuses to Follow a Diet', *Financial Times*, 25 February 1991

Ragsdale, Rose, 'Liberty Called Tip of Offshore Oil, Gas Riches', *Alaska Oil and Gas Reporter*, 5 February 2002, online: available http://www.oilandgasreporter.com/stories/020502/nor_liberty_hopeful.shtml (15 February 2002)

Rahman, Bayan and Jack, Andrew, 'Japan Lures Russia with $7bn Offer on Pipeline', *Financial Times*, 14 October 2003

Ricks, Thomas E., 'Briefing Depicted Saudis as Enemies', *Washington Post*, 2 August 2002

Rohloff, Greg, 'Cheney's Experience Pays off as a CEO', *Amarillo Business Journal*, 13 June 1998, online: available http://businessjournal.net/stories/061398/ABJ_pays.html (21 November 2002)

Rosenbaum, David E., 'Two Sides Push on Arctic Oil, but Proposal Lacks Votes', *New York Times*, 18 April 2002

Royce, Knut and Heller, Nathaniel, 'Cheney Led Halliburton to Feast at the Federal Trough', Center for Public Integrity, online: available http://www.public-i.org/dtaweb/report.asp?ReportID=172&L1=10&L2=70&L3=15&L4=0&L5=0&S

Sachs, Jeffrey, 'The Real Target of the War in Iraq was Saudi Arabia', *Financial Times*, 13 August 2003

Sampson, Anthony, 'West's Greed for Oil Fuels Saddam Fever', *The Observer*, 11 August 2002

Sampson, Anthony, 'Oilmen Don't Want Another Suez', *The Observer*, 22 December 2002

Sampson, Anthony, 'Why is Britain so committed to this war?', *The Observer*, 16 February 2003

Sevastopulo, Demetri, 'Bush and Kerry Clash on Surging Fuel Price', *Financial Times*, 25 March 2004

Shlaes, Amity, 'Oil Must be Seized from the Hands of the State', *Financial Times*, 26 March 2003

Shlaes, Amity, 'Team Bush Polishes its Green Credentials', *Financial Times*, 15 September 2003

Shlaes, Amity, 'Free Markets Are the Key to Rebuilding Iraq', *Financial Times*, 29 September 2003

Simon, Bernard, 'Canada Oil Group To Be Privatised', *Financial Times*, 14 May 1991

Somerville, Glenn, 'Iraq to Allow Full Foreign Ownership Outside Oil' *Reuters*, 21 September 2003, online: available http://biz.yahoo.com/rf/030921/group_iraq_5.html (26 September 2003)

Stelzer, Irwin M., 'Can We Do Without Saudi Oil?', *The Weekly Standard*, 19 November 2001, online: available http://www.weeklystandard.com/content/public/articles/000/000/525pggsa.asp (9 August 2002)

Tatom, John, 'Iraqi Oil is Not America's Objective', *Financial Times*, 13 February 2003

Thompson, Scott, 'Dick Cheney Has Long Planned to Loot Iraqi Oil', *Executive Intelligence Review*, 1 August 2003

Tran, Mark, 'Bush and Harken Energy', *Guardian Unlimited*, 10 July 2002, online: available http://www.guardian.co.uk/theissues/article/0,6512,75270,00.html (9 November 2002)

Tully, Andrew F., 'Iraq: After Hussein, How Will Iraqis Assert Control Over Their Oil?', *Radio Free Europe*, 28 April 2003, online: available http://www.rferl.org/nca/features/2003/04/28042003151159.asp(26 September 2003)

Wagoner, Rick, 'Carmakers Are Vying to Meet China's Needs', *Financial Times*, 7 November 2003

Williams, Garry, 'Dick Cheney Ain't Studying War No More', *Business Week*, 2 March 1998, online: available http://www.businessweek.com/1998/09/b3567127.htm (18 November 2002)

Wolf, Martin, 'The Long March to Prosperity: Why China Can Maintain Its Explosive Rate of Growth for Another Two Decades', *Financial Times*, 9 December 2003

Wolffe, Richard and Webb-Vidal, Andy, 'US Insists it Rebuffed Approaches by Anti-Chavez Opposition', *Financial Times*, 17 April 2002

Wonacott, Peter, Whalen, Jeanne and Bahree, Bhushan, 'China's Growing Thirst for Oil Remakes the World Market', *Wall Street Journal*, 3 December 2003

Yergin, Daniel, 'Gulf Oil: How Important is it Anyway ?', *Financial Times*, 22/23 March 2003

NON-AUTHORED PRESS, RESEARCH GROUP AND 'THINK TANK' WEBSITES

ABC News, 'Spencer Abraham, Friend to Oil and Immigrants', 3 January 2001, online: available http://abcnews.go.com/sections/politics/Daily News/Abraham_ profile.html (25 January 2003)

AFX Europe, 'Halliburton Reportedly Dealt with Iraq While Cheney Was CEO', 24 June 2001, online: available http://search.ft.com:80/search/articles.html (18 November 2002)

Alexander's Gas and Oil Connections, 'National Security Act of 2001', Vol.6, Issue 11, 18 June 2001, online: available http://www.gasandoil.com/goc/news/ntn12531.htm (9 February 2003)

Alexander's Gas and Oil Connections, 'Iraq to Invite 60 Foreign Companies to First-Ever Oil Conference', online: available http://www.gasandoil.com/goc/news/ntm34438.htm (10 January 2004)

Alexander's Gas and Oil Connections, 'Iraq is a Field of Dreams for Big Oil Firms', 1 May 2003, online: available http://www.gasandoil.com/goc/company/cm31821.htm (18 December 2003)

ANNOCOL, News Agency New Colombia, February 2002, online: available http://www.annocol.com

anwr.org., 'ANWR, Top 10 Reasons to Support Development in ANWR', online: available http://www.anwr.org/topten.htm (4 February 2002)

Associated Press, 'Cheney, Oil Executives Raise $8 Million for GOP', 28 September 2000, online: available http://quest.conline.com/stories/092800/gen_0928006149.shtml (24 October 2002)

Associated Press, 'Abraham To Lead Department He Wanted Shut', 3 January 2001, online: available http://quest.cjonline.com/stories/010301/gen_013017592.shtml (25 November 2003)

Associated Press, 'Abraham Sees Nation Threatened by Energy Crisis', *Arizona Daily Wildcat*, 9 March 2001, online: available http://wildcat.arizona.edu/papers/94/118/01_93_m.html (8 December 2003)

Associated Press, 'GM to Launch Chevrolet Mini-Car in China', *AP Biz Wire*, 1 December 2003. online: available http://seatlepi.nwsource.com

Atlantic Council of the United States et al., 'US Challenges and Choices in the Gulf: Saudi Arabia', *Policy Brief 1*, Atlantic Council of the United States, Middle East Institute, Middle East Policy Council and Stanley Foundation (Washington, 2001)

Atlantic Council of the United States et al., 'US Challenges and Choices in the Gulf: Energy Security', *Policy Brief 3*, Atlantic Council of the United States, Middle East Institute, Middle East Policy Council and Stanley Foundation (Washington, 2002)

Baku Ceyhan Campaign News, January 2003

BBC News/Business, 'Halliburton Iraq Contract Queried', 30 May 2003, online: available http://www.bbc.co.uk/2/low/business/2950154.stm (21 January 2004)

BBC News, World Edition, 'Poland Seeks Iraqi Oil Stake', 3 July 2003, online: available, http://news.bbc.co.uk/2/hi/europe/3043330.stm (17 June 2004)

Center for Responsible Politics, online: available http://opensecrets.org/industries/ (17 November 2002)

Center for Strategic and International Studies (CSIS), online: available http:// www.csis.org/sei/event991208bioGiusti.html (7 September 2002)

Center for Strategic and International Studies (CSIS), 'Crude Business: Corruption and Caspian Oil.' 1 September 2000, online: available http://www.csis.org/turkey/ CEU000901.htm (15 January 2003)

Christian Science Monitor, 25 October 2001, online: available http://www.csmonitor.com/ 2001/1025/p8s1-comv.html (14 January 2003)

CNN Money, 'Gas Doesn't Bite SUV Sales', online: available http://money.cnn.com/ 2004/06/02/pf/autos/suv_sales/ (12 June 2004)

Competitive Enterprise Institute, 'Statement on the National Energy Policy Security Act of 2001', 16 February 2001, online: available http://www.cei.org/ utils/printer.cfm?AID=2506 (9 February 2003)

Cooperativeresearch.org, online: available http://www.cooperativeresearch.org/ organizations/corporate/usacc.htm (3 March 2003)

El Universal, 11 June 2002, online: available http://archivo.eluniversal.com/2002/ 07/11/11204DD.html (8 September 2002)

Fortune Magazine, 26 April 1999

Independent Petroleum Association of America, *Press Release* 30 June 1999, online: available http://www.ipaa.org.departments/communications/PR1999/PRO6301999.htm (26 February 2001)

Independent Petroleum Association of America (IPAA), Information Services, *1998 Profile of Independent Producers* (no place of publication given, 1999)

Infoplease.com, *US Light Vehicles Production by Manufacturer*, online: available http://www.infoplease.com/ipa/A0104789.html

Institute for Policy Studies, SEEN Project, *Press Release,* 23 July 2003, online: available http://www.seen.org/BushEO.shtml (5 June 2004)

Interstate Oil and Gas Compact Commission (IOGCC), *A Battle for Survival? The Real Story Behind Low Oil Prices* (Oklahoma City, April 1999)

Middle East International, 21 November 2003

Modern Transit Society, online: available http://www.trainweb.org

Natural Resource Defense Council, *Oil and the Arctic National Wildlife Refuge*, online: available http://www.nrdc.org/land/wilderness/artic.asp (5 February 2003)

Natural Resource Defense Council, 'The Bush Administration's Fuel Cell Fake-out', online: available http://www.nrdc.org/air/transportation/ffuelcell.asp (11 October 2003)

New York State Society of Certified Public Accountants, 'Bush's Harken Past Becoming Clearer', online: available http://www.nysscpa.org/home/2002/702/3week/ article19.htm (24 October 2002)

Oil and Gas Investor, editorial, 'U.S. Interest in Canadian Mergers Not a Cause for Concern, Analysts Say', online: available http://www.oilandgasinvestor.com/ comment/994111170.html (3 January 2003)

Oil and Gas Journal, 15 June 1998

Oil and Gas Journal, 21 December 1998

Oil and Gas Journal, 4 January 1999

Oil and Gas Journal, 8 March 1999

Oil and Gas Journal, 29 March 1999

Oil and Gas Journal, 16 March 2001

Open Letter to the President, 19 February 1998, online: available http://www.cooperativeresearch.org/archive/1990s/openletter021998.htm (24 December 2003)

Opensecrets.org, 'Oil and Gas Top 20 Recipients', online: available http://www.opensecrets.org/industries/recips.asp?Ind=E01&Cycle=2000&recipdetail=A&mem=N&sortorder=U (14 February 2004)

Platts, *The Future of Iraq's Oil*, Platts.com, online: available http://www.platts.com/features/oilprices/iraqoutlook.sthml (14 January 2003)

Project for the New American Century, *Statement of Principles*, 3 June 1997, online: available http://www.newamericancentury.org/statementofprinciples.htm (12 December 2003)

Project for the New American Century, *Rebuilding America's Defenses: Strategy, Forces and Resources for a New Century*, (Washington, September 2000)

Reuters, 21 September 2002, quoted in 'US Oil Diversity Drive Comes Back to Middle East', *New Zealand Herald*, 22 September 2002

Reuters, 'US-Iran Standoff over Nuclear Policy Disappoints Conoco', 22 June 2003, online: available http://www.iranexpert.com/2003/usiranstandoff22june.htm (30 September 2003)

Reuters, 'Iraq Seeks Quick Infusion of Foreign Oil Money', 24 September 2003, online: available http://www.chron.com/cs/CDA/ssistory.mpl/business/2117622 (26 September 2003)

Rusenergy.com, 'AGIP KCP Revises Valuation of Northern Caspian Reserves under Kazakh Pressure', 19 July 2002, online: available http://www.rusenergy.com/eng/caspian.htm (19 January 2003)

Saudhouse.com, 'Al-Al-Yamamah Scandal', online: available http://www.saudhouse.com/saudi_al_Al-Yamamah_scandal.htm (25 November 2003)

Savedomesticoil.com, online: available http://www.savedomesticoil.com/hhammdoc.htm (12 January 2002)

Texans for Public Justice, 'George W. Bush's $100,000 Club', online: available http://tpj.org/pioneers (17 November 2002)

Veneconomia.com, 'Quien es Quien: Luis Giusti', online: available http://www.veneconomia.com/esp/aldia/resumenQuien.asp?pub=141 (7 September 2002)

Wall Street Journal, 'Kazakhstan: US Investigates Possible Payments to Government Officials from Oil Firm Funds', 30 June 2000

Wall Street Journal, 'CAFE Society', 28 February 2002, reproduced in the Competitive Enterprise Institute NewsCenter, online: available http://www.cei.org/gencon/003,02417.cfm (10 July 2002)

Whatreallyhappened.com, 'What was Mobil up to in Kazakhstan', online: available http://www.whatreallyhappened.com/mobil.html (17 January 2003)

World Economic Forum, *The Geopolitics of Oil*, Extraordinary Meeting, 21 June 2003, online: available http://www.weforum.org/site/knowledgenavigator.nsf/The%20geopolitics%20oc%20Oil_2003?open&event_id (1 January 2004)

World Resources Institute, 'Resource Consumption', *Earth Trends: The Environmental Portal*, online: available http://earthtrends.wri.org

World Resources Institute, *Global Topic: Size Distribution of Oil Fields*, online: available http://www.wri.org/wri/climate/jm_oil_006.html (29 September 2002)

COMPANY REPORTS

Chevron Corporation, *Annual Report on Form 10-K for 1995*
Chevron Corporation, *Annual Report on Form 10-K for 1993*
Halliburton Company, *Annual Report on Form 10-K for 1994*
Halliburton Company, *Annual Report on Form 10-K for 2001*

INDEX